The Nature of Empires and the Empires of Nature

Indigenous Studies Series

The Indigenous Studies Series builds on the successes of the past and is inspired by recent critical conversations about Indigenous epistemological frameworks. Recognizing the need to encourage burgeoning scholarship, the series welcomes manuscripts drawing upon Indigenous intellectual traditions and philosophies, particularly in discussions situated within the Humanities.

Karl S. Hele, editor

The Nature of Empires and the Empires of Nature

Indigenous Peoples and the Great Lakes Environment

WILFRID LAURIER
UNIVERSITY PRESS

LAURIER
Inspiring Lives.

Wilfrid Laurier University Press acknowledges the support of the Canada Council for the Arts for our publishing program. We acknowledge the financial support of the Government of Canada through the Book Publishing Industry Development Program for our publishing activities. This work was supported by the Research Support Fund.

Canada | Canada Council for the Arts | Conseil des arts du Canada | ONTARIO ARTS COUNCIL CONSEIL DES ARTS DE L'ONTARIO an Ontario government agency un organisme du gouvernement de l'Ontario

Library and Archives Canada Cataloguing in Publication

The nature of empires and the empires of nature : Indigenous peoples and the Great Lakes environment / Karl S. Hele, editor.

(Indigenous studies series)
Includes bibliographical references and index.
Issued in print and electronic formats.
ISBN 978-1-55458-488-8 (paperback).—ISBN 978-1-55458-421-5 (pdf).—
ISBN 978-1-55458-422-2 (epub)

1. Native peoples—Great Lakes Region (North America)—Historiography. 2. Great Lakes Region (North America)—Environmental conditions—History. 3. Human ecology—Great Lakes Region (North America)—History. 4. Native peoples—Land tenure—Great Lakes Region (North America)—History. 5. Native peoples—Colonization—Great Lakes Region (North America)—History. 6. Great Lakes Region (North America)—Historiography. I. Hele, Karl S. (Karl Scott), 1970– II. Series: Indigenous studies series

E78.G7N38 2013 971.3004'97 C2012-904308-7
C2012-904309-5

Cover design by Blakeley Words+Pictures. Cover image: *Shingaba W'Ossin*, by Charles Bird King (1785–1862). MPI /Getty Images photo from iStockphoto. Text design by Sandra Friesen.

First paperback printing 2016

Waterloo, Ontario, Canada
www.wlupress.wlu.ca

This book is printed on FSC® certified paper and is certified Ecologo. It contains post-consumer fibre, is processed chlorine free, and is manufactured using biogas energy.

Printed in Canada

This volume is dedicated to
all those living under both the sublimity of the natural world
and the shadow of empires in the Great Lakes.

CONTENTS

Preface

Karl S. Hele

This book, and the conference that sparked its creation, originated from John MacKenzie's monograph *Empires of Nature and the Nature of Empires* (1997).[1] Growing up Anishinaabe in the Great Lakes, which are subdivided between two imperial–colonialist states, has made me intimately familiar with the natural world, its sublime power, and the ongoing attempts by states to impose their wills upon the land, water, and people. Displays of power both subtle and overt are a fact of life in the history and contemporary lives of Indigenous peoples in Canada and the world over. Denials by Prime Minister Stephen Harper of Canada's colonial history are only the most recent examples of the dominant empire's ignorance of its past.[2] Indeed, the prime minister's insistance at a "historic" Crown–First Nations gathering on 24 May 2012 that the key piece of colonial legislation—the Indian Act—would remain is the most recent example.[3] Moreover the ignorance about First Nations and Aboriginal issues in Canada is best summed up by John Ivison's opinion column in the *National Post,* where he notes that the chiefs continue to "air old grievances" while a "pragmatic PM looks ahead."[4] Ivison and many other Canadians fail to realize that the "pragmatism" evidenced by the prime minister is simply one element of the government's historic and ongoing colonial relationship with First Nations. Canadians seem to think that France and Britain were the colonial powers and that the slate was wiped clean in 1867 with the birth of Canada as a nation. Sadly, this is a failure to grasp the reality that Canada and its provinces are and remain colonial empires with the subjugation of Indigenous population resting at the nation's core.

Regardless of various attempts by "civilization" to control or thwart the empire of nature, nature has eons to achieve ultimate victory. The ruins of countless empires of man around the globe attest to this. An article in *Discover* magazine describes how nature would recolonize the environment once humanity is gone; many aspects of "civilization" would simply crumble with very fleeting physical records remaining of our presence within ten to twenty thousand years.[5] A similar conclusion is vividly presented in the 2009 television series airing on the History Channel titled *Life after People*.[6] Today, melting icecaps, disappearing bees, declining species, global warming, pollution, and increasing desertification are recognized as the result of humanity's (read empire's) attempt to promote itself over nature. Nature as an entity is damaged. Mother Earth cries in pain, her body and bones are contaminated and weakened, her blood increasingly poisoned, and her breath is becoming ever more fouled; yet, despite the accumulating evidence that empires of man are destroying our world, capitalism and its supporters continue to deny this basic fact.[7] Recent discussions about the seeming lack of will to explore and colonize space—apparently humanity's long-term survival rests upon establishing off-earth settlements—only illustrate the failure to listen to the earth; such plans present empires with the opportunity to export their visions of dominance and subordination.[8] It is time we listened to those who speak to the earth and learn the lessons about how to live upon this planet without destroying it before ruining other worlds.

To Indigenous peoples, humanity is but one occupant of a diverse and interconnected world of beings that are bound together in a variety of known and unknown ways. This is often referred to as the circle of life, the circular movement of which can be seen in the movement of the seasons and animal life patterns, as well as a plethora of other cycles. Modern Western, and even Eastern societies, through the growing empire of statistics, are seeking ways in which to predict and eventually control the cycles of life as they are understood through a superimposed linear pattern. However, this effort is counterintuitive to the whirlwind of our existences. The sense of interconnectedness that shapes Indigenous interactions with the environment is key to understanding how to restore nature to its central position in the human relationship. Non-Indigenous people may scoff at the idea that rocks, trees, waterfalls, birds, bears, humanity, and all matter of life can be both animate and inanimate depending on the circumstances and essence of the thing, but the binary division of animate and inanimate, developed by Western thought as a way to categorize Indigenous belief and views of their natural world, fails to grasp the complexity of this knowledge while serving to belittle it in the process. To break this habit of mind that Western knowledge is supreme in all things, we must listen and hear what knowledgeable Indigenous people have to say. We must begin to cross the epistemological divide between Indigenous and non-Indigenous, or between the "modern" and the "other."

MacKenzie's work focuses on the environmental history of the British Empire and suggests fresh modes of analysis and connections with the Scottish experience. The Great Lakes region were a part of that empire, and many of its colonizing agents in the Americas were Scottish.[9] Therefore, Dr. MacKenzie's work is directly applicable to the study of the Great Lakes watershed. This conclusion led to the call for papers for a conference sponsored by the former Atkinson Faculty of Liberal and Professional Studies at York University, Center for the Study of Indigenous Border Issues, and the Bkejwanong (Walpole Island First Nation) community. Papers presented at this conference took their cue from MacKenzie's foundational studies. Drawing on both documentary and oral records, conference participants presented a series of papers that discussed the relationship between nature and empires in the context of the Great Lakes watershed. This volume in turn draws upon the conference's theme, the papers presented there, and contributions solicited through a call for papers.

This volume has two primary objectives. First, it explores the power of nature and the attempts by empires (United States, Canada, and Britain) to control the environment. Second, it touches upon contemporary threats facing First Nations communities in the Great Lakes region from ongoing political, environmental, and social issues, as well as efforts to confront and eliminate these threats to peoples and the environment. These two objectives served as the focus of the papers presented at the conference and for those collected to form this volume. The resulting collection seeks to address the epistemological chasm between the cultures and nations living within the Great Lakes watershed.

The essays collected in this volume explore the interconnections between the nature of empires and the empires of nature. A series of events sparked by the intrusion of empires and their attempts to suppress and claim dominance while extending their influence have indisputably affected the environment and Indigenous peoples. Contributions to this volume emphasize how either nature or Indigenous peoples attempted to mediate the effects of empire. The issues addressed can be configured within a metaphysical and epistemological framework as well as through case studies. All discussions centre around the concept of the "civilized" attempting to control the "savage," and how the "savage" is forcing the "civilized" to alter its trajectory. It is readily apparent that empire, despite all its manifest power, has failed to control or discipline humanity and nature. In short, all the conversations about nature and empire are constructed through a multifaceted lens.

As such, this volume hopes to inspire new ways of looking at the Great Lakes watershed and the peoples and empires contained within it. The essays cover a wide range of interdisciplinary and multidisciplinary research being undertaken by Indigenous and non-Indigenous scholars in environmental studies, native studies, history, anthropology, and literature. Each paper is informed by Dr. MacKenzie's work, oral tradition, and an awareness that we need to place the environment at the forefront of our discussions. This research will be of interest to all who are interested in the Great Lakes watershed, environmental knowledge, and new ways of looking at the world. It is hoped that by addressing some of the fundamental elements of humanity's various empires, this volume will begin a process of positive social change. Part of this change is seen in the partnering of York, Bkejwanong, and the Center for the Study of Indigenous Border Issues to undertake a conference exploring these questions. It is part of the ongoing process between Indigenous communities and academic institutions to help understand and decolonize attitudes that have historically been Eurocentric.[10]

Although not written as an introduction, the first chapter in this volume, "A Meditation on Environmental History," by John MacKenzie, serves as an excellent introductory reading for the papers that follow. His observation that environmental history has traditionally been written within the cultural frameworks of the West is underscored by other contributors' efforts to recast this same history from Indigenous perspectives. Moreover, MacKenzie's view that nature's power is often underestimated and that efforts to control it are met with disaster is carried through in a number of contributions. His argument that Western missionaries removed the spirit from nature is also found in discussions about modern society's new missionaries—educators—and their continued efforts to separate man from nature. Finally, MacKenzie's call for scholars to examine the Indigenous and the local before addressing national or global narratives forms the underlying basis of the conference, this volume, and all the papers it contains. Simply, MacKenzie's contribution is the foundational block from which all other contributions are hewn.

Chapters 2 through 5 offer a discussion of how education, knowledge, and the environment are intimately bound. In chapter 2, Heather Marie Annis utilizes the idea of the clown as trickster as a means to cross the cultural divide when it comes to understanding the environment and to reconnect humanity with nature as a daily lived experience. Chapter 3 builds upon the idea of the need to reconnect with nature. Alesha Jane Breckenridge maintains that the empire of Western knowledge as taught in modern educational institutions has striven to separate humanity and nature. She maintains that to overcome the many concerns of modern society we need to reconnect humanity and nature through education. In chapter 4, Lori Hallock takes these broad brush strokes and encapsulates them in a case study of place-based education in Northern Ontario. Here, similar to the preceding chapters, she discusses the importance of rethinking education in terms of the environment, orality, and specificity of place. By focusing on how stories create sense and meaning in terms of place, Hallock successfully shows that to re-establish the link between nature, education, and place we need to invest in developing knowledge that is place-orientated. Simply, one cannot pick a particular area or region to serve as the basis for educating everyone. As obvious as it sounds, the environment of Toronto is vastly different from that of Sault Ste. Marie. Brian Rice in chapter 5 discusses the colonization of Native/Aboriginal/Indigenous studies programs by colonial demands for modern and practical training and by anthropological theories. He argues that programs need to return to an Indigenous methodology that reflects a holistic approach. Simply, Rice argues that Indigenous knowledge's focus on balance between all the components that make up the environment (by which he means everything and everyone) must be central to programs' intellectualism. Thus, these authors effectively tie the need to truly reform all aspects of education as a means to reconnecting the empire of nature with the empires of humanity, thereby regaining and bringing to the fore an Indigenous way of looking at the world.

Chapters 6 through 10 look at specific examples of the nature of empire. Karen J. Travers in chapter 6 argues that the standard view of the Royal Proclamation and Indian agents' role in Aboriginal land transactions must be reconsidered. First Nations had different understandings of land transactions and treaties, based on oral promises, while Euro-Canadians came to different conclusions, particularly after Indian agents who were involved in treaty negotiations died. These Indian agents, she argues, worked with some First Nations communities to protect the lands. This is seen in the large tracts of land that Indian agents held in speculation, according to settlers and colonial governments, while First Nations members continued to access these holdings. Simply, the agreements and understandings surrounding early land transactions need to be examined from both Native and Euro-Canadian perspectives. In chapter 7, Rhonda Telford follows Travers's arguments that the early agreements were oral documents that emphasized the sharing of the land, not its acquisition. She illustrates the complexity of running and describing survey lines by the empire's agents, showing how the very same government records document Aboriginal occupation. For Telford, the lines drawn upon the land for the purpose of empire were anything but straight and clear.

Lianne Leddy in chapter 8 brings the discussion into the mid-twentieth century through her study of the uranium industry's effects on Serpent River First Nation. This chapter is a wonderful example of how a First Nation and local interests were ignored and trampled upon in favour of industrialization, employment, and most importantly global geopolitics. In the interest of maintaining the Western lifestyle at the height of the Cold War, Indian and Northern Affairs, the uranium industry, and the American military complex complicity poisoned a community's lifeblood with no regard for people or nature. In another contemporary example, Maureen Riche in chapter 9 examines the efforts to aid a northern community to control a dog problem; her paper explores the dialogical differences between north and south regarding animal ownership. Through well-intentioned attempts to control what seemed to be an out-of-control animal population, southern (Great Lakes region) veterinarians, unintentionally, illustrated how Western empires of thought impinge upon Indigenous knowledge. The author refers to this as a case of canine colonialism, whereby the south attempted, through spaying or neutering, to impose its version of how to care for dogs on an Indigenous community.[11] Lastly, chapter 10, by María C. Manzano-Munguía, looks at how empires by their very nature seek to create legible subjects, in this case Aboriginal peoples, in order to offer programs to or engage in social engineering. Part of the legibility project that Canada has and continues to undertake involves turning Aboriginal peoples into sedentary citizens who are readily quantifiable through the census or other means; such efforts are resisted by Aboriginal peoples through continued movement upon the landscape as well as a simple refusal to stand up and be counted. In short, statisticians through government programs may attempt to recast Aboriginal peoples as legible subjects who can be shown to undergo progress through civilizing or modernizing policies that in turn fail to understand or correctly map these communities.[12] Manzano-Munguía illustrates Mackenzie's argument that statisticians may attempt to quantify and qualify nature and Indigenous peoples, but both continue to defy the linear mentality necessitating newer and ever more complex schemes to straighten the circle.

The remaining five chapters continue the exploration of the nature of empires and the empires of nature through a literary or narrative framework.

The joint chapter by Christianne V. Stephens and Regna Darnell represents a foray into understanding how oral narratives can illuminate health and environmental conditions on Walpole Island First Nation and more generally on any First Nations territory. Chapter 12, by David T. McNab, uses an oral and documentary analysis to understand both the changing mindscape and landscape of the Reverend William A. Elias. McNab's creative combination of these diverse sources offers a unique perspective into an Ojibwa man's life in the late nineteenth and early twentieth centuries. By tying together Elias's life in both the Aboriginal and Euro-Canadian world, McNab shows how for the Reverend these worlds were intimately joined by the empire of nature. Ute Lischke in chapter 13 offers a reading of how Louise Erdrich's narrative works represent nature, place, and person. For Lischke, Erdrich's fiction uses local and personal understandings of the empire of nature to create narratives that are intimately personal and drawn from Aboriginal culture, yet speak to a wider audience. When read together, McNab and Lischke offer an examination of how landscapes, nature, and narrative are born of traditions that are adapted for the written word. Similarly, Rick Fehr in the fourteenth chapter looks at the competing narratives surrounding a mystery in Southwestern Ontario known as the Baldoon mystery. He presents the mystery's narrative as an illustration of Western man or empire's need to conquer and subdue nature to the ordered realm of the farmer. Additionally, the myth itself contains elements that illustrate empire's failure to conquer nature as well as its inability to subdue Aboriginal people to its dictates. For Fehr the myth is a prophetic device demonstrating the futility of imperial efforts to dominate a landscape or to recast it in the image of the homeland. The last paper of this collection, chapter 15, is a narrative of the Great Indian Bus Tour of Toronto. Jon Johnson's piece serves as an excellent end point, for it demonstrates that through oral narrative, Aboriginal storytellers/tour guides undermine the efforts of the Canadian empire to erase the history of First Nations by imposing itself upon the landscape. The bus tour is a modern form of storytelling. By illustrating that old and new narratives of Aboriginal use and occupation of the region overlay the contemporary and past landscapes of the city, the tour and its guides un-erase Toronto's Indigenous past and present. In short, Johnson draws the conclusion that the efforts by Britain, and then Canada, to recast the stories surrounding the use and occupation of the landscape of Toronto are failing.

Taken together, these fifteen chapters constitute a unique look at the idea presented by John MacKenzie in 1997. Each author brings his or her own interpretation and understanding to the idea. This collective effort has resulted in a set of papers that offer individual explorations to effectively move the debate surrounding how empires have affected local populations and nature in an effort to superimpose themselves upon the globe. Although this volume is by no means the final word on the nature of empires and the empires of nature, it does offer a starting point and a new way of understanding the complex conversation between newcomer, Indigenous, and environment. This conversation needs to take place, in order for Canada, and the world, to move forward in terms of our relationships with each other and nature. It is also part of a new and growing field of study, represented by scholars who see nature not as a force to conquer but as an empire that acts as a crucible. This crucible of nature forges local and national communities' identities, concepts, and nationhood.

Notes

1 John M. MacKenzie is the Professor of Imperial History at the University of Lancaster in England. John M. MacKenzie, *Empires of Nature and the Nature of Empires: Imperialism, Scotland and the Environment* (East Linton: Tuckwell, 1997).

2 Harsha Walia, "Really, Harper: Canada Has No History of Colonialism?" *The Dominion*, 28 Sept. 2009, accessed 19 Oct. 2009, www.dominionpaper.ca/articles/2943; and "Where Was the Outcry: At the G20 Conference, Stephen Harper Claims that Canada Has 'no history of colonialism,'" *Journal*, 29 Sept. 2009, accessed 19 Oct. 2009, www.queensjournal.ca/story/2009-09-29/opinions/where-was-outcry/.

3 "PM Stephen Harper's Speech to Crown–First Nations Gathering," *The Gazette*, 25 Jan. 2012, accessed 26 Apr. 2012, www.montrealgazette.com/life/Stephen+Harper+speech+Crown+First+Nations+Gathering/6046010/story.html; and Daniel David, "Not Quite Historic: Meeting Harper in Ottawa Proves Disappointing for First Nations Leaders," *The Nation*, 12 Feb. 2012, 10–12.

4 Apparently Ivison, like many Canadians, believes that First Nations' demands for our treaties, sovereignty, and rights to be respected are old grievances that obviously need to be consigned to the dust bin of history. Sadly these "old grievances" are ongoing and remain central to Canada's liberal colonial project. To forget or ignore the continued violation of our treaties, sovereignty, and rights is comparable to forgetting or ignoring acts of genocide the world over. Ironically, in linking Prime Minister Harper to Sir John A. Macdonald, Ivison fails to realize that he is comparing the keeper of the Indian Act to its creator—the pragmatism of civilization/assimilation/integration remains at the forefront of Canada's Indian policies and in the mindset of many of its citizens. John

Ivison, "Pragmatic PM Looks Ahead as Chiefs Air Old Grievances," *National Post*, 24 Jan. 2012, accessed 20 Apr. 2012, http://fullcomment.nationalpost.com/2012/01/24/john-ivison-pragmatic-pm-looks-ahead-as-chiefs-air-old-grievances/. See also "Canada Keeps forgetting First Nations," *Anishinabek News*, Jan.–Feb. 2012, 1–2.

5 Alan Weisman, "Earth Without People: What Would Happen to Our Planet If the Mighty Hand of Humanity Simply Disappeared?" *Discover Magazine*, Feb. 2005, accessed 19 Oct. 2009, discovermagazine.com/2005/feb/earth-without-people/article_view?b_start:int=1&-C=.

6 *Life after People: The Series*, History Channel, A & E Television Networks, accessed 19 Oct. 2009, www.history.com/content/life_after_people/about-the-show.

7 One of the most recent denials of climate change came from the leader of the Wildrose party during the April 2012 provincial election in Alberta. "Smith's Views on Climate Change May Have Turned Tide," *Financial Post*, 24 Apr. 2012, http://business.financialpost.com/2012/04/24/smiths-views-on-climate-change-may-have-turned-tide/?_lsa=bb963709.

8 "Is Humanity Quietly Abandoning a Future in Space?" *Thestar.com*, 17 Apr. 2012, accessed 25 Apr. 2012, http://www.thestar.com/news/world/article/1162987-is-humanity-quietly-abandoning-a-future-in-space?bn=1.

9 Michael Fry, *Bold, Independent, Unconquer'd and Free: How the Scots Made America Safe for Liberty, Democracy and Capitalism* (Ayr: Fort, 2003); Patrick Griffin, *The People with No Name: Ireland's Ulster Scots, America's Scots Irish, and the Creation of a British Atlantic World, 1689–1764* (Princeton: Princeton University Press, 2001); T. M. Devine, *Scotland's Empire, 1600–1815* (London : Allen Lane, 2003); Jenni Calder, *The Scots in Canada* (Edinburgh: Lauth, 2003); and J. M. Bumsted, *The Scots in Canada* (Ottawa: Canadian Historical Association, 1982).

10 MacKenzie, *Empires of Nature and the Nature of Empires*; and David McNab, *Earth, Water, Air and Fire: Studies in Canadian Ethnohistory* (Waterloo: Wilfrid Laurier University Press, 1998).

11 For more on the issue of colonialism and treatment of canines, see "Canada: Providing Veterinary Care in Remote Cree Communities," IFAW: International Fund for Animal Welfare, accessed 25 Apr. 2012, www.ifaw.org/ca/our-work/cats-and-dogs/canada-providing-veterinary-care-remote-cree-communities.

12 For example, see the various publications that the Aboriginal Policy Research Consortium (International) contribute to the state's efforts at making Aboriginal people in Canada more legible for good or bad.

View of the "modern" Empire: Is this really the way to behave? Drawing by Lorraine Trecroce.

Acknowledgements

This collection and the workshop that gave birth to it originated in David T. McNab's and John M. MacKenzie's experiences researching and writing about empires and colonialism. It was Dr. McNab's desire to encourage scholars to apply to the Canadian and American experiences the concepts found in Dr. Mackenzie's work, particularly *Empires of Nature and the Nature of Empires: Imperialism, Scotland and the Environment* (1997). After all, both Canada and the United States are colonial empires. For this encouragement, I say *meegwetch*.

I would like to thank the various editors for seeing this volume through to completion. Additional thanks are extended specifically to Dr. Tanya Gogan for her judicious editorial advice and moral support. On behalf of all the contributors, it is necessary to thank all unnamed individuals for advice offered. I would like to thank all the contributors for bearing with the various delays, editorial inquiries, and most of all their patience.

Finally, without the support of the former Atkinson Faculty of Liberal and Professional Studies at York University, the Centre for the Study of Indigenous Border Issues, and the Bkejwanong (Walpole Island First Nation) community, the workshop would have never taken place; and without the support of Concordia University through the Vice-President, Research and Graduate Studies' Aid to Research-Related Events, the publication of this volume would have been impossible.

CHAPTER 1 | INTRODUCTION

A Meditation on Environmental History

John MacKenzie

David McNab, the organizer of the conference on which this collection was based, was a Ph.D. student of mine at Lancaster University more than thirty years ago. He worked on the very important British colonial bureaucrat Herman Merivale, a fascinating man whose ideas and viewpoints mark him out as representative of a particular intellectual tradition in the early nineteenth century, generally very different from the views that prevailed later in that century. The flavour of the man is encapsulated in the fact that he considered miscegenation a good thing, even if he saw this in a patronizing way, as a means by which Westerners could assimilate what he would have called "savage races." Later in the century, miscegenation became abhorrent to those who thought in terms of the full-blown racism of the time and insisted on, for us, obnoxious notions of racial purity. Even less attractively, Merivale was opposed to reserves for indigenous peoples, yet his reasons were good. He was not an admirer of the United States and he felt that reserves, as there, simply led to the further cupidity of white people. He argued that reserves would always inevitably contract and were not, therefore, an effective means of protection. Perhaps the Canadian experience has indicated that, at least in one respect, his scepticism was justified. McNab cut his historical teeth on some of these issues before working so assiduously, humanely, and effectively in the realm of First Nations land rights and claims in Canada. When I read his book *Circles of Time*,[1] I become aware of the all the work that he did in this field, the many communities that he had contact with, and the enormous respect that he developed for First Nations peoples, as I am sure they did for him.

What follows is something of a personal account of my relationship with environmental history. I literally stumbled into this important field at a time when it was a relatively new discipline. The story offers a good indication of how historical research can proceed as much by accident as by design. In the mid-1980s, two sports historians wrote to me out of the blue, inquiring if I would contribute to a book they were intending to edit with the title "Sport in Africa." I very nearly refused. I considered it to be a very interesting subject, but not one on which I would have anything useful to say without changing the direction of my research more fundamentally than I was inclined to do. Almost at the moment when I was poised to decline, however, I had a thought. In many books of African exploration and the memoirs of colonial officials and others, I had encountered seemingly endless accounts of hunting African animals. These were passages that I had generally skipped, finding them not very congenial. Other Africanists subsequently told me that they had always done the same. I thought I would return to these and perhaps "give it a go." I would define *sport* not as team games, but in order to reinvoke the uses of that word in the eighteenth and nineteenth centuries: for the British, *sport* always meant shooting.

I was soon enthralled. Whereas it is obvious that hunting has always been central to white expansion and interaction with indigenous peoples in Canada, I realized that this had not been the case in Africa. The myopia of historians had led them to think about the geography, the politics, the diplomacy, and the warfare inherent in the conquest and partition of the so-called Dark Continent, but the great and strikingly characteristic African fauna had tended to be overlooked. Even ivory had been dealt with very much as a commodity and not in terms of the means by which it was extracted. I wrote the article for the *Sport in Africa* collection,[2] and was now enthused enough to write a full-length book.[3] Africa, it seemed to me, had been conquered on the back of its animals. Ivory had been a vital subsidy for missionaries, explorers, and early administrators. Much more than this, animals had provided a crucial protein supplement: whites shot animals in order to feed their porters, their soldiers, their workers, and others. Even the labourers on railway construction had been fed on the products of the gun. As a result, white hunters greatly reduced the animal resources of the new colonies through a dramatic process of asset-stripping. They denied Africans access to the hunt, always a vital component of the African diet, a prohibition that whites eventually backed up with legislation in which they disguised a whites-only right to hunting as a means of conserving a rapidly scarce resource. Such legislation ultimately led to the creation of game reserves and national parks, and all of this was again characterized by the denial of the age-old hunting practices of Africans. As a further twist, these practices were dubbed cruel, unacceptable to modern susceptibilities. Africans, with their long history of finding means of accommodation with often-dangerous animals, defending their crops, supplementing their diet, and utilizing economically valuable products, were now turned into poachers by the intrusion of legal concepts imported from Europe, where class and supposed ownership had long been the key conditioning factor in people's access to the animal resource. Now, in Africa, class was transformed into race.[4]

When you are a pioneer in a field, as seems to have been the case for me, you tread in ways that you would fear to do at a later and more sophisticated time. My ambition was boundless, so I examined hunting in East, Central, and Southern Africa, and, since I was interested in comparative imperial perspectives, I even turned to India. There was a similar, if not entirely parallel, story there. There were other connections too. British army officers in India, and some wealthy compatriots, liked nothing better than planning an African hunting trip as a vacation. Now the point about this lengthy preamble is that when I published a book and several articles in this area,[5] I was naïve enough to fail to realize that I had turned myself into an environmental historian. The distribution of animal species, their relationships with humans, and their fortunes within a multi-use environment were clearly a crucial aspect of the history of the environment, an aspect that also had a very real global dimension. The human interaction with animals, in peoples' mythologies, oral literatures, spiritual responses to their environment, and taboos, as well as in their economic and dietary well-being, was and is a global phenomenon, exhibiting many continental parallels and also disjunctions.[6]

In reality, this new concern with the human/animal relationship merely re-created an interest from my own past. A period of living in Zimbabwe in the early 1970s had already provided me with a fascination with hunting and gathering peoples, notably the so-called Bushmen, sometimes called the San (although that is also a problematic designation). In particular, the Bushmen interacted with and meditated upon their environment through their cave paintings, great artistic achievements that also sparked thoughts about transcontinental parallels. Outside Harare in Zimbabwe, I saw one of the most moving of all Bushmen paintings. It depicts a man chopping down a tree, probably several centuries ago. Now, Bushmen did not chop down trees: they hid behind them while hunting; they gathered their fruits and nuts; they respected them as a source of food and as a spiritual presence in their landscape. For these reasons, trees often appeared in their paintings. So who is this man who is performing this sacrilege? He is a Bantu-speaking African. He is depicted in the painting with a different and heavier physique than the Bushmen. He is an agriculturalist. He is a user of iron, for chopping down trees without iron is difficult. He has arrived to transform the landscape, to rearrange it for a new economic order. His arrival heralded many changes for the Bushmen. They would now become marginal people. They would be partially genetically assimilated by the iron-users, but they would also retreat into less favourable lands, ultimately surviving until modern times. Many now live in Botswana, where they are still under threat. They pursue their traditional lifestyle on poor land, which is now suspected of bearing mineral riches. The government of Botswana is seeking to settle them so that the developers can move in or alternatively to ensure that game reserves are free of people. The Bushmen are seen as standing in the way of progress.

If this all sounds familiar, that is because it is representative of a story that has been repeated many times throughout the globe. Whether it is the Bushmen, or the so-called tribals of the Indian forests, or the Australian Aborigines, or the Gypsies of Europe (whom the Nazis attempted to exterminate), or the travelling people in Britain, sometimes known in Scotland as the tinkers, people who move about are alien to, and unsettling for, the modern state. People should be settled and pinned down. The Bushmen, whose lifestyle was incompatible with iron-age Bantu speakers and with whites in southern Africa (after all, hunters never co-exist comfortably with pastoralists), were themselves hunted down and pushed to the fringes as their numbers declined. Later I read the enthralling book by Marshall Sahlins, *Stone Age Economics*, in which that distinguished anthropologist wrote of hunting and gathering peoples as representing the first affluent societies.[7] Again this is a global story, familiar in Canada, where we think of the potlatch and other distributive systems as representative of such affluence. The universality of this story provides me with my theme for this paper. My intention is to offer further reflections, more than ten years on, about the nature and writing of environmental history. How has it developed during that period?

In 1995, I gave a series of lectures at the University of Aberdeen that were published in 1997 with the title *Empires of Nature and the Nature of Empires* and with the subtitle *Imperialism, Scotland and the Environment.*[8] In offering an initial retrospect to those lectures, perhaps I should start by explaining that subtitle. I adopted it not just because I was delivering the lectures in Scotland, but also because it seemed to me that in the business of imperialism, Scots had had a particular significance when it came to environmental matters. Scots and Scotland were an interesting case. They were in a sense both victims and perpetrators, victims of the extension of English authority and of the power of landlordism, but also perpetrators in the sense that, as one of the most notable of all European emigrant peoples, both in numbers and in prominence, they had so often transferred the problems inflicted upon them at home on to other peoples abroad. This is a familiar and potent theme in Canada.[9] It also illustrates the manner in which so-called metropole and periphery are, in the modern phrase, mutually constitutive. Imperial history, not least of the environment, is never a one-way process.

There were further reasons for using this focus. Scotland was and is a marginal place in terms of the European continent, and its people are in many respects also marginal. Much of the country, in the Highlands and Islands, and in the uplands elsewhere, is made up of marginal land. Through the Highland Clearances, Scots had been dispossessed and their mixed pastoral and agricultural economy (the latter small-scale and largely subsistence) had been replaced by a monoculture, the running of sheep. An extensive pastoralism had removed the need for intensive labour and therefore for closely settled people. Later still, in many areas, the sheep had themselves been replaced. As Scotland had become a playground for the aristocracy and the nouveaux riches of the industrial and commercial worlds, it had been re-created as a landscape suitable for the shooting of grouse, the hunting of deer, and the fishing of trout and salmon.[10] The heather-clad moors that we associate with Scotland were in many respects synthetically created for grouse, since grouse, like tourists, love heather. So-called deer forests were actually open land where stags could be stalked and shot. Scotland was a land of great estates, with landlords of considerable economic and social power. Scottish migrants often wished to recreate such conditions for themselves. Scottish university education, with four universities, was sympathetic to the environmental professions. Scots made good botanists, plant-hunters, foresters, and engineers. They were also highly influential in the worlds of medicine and microbiology, the new science of the late nineteenth century; perhaps the environment could now be cleaned up of diseases both of cattle and of humans. As such, Scots were to have an influence far beyond their numbers throughout the world.

In those lectures, I identified different imperial responses to the environment (and here I am expanding a little by incorporating later work). Initially, explorers and early imperial rulers were convinced of their capacity to transform the environment. For missionaries, the environment was part of the dark forces of the world, mirroring those of the Western conception of hell itself, which Christianity and the elements of modernity that went with it were capable of transforming into a new state of grace.[11] As people found the Christian form of salvation, so too would the environment be saved. Mission stations and European townships, neatly ordered in straight blocks and surrounded by fences, would impose a new order on the land.[12] According to this view, and it was one that was also promulgated by the Victorian art critic John Ruskin, the straight line was emblematic of order and civilization, the curving was symptomatic of disorder and a lack of enlightenment. There are illustrations of African missions, of white settlements in Canada and in New Zealand, which, across the globe, neatly illustrate these Eurocentric and time-specific perceptions. Meanwhile, self-confident imperial figures, both rulers and the new breed of environmental professionals that emerged from the late nineteenth century, were convinced that imperial rule could transform human control of environments. At the beginning of the twentieth century, the commissioner of the East Africa Protectorate, Sir Charles Elliott, considered that Europeans had the capacity to reclaim, discipline, and train nature: "Marshes must be drained, forests skilfully thinned, rivers be taught to run in ordered course and not to afflict the land with drought or flood at their caprice."[13] Deserts and jungles should be conquered and war waged against fever and other diseases. Indigenous peoples, in this world view, were victims and not controllers of their environment. Europeans, in contrast, could subject it to a regime of command and control.

By the interwar years, however, such an overweening imperial sense of mission was already being overtaken by a new scepticism.[14] Grand engineering works and schemes of environmental transformation had not always worked. Self-confidence in theorizing and planning was overtaken by self-consciousness and the possibility of failure. Just as the interwar years were a period of discouraging, confidence-sapping cyclical slump in the world economy, so too was this a time of environmental problems, inducing what we may call the "dust-bowl mentality." Intriguingly, the subsequent writing of environmental history, once the discipline had been fully founded, followed these two moods, though different historians often pursued them in the same period rather than sequentially. The first school was one I identified as Whiggish: a group of writers who adhered to concepts of progress in the human thinking about the environment. This is, it seems to me, largely a Eurocentric school that sees understanding of the environment arising out of the eighteenth-century Enlightenment and from Romantic ideas. In that age-old shibboleth, dating from at least the seventeenth century, knowledge represents power. As studies of the environment increase human understanding, the opportunities to control that environment and render it more benign become more possible. The second school I called the *apocalyptic*, the school for whom present fears are projected on to the past. Thus the collapse of the Mayan and other civilizations of Central and South America, or of the cultures of the Indus Valley, or the society of Easter Island, or again the African culture based upon Great Zimbabwe, all originate from environmental crises, carrying powerful lessons for today.[15]

The third school seemed to me to be a rather more sober one, although I was anxious to avoid anything so reductionist as a dialectical triad. In this third historical strand, it seemed that the imperial period was reduced in scale. It became but one era in a much longer history of human grappling with the environment. Later, in an article in a volume edited by Griffiths and Robin, *Ecology and Empire* (1997), I expanded this phase into a new one which I called, perhaps rather optimistically, the *fully integrated cultural school*.[16] These historians, it seemed to me, attempted to set environmental issues into their full economic, political, and cultural contexts. The major problem with this development in the historiography was that it tended to renationalize environmental history. The massive strength of histories of the environment was that they had broken down or ignored the old nationalist categories. History of this sort could no longer be written in terms of the international boundaries that had been established in Europe and then, partly through the agency of imperialism, around the world. Environmental history transcended such boundaries, for the environment does not respect the lines drawn on maps by humans. If a fully contextualized environmental history were being attempted, however, then the consideration of all the ethnographic, political, economic, and cultural settings in which human interaction with the environment took place tended to bring those boundaries back into play. To write about too many multiple contexts would be a near-impossibility in terms of the practicalities of the historian's range and grasp.

The great virtue of environmental history has been its capacity to globalize the historical vision. Alfred Crosby had done this in his celebrated work *Ecological Imperialism* (1986).[17] So had Richard Grove in his audaciously titled *Green Imperialism* (1995), in this case pursuing the development and application of one concept, desiccation theory, across two centuries, in oceanic islands, and ultimately across the world.[18] If Crosby's book charted what he seemed to see as the malignant in history, the European export of plants and pathogens across the globe, Grove sought out something more benign, the development of an alleged understanding of natural phenomena and the application of policy ideas, for example in the extension of sustainable forestry, based upon them. The flaws of Crosby's book, groundbreaking as it was, are now all too apparent. He dealt only in one-way traffic, failing to recognize that there were processes of exchange taking place that took the grey squirrel, North American conifers, and ultimately such horrors as Himalayan balsam, Japanese knotweed, and the New Zealand flatworm into Europe. He dealt only with what he called neo-Europes, largely ignoring Asia and Africa. Casting the net more widely, the eucalyptus and the wattle were trees with highly specific non-European origins; they have swept the world, sometimes with damaging environmental consequences, but were also ignored by Crosby. Moreover, there were other continental exchanges that took place independent of the imperial process.[19] It is a great pity that, in the 2004 edition of the book, Crosby made no attempt to examine the historiography that he had stimulated over the preceding fifteen to twenty years.

Nevertheless, Crosby and Grove set a global agenda pursued by others. Subsequent works, such as David Arnold's *The Problem of Nature: Environment, Culture and European Expansion*[20] of 1996 and Thomas R. Dunlap's *Nature and the English Diaspora: Environment and History in the United States, Canada, Australia and New Zealand* of 1999,[21] were much more concerned to examine nature as a cultural construct. However, neither of these confronts the major requirement of environmental history in a modern historiography, namely the interconnections and interrelationships of the perceptions and productive use of nature by indigenous peoples on the one hand and imperial people and white settlers on the other, as well as in negotiations between men and women. Even in my own small way, back in the 1980s, I was very much aware of the manner in which hunting was valuable in analyzing such relationships. After all, almost all peoples hunt. Throughout history, hunting has been a source of tension between peoples and classes. It was sufficiently central as a value-laden activity, so important in all manner of economic, cultural, social, even propagandist contexts that it has been a source of conflict since at least ancient times. It has long stimulated the creation of legal provisions, taboos, and sumptuary law. Not surprisingly, hunting has also been a major point of contact and conflict among whites and indigenous peoples throughout the era of imperial conquest. Moreover, we should extend the investigation of the exploitation of the animal resource from the land to waters, to rivers, lakes, and the ocean itself, all of these so important in Canada. As editor of the journal *Environment and History* from 2000 to 2005, one of my complaints was that we never seemed to receive sufficient articles on riverine, lacustrine, and oceanic subjects, never enough on fisheries;[22] yet they have been so central to so many peoples' wellbeing across the world, and also, so significant in so many imperial/indigenous conflicts. To make a broader but related point, it seems to me that the writing of environmental history has arrived at a point where the micro-study, rooted in its locality, examining both the concepts and the potential conflicts of peoples, should be set into these wider macro, even global, issues.

Moreover, the nature and scale of conflict are absolutely rooted in the specifics of the conceptualization of opposing modes of exploitation, themselves embedded in world views and in more prosaic ways of seeing. Many years ago, I stopped a car in the Highlands of Scotland and jumped out to take a photograph of a beautiful view. An old man sat on a chair outside a cottage and, almost in a spirit of embarrassment at my all-too-touristic invasion of his space, I said, "It is so beautiful here." The old man turned a practical and slightly condescending eye upon me. "Aye," he said in his lilting Highland accent, "it's beautiful if you like farming stones." I had not only invaded his space, where he may well have been for many decades, following the lives of his ancestors, but I had failed to look properly and to think deeply. Although that happened nearly forty years ago, the moment has always stayed with me. My gaze was that of the tourist, the far-away romantic gaze looking out mistily over the landscape. His gaze was that of the local, the practical man, for whom romantic images were less important than the immediate problems of getting the land to work, to produce. My view was distant, generalized; his was closer and precise. When I later spent years collecting oral evidence in Africa, I always reminded myself of the different perspectives that I brought to bear as a visiting scholar who would come, see, perhaps evaluate, and go, compared with the people who remained, with their construction of the land in which they set out to survive and to understand the mysteries of life and existence, of the relationship of past, present and future, of the mix of dangers and opportunities, both productive and spiritual, presented by their environment.

These conflicts in perceptions are generally well known, but it is perhaps not too glib to repeat them. Throughout the world, Europeans have tended to see land and nature in terms of ownership, while indigenous people see them in terms of use and relationship. Ownership is divisible into fractions, estate, farm, domestic plot. Ownership of this sort implies individuality. An approach that emphasizes use implies the agency of community, of techniques implying the operation of communal support systems of central relationships to the land and to both kin and other people. It is of course this contrast that lies behind most of the conflicts between First Nations ways of thinking and the developmental notions of modernity. The recent stand-off in Caledonia—it's that Scottish connection again—between the Six Nations of the Haudenosaunee, house-building developers, and the provincial government is of course precisely rooted in this conceptual clash. Euro-Canadians claim that some kind of immutable sale took place. The First Nation understandably cannot conceive of such a sale, particularly as they received no monetary or any other kind of benefit from it. They say the land for the railway line was leased. The notion of leasing fits their communal perceptions much more readily. It is not by any means that they do not understand the notion of a treaty; it is that they do not understand injustice, whatever the quasi-legal forms behind it. Even in the small Scottish town where I live this conflict survives, though in a much less significant form. Alyth Hill is regarded as a commonalty, an area of communal pasture. My own house deeds say that I can take a flock of sheep on to it. Farmers have tried to annex it, and when they do, the villagers in the relatively recent past have marched up the hill and thrown down their fences. The villagers no longer have flocks, but the principle of communal ownership and access still appeals. Such a local case can surely lead to cross-continental sympathy if we just make the connection.

The point is that these communal ways of seeing are in conflict with European notions of change, transformation, and so-called development. Although these European ideas are rooted in the soil of modernity, they have also led to failure. Settlers everywhere had a tendency to underestimate the power of nature in their new lands, not least in the seasonal supply of water and consequent inundations or droughts. We now know that Europeans often seriously misread the environment, projecting one season's characteristics on to another. In consequence, their efforts at control could often fail. Just such an example is the manner in which the environment defeated the Scottish settlement at Baldoon, Ontario, as revealed by Rick Fehr in his current research for York University.[23] His work demonstrates the manner in which settler confidence could be so readily misplaced, not least in failing to understand the conceptions and modes of utilization of the environment of the Odawa, Ojibwa, and Potawatomi peoples of the area. Moreover, settlers, it has been said, hated trees.[24] Whether in Canada or South Africa, Australia or New Zealand, trees were in the way of productive agriculturel; but trees for so many of the indigenous peoples were an essential part of the landscape, not immutable perhaps, but still there and to be respected. We are back with my Bushmen: where settlers did love trees for their considerable economic returns, as in the early—and some would say more recent—period of the Canadian lumber industry, they attacked them with such a will that they seemed to imagine that this bounty could go on for ever.

Indigenous peoples were seldom so profligate, although they were of course perfectly capable of transforming their landscape, mainly through the agency of fire. Fire can be regenerative as well as destructive, but changes in tree cover and the extension of desertification can also arise from indigenous use. Nevertheless, most indigenous people have a sense of the seasonal productivity of the landscape, of multiple and sequential exploitation (in the best sense of the word) in which nature offers opportunities for different areas of productivity. The Enlightenment notion that societies pass through evolutionary stages from hunting and gathering to pastoralism to agriculture has never been quite true, even though it has been a central part of the vision of the imperial world view. Pastoralists and agriculturalists everywhere also hunt and gather, sometimes as a matter of course, sometimes in time of dearth. Europeans found it difficult to grasp this: if a people secured their principal mode of subsistence from herding or cultivating, why should they apparently regress into an older mode from time to time? Consequently, to the European mind it somehow made people more civilized to impose hunting restrictions upon them. In a way, this was odd, since we know that in Europe both rural and even sometimes industrial people tried to diversify, from time to time, into hunting and gathering, although that often turned them into poachers. This is a reminder, to develop an earlier thought, that the word *poacher*, almost more than any other, is profoundly symbolic of social hierarchies and the notion that hunting should be a sporting and not a subsistence activity; yet when emigrants arrived in the colonies of white settlement, they often extolled the fact that they were no longer poachers, but could almost hunt at will, while displacing the term *poacher* onto the newly disadvantaged indigenous people. Those who have been oppressed all too easily become oppressors themselves. That is another of the lessons of modern history.

It was, however, this vision of appropriate and inappropriate activities, of a supposedly civilized use of nature, that helped to elevate the concept of the monoculture in European eyes. Land should be assessed for the product that was most appropriate to its characteristics and qualities. In this respect, humans could do better than God. Indeed the new deity, in a sense, was the market. The monoculture existed because of the market; monoculture's role was to feed the market and respond to its will and caprice. Sugar did well in the Caribbean islands, in the southern States of America, or in the islands of the Indian Ocean, so why not cover the whole place with sugar? Rubber did fantastically well in Malaya, so why not fill it with non-indigenous rubber trees? Of course, there are many Canadian examples, not least in western Ontario. Monocultures globalized approaches to land use and attitudes toward the land's product. They rendered one people on one continent dependent on others in another, a phenomenon that should of course be seen as two-way. The vulnerabilities of such an approach were to become all too apparent in the future. Another major result of this monocultural obsession was to elevate the productivity of land and nature over all other roles. For indigenous people, the land and its products were certainly part of subsistence, possibly even a means of creating exchange relations with neighbours, but the land performed many other functions. It was the place where ancestors had lived and worked. In death, those ancestors had become part of the landscape. They had entered into the spiritual relations of the people of the here and now. Indigenous eyes saw spiritual connections throughout their vision of nature: it was the only way to understand the relationships of humans with the environment.[25] Europeans tended to erase the spiritual. When they introduced missions, they located the spiritual in a particular place; their notion was to penetrate the spiritual into individual hearts and heads. Missions removed spirituality from nature—that smacked too much of pantheism.

According to European interpretations (not necessarily to reality), one common difference between Europeans and non-Europeans is that the former thought in terms of linearity, the latter of circularity. The straight line and the curve to which I have already referred also applied to concepts of time and notions of supposed development or progress. Cliché as this is, we should add other ways of looking to it. When it comes to monocultures and the market, Europeans thought in terms of statistics. From the early nineteenth century, statistics became central to the ways in which Europeans constructed the world. The Statistical Accounts of Scotland were first produced in the late eighteenth century, with the ministers of every parish in the land supplying statistics of agricultural and industrial production, wages, markets, and much other qualitative and quantitative information.[26] Scots took that statistical approach around the world with them.[27] Statistics could be arranged in linear patterns, and those linear arrangements supposedly bespoke progress or the lack of it. What could be more linear than the graph? Of course indigenous peoples recognized times of plenty and periods of dearth, often naming years or seasons according to such recollections. Statistics are a function of writing. Oral cultures (although it must be said that there are of course different forms of literacy) can often deal in combined qualitative and quantitative assessments, in which a more generalized approach to numeracy is endowed with memories and spiritual associations that belong to the society as a whole in ways that cold statistics never could. Statistics came to be attached to a whole range of functions: to water flows, to tree planting and growth, to agricultural production, to all forms of extraction, to shipbuilding and shipping to feed the market, to urban spread, and to port development. Nature in its widest form was counted and pored over, reduced to numbers and sliced up into portions, just like the later development, the pie chart. Land itself was counted. Square miles, acreages, and hectares, however approximate, became the handmaidens of forms of national identity, of concepts of ownership, of demarcations of land in terms of access, use, and productivity. Statistics took on their own logic and could inspire confidence and apprehension at the same time.

The irony of all of this is that the linearity that Europeans brought to all their concepts of time, space, place, and production actually fell down before the cyclical character of markets, modern economies, and nature itself. The ancient writers of the Judaeo-Christian Bible were well aware of cycles, with their seven years of plenty and seven years of want. Strikingly, in Africa, rainfall patterns sometimes do seem to operate in something approximating to seven-year cycles. It was soon discovered that markets and modern economies also operated in cyclical ways, with each good period carrying the seeds of the succeeding bad one. Economists in the twentieth century pondered such cycles and pursued the economic holy grail of breaking them; but, fascinatingly, the observers of the natural world have today become terrified of the breaking of the environmental cycle in new, human-made, and alarming forms. We now know that natural cycles operate at two levels, the short term where good and poor rains with all their concomitant effects in wind flows and temperatures can alternate over periods of years, and the longer term where temperature changes—like the northern hemisphere's little ice age of the seventeenth century—and rainfall patterns, with consequent effects upon vegetation, insect distribution, and animal numbers, can vary across centuries.[28] The major question, today, of course is the extent to which global warming represents one of these longer term cycles. Scientists seem generally to agree that it almost certainly does not, that it is something unique in relatively recent history, that it has been induced by human activity, and that it is probably irreversible. The cycle has been broken in exceptionally disturbing ways. In the spring of 2006, the British government's chief scientific officer, Sir David King, was castigating politicians for failing to view global warming seriously enough. The belief that such warming could be restricted to something of the order of two degrees Celsius was, in his view, unrealistic—and there is, he said, "no planet B."[29] The rapid retraction of the Arctic ice cap, so familiar in Canada, the melting of the Siberian permafrost (perhaps for the first time in 40,000 years), and the astonishing decline in the ice surrounding the Antarctic continent indicated that we are heading for warming in the order of at least three degrees. This is an alarming phenomenon induced by the profligacy of the developed and rapidly developing world, but impacts upon the poorest of the globe. Suddenly, the apocalyptic approach to environmental history, about which I felt sceptical in the past, seems to take on a new but different twist.

It is perhaps our current concern with CO_2 emissions and their effects upon our planet, together with a realization that extreme climatic events seem to be more common, that has helped to develop a new interest in the history of climate upon human history. Since I gave those lectures more than ten years ago, there have been many studies of global patterns, such as the periodic El Niño and other meteorological phenomena throughout human history. In 2006, Greg Bankoff suggested that we should arrive at a better understanding of Spanish colonization in the Pacific between 1521 and 1898 in terms of meteorological history.[30] Weather systems influenced the form and extent of empire at the macro level while also mediating Spanish relationships with indigenous people (e.g., in relationship to periodical floods in the Philippines). This article represents another welcome characteristic of some modern approaches, namely the tendency to deal in deeper time periods as well as wider geographical frames.

To sum up the changes that have taken place over the past ten years, I would suggest the following. Early works in any field have a tendency to be sweeping and perhaps underspecialized. An opening bid goes where successors may fear to tread. Objections, additions, and modifications soon follow, sometimes disabling the original thesis, sometimes confirming it in certain respects. The original hypothesis may be shown to be both part of an even bigger picture and also amenable to evaluation in many more local studies. In these ways have early ideas been partially confirmed or denied; yet as this work has progressed, we have at least largely escaped from older Western and imperial perceptions. Moreover, we have begun to realize that many cultural artefacts can lead us into aspects of the history of the environment. We have developed an increasing interest in visual depictions of the natural world, not just on the surfaces of caves, as with the Bushmen, but in the many abstract and geometrical representations of Australian Aborigines, or in the carvings and images on bark of other peoples in North America and elsewhere. Meanwhile, paintings by European migrants passed through a fascinating progression that tells us a great deal about the imperial vision: they started by attempting to make the exotic look like the familiar, by transferring Western artistic conventions (e.g., the picturesque and the sublime) into unfamiliar contexts. They moved on into efforts to render the essence of difference, in climate, light effects, trees, snow, and ice. In the twentieth century, they realized that the true route to a nationalist art lay in taking up, celebrating, and perhaps adapting indigenous art forms.[31] They thus returned to the people and to the land. This was one important way in which Western perceptions were, if not entirely abandoned, at least modified.

We have in some respects risen above the obsession with the imperial era, though in a country like Canada it is in many ways always with us. We are more aware of environmental histories in deeper time and of the ways in which indigenous peoples have changed their environments. At least in Africa and some other places, we no longer see the imperial period as uniquely evil in terms of environmental change; some conservationist practices were relatively benign. As the imperial period sinks into history, we are now aware of the fact that inheritor regimes, such as some of the nationalist governments in Africa, have actually pursued policies more destructive of the environment, and less sympathetic to indigenous peoples (in this case fellow citizens of the politicians) and their practices than was the case under European rule. One or two studies in East and West Africa, for example, have demonstrated that this might be true.[32] Moreover, new nationalist governments have invariably clung to individualistic and class relations, not to mention the strict demarcations of land ownership and use that characterized their imperial predecessors. Western forms of mapping the land, as well as the mind, still prevail.

Only the hopelessly naïve can continue to see the supposed scientific study of the environment as some kind of objective and progressive system of knowledge. Science is rooted in its social, cultural, and economic contexts, and one person's scientific certainty is another's dubious theory. This is not to say, of course, that such research is entirely bereft of valuable quantifiable data and theoretical ideas, as perhaps the science of global warming among much else reveals; but skeptical contextualization is always necessary. The scientist invariably needs the correctives supplied by the social sciences and the humanities.

Another significant development that has taken place in recent years is a welcome gendering of the environment. Scientists of the past, and perhaps some of the present, seldom gendered their work, yet it is quite clear that the relationship of men and women with their environments can be different. As always, the prime focus has been on men, but women also conceptualized and modified their ecological contexts. We need far more studies in this area, though there have been some significant ones in Africa.[33] In a similar way, local environmental histories must be rooted in the experiences of real people, in their oral traditions, and in their myths, legends, and histories, transmitted from generation to generation. This is clearly a very important consideration in Canada, and significant studies in India and Africa have taken these considerations on board.[34] Moreover, the relationships of communities, between Euro-Canadians and First Nations peoples, but also between different religious and ethnic communities elsewhere, must remain central to all forms of a human-centred environmental history.

Some areas remain underexamined, however. I have already mentioned human interactions with water, fisheries, and marine life. We need more on the history of environmental degradation caused by urbanization and industry, more on catchments and water supply, more on towns, cities, parks, and gardens. Some work has been done on all of these, not least in the environmental histories of New Zealand[35] and in some corners of Canada. I would add to these the apparent reluctance to deal with the environmental effects of war.[36] With some notable exceptions, this reluctance stems from the disruptions in the supply of data that are occasioned by war, in the difficulties of entering war zones when dealing with recent wars, and in the sensitivities of such studies, particularly when other political, economic, and social considerations may seem more pressing. In the recent Iraq War, it is quite clear that environmental effects have been enormous. When will it be possible to study these? On the one hand, we know that, among his many iniquities, Saddam Hussein tried to destroy an entire people, the Marsh Arabs, by draining and thereby transforming their landscape such that their traditional economy and the culture based upon it would be unsustainable. It is now possible that their lands will be flooded once more and their culture revived. However, much else has been highly destructive: the disruption of oil pipelines and many other sources of pollution and damage. The activities of soldiers are seldom environmentally friendly, and we must include archaeological sites among key aspects of the environment, vital in a people's sense of identity and relationship with the past. The immense damage caused to the great site of Babylon, archaeology that in many ways is a possession of the entire world, has been a highly disturbing aspect of the Allied occupation. Turning one of the great sites of the world into a military base seems all the more crass when its partial destruction is justified on the basis of alleged efforts to preserve it. Such crassness, of course, comes from the top, from politicians, senior officials, and generals in the Pentagon. It comes as no surprise to find that those who fail so utterly to respect the past also have no respect for the future. That archaeological and cultural destroyers and global warming deniers are to be found within the same warped minds should perhaps come as no surprise.

This leads me to my final point. It is hard to study environmental history without being, in some senses, an environmental activist. Those of us who are concerned with the past need to maintain a certain coolness, a degree of scepticism, a refusal to be blown hither and thither by passionate fads, but, that said, it is difficult not to be committed to certain ideals. Environmental historians have, in so many respects, to be idealists. They study the past precisely because they have a care for the present and a concern for the future. Their manifesto embraces a sympathetic understanding and a commitment to more benign relationships among peoples and between people and their ecological contexts.

Notes

1 David T. McNab, *Circles of Time: Aboriginal Land Rights and Resistance in Ontario* (Waterloo: Wilfrid Laurier University Press, 1999). See also David T. McNab, ed., *Earth, Water, Air and Fire: Studies in Canadian Ethnohistory* (Waterloo: Wilfrid Laurier University Press, 1988), which contains many environmental insights.

2 John M. MacKenzie, "Hunting in Eastern and Central Africa in the Late Nineteenth Century, with Special Reference to Zimbabwe," in *Sport in Africa: Essays in Social History*, ed. William J. Baker and James A. Mangan (New York: Africana Publishing, 1987), 172–95.

3 John M. MacKenzie, *The Empire of Nature: Hunting, Conservation and British Imperialism* (Manchester: Manchester University Press, 1988).

4 A recent, excellent survey of these tendencies in the case of Kenya is to be found in Edward I. Steinhart, *Black Poachers, White Hunters: A Social History of Hunting in Colonial Kenya* (Oxford: James Currey, 2006).

5 John M. MacKenzie, "Hunting and the Natural World in Juvenile Literature," in *Imperialism and Juvenile Literature*, ed. Jeffrey Richards (Manchester: Manchester University Press, 1989), 144–72, and "Chivalry, Social Darwinism and Ritualised Killing: The Hunting Ethos in Central Africa up to 1914," in *Conservation in Africa: People, Policies and Practice*, ed. David Anderson and Richard Grove (Cambridge: Cambridge University Press, 1987), 41–62. See also John M. MacKenzie, ed., *Imperialism and the Natural World* (Manchester: Manchester University Press, 1990).

6 From an extensive literature, useful works include Tim Ingold, David Riches, and James Woodburn, eds., *Hunters and Gatherers: History, Evolution and Social*

Change (New York: Berg, 1988); Tim Ingold, *The Appropriation of Nature: Essays on Human Ecology and Social Relations* (Manchester: Manchester University Press, 1986); and Robert L. Kelly, *The Foraging Spectrum: Diversity in Hunter-Gatherer Lifeways* (Washington: Smithsonian Institution Press, 1995). A recent sophisticated work on hunting is one relating to Canada: Greg Gillespie, *Hunting for Empire: Narratives of Sport in Rupert's Land, 1840–70* (Vancouver: University of British Columbia Press, 2007).

7 Marshall Sahlins, *Stone Age Economics* (London: Aldine-Atherton, 1974); see also his "Notes on the Original Affluent Society," in *Man the Hunter*, ed. R. Lee and I. DeVore (Chicago: Aldine, 1968).

8 John M. MacKenzie, *Empires of Nature and the Nature of Empires: Imperialism, Scotland and the Environment* (Edinburgh: Manchester University Press, 1997).

9 There is now a considerable bibliography on Scots in Canada. Useful overviews and more detailed research are provided by Jenni Calder, *The Scots in Canada* (Edinburgh: Lauth, 2003), and Marjory Harper and Michael E. Vance, eds., *Myth, Migration and the Making of Memory: Scotia and Nova Scotia, c. 1700–1990* (Halifax: Fernwood, 1999).

10 Willie Orr, *Deer Forests, Landlords and Crofters* (Edinburgh: John Donald, 1982).

11 John M. MacKenzie, "Missionaries, Science and the Environment in Nineteenth-century Africa," in *The Imperial Horizons of British Protestant Missions, 1880–1914*, ed. Andrew Porter (Grand Rapids, MI: W.B. Eerdmans, 2003), 106–30.

12 An excellent example of this is the image of the mission station to be found in Robert Moffat, *Missionary Labours and Scenes in Southern Africa* (London: John Snow, 1846), 147. Moffat was particularly keen on the notion of environmental redemption through Christianity.

13 Sir Charles Eliot, *The East Africa Protectorate* (London: F. Cass, 1905), 4.

14 Some of these themes were developed in John M. MacKenzie "'This year's forest is next year's fire': The Colonial Official and the Environment," in *How Green Was Our Empire: Environment, Development and the Colonial Service*, ed. Terry Barringer (London: Institute of Commonwealth Studies OSPA Research Project, 2005), 7–22. See also John M. MacKenzie, "Green Pasts and Presents: The Paradox of Environmental Histories and Current Anxieties of Damage and Destruction," in *How Green Was Our Empire: Environment, Development and the Colonial Service*, ed. Terry Barringer (London: Institute of Commonwealth Studies OSPA Research Project, 2005), 145–51.

15 A popular example of this kind of apocalyptic view is Clive Ponting, *A Green History of the World* (Harmondsworth: Penguin, 1992).

16 John M. MacKenzie, "Empire and the Ecological Apocalypse: The Historiography of the Imperial Environment," in *Ecology and Empire: Environmental History of Settler Societies*, ed. Tom Griffiths and Libby Robin (Edinburgh: Keele University Press, 1997), 215–28.

17 Alfred W. Crosby, *Ecological Imperialism: The Biological Expansion of Europe, 900–1900* (Cambridge: Cambridge University Press, 1986); the second edition (actually an impression) appeared in 2004.

18 Richard H. Grove, *Green Imperialism: Colonial Expansion, Tropical Island Edens and the Origins of Environmentalism, 1600–1860* (Cambridge, UK: White Horse Press, 1995).

19 William Beinart and Karen Middleton, "Plant Transfers in Historical Perspective: A Review Article," *Environment and History* 10, no. 1 (2004): 3–30. A notable overview of environmental history of the British Empire, published since this paper was written, is William Beinart and Lotte Hughes, *Environment and Empire* (Oxford: Oxford University Press, 2007).

20 David Arnold, *The Problem of Nature: Environment, Culture and European Expansion* (Oxford: Oxford University Press, 1996).

21 Thomas R. Dunlap, *Nature and the English Diaspora: Environment and History in the United States, Canada, Australia and New Zealand* (Cambridge: Cambridge University Press, 1999).

22 One notable exception is Michael J. Chiarappa, "Overseeing the Family of Whitefishes: The Priorities and Debates of Coregonid Management on America's Great Lakes, 1870–2000," *Environment and History* 11, no. 2 (2005): 163–94.

23 I am grateful to David McNab and to Rick Fehr for allowing me access to some of Fehr's insights.

24 Brian S. Osborne, "The Iconography of Nationhood in Canadian Art," in *The Iconography of Landscape: Essays on the Symbolic Representation, Design and Use of Past Environments*, ed. Denis Cosgrove and Stephen Daniels (Cambridge: Cambridge University Press, 1988), 165. This volume contains a good deal on the symbolism and representation of trees. See also Warwick Frost, "Did They Really Hate Trees? Attitudes of Farmers, Tourists and Naturalists Towards Nature in the Rainforests of Eastern Australia," *Environment and History* 8, no. 1 (2002): 3–20.

25 These searches for the spiritual and the ancestral in nature, so often illustrating the great oral myths through which origins and continuities can be explained, are common in the artistic traditions of Canadian First Nations peoples. I have long argued that museums must be alert and sensitive to this. See John M. MacKenzie, "People and Landscape: The Environment and National Identities

in Museums," in *National Museums: Negotiating Histories*, ed. Darryl McIntyre and Kirsten Wiener (Canberra: National Museum of Australia, 2001), 173–82.

26 There is some useful information on this in Charles W.J. Withers, *Geography, Science and National Identity: Scotland since 1520* (Cambridge: Cambridge University Press, 2001).

27 For the application of these phenomena in a particular environment, see John M. MacKenzie, *The Scots in South Africa: Ethnicity, Identity, Gender and Race* (Manchester: Manchester University Press, 2007).

28 These issues can be followed through in Raymond S. Bradley and Philip D. Jones, ed., *Climate since 1500* (London: Routledge, 1992); A.M. Mannion, *Global Environmental Change* (Harlow: Prentice Hall, 1991); and Richard H. Grove, *Ecology, Climate and Empire: Colonialism and Global Environmental History, 1400–1940* (Cambridge, UK: White Horse Press, 1997).

29 King continued to use this phrase in later years—as at the Third Annual Forum on Enterprise and the Environment in June 2011. See www.smithschool.ox.ac.uk/thereisnoplanetB, accessed 6 October, 2012.

30 Greg Bankoff, "Winds of Colonisation: The Meteorological Contours of Spain's Imperium in the Pacific, 1521–1878," in *Environment and History* 12, no. 1 (2006): 65–88.

31 These themes are developed in John M. MacKenzie, "Art and the Empire," in *The Cambridge Illustrated History of the British Empire*, ed. P.J. Marshall (Cambridge: Cambridge University Press, 1996), 296–315.

32 See, among other examples, Dan Brockington, *Fortress Conservation: The Preservation of the Mkomazi Reserve, Tanzania* (Oxford: International African Institute in association with James Currey, 2002); some of the contributions to William Beinart and Joann McGregor, ed., *Social History and African Environments* (Oxford: James Currey, 2003); and William G. Moseley and B. Ikubolajeh Logan, ed., *African Environment and Development* (Aldershot: Ashgate, 2004).

33 L. Muthoni Wanyeki, ed., *Women and Land in Africa: Culture, Religion and Realizing Women's Rights* (London: Zed, 2003).

34 A good example in the case of India is Ajay Skaria, *Hybrid Histories: Forests, Frontiers and Wildness in Western India* (Delhi: Oxford University Press, 1999); and for Africa, Christopher A. Conte, *Highland Sanctuary: Environmental History in Tanzania's Usambara Mountains* (Athens: Ohio University Press, 2004); see also Brockington, *Fortress Conservation*; MacKenzie, "People and Landscape"; and Withers, *Geography, Science and National Identity*.

35 Geoff Park, *Nga Ururoa: Ecology and History in a New Zealand Landscape* (Wellington: Victoria University Press, 1995); Eric Pawson and Tom Brooking,

eds., *Environmental Histories of New Zealand* (Oxford: Oxford University Press, 2002); and Tom Brooking and Eric Pawson, eds., "New Zealand," special issue, *Environment and History* 9, no. 4 (2003).

36 A relatively rare example is Judith A. Bennett, "War, Emergency and the Environment: Fiji, 1939–1946," *Environment and History* 7, no. 3 (2001): 255–88.

CHAPTER 2

Tricky Medicine: Something Old for Something New

Heather Marie Annis

> I think it's up to us, particularly as artists, people working with spiritual lives—which is essentially what artists do—they're kind of priests of a sort, they serve that kind of purpose in the culture—without the revival and the bringing back of that essential character, the Trickster—Weesageechak [in Cree], Nanabush in Ojibway—I think we've had it. We're up shit creek.
>
> — *Tomson Highway*

Misery: the sign that hangs sluggishly above the heads of Torontonians as they walk down the bustling streets, ride the subway, or enter one of the many financial institutions. Trickster watches from her window as the crowds move in synchronicity rushing to work, or to a meeting, or to lunch—and although they rush to lunch, they seem to rush through lunch so they can rush back to work again. She wonders, because she herself is not in a rush, if she is in someway abnormal, or has too much time on her hands.

"How did we get ourselves into such a state of unhappiness and decay?" she asks aloud. It might have something to do with the disconnection that exists between us and the world around us, including the natural environment and other people (human and non-human). The fact that we are able to rush by so many people is only possible because we do not know them. Knowing them would slow us down, which is unacceptable if speed is directly connected to efficiency, which in turn is connected to productivity or success. The possibilities run through Trickster's mind. Trickster is very smart.

In North American Western society, most people are very busy working towards being happy, and the harder they work (i.e., the more they work) the faster they can get there (or so they have been told). This is where the conflict sits. We get caught up with working so very hard, and after a while start to get sick and miserable. Getting sick is usually a tell-tale sign that you need a rest, but not here. Here it means that you should work even harder because if you are feeling less happy, you are obviously not working hard enough. Soon we begin to forget what our families look like because we see them only on holidays, our friends fade into the background, and the natural environment ... well, we do not even have to worry about that because we only need to be outside to get in and out of our cars.

Sometimes we even forget about ourselves, and then we cannot even remember what we are working for in the first place. Trickster knows this first-hand because she tried it for a while, and soon enough she realized that she had not taken a holiday for over two years. One day she went to the movies and recognized herself as a zombie in a sci-fi flick. "It seems that this world is in desperate need for some medicine," she says. None of that new stuff, though. She has seen what that does to people—temporary relief to help get them back to work (side effects may include nausea, heartburn, indigestion, and difficulty sleeping, but not addiction even though you may be tempted to continue taking this particular medication for weeks—maybe even months—to follow). We need something tried and true, something that will work worldwide, something that someone (nudge, nudge) has been keeping safe up her sleeve.

In his book *Dialects of the Concrete,* Karel Kosik addresses the habits of Western society; living always for the future and for the joy that we can feel tomorrow if we work hard today: "the individual always finds himself in the future and he uses the present as a means or instrument to realize his projects."[1] Due to this ever-increasing focus on "success" and economy, attention is removed from everyday life and goals are made distant and unattainable. The problem, of course, with unattainable goals is that they very often fail to be attained.

In *The Spirit of Regeneration,* Eduardo Grillo Fernandez describes this idea of happiness as the "legal drug" that the capitalist society produces for itself, known as "Utopia." The utopia he describes "is the image of a world which does not yet exist but which can be constructed in the future ... a flight from the present [which] can only emerge as the expression of a profound discontent on the part of people with the world in which they live, as well as from the conviction that it can indeed be modified."[2] This drug then created a dichotomy between what could one day exist and reality, positioning the former much higher than the latter despite its often being yet another unattainable imagining. This is not to discredit the idea of creating goals or dreams to strive for, but the distance that exists between the reality and the utopia prevents pleasure or happiness from existing in the now.

The idea of utopia being located always in the distant future, Fernandez explains, is specific to and a direct result of the Judeo-Christian religion and conception of the world, which "finds support in the doctrine of unlimited progress and in technology as the instruments of the domination of nature by man."[3] Moreover, within this pursuit to modify, in accordance with the needs of humanity, we become as beings separated from others in society, focused on the needs and desires of the self—a perception that easily results in a consumer society.[4]

The response to this fulfillment of individual satisfaction is gargantuan. Everywhere we look, there is someone or something that can be at our disposal for a mere exchange of dollar bills, and suddenly we are that much closer to being happy. One does not even need to think very much because the products, and little bits of temporary happiness, are brought to us via television and billboards, sales and price rollbacks.

Within this prescription however, exists the demise of imagination and of the ability to create one's own definition of "success" because it is supplied *for us* very clearly: the more we have the happier we are. As preparation for this, children learn from a young age that anything outside of this dominant methodology is not effective and inadequate; they learn to comply.

This system is a difficult one to challenge because we are constantly reminded of our good fortune and thus we have no right to complain. Urged to look to the misfortune of others, we learn to hold our position as privileged. Even though we are unhappy, we dare not question privilege, and we suppress emotions that tell us that maybe things could be different. The flooding of bad news from other parts of the world justifies for us that we are the lucky ones. It is this denial that allows the system to remain intact and allows some to be oppressed while others possess. Every empire has its ways of ensuring and maintaining its dominance.

In *Pedagogy of the Oppressed,* Paulo Freire says that "for the oppressors, what is worthwhile is to have more—always more—even at the cost of the oppressed having less or having nothing. For them, to be is to have and to be the class of the 'haves.'" He goes on to say that "in the egotistic pursuit of having as a possessing class, they suffocate in their own possessions and no longer are; they merely have."[5] The system is then perpetuated and we continue to look to the future for our happiness, while measuring ourselves against others, positioning ourselves in competition with others. The most dangerous conflict is that we are no longer active beings, since we are disconnected by the technologies that separate us from the real world, from real communication, and from real interaction. News of injustice does not have the same impact when delivered through the television or computer, which can be turned off, or when it is received through a Facebook feed. Although we remain unhappy we cannot act upon this competition because we are numbed and appeased from the interference of white noise.

Throughout her work, Patricia A. O'Riley suggests that this is particularly a problem for future generations that are experiencing overexposure to technology from a young age in the current education system. She says that to combat the negative aspects of this technological implementation into the educational system we need "to have silence in the dominant technology discourse so that other voices may be heard, so that students might hear their own voices and the voices of others."[6] This likewise applies to technological involvement in daily life as well as in the workforce, not in an effort to abolish technological discourse completely, but to allow space and interaction of other forms as equal.

O'Riley calls this reconfiguration of meaning-making a "methodology of difference,"[7] in which we can create a respectful and encouraging space for variation and acceptance. To achieve this, societies (especially North American Western society) must be willing to research and examine their own flaws, instead of pointing them out in others to maintain their own credibility and status as the dominant culture. Cultural competition and comparison must be halted in order for humanity to progress in a positive manner.

Back to the Beginning

Theatre creator Jerzy Grotowski once said, "I don't want to discover something new but something forgotten."[8] Let us for a minute consider returning to a healthy lifestyle through the sharing of times gone by—let us consider storytelling. Kieran Egan discusses the qualities of oral tradition that are missing in literacy, and how this affects development: "If a story is the machine we have for fixing the affective meaning of events, we may be approaching a reason why young children find them so engaging. In a world where the meaning of events and incidents must be quite puzzling, the story offers a haven of clarity."[9]

Since children are brought up in oral-language environments, storytelling, as Egan points out, is a natural progression from story as entertainment and stimulation to story as a means of education. Traditional stories worldwide have been developed by the history of our ancestors and their relationship with the land. Often the stories are said to come from the land itself and to have been overheard by our ancestors, who necessarily had close and reciprocal relationships with the natural world. This reciprocity has been passed down as tradition, and when a storyteller embodies the power of oral culture, the teller "reawakens a people's whole memory by an act of handing on."[10]

As a time-honoured tradition in oral cultures storytelling provides the impetus for teaching, building and maintaining social moralities and relationships, "with all the necessary emotional warnings and encouragements built into it."[11] Oral traditions have been slowly gaining long-overdue validation in Western culture, although due to its complexity, oral culture is still largely misunderstood.

This part of the paper could very well be about storytelling and its endless attributes. It could very well be about stories because "the truth about stories," as Thomas King would say, "is that that's all we are."[12] We are in this moment, however, going to focus on one aspect of the story in particular. A key player, actually. One that might be able to help heal the stunted communication that has occurred in North American Western culture and throughout the world: the trickster. "It is about time," Trickster pipes in. "I've been waiting in the margins since paragraph four."

Other than a funny character that plays pranks or is being pranked, and therefore provokes laughter, the trickster is a complex character that is constantly changing and adapting. In his work on trickster discourse in art, Allan Ryan describes the traditional Native North American trickster as "transcending geographical boundaries and tribal distinctions, it is most often characterized by frequent teasing, outrageous punning, constant wordplay, surprising association, extreme subtlety, layered and serious reference, and considerable compassion."[13] It is important to note that the trickster appears, in some form, in every culture throughout the history of the world. It is a universal trait, an archetype.[14] Be it the clown, the jester, coyote, raven, fool, Nanabojo, Weesageechak, hare, half hero or Napi (and the list goes on) this character is always waiting and ready for action.

It is also important to note that this idea of a trickster and even the term trickster itself is grossly problematic. In her work, "What's the Trouble with the Trickster?" Kristina Fagan addresses how in studies of the Aboriginal trickster many literary critics have categorized and contained a trickster "stripped of the burden of belonging to any particular time of place," making the trickster so vague that it was "free to represent the critics' ideals."[15] She questions an approach to humour and comedy, a "mythical strain," as she quotes from Susan Purdie, in which mythical forms such as the trickster or fool are seen as "expressing certain universal forces ... and arising out of the unconscious, of lower classes, of past cultures, or of 'primitive' cultures," rather than "focusing on the social uses of humour." She also criticizes how, in such studies, the laughter generated from such characters or the actions of such characters is seen as intrinsically valuable and involved with energies that are "distinct from social convention."[16] To counter this argument for the trickster's intrinsic value, Fagan cites examples of how the trickster has been used for negative purposes and demonstrates that the trickster does indeed have its "dark side" as well.

Whether labelled *trickster* or *clown*, these beings come with a great variety of uses depending on the artist using them (as there is always an artist behind the scenes—be it writer, performer, storyteller, or other creator). Where this artist lives, when he or she lives, the context in which these artistic expressions are used, and the learned history and tradition from which the individual artist draws, all change the use and meaning of a specific rendering.

Fagan also critiques *The Trickster Shift* and its examination of artists' uses of the trickster, saying that "artists and their practices are presented not as using and drawing on tradition, but as guided by a tradition and a 'worldview.'"[17] She critiques the fact that, in this understanding, the trickster is making choices rather than the artist and the term *trickster* begins to refer to everything Indigenous artists are involved in; the term thus becomes meaningless and "loses its usefulness as a term of analysis." In using the trickster, the artist does so with specific personal goals and choices motivated by personal agendas, sometimes positive and sometimes negative. Therefore it is important to look at the context in which a writer or artist is using "trickster methodology," in order to better understand why the creator has produced this particular rendition of trickster or clown and what it is a reaction to; idealizing and generalizing such choices removes the artist's agency.

Fagan also notes that "'tradition' is continually reinvented, with contemporary cultural responses being framed in reference to the past and to 'traditionality.'"[18] Every work of art is moving forward with the past and using the traditions of specific tricksters "recreated because of specific and current needs."[19] In this paper, then, the term *trickster* is used generally not in order to simplify or reduce that span of the many, many traditions but as a contemporary critical term to reference a variety of artists using tradition and drawing from the world around them to communicate a message that is sometimes subversive, sometimes silly, sometimes healing, and always dependent upon the context, the current environment, and the individual artist.

Serious Play

At this point, perhaps we should attempt to define the word *clown*. "Good luck!" says Trickster. As typically defined, the clown is someone who jokes, plays, and is involved in antics, or someone who acts comically. Although these descriptions are vague, it is as difficult to define or pinpoint Clown as it is Trickster, and the word is just as problematic, since (particularly in Western culture) it conjures images big shoes, big colourful hair, and big makeup. Traditions of clowning in terms of performance, social reaction, and commentary, or as a form of connection and communication, however, are limitless and span the globe as well as history. In many traditions, the clown figure is seen as a messenger or shaman and was, sometimes still is, perceived as being above the leaders of a tribe, kingdom, or community. The clown could speak truthfully and ridicule the leader when he was out of line.[20]

There are as many ways or methods to explore, learn, approach and draw on such traditions, including the Pochinko Clown. To learn this specific tradition of clowning, one must face oneself in the six directions: earth, sky, north, south, east, and west. This exploration is done through both the making and the (re)discovery of masks for each direction in innocence (past) and experience (future). Within this unveiling of the self, a seventh mask is then discovered, the mask of the trickster, clown, fool, *Heyoka*, or messenger of the gods. This mask is able to discover joy within an individual. From this joy, the clown being can take in the world around him or herself and discover what effect he or she will have on society and, by extension, how society can be altered and transformed into good.

In Canada, the mainstream exploration of clown has undergone renewed interest of late. This began with Canadian performer Richard Pochinko (after whom Pochinko Clown is named), who studied clowning throughout Europe and returned unsatisfied, with the impression that this clown work lacked emotional and spiritual range. After exploring several types of clown, he then allegedly met a Native American clown named Jonsmith, who taught Pochinko a traditional form of clown. Pochinko immediately fell in love with the purpose of this work and has been integral in facilitating and nurturing a new generation of clowns, with the intent to help other people rediscover the joy that resides within them by addressing what inhibits or enables this joy. Pochinko Clown has become recognized and celebrated as one of the most important techniques for exploring the art of clown today in North America, and this has allowed the trickster to become more prominent in Western culture. Ironically enough, this practice has been around for thousands of years.

One of the most important aspects of the clown figure is that the audience has the opportunity to share the experience of joy discovered by the character, even when discovery takes place through a painful process. The audience's participation in this act is crucial to the performance since without the act of sharing the clown cannot travel through his or her journey and therefore cannot reach joy: "You can't act in a comic way in isolation. You have to be included. There has to be a collective of some kind.... It's a positive, compassionate act of survival, it's getting along."[21] This can be easily achieved when the audience is able to relate to a similar circumstance in their own lives, one of youthful abandon, an open heart and, hopefully, good old fun.

This type of relationship and sense of abandon is often perceived as a waste of time or invalid as a form of medicine in Western culture. The Indian tradition of *maya-lila* (*Sanskrit* for *illusion and play*), however, rejects the Western perspective that play is an interruption of ordinary life. To the *maya-lila*, play is permanent and is seen as a privilege held in great esteem. In *The Future of Ritual*, Richard Schechner writes of the *maya-lila*: "playing is what the world consists of. To be 'at play' is to recognize that all relationships are provisional.... The only realities that can be experienced are the interpenetrating, transformable, non-exclusive, porous, multiple realities."[22]

So why is it that Western culture reserves play for children, positioning it as something that is grown out of as one matures? Why and when is play denied or repressed, and when is it sustained or invited? Schechner argues that play is in fact an integral part of society and explains that it fulfills aspects of human need. This occurs through the expressive and communicative behaviour that accesses "ambivalent symbolic actions pointing at the real transactions." Schechner continues, explaining that accessing these interactions through play "help[s] people avoid too direct a confrontation with these events."[23] In this way, play is necessary for the betterment of society. Trickster, as primary figure of play or as a form of play, plays at realities so we can watch/observe and learn from the mistakes.

How then can play work in the Western world? Is it an idea worth pursuing? On the street, about their daily rush, people are caught off guard by anything out of the ordinary, such as play. In public, they do not have the ability to dismiss play by separating themselves from the action with the fourth wall (a device used in the theatre when we go to see a play, which separates the audience from the performer). In this situation, the clown or the play becomes an event because it appears in life, not in abstraction. This event of "transport[ing] everyday reality into something more ideal"[24]—that is, bringing the ideal into the now—is more likely to have a lasting impact on an audience member/participant/viewer than something officially prescribed for that purpose. The viewer goes home to tell someone about the strange and exciting thing that was witnessed, and then the story is alive and contagious—and when a story is active, it spreads like wildfire.

More importantly, a theatre suggests a limited or specific audience, usually confined to those that can pay. The clown figure, due to its playful nature, is not confined to a theatre or to a select group of people, or even to performance. The clown instead transforms spaces and creates celebration. Richard Schechner stresses that one of the most important aspects of street performance, one way in which the clown often appears, is the celebration: "A big part of the celebration is experiencing the transformation of work space, or traffic space, or some kind of official space into a playfield."[25] Schechner believes play to be a non-exclusive, unifying act. Anyone has the ability to play at any time and anywhere, despite cultural inhibitions, and clown/trickster is an excellent facilitator in play.

Carl Beam expands on this point, classifying the trickster's work as "serious play, the ultimate goal of which is a radical shift in viewer perspective and even political positioning by imagining and imaging alternative viewpoints." The play allows the spectator to realize that "an accepted pattern has no necessity."[26] One example of this is a Pueblo clown who, in Jill Sweet's telling, borrows a visitor's camera to reverse the usual photographic process that comes with tourism: "The clown became the tourist with camera while the tourist became the photographic subject."[27] This simple reversal raises several questions about power, identity, social "norms" and habits, and asks us to reconsider our actions. In doing this we can learn to laugh at ourselves by gaining new perspectives.

Beginning with the unique individual clown serves primarily as a self-critique and self-revelation. It differs from general acting in that at its core an actor in the art form of clown draws more directly on the self and internal struggles of his or her own person, the way that all actors can; but with the clown there is less of a separation between the character and the actor. Although the idea is sometimes disputed, Pochinko was a firm believer that anyone could be a clown, and he taught workshops to both performers and non-performers: to anyone who wanted to rediscover joy. Additionally, the theatrical aspect of the clown allows a further forum for communication, in which not everyone has to become a clown. Pochinko observes,

> between the panic and possibilities lies your clown. The panic and the possibilities are universal. If you can learn to laugh at your panic and together we can find a way to express it, then people will identify with it and go through their panic with you and release it. So you see what you're doing for an audience? The audience identifies with the clown. That's the difference between an actor and a clown. While an actor is playing someone else, a clown is playing himself and you. A clown doesn't act; he pretends, like a child does, but is the innocence after experience.[28]

Ian Wallace, a student of Pochinko, adds, "The gift that he [Pochinko] gave to so many of us is like a mirror. He led us to face our essential uniqueness and encouraged us to love and celebrate it."[29] This discovery of uniqueness allows people to rejoice in the events of their lives and "celebrate them instead of crying about them" as Fiona Griffiths, another of Pochinko's students, claims.[30]

The art of the clown refuses to ignore life or distract us from it; rather it embraces even the ugliest parts of life and allows us a new perspective on everyday life—one in which we allow this life to unfold on its own terms. Life is always changing and evolving, so clown must do the same, since it exists in direct relation to life. Pochinko said, "Clowning for me is the most immediate expression of our artistic natures because what you are doing is learning ways to celebrate not only the normalcy of you but the extremity of you ... it allows us first of all to learn how not to judge ourselves. If you face all the directions yourself, you'll be able to laugh at the sheer beauty of that that's inside you."[31] The clown relocates the idea of utopia from existing in the future to existing within ourselves, and in the present. The clown does not strive for something outside and beyond, but is capable of finding all the answers and emotions within the self because clowns know how to access them and express them in the present. Pochinko says that the only responsibility of the clown is to know how to find joy within him- or herself, and to be able to share this with others. He calls this "that magic that no one else has,"[32] identifying the idea that while learning the importance of the self, one also learns the importance of the individuality of others. Despite the opposing or similar values/beliefs that a group of people may possess, each is greatly honoured and celebrated without end.

The trickster, whether in story, street theatre, or on a stage, is an important part of popular education and social development. It can provide means of self-critique and expression. As an art form that has appeared in various incarnations, and in numerous cultures all around the world, the trickster interacts directly with life and thus, with people. With the clown, there is never a world so far removed that the general public cannot recognize it, as the clown world is always a direct response to the one we live in constantly evolving, never bring pinned down (thus making it very hard to define or categorize). Thus, the clown has been able to transcend time and can still have an important role in affecting social and environmental justice.

Here comes the medicine!

Notes

The epigraph is taken from Tomson Highway, quoted in Allan J. Ryan, *The Trickster Shift* (Vancouver: University of British Columbia Press, 1999), 3–4.

1 As quoted in Frederique Apffel-Marglin, "Development or Decolonization in the Andez?" (193–243), in *The Spirit of Regeneration*, ed. Frederique Apffel-Marglin (New York: Zed, 1998), 203.
2 Fernandez, "Development or Decolonization," 194.
3 Fernandez, "Development or Decolonization," 194.
4 Apffel-Marglin, *The Spirit of Regeneration*.
5 Paulo Freire, *Pedagogy of the Oppressed* (New York: Continuum International, 2000), 59.
6 Patricia A. O'Riley, *Technology, Culture and Socioeconomics: A Rhizoanalysis of Educational Discourses* (New York: Peter Lang, 2003), 36–37.
7 O'Riley, *Technology, Culture and Socioeconomics*, 51.
8 Quoted in Richard Schechner, *The Future of Ritual: Writings on Culture and Performance* (New York: Routledge, 1995), 254.
9 Kieran Egan, "Individual Development in Literacy," in *Literacy, Society, and Schooling: A Reader*, ed. Suzanne de Castell, Allan Luke, and Kieran Egan (Cambridge: Cambridge University Press, 1986), 248.
10 Sean Kane, *Wisdom of the Mythtellers* (Peterborough: Broadview, 1995), 186.
11 Kane, *Wisdom*, 205.
12 Thomas King, *The Truth about Stories* (Toronto: House of Anansi, 2003), 92.
13 Ryan, *The Trickster Shift*, xii.
14 Kane, *Wisdom*.
15 Kristina Fagan, "What's the Trouble with the Trickster? An Introduction," in *Troubling Tricksters: Revisioning Critical Conversations*, ed. Deanna Reder and Linda M. Morra (Waterloo: Wilfrid Laurier University Press, 2010), 5.
16 Fagan, "What's the Trouble," 6.
17 Fagan, "What's the Trouble," 9.
18 Fagan, "What's the Trouble," 11.
19 Fagan, "What's the Trouble," 12.

20 Diane Peters, "Fears of a Clown," *Eyeopener,* 22 March 1995.
21 Gerald Vizenor, quoted in Ryan, *The Trickster Shift,* 4.
22 Schechner, *The Future of Ritual,* 34.
23 Schechner, *The Future of Ritual,* 230.
24 Jan Cohen-Cruz, "General Introduction," in *Radical Street Performance* (New York: Routledge, 1998), 1.
25 Schechner, *The Future of Ritual,* 49.
26 Mary Douglas, quoted in Ryan, *The Trickster Shift,* 5.
27 Quoted in Ryan, *The Trickster Shift,* 161.
28 Eileen Par, "A Clown for Our Times," *En Route Magazine,* December 1981.
29 Ian Wallace, "Waving Goodbye to Someone You Love," *Impact,* Fall 1989.
30 Quoted in Theresa Hefferman, "Power in the Clown," *Toronto Theatre Magazine,* Fall 1998.
31 Quoted in Hefferman, "Power in the Clown."
32 Quoted in Hefferman, "Power in the Clown."

CHAPTER 3

Rediscovering Relationships

Alesha Jane Breckenridge

> We need stewardship of our own species. Rather than thinking of healing the Earth, we should be looking to the Earth to heal us ... heal the underlying sickness—*our relationship* with the planet, *our worldview*.
>
> — Paul Devereux, *Re-visioning the Earth*

This chapter is an excerpt from a paper I completed in May 2006 as part of York University's Master in Environmental Studies Program, and at the time of the Indigenous Education Conference on Walpole Island. I thoroughly enjoyed the diversity of approaches to the conference's theme "The Nature of Empires and the Empire of Nature" and the hospitality of the Walpole Island community. This paper contributes to the conversations about cross-cultural relationships that began at the conference, by exploring the wellspring of indigenous education (theories and practices), in hope that—through dialogue and co-operation—such exploration might provide contemporary education in Ontario with much-needed ecological and spiritual renewal during this era of human disconnection to the wisdom of nature.

There is an inseparable connection between humans and nature held fast by physical, emotional, spiritual, aesthetic, and cultural bonds.[1] Currently, most humans live in urban areas predominantly marked by human-to-human interactions. These interactions take place within human-built, technologically enhanced environments that obscure innate biological realities (connection to water, soil, and food) and non-human species—nature. Arguably, ecological deterioration is the price that all of life on earth is paying for the disconnection and estrangement of large populations of humans from the natural world. For Arundhati Roy, the twentieth century is "a point in time when human intelligence has outstripped its own instinct for survival."[2] In *The Cost of Living,* she argues that twentieth-century technologies (such as massive hydroelectric dams) "represent the severing of the link, not just the link—the *understanding*—between human beings and the planet they live on. They scramble the intelligence that connects eggs to hens, milk to cows, food to forests, waters to rivers, air to life, and the earth to human existence."[3] Generally speaking, I believe that this illusion of biological separation is perpetuated by contemporary Western culture and its world view, and therefore is not restricted simply to urban lifestyles. Rural areas, or other communities that lie between the constructed urban/rural divide, demonstrate similar scrambled and limited interpretations of nature: "The conservation of natural spaces is often seen as a luxury that has little to do with the well-being of local peoples—a swamp, for example, might be viewed as wasted land, whose only value is in the crops that could be planted if it were to be drained."[4]

A powerful dynamic of cultural and socio-economic forces combine to create contemporary Western culture's world view, which sees nature in disconnected and limited terms. As Thomas Berry explains in *The Great Work: Our Way into the Future,* our current anthropocentric-based culture only places value upon the natural world once it has *use* by and for humans.[5] Thus, modern Western social structures, such as educational, legal, political, or economic discussions of nature, are in essence limited. They do not consider, nor fully understand, nature as having intrinsic value or worth, even for other-than-human entities. The powerful global influence of modern Western economics, corporations, science and technology, and, most importantly, education has spread this restricted view of nature. In essence, a pandemic of blatant disregard for deep human connections to nature has expanded across the globe, leaving in its wake a monoculture of *bio-estranged* human beings. Paul Devereux, author of *Re-Visioning the Earth,* explains, "So impermeable and dense is this *monoculture* becoming that it has eclipsed our view of the natural world, except through carefully controlled windows that ensure that we see nature in certain limited ways."[6] Devereux observes that culture "stands between the individual and the natural world," and thus becomes an "expression of the collective worldview of its inhabitants."[7]

As an educator and environmentalist, I struggle with the limited and unrealistic world view my culture provides and disseminates through standardized, formal public education. By formalizing this limited world view in educational structures and mandates, we erode the uniqueness of places, communities, and biodiverse geographical differences of the province of Ontario. The theme of the Walpole conference, "The Nature of Empires and the Empire of Nature," is relevant here: much like the assimilative power of an empire, a standardized educational mandate brushes over the complexities of local knowledge of place and community, and instead provides a one-size-fits-all educational directive. Given the powerful role education plays in perpetuating a world view, and in light of a crippling human–nature divide and the subsequent ecological crisis, we need to consider an educational mandate that will broaden the existing and inadequate world view ecologically and spiritually. A new educational vision for Ontario is needed.

In attempting to rediscover relationships and restore intimacy with nature, the purpose and role of education for bio-cultural perpetuation needs to be explored. Since the 1980s, educational reform in North America has been held captive by educators' "belief that their primary purpose is to prepare all children to compete successfully in the race for social mobility and contribute to ... economic domination."[8] Berry proclaims that modern education in North America, is preoccupied in "initiat[ing] our children into an economic order based on the exploitation of the natural life systems of the planet."[9] This approach is outdated. It is not of dire importance while the stability of ecosystems and human health everywhere are under threat.[10] Current educational commands are ruled by short-term agendas, whereas there are growing demands for educational directives that embrace long-term strategies supporting a broadened, sustainability-oriented approach to teaching and learning that will aid diverse communities in Ontario to bridge the human–nature divide.

Attempts to increase students' awareness of nature through mandated environmental education have fallen short. In June 2007, a Working Group on Environmental Education (created by the Ontario Ministry of Education) released a framework for environmental education in schools. In the introductory statements in their final report, *Shaping Our Schools, Shaping Our Future: Environmental Education in Schools* (the Bondar Report), the working group confessed that "in the absence of a comprehensive framework for environmental education ... efforts remain fragmented and inconsistent."[11]

By personally experiencing and assessing the limitations of modern education, both as a student and a teacher, in effectively teaching ecological content in a standardized setting, I have come to realize (as have Gregory A. Cajete and Thom Henley)[12] that indigenous educational ideologies offer a tremendous transformative prospect for educational authorities in Ontario. Practically speaking, I would like to propose a new vision for education in

Ontario—a vision for social change in light of the ecological crisis and the need to live sustainably for the sake of future generations and the remainder of the "more-than-human world."[13] By researching Aboriginal educational traditions, I hope to identify an ideological map to guide educational renewal and reform within Ontario (and add to the dialogue begun by the Bondar Report) and to reawaken an environmental consciousness, while maintaining and respecting the unique cultural communities and bioregions across the province.

Given the highly debated context of the terms *sustainability* and *sustainable development,* I felt it necessary to define sustainability as it is referred to in this paper. I recognize that the notion of sustainable living has its roots in Aboriginal cultures; this term has been used in practice for millennia, and it has been adopted by non-Native cultures for its ability to aid non-Native peoples in the rediscovery of their lost relations to the earth. As Thom Henley states in *Rediscovery: Ancient Pathways, New Directions,* "Sustainable development in its truest form was the guiding principles of indigenous cultures long before it became a term coined by a United Nations commission and a blueprint for global survival."[14] For the purpose of clarification within this report, *sustainability* is defined as the building of a community that has extended its ethical boundaries to incorporate both social and environmental realms; and in turn works collaboratively and democratically to reduce harm and live both appropriately in order to enhance the local community and environment.

Globally, the concept of sustainable development is flourishing (albeit in a controversial manner). The United Nations Educational, Scientific, and Cultural Organization (UNESCO) has declared the years 2005 to 2014 to be the Decade for Education for Sustainable Development. The purpose of this declaration is to reinforce and reiterate the importance of education for behaviour change and for rediscovering more sustainable relationships with the earth:

> As people we seek positive change for ourselves, our children and grandchildren; we must do it in ways that respect the right of all to do so. To do this we must learn constantly—about ourselves, our potential, our limitations, our relationships, our society, our environment, our world. Education for sustainable development is a life-wide and lifelong endeavour which challenges individuals, institutions and societies to view tomorrow as a day that belongs to all of us, or it will not belong to anyone.[15]

This statement emphasizes that a collective vision of living appropriately and sustainably is occurring as ecological limits to human growth are recognized.

Action, dialogue, and passionate participation in all sectors of contemporary society are underway. Keep in mind that sustainability is not a Western concept, and that this process—in order to be achieved properly—should incorporate a cross-cultural approach. After all, to prepare a culture for a cultural change of this magnitude, educational authorities must lead the transformation.[16] The way in which formal, public education is envisioned and delivered will guide this cultural transition. The remainder of this paper's discussion represents a journey of thought and a continuation of the education for the environment discourses at play in the rediscovery of humanity's relationship with the earth. It is critical that educational authorities in Ontario navigate the controversial and highly debated question "what is education for" in this postmodern era?[17]

The separation between humanity and nature is historically rooted in reductionist notions of the world as a machine—an inanimate object. According to Ann Dale, the eighteenth-century philosopher René Descartes defined "the material universe [as] a machine and nothing but a machine. 'Matter' had no purpose, life, or spirituality."[18] Descartes' philosophy concerning nature became the central tenet of the scientific (and technological) revolution, which unfortunately positioned "human beings as living in a dead world, a lifeless universe."[19] This philosophy works to reinforce contemporary, imperialistic Western views of nature in order to legitimize the oppression, domination, control, and use of nature for socio-economic ends.

As we begin to see the consequences of "stripping nature of its sacredness," the true cultural roots of the control and domination of nature are revealed.[20] It is certain that "in spite of our great achievements in science and technology, we [modern Western culture] remain incredibly ignorant about the natural world."[21] In light of the ecological crisis, it should become an educational imperative to restore ecological integrity and human dignity, a reverence for the earth, and an understanding of living sustainably (respectfully) within local communities and their respective bioregions.

Currently, the machine cosmology is being renounced and rejected, as biological connections and natural realities are being rediscovered through contemporary Western science and research. For example, it is now known that there are ecological limits to growth, that toxins in the environment exist also within human bodies, that the highly debated consequences of climate change mean that humans do not understand and cannot control the negative implications of human activities at an atmospheric level, and that "a growing body of evidence indicates that direct exposure to nature is essential for the physical and emotional health" of children.[22] Humanity is deeply immersed in and indivisible from ecological life-support systems and exists in a "more-than-human" world whose characteristics are far from machine-like.[23] Unfortunately, whole communities in Ontario have been established on the premise of this ruling ideology and view themselves as separate from the environment (or, at least capable of technological control and independence). Today, the consequences of the illusion that humanity can exist without its umbilical life connections are being recognized on a grand scale. The gravity of this realization increases one's awareness of the critical role education can play in reversing dominant cultural notions that remain the instigators and perpetuators of the ecological crisis. The question remains: how can Western society, structured around the human–nature dichotomy, rediscover and re-establish whole cultures and societies based on notions of interdependence and ecological sustainability? Before teaching and learning can spur this revolution, it is necessary to explore initial educational structural and methodological obstacles to ecological education for sustainability.

Education in Ontario schools disseminates contemporary Western cultural messages that explicitly and implicitly reinforce the roots of the modern era and, consequently, the roots of the ecological crisis: the separation between humanity and nature. Education and schools are built upon deep-rooted cultural metaphors that gave birth to the modern industrial era.[24] Thus the most significant institution to play a dominant role in the reiteration of the modern illusion is contemporary education. Education is after all a powerful tool for cultural perpetuation; indeed, this can be defined as its purpose. However, education can, in turn, be a tool for cultural change and transformation. In order to place environmental realities on par with social and economic concerns, ecological issues need to be reprioritized and demarginalized within educational institutions.

As we know, children and youth spend the majority of their formative years in school institutions that perpetuate deep-rooted explicit and implicit cultural assumptions of nature. In addition, students' experiences with nature have drastically declined due to rapid urbanization and suburban landscape changes, ecological destruction, and funding cuts to—and consequent delegitimization of—outdoor and experiential education.[25] Given this reality, how can schooling become more ecologically immersed, in order to reveal the cultural dimensions of ecological degradation? Initial recommendations should include reducing notions of human domination, awakening others to the illusion of the human–nature separation by rekindling a sense of place, and exposing the cultural dimensions of ecological degradation. In light of the need to live sustainably, these actions seem all the more pressing. Formal education at all levels should embrace a non-anthropocentric extended ethic of care, respect, and responsibility toward nature due to the ecological predicament we all find ourselves in.

In terms of rediscovering human relationships with nature, it is important to eliminate notions of nature as an exploitable resource within educational curricula, and to nurture an ethic that sees the earth as more than a resource for human use and domination.[26] Shockingly, the act of schooling requires that children and youth are separated from their communities, life experiences, and opportunities that exist beyond the school. The school and the indoors become the only environments in which learning takes place.[27] This basic act of schooling is a primary obstacle to overcoming ecological estrangement. Gregory Smith observes, "Nearly all school instruction occurs in classrooms cut off from the natural environment. Within four walls, the world is generally studied at a distance, from books or behind glass, or from the images of films and videotapes. The contact with the earth, animals, plants, and weather that would have been the stuff of the education of children in pre-modern societies is mediated in contemporary schools."[28]

Once students are separated out of society and placed in schools, Smith points out that what is missing is contact with nature. Without this contact, children and youth become estranged from the characteristics of nature and become familiar and comfortable with the indoor environment. Professor of landscape architecture Robin Moore discusses the loss of natural play areas in urban England: "Either indoor spaces have become more attractive, or outdoor spaces have become less attractive." He then highlights "state-mandated school curricula that do not allow time for study outdoors."[29] This lack of outdoor experience is similar to neglecting a relationship with a friend—as the bond diminishes, you become as strangers.

Notes

The epigraph is taken from Paul Devereux, *Re-visioning the Earth: A Guide to Opening the Healing Channels Between Mind and Nature* (New York: Fireside, 1996), 17; the italics are mine.

1 Thomas Berry, *The Great Work: Our Way into the Future* (New York: Bell Tower, 1999); David Abram, *The Spell of the Sensuous: Perception and Language in a More-Than-Human World* (New York: Pantheon, 1996).

2 Arundhati Roy, *The Cost of Living* (New York: Modern Library, 1999), 80.

3 Roy, *Cost of Living*, 81.

4 Millennium Ecosystem Assessment Board, *Living Beyond Our Means: Natural Assets and Human Well-being,* March 2005, accessed 25 June 2012, www.millenniumassessment.org/documents/document.429.aspx.pdf.

5 Berry, *Great Work,* 4.

6 Paul Devereux, *Re-visioning the Earth: A Guide to Opening the Healing Channels Between Mind and Nature* (New York: Fireside, 1996), 25; the italics are mine.

7 Devereux, *Re-visioning the Earth,* 24–25.

8 Robert Labaree, quoted in Gregory Smith, "Cultivating Care and Connections: Preparing the Soil for a Just and Sustainable Society," *Educational Studies* 36, no. 1 (2004): 73.

9 Berry, *Great Work,* 15.

10 Millennium Ecosystem Assessment Board, *Living Beyond Our Means.*

11 Ontario, Working Group on Environmental Education, *Shaping Our Schools, Shaping Our Future: Environmental Education in Ontario Schools,* Chair Roberta Bondar (Toronto: Working Group on Environmental Education, 2007), 1, accessed 26 June 2012, www.edu.gov.on.ca/curriculumcouncil/shapingSchools.pdf.

12 Gregory Cajete, "Chapter 6: Sense of Place," in *Native Science: Natural Laws of Interdependence* (Sante Fe: Clear Light, 2000), 178–213; *Look to the Mountain: An Ecology of Indigenous Education* (Durango: Kivaki, 1994); Thom Henley, *Rediscovery: Ancient Pathways, New Directions* (Edmonton: Lone Pine, 1996).

13 Abram, *Spell of the Sensuous.*

14 Henley, *Rediscovery,* 25.

15 United Nations Education, Scientific, Cultural Organisation (UNESCO), *United Nations Decade for Education for Sustainable Development (2005–2014): Draft International Implementation Scheme,"* October 2004, 7, accessed 26 June 2012, http://portal.unesco.org/education/en/file_download.php/03f375b07798a2a55dcdc39db7aa8211Final+IIS.pdf.

16 The Province of Ontario should consider the following document (and process) from the New Zealand Parliamentary Commissioner for the Environment, *See Change: Learning and Education for Sustainability* (Wellington, NZ: Parliamentary Commissioner for the Environment, 2004), accessed 6 February 2006, www.pce.parliament.nz/assets/Uploads/Reports/pdf/See_change_report.pdf. This report provides a model for cross-culture action and dialogue; the title *See Change* refers to a traditional Maori concept meaning transformation. The report highlights the importance of enhancing the capacity of *tangata whenua* (local, Maori schools), and presents a unique analysis of modern education with a focus on policies, curriculum, and teacher training in environmental education, education for sustainable development, and ecological

literacy (as a form of resistance to globalization and market forces). The report states that current educational programs and policies do not make the vital connections between issues (environmental, social, cultural, and economic), and that the root causes of environmental degradation are rarely addressed. The report findings suggest that the government at all levels should focus on quality of life, keeping an eye on the bigger picture (root causes of environmental, social, and economic problems), developing capacity, learning across society, pursuing social marketing for sustainability, and being responsive to cultural diversity.

17 This question is posed by both Aldo Leopold, *A Sand County Almanac: With Essays on Conservation from Round River* (1949; reprint, New York: Oxford University Press, 1966), and David Orr, *Ecological literacy: Education and the Transition to a Postmodern World* (New York: State University of New York Press, 1992), 143. Thomas Homer-Dixon refers to this postmodern era as "the Age of Nature." Thomas Berry refers to this post-"Cenozoic Era" as entering into an "Ecozoic Era, the period when humans would become a mutually beneficial presence on the Earth." Thomas Homer-Dixon, *The Upside of Down: Catastrophe, Creativity, and the Renewal of Civilization* (Toronto: Knopf, 2006), 13; Berry, *Great Work*, x.

18 Ann Dale, *At the Edge: Sustainable Development in the 21st Century* (Vancouver: UBC Press, 2001), 16.

19 J.L. Kincheloe, "Critical Ontology: Visions of Selfhood and Curriculum," *Journal of Curriculum Theorizing* 19, no. 1 (2003): 49.

20 Jill H. Gill, *Native Worldviews: An Introduction* (New York: Prometheus, 2002), 177.

21 David Suzuki, "Foreword," in Henley, *Rediscovery*, 13.

22 Richard Louv, *Last Child in the Woods: Saving Our Children from Nature-Deficit Disorder* (Chapel Hill: Algonquin, 2005), 34.

23 Consider the difference between *complicated* and *complex*, as defined by Homer-Dixon, *Upside of Down*, 22–23: "Complex systems ... they generally have a wider range of potential behaviours.... So machines like wind up clocks or car engines aren't complex.... They may be extremely complicated ... but their parts work together to produce a system with a relatively narrow and predictable range of behaviours."

24 See C.A. Bowers, *Educating for Eco-justice and Community* (Athens: University of Georgia Press, 2001); and C.A. Bowers, *Let Them Eat Data: How Computers Affect Education, Cultural Diversity, and the Prospects of Ecological Sustainability* (Athens: University of Georgia Press, 2000).

25 For more information on the decline of outdoor and experiential education see Louv; and, David Sobel, *Beyond Ecophobia: Reclaiming the Heart in Nature Education* (Great Barrington, MA: Orion Society, 1996).

26 David Hutchison, *Growing Up Green: Education for Ecological Renewal* (New York: Teachers College Press, 1998), 19.

27 Sandy Steen, "Bastions of Mechanism, Castles Built on Sand: A Critique of Schooling from an Ecological Perspective," *Canadian Journal of Environmental Education* 8 (2003): 195.

28 Gregory A. Smith, *Education and the Environment: Learning to Live with Limits* (Albany: State University of New York Press, 1992), 61.

29 Quoted in Louv, *Last Child in the Woods*, 33.

CHAPTER 4

Learning to Relate: Environmental and Place-Based Education in Northern Ontario

Lori-Beth Hallock

> Knowledge is to be shared. Each person is blessed by both the opportunity to teach and to learn, to give and to receive. Knowledge, once shared, is the greatest equalizer.

The sharing of knowledge allows connections between individuals and communities, between communities and regions, and between regions and the world. The stories and the knowledge we share about ourselves and the places we call home begins the process of helping communities practise sustainable community development. The strength of these stories lies in the way we learn to see ourselves in relation to a place and helps us to better understand the wisdom of how to live sustainably within that place. This chapter examines contemporary public education in Northern Ontario and argues that it should encourage sustainable community development by educating and equipping students with the necessary skills to be actively engaged. I argue that students can acquire these skills through environmental and place-based education. This is relevant today in Northern Ontario because of the lingering effects of at least a century of unsustainable development practices in resource industries, which have led to short-lived economic gains. The result has created an economic pattern of resource dependency across Northern Ontario. This type of environmental relationship is not only unsustainable, but it also encourages the continued exploitation of lands and resources leading to ongoing power struggles related to rights and ownership, creating conflict and uncertainty. Environmental and place-based education can help students rediscover their communities by learning from the shortcomings of the boom-and-bust cycles of development that have come to dominate the region and by better understanding older ways of knowing through local and traditional knowledge. The result can be the creation of an environmentally literate population, committed to practising and encouraging sustainable community development, made up of people who have a deep understanding of their place in the world.

Sustainable community development should integrate economic, social, and environmental objectives into community development that is participatory and leads to positive, concrete outcomes. In doing so, sustainable community development can create employment, reduce poverty, restore the health of the natural environment, stabilize local economies, and increase community control.[1] The success of sustainable community development depends on a number of factors and activities that are unique to each community. One constant is the importance of having a community that supports environmental learning. Environmental education aims to explore and to better understand the relationships between social, built, and natural environments. Since environmental learning needs are different from one community to the next, the learning lens needed in public education largely depends upon the development of local or place-based environmental education.

Environmental and place-based education recognizes that humans are all storytelling creatures and that stories help to shape and give meaning to places. Local knowledge plays an important role in shaping place-based education and making it an effective tool for sustainable community development. Chet A. Bowers proposes that we must present students with the opportunity to develop a deeper understanding and appreciation of what Sim Van Der Ryn and Stuart Cowan refer to as "ecological design": "The collective memories of those who inhabit a place provide a powerful map of its constraints and possibilities. In a sense, ecological design is really just the unfolding of place through the hearts and minds of its inhabitants. It embraces the realization that needs to be met in the potentialities of the landscape and the skills already present in a community."[2] In this chapter, I attempt to demonstrate the importance of both indigenous and non-indigenous local knowledge to the development of place-based education, as both provide opportunities for an enhanced dialogue around sustainable community development. Additionally, I explain how the public education curriculum in Ontario continues to ignore the intimate connection between place-making and the creation of sustainable communities and an environmentally engaged population.

Lighting the Fire

The Anishinaabe have stories and prophecies that relate learning to a journey or a path. Stories of the Seven Fires Prophecies and the migration of the Anishinaabe are good examples of this.[3] The Seven Fires (Neesh-wa-swi' ish-ko-day-kawn) are seven prophecies that were given to the Anishinaabe by seven prophets. Each prophecy is supposed to help guide the Anishinaabe in the direction of the eighth and final fire, which is an eternal fire of peace, love, brotherhood, and sisterhood.[4] Today, the Anishinaabe look to these prophecies for strength and courage.[5]

The path to learning can also be seen as a process that functions at different scales of community, from the individual to the collective, and at the regional, national, and transnational levels. David Havlick and Marion Hourdequin refer to learning on multiple scales as a "practical wisdom," they identify three elements that can contribute to integrated learning of this sort: "first, greater emphasis on *contextualized knowledge*, grounded in particular places and cases; second, *multi-modal learning* that engages students as whole persons both cognitively and affectively; third, stronger connections between knowing and doing or between *knowledge and responsibility*."[6] These models of learning can be regarded as principles of environmental education. Other explicitly named pedagogical models that can be counted as part of the repertoire of environmental education include experiential learning, contextual learning, problem-based learning, constructivism, outdoor education, bioregional education, democratic education, multicultural education, place-based education, and critical pedagogy.[7] Since the focus of these models is more narrowly defined, they can be usefully applied in specific situations and create a more holistic definition of environmental education that includes natural, as well as social and built, environments.

All of these models of environmental education can be linked to sustainable community development and lend themselves to a greater consciousness of place. The interpretation of environmental education that I am presenting here is one that sees the need for place-based education and local knowledge within the Ontario curriculum. The fulfillment of the Seven Fires Prophecies centres on the choices we make, which can either lead to great wisdom and renewal or destruction and suffering. We can forge a new relationship with each other and the places we call home if we so choose. In the next sections of this chapter, I explore the relationship between environmental, place-based, and indigenous education in an attempt to demonstrate that other ways of learning are possible and desirable.

Environmental and Placed-Based Education

The concept of environmental education is premised on notions of sustainability and is widely regarded as a means for addressing historic and contemporary environmental neglect. As a result, environmental education can be regarded as an essential pedagogy, teaching us how to reshape the way we view the world around us and to see ourselves as an intricate part of the complex and diverse world in which we live. The North American Association for Environmental Education (NAAEE) defines six essential underpinnings of environmental education, one of which includes "the importance of where one lives."[8] According to NAAEE, "Beginning close to home, learners forge connections with, explore, and understand their immediate surroundings. The sensitivity, knowledge, and skills needed for this local connection provide a base for moving out into larger systems, broader issues, and an expanding understanding of causes, connections, and consequences."[9] When properly understood and applied, environmental education can be an essential tool for encouraging sustainable community development by integrating an environmental awareness of diverse objectives. Tom Puk and Dustin Behm support this idea by drawing upon the work of T.W. Luke to explain that "ecological education must look at the interrelationships between the environment and 'economics, politics and technics of social ecologies.'"[10] I would add that environmental education must also explicitly incorporate the use of local knowledge in order to root education in an understanding of place.

Focusing the concept of environmental education around place-based education and local knowledge can be useful to the design of curricula and can appeal to a broader range of participants within a community: "Whether people identify with or are alienated by 'environmentalism,' they can still appreciate and care about the places where they live."[11] The work of Paulo Freire offers some early clues relating to the importance of place-based education in critical pedagogy: "People as beings 'in a situation,' find themselves rooted in temporal-spatial conditions which mark them and which they also mark. They will tend to reflect on their own 'situationality' to the extent that they are challenged by it to act upon it. Human beings *are* because they *are in* a situation. And they *will be more* the more they not only critically reflect upon their existence but critically act upon it."[12] Although rooted primarily within the field of critical pedagogy, Freire's concept of *situationality* can be understood as a means of exploring and implementing the processes of *reinhabitation,* or learning to live-in-place in an area that has been disrupted and injured through past exploitations.[13]

As stated above, some people might feel alienated by the concept of environmentalism and link environmentalism solely to natural environments. In Northern Ontario, the relationships between (or the stories we tell about) environmentalism and natural environments are shaped by the resource economies that have come to define the region. Overall, these stories reveal a history of dependency, pollution, and environmental destruction.[14] This is what Bruce W. Hodgins calls *hinterland politics*:

> Hinterland politics are linked to the so-called demographic imperative ... and to the influence of the metropolitan economic-power base.... The north is seen primarily as a source of wealth for the provincial economy or as an embarrassingly depressed area of mass unemployment. [Provincial political] elites help prop up local entrepreneurs and the government relies mainly on them to keep the economy going and unemployment under some control. They promote the extraction of resources for the short-term wealth of the province, public and private, and the government pays something back in welfare and subsidies.[15]

Hinterland politics reveal the challenges inherent in applying environmental education in a community where the local economy is largely dependent upon resource extraction and development. Even though the goals of environmental and place-based education are the same, the latter is likely to be a more effective pedagogical tool for environmental education in Northern Ontario. Place-based education creates the space for the dialogue between place and sustainable community development to occur. David A. Gruenewald explains that "Place becomes a critical construct not because it is in opposition to economic well-being (it is not), but because it focuses attention to analyzing how economic and political decisions impact particular places.... Articulating a critical pedagogy of place is thus a response against educational reform policies and practices that disregard places and that leave assumptions about the relationship between education and the politics of economic development unexamined."[16] In applying place-based education to the curriculum, communities across Northern Ontario can find ways to encourage sustainable community development and to eliminate (or at least reduce) the continued effects of unsustainable development practices.

Indigenous Education

Within the model of place-based education, indigenous pedagogies can also contribute to a sense of place by understanding and celebrating older ways of knowing and tradition. Eber Hampton, a leading scholar on indigenous education in Canada, identifies a number of points that can help define indigenous education (what Hampton refers to as Indian education). Of these, the first three are of particular importance for our purposes here:

- Spiritual concerns are an important part of Indian education.
- There are distinctive Indian styles of thought and communication with educational implications.
- For most Indians, education has the dual purpose of promoting Indian features as well as providing skills and information relevant to non-Indian society.[17]

The first point suggests that indigenous education necessarily includes a spiritual element. Regardless of how objective we choose to imagine Ontario classrooms to be, publicly funded schools are inevitably infused with some form of belief, from the Catholic-infused curricula in the separate school system to "character education" in the public school system. What is important to take note of in Hampton's first step is that spiritual concerns in indigenous education go beyond simply adding a mixture of moral and cultural values into a student's education. Rather, spirituality can and should be understood more holistically as traditional knowledge, an important component of local knowledge.[18] In general, indigenous education necessarily includes a balance of both tradition and knowledge and "is based on the belief that all things are connected and must be considered within the context of that interrelationship."[19] This balance is useful to environmental and place-based education because it reinforces the use of local knowledge and has the power to reconcile relationships, not just with places but between communities too. This is especially important in Northern Ontario, where Aboriginal people comprise nearly 13 percent of the total population.[20]

Hampton's second step takes the concept of spirituality further by recognizing the distinctive modes of thought and learning in indigenous education. The most significant of these modes is the model of the six directions (also sometimes referred to as the four directions teaching), which is premised upon the traditional Medicine Wheel or Circle Teachings that exist in many North American indigenous cultures. These teachings are also the foundation of most North American indigenous pedagogies and are at the core of contemporary scholarship on the subject of indigenous education.[21] For instance, Robert Regnier states that the Circle Teachings are the ultimate representations of unity, interdependence, and harmony among all beings in the universe.[22] They represent the natural patterns whose recurrences "constitute the reality in which humans can understand purpose and meaning."[23]

Hampton explains the six directions as the holistic teachings of the spirit, east, south, west, north, and earth.[24] This method of relating to the directions and to environmental patterns is the result of prolonged cultural connections and relationships to place and land. Leroy Little Bear writes, "When our people say, 'I am the environment, for the land and me are the same,' a lot of non-Indians interpret those statements metaphorically. Why? Because in non-Indian society, everything is metaphorical."[25] In this statement, Little Bear is reminding his readers of the distinction that Hampton makes between indigenous and non-indigenous models of education. Little Bear is demonstrating an important relationship to land that is uniquely indigenous and not often reproduced in dominant institutional learning models. As a result, indigenous education offers a different perspective within environmental education and different tools for place-based education.

Hampton's third point requires the most attention since he comments on the usefulness of indigenous education for Aboriginal peoples *and* non-Aboriginal peoples. Indigenous education for Aboriginal peoples is not only culturally appropriate but is also useful in order to fully understand the long history and effects of colonialism in Canada. This can similarly be applied to Northern Ontario. Although many scholars of indigenous education reflect on the importance of this type of learning for Aboriginal students, there are some, such as Nancy Turner, who support its use for non-Aboriginal students as well. Turner examines the concept of the "Earth's Blanket," in relation to sustainable living. The term "compels people to consider that which is valuable to *Earth*, and to link Earth's wealth and important possessions—the flowers, the grass and other vegetation—to human action."[26] Turner, along with others such as C.A. Bowers and Stephen A. Marglin, advocates for the recognition and reinstatement of older ways of knowing in education and community development. The significance of this in relation to environmental and place-based education is the recognition of organic sciences and knowledge, which helps to create a more diverse and yet localized curriculum that is relevant to the day-to-day experience of students.[27] Indigenous education also functions as a way of providing skills and information relevant to non-Aboriginal students and society. In the next sections, I consider the role of environmental education in the Ontario curriculum. First, I want to consider the applicability of local knowledge to environmental and place-based education.

Lost Lifeways

> [The town of] Cobalt ... exists today like a shipwrecked survivor in a surrounding sea of normalcy and prudence. The generations born and raised along its tottering streets and scarred hills carry within them the mark of a tragic glory.... They [mining towns] defy history with the rousing chorus "we lived a life and then some." Yes, your towns might be well-ordered and pretty, but we once entertained princes and danced on the stage of the world.[28]

The boom-bust cycles associated with primary-sector industries, such as mining and logging, have had lasting cultural and environmental effects in Northern Ontario. As Charlie Angus and Brit Griffin demonstrate in their case study of Cobalt, Ontario, communities have fallen pray to the vicious effects of resource development. Industries like mining are often cherished or celebrated under the influence of nostalgia. In place-based education, however, the recognition of local knowledge means constantly checking to make sure we are telling the right stories. Trevor Herriot explains how nostalgia can be interpreted as a yearning that should not always be trusted: "A people who fall easily under its spell are living in exile from something—a life or a home that they or their ancestors forsook."[29] Herriot demonstrates how nostalgia and migration, or what Harriot refers to as "exile," can work together to provide a glimpse of what is possible when people come to see themselves and their communities for what they truly are:

> Something in our blood remembers, yearns hopelessly for lost lifeways and the time when we were native and kin to the soil, the water, the creatures, and the plants.... Getting there from here would require, among other revolutions, a willingness to make actual, hand-and-foot contact with the land, to accumulate an intimate knowledge of local lives and ecologies, and to tell and retell the right stories. An unlikely journey, perhaps, but the right kind of nostalgia, a selective yearning that remembers our failures and imagines our possibilities, would be enough inspiration to allow us to embark.[30]

Nostalgia is a useful tool for considering a relationship to place because it helps us to recall our "lost lifeways," as Herriot puts it, and to recognize the cultural and environmental forces that have eroded our connection to place.

However, we must be wary of the wrong kind of nostalgia as well—the kind of nostalgia that Dan Flores refers to as "pioneer family ancestor worship."[31] In Northern Ontario, we must be mindful of the history and stories of domination and cultural erasure that are a fundamental part of the local knowledge of that place. In his article "Jack Pine: Wilderness Sublime or the Erasure of the Aboriginal Presence from the Landscape," Jonathan Bordo argues that the image of the jack pine in the works of the Group of Seven effectively endorses this wrong kind of nostalgia. Many of these images were crafted in the woods of Northern Ontario, making them useful to our discussion here. Apart from the obvious erasure of the Aboriginal presence in a number of the landscape paintings, Bordo argues that the jack pine in the work of the Group of Seven artists becomes a symbol of otherness and is thereby anthropomorphized, losing its own reality and becoming a device for empowering the subject (in this case, the non-Indigenous voyeur).[32] By the same token, the jack pine can also become a costume or cloak that masks what Bordo calls "a finitizing architecture upon the wilderness symbolic," which has the ability to reduce the environment in question to the condition of the park, or a kind of real estate that can be manipulated by the artist (in this case, the relationship between non-Indigenous people and Northern Ontario).[33] The jack pine is only one of many symbols that could be considered here.

With the right kind of nostalgia that "remembers our failures and imagines our possibilities" we are capable of relating the endearing human qualities that link us so intimately to place. With this in mind, Simon Schama argues that

> the cultural habits of humanity have always made room for the sacredness of nature. All our landscapes, from the city park to the mountain hike, are imprinted with our tenacious, inescapable obsessions. So that to take the many and several ills of the environment seriously does not, I think, require that we trade in our cultural legacy or its posterity. It asks instead that we simply see it for what it has truly been: not the repudiation, but the veneration, of nature.[34]

On one hand, we ought to be conscientious about the wrong kind of nostalgia described by Bordo, but we can also learn to acquire and celebrate the right kind of nostalgia that both Herriot and Schama discuss. In many ways, this can be described as a type of reconciliation or a means of understanding who we are, as individuals and communities, and our place in the world. If we take nostalgia as a tool for interpreting local knowledge, then we must treat it carefully. We must admit that a fine line also exists between the right and the wrong kind of local knowledge. This must be clearly understood and assessed before creating a place-based curriculum. However, once this has been established, we can begin the journey of defining and designing environmental and place-based education in Ontario.

Shaping Our Schools, Shaping Our Future

> We shall not cease from exploration
> And the end of all our exploring
> Will be to arrive where we started
> And know the place for the first time.[35]

Demand for the increased recognition of environmental education is widespread and is continually promoted by organizations such as the North American Association for Environmental Education (NAAEE) and the Canadian Network for Environmental Education and Communication. In Ontario, the Council of Outdoor Educators of Ontario (COEO) and the Ontario Society for Environmental Education (OSEE) are professional organizations with the mandate to support and raise the profile of environmental and outdoor education in Ontario.[36] As well, OSEE is part of Environmental Education Ontario (EEON), a larger network of individuals and groups involved in environmental education initiatives. This network came about largely as a response to the removal of environmental sciences and environmental studies from the Ontario curriculum in 2000.

The work of EEON includes the facilitation, development, and implementation of a strategic plan for environmental and sustainability education. For clarity, sustainability education encompasses a broad range of different types of environmental education, including place-based education. According to EEON, "Environmental and sustainability education today is perhaps best defined by its desired outcomes. To EEON, E&SE [environmental and sustainability education] means the transmission, growth, and application of environmental knowledge across all sectors of society. Such learning is essential for the cooperative building of an ecologically literate and sustainable society, and for the decision-making and behavioural choices required to maintain a healthy environment."[37] EEON suggests that, in order to implement this type of education, a shift is required in current learning to include a systematic examination of what is ecologically sustainable, with consideration for social, environmental, and economic needs.[38] EEON released its strategic plan, entitled *Greening the Way Ontario Learns: A Public Strategic Plan for Environmental and Sustainability Education,* in 2003. The plan highlights some of the guiding principles that EEON believes are relevant to environmental and sustainability education, including the recognition that

- humans are a part of, not separate from, the natural environment
- environment must be considered in its totality, with a focus on the dynamic interactions among human systems and natural systems
- environmental learning, to be coherent, must be interdisciplinary
- the scope of learning encompasses both short and long-term futures, as well as issues from the local and regional, to the national and global levels
- critical thinking, problem-solving, and the ability to consider a diversity of viewpoints are core skills
- values and ethics guide environmental attitudes, actions, and decision-making
- citizens' participation in sustainable solutions is essential ...
- environmental and sustainability education is a process of lifelong learning.[39]

EEON also proposes that environmental and sustainability education include the representation of Aboriginal peoples, business and industry, consumers, families, governments and agencies, labour organizations, media, medical and public health professionals, and new Canadians.[40] Essentially, the implementation and function of environmental education must include the input of local knowledge from a variety of social and environmental actors and organizations in order to tell the right stories. These elements of environmental education are fundamentally important considerations for both place-based education and sustainable community development.

One of the most obvious ways that local knowledge can be incorporated into locally developed programs is through contemporary, as well as traditional, storytelling. As Chet A. Bowers suggests, "The ensuing discussion could cover such issues as how the values and assumptions in the student's own stories differ from those of a traditional folk tale and from the oral tradition still anchored in generations of experience within a [place]."[41] Also, schools and teachers could work closely with community groups to promote outdoor education that incorporates historic landmarks, the ecology of relevant communities, and sacred, recreational and industrial sites. An oral history or story could also be presented to students by community members, and this can be followed by a trip to important and relevant sites. As well, a good portion of the standard Ontario school year falls during the winter months, a time when specific Anishinaabe stories can be told. Anishinaabe elders and storytellers can be invited to interact with students and to share their stories and discuss the significance and importance of the ecology of plants, animals, and cultural sites. Suggestions such as these are ways to begin thinking about the classroom and local sites as a place for mediating place-based knowledge and for infusing a static, standardized curriculum with meaningful local knowledge.

In June 2007, the Working Group on Environmental Education, appointed by the Curriculum Council on behalf of the Ontario Ministry of Education, was requested to deliver an assessment of environmental education values and practices in the Ontario public education system. The result was a report entitled *Shaping Our Schools, Shaping Our Future: Environmental Education in Ontario Schools,* which included thirty-two recommendations. The Ministry of Education responded positively and publicly announced its intent to implement the recommendations. At the time of the report, EEON expressed concern for the committee's omission of sustainability in its comprehensive definition of environmental education[42] and in any of the thirty-two recommendations. EEON places equal importance on both environmental *and sustainability* education as strategic goals, and proposed the expansion of the term *environmental education* to *environmental and sustainability education*: "The environment is our home. Sustainability is about the choices we make in how we choose to maintain it. Both are equally important as learning goals, and both need to be examined, specifically."[43] Since 2007, the Ministry of Education has published *Acting Today, Shaping Tomorrow: A Policy Framework for Environmental Education in Ontario Schools* and two resource guides to be applied to Kindergarten–Grade 8 and Grade 9–12 curricula entitled, *Environmental Education: Scope and Sequence of Expectations.*[44] Although the concept of sustainability appears throughout each of these documents, none of them directly identify sustainability as an integral element of environmental education.

The Working Group made a number of recommendations yet did not formally acknowledge the importance of environmental, place-based, or indigenous education.[45] Even with the recent development of environmental education policy, education in Ontario, and particularly Northern Ontario, still lacks adequate resource materials and guides for the development of place-based programs. Nevertheless, Ontario has taken a major first step by acknowledging the importance of environmental education in public education. Options presently exist for introducing locally developed elements into the curriculum. The burden now rests with the community, such as the local and regional school boards and educators, to find ways to infuse the curriculum with place-based programs and materials.

Environmental education needs to incorporate an understanding of local environments, resources, and knowledge in order to be effective and meaningful in the lives of students. In Northern Ontario, this means the thorough and formal recognition of Aboriginal cultural landscapes, traditional knowledge, and place-names, and the ways in which these aspects of place-making have been, and continue to be, ignored. Real, deep, and effective environmental and place-based education cannot occur in the north until this is acknowledged. Local and regional school boards and educators, with the support of the community, must personally as well as professionally acquire and prepare the necessary knowledge, skills, and resources to begin the process.

Teacher Education and Transformative Learning

> There is, in many Indigenous teachings, a great optimism for the potential to make positive change. Change *will* come. As always, it is just a matter of who determines what that change will be.[46]

Regarding environmental and place-based education, educators have the important job of interpreting, mediating, and sharing concepts related to local knowledge and sustainable community development. Bowers refers to this task as "primary socialization," meaning "the way individuals, when learning about a new aspect of cultural experience, initially depend on other people ... who are sharing what they have already learned."[47] The role of educators is to mediate these new aspects of cultural experience and to revise and reaffirm the past in terms of the ever-changing state of communal and environmental relationships.[48] In order to do so, educators will need to contextualize their own experiences and knowledge of the community in question as part of this socialization process. This requires consideration of teacher education.

Teacher education consists of two parts: initial training and certification, and ongoing in-service training. In the first instance, faculties of education and the Ontario College of Teachers set standards that are required in order for educators to acquire certification in Ontario. The requirements of teacher certification are coupled with the expectations of educators as outlined in Ontario K–12 curricula, which is set by the Ministry of Education. EEON argues that, in order for educators to effectively provide students with the necessary understanding of environmental and place-based education, teachers need an education system that is committed to environmental and sustainability education and ecological literacy.[49] Teacher certification programs must be designed so that educators can acquire the necessary skills, such as learning to work collaboratively on educational projects with local Aboriginal communities or planning a local knowledge field trip.

Another tool for educators includes the theory and practice of transformative learning. This type of learning involves a deep, structural shift in basic premises of thought, feelings, and actions, and is a shift of consciousness that dramatically and permanently alters our way of being in the world.[50] In Ontario, implementing environmental and place-based learning may in fact necessitate a shift away from simple educational reform towards a greater emphasis on transformative learning. This type of learning has the potential to dramatically change public education, but can also be a valuable tool for addressing the interests of place-based education and local knowledge.

Storytelling is at the very core of local knowledge, so in order to incorporate local knowledge in the classroom, the educator must also be able to incorporate storytelling in the classroom. Mary Anne Lanigan examines the importance of transformative learning through storytelling and also demonstrates its use. She explains that "it is through cultural stories that children learn how they fit in their world."[51] Lanigan goes on to explain the difference between stories as myth (the sacred truths of a group of peoples) and stories as narratives (providing an oral account of historical events), which are both important and essential, and can be integrated across all subjects.[52] She also incorporates the use of storytelling in her own classroom and demonstrates its effectiveness as a method of learning through a small experiment that she conducts with an oral and written story. The results of Lanigan's experiment are demonstrated in a chart at the end of her article, where she summarizes these results with five important points about the quality of learning achieved through storytelling:

> First, I found that all levels of students were equally successful at listening skills, comprehension skills and writing skills with the oral story.... Second, the students appeared to have greater confidence in their ability after the oral stories.... Third, the students wrote more and expressed themselves more grammatically when answering the questions about the oral story. Fourth, all students performed better on the questions for the oral story than those for the story that was read silently. Fifth, students who were academically challenged showed the greatest discrepancy in successful answers for questions between the oral and written stories.[53]

Although the findings and the experiment itself are fairly simplistic in their scope, what is interesting about Lanigan's experiment is that even though the students are quizzed on two stories, they perform overwhelmingly better on the oral story. Both are Aboriginal stories whose lessons are rooted in environmental and place-based education, revealing how transformative learning can be a useful tool when applied in this way. Additionally, Lanigan's experiment signifies how environmental and place-based education is not only a matter of content, but also a matter of presentation. Students are able to more easily absorb and make meaning of the stories they hear and apply that meaning to their daily lives and to their educational experiences.

Bringing It All Back Home

> Times likes these call us with more urgency than ever to know our place, to learn its history, to engage with its material reality, to love and protect it. This does not require that we never travel, nor that we live in one particular place for the rest of our lives. But it does require that we ask ourselves "Where is my soul's landscape?" and that we wonder hard to ourselves what it would actually mean to make a commitment to be in that place, to come to know its outlines—its smells, its history, its plants and animals, its people, its geography, its special magic—and ultimately to commit to its preservation and flowering. We must risk actually *loving* that place enough to preserve it.[54]

In relation to concerns about sustainability and place in public education, David Orr poses an important question: "do we equip students morally and intellectually to be a part of the existing pattern of corporate-dominated resource flows, or to take part in reshaping these patterns toward greater sustainability?"[55] Orr reminds us that education should become increasingly concerned with the question of sustainable community development, such that "education appropriate for sustainability will give greater emphasis to place-specific knowledge and skills useful in meeting individual local needs, and for rebuilding local communities. The rise of the modern nation-state, corporation, and megalopolis has drained talent, initiative, power, capital, and responsibility from the fine grain of society. The results have been devastating, both ecologically and socially."[56] The goals of environmental, place-based education include the re-evaluation and reconciliation of cultural and environmental relationships that are often easily ignored or forgotten, and are not currently a part of contemporary public education in Ontario. These goals may necessitate the implementation of true transformative learning in order to be successful, or they may be simply resolved through the increased awareness and participation of local and regional school boards and teacher education.

Trevor Herriot wrote that "A landscape in which people dwell is a fully named place. Everything—hills, crossings, rivers, rocks, even the winds—has a name. Most are not on any maps, save those we carry in our heads."[57] Herriot forgot to add that behind every name a story exists that begs us to ask questions: What does the name mean? Where does the name come from? Who is responsible for the name? The stories that answer these questions remind us that we are intimately affected and influenced by our environments and specifically by the places that we call home. Unfortunately, contemporary environmental education in Ontario has not yet fully recognized the impact these influences have on sustainable community development.

Change is not only necessary, but possible. On the journey to change, many critics will ask if this way of thinking and acting is necessary. Many will doubt that environmental and place-based education can provide any insight for the future; yet there is a tremendous need for this type of learning and thinking, especially in Northern Ontario, and specifically in those communities in the north with resource-dependent economies. These places have endured the long-standing tradition of regarding our natural and geo-cultural histories as secondary to human development. These views persist today, steering past and present development initiatives and impacting contemporary perceptions of place and place-making in the north. By not educating and preparing students for the complex challenges that lie ahead for Northern Ontario communities, we risk missing the opportunities to make the right choices for the future today. We have a responsibility to be the best ancestors we possibly can, "seven generations from now, when we are leaves."[58]

Notes

The ideas and arguments presented in this chapter came out of my graduate work on environmental education and Northern Ontario, which I completed as part of the Master in Environmental Studies (MES) program at York University in 2007. I am grateful to Karl Hele, Matthew Tegelberg, and the anonymous reviewers of this chapter for providing me with helpful and encouraging feedback. The epigraph is taken from The Circle of Turtle Lodge, *Anishnabe 101: The Basics of What You Need to Know to Begin Your Journey on the Red Road* (Golden Lake, ON: Circle of Turtle Lodge, 2002), 15.

1 Centre for Sustainable Community Development, "What Is Sustainable Community Development?" Simon Fraser University, www.sfu.ca/cscd/about-us/what-is-sustainable-community-development.html.

2 Sim Van Der Ryn and Stuart Cowan, *Ecological Design*, 10th anniversary ed. (Washington: Island Press, 1996), 85; Chet A. Bowers, "The Role of Education and Ideology in the Transition from a Modern to a More Bioregionally-oriented Culture," in *Bioregionalism*, ed. Michael Vincent McGinnis (London: Routledge, 1999), 191–204.

3 For more information about these stories, see Edward Benton-Banai, *The Mishomis Book: The Voice of the Ojibway* (St. Paul, MN: Indian Country Press, 1979), 89–102.

4 Benton-Banai, *Mishomis*, 93.

5 Benton-Banai, *Mishomis*, 102.

6 David Havlick and Marion Hourdequin, "Practical Wisdom in Environmental Education," *Ethics, Place and Environment* 8, no. 3 (2005): 386. Italics in original.

7 David A. Gruenewald, "The Best of Both Worlds: A Critical Pedagogy of Place," *Educational Researcher* 32, no. 4 (2002): 3.

8 The other five essential underpinnings of environmental education include systems, interdependence, integration and infusion, roots in the real world, and lifelong learning. North American Association for Environmental Education (NAAEE), *Excellence in Environmental Education: Guidelines for Learning* (Washington, DC: NAAEE, 2004), 2–4.

9 NAAEE, *Excellence in Environmental Education*, 3.

10 Tom Puk and Dustin Behm, "Ecological Literacy as the First Imperative: The Role of Government in Developing Ecological Literacy in Ontario Secondary Schools; The Diluted Curriculum" (research report, Faculty of Education, Lakehead University, 2002), http://flash.lakeheadu.ca/~tpuk/Ecological%20Literacy%20as%20the%20First%20Imperative%20Research%20Report.PDF.

11 David A. Gruenewald, "Accountability and Collaboration: Institutional Barriers and Strategic Pathways for Place-based Education," *Ethics, Place and Environment* 8, no. 3 (2005): 263.

12 Paulo Freire, *Pedagogy of the oppressed*, 30th anniversary ed. (New York: Continuum International, 2000), 109. Italics in original.

13 Doug Aberley, "Interpreting Bioregionalism: A Story from Many Voices," in *Bioregionalism*, ed. Michael Vincent McGinnis (London: Routledge: 1999), 23. For more information about the concept of *reinhabitation*, see Peter Berg and Raymond F. Dasmann, "Reinhabiting California," in *Home! A Bioregional Reader*, ed. Van Andruss, Christopher Plant, Judith Plant, and Stephanie Wright (Philadelphia: New Society, 1990), 35–38.

14 Although the scale of mining development generally takes up a smaller geographical footprint than logging, the environmental impact can be far more disastrous. A particular concern lies with the responsibility of orphaned mine sites; liability falls to society through the government. There are potential environmental impacts in each phase of mining. For a detailed account of these impacts see Table 1: Key Activities and Potential Environmental Impacts in the 2nd Report of the Standing Committee on Natural Resources, November 1996, http://www.parl.gc.ca/Content/HOC/Archives/Committee/352/natu/reports/02_1996-11/report-e.html.

15 This concern is most clearly depicted in the logging conflicts of the late 1980s in Temagami, Ontario. According to Bruce W. Hodgins, environmentalists and preservationists tend to reside outside of northern communities and impose their views of environmentalism upon community members. These views often disregard the reality of Northern Ontario resource economies. Bruce W. Hodgins, "Gary G. Potts," in *Blockades and Resistance: Studies in Actions of Peace and the Temagami Blockades of 1988–89*, ed. Bruce W. Hodgins, Ute Lischke, and David T. McNab (Waterloo: Wilfrid Laurier University Press, 2003), 133.

16 Gruenewald, "The Best of Both Worlds," 3.

17 Eber Hampton, "Towards a Redefinition of Indian Education," in *First Nations Education in Canada: The Circle Unfolds*, ed. M. Battiste and J. Barman (Vancouver: University of British Columbia Press, 1995), 14–15.

18 Stephen J. Augustine, "Traditional Aboriginal Knowledge and Science versus Occidental Science," report prepared in 1997 for the Biodiversity Convention Office of Environment Canada, unpublished.

19 Augustine, "Traditional Aboriginal Knowledge and Science," 2.

20 Chris Southcott, *The Aboriginal Population and the Economy of Northern Ontario: Census Research Paper Series Report #12* (Thunder Bay: Local Boards of Northern Ontario, 2009), 5. By contrast, Aboriginal peoples in the whole of the province of Ontario make up about two percent of the total population. Statistics Canada. *Ontario (Code 35): Aboriginal Population Profile, 2006 Census* [table], cat. no. 92-594-XWE (Ottawa: Statistics Canada, 2007), www12.statcan.ca/census-recensement/2006/dp-pd/prof/92-594/index.cfm?Lang=E.

21 For more information on indigenous education, see Hampton "Towards a Redefinition," 5–46; Sharilyn.Calliou, "Peacekeeping Actions at Home: A Medicine Wheel Model for a Peacekeeping Pedagogy," in *First Nations Education in Canada: The Circle Unfolds*, ed. M. Battiste and J. Barman (Vancouver: UBC Press, 1995), 47–72; Sharilyn Calliou, "Us/Them, Me/You: Who? (Re)thinking the Binary of First Nations and non-First Nations," *Canadian Journal of Native Education* 22, no. 1 (1998): 28–52; Robert Regnier, "The Sacred Circle: An

Aboriginal Approach to Healing Education at an Urban High School," in *First Nations Education in Canada: The Circle Unfolds*, ed. M. Battiste and J. Barman (Vancouver: UBC Press, 1995), 313–29; Angelina Weenie, "Aboriginal Pedagogy: The Sacred Circle Concept," in *As We See ... Aboriginal Pedagogy*, ed. L.A. Stiffarm (Saskatoon: Extension Division at the University of Saskatchewan, 1998), 59–66; and Mary Anne Lanigan, "Aboriginal Pedagogy: Storytelling," in *As We See ... Aboriginal Pedagogy*, ed. L.A. Stiffarm (Saskatoon: Extension Division at the University of Saskatchewan, 1998), 103–20.

22 Regnier, "Sacred Circle," 316.

23 Regnier, "Sacred Circle," 316.

24 Hampton, "Towards a Redefinition," 17.

25 Leroy Little Bear, "Aboriginal Relationships to the Land and Resources," in *Sacred Lands: Aboriginal World Views, Claims and Conflicts*, ed. J. Oakes, R. Riewe, K. Kinew, and E. Maloney (Winnipeg: Canadian Circumpolar Institute and Department of Native Studies, 1998), 15.

26 Nancy J. Turner, *The Earth's Blanket: Traditional Teachings for Sustainable Living* (Seattle: University of Washington Press, 2005), 28. Emphasis in original.

27 C.A. Bowers defines organic science as "a cumulative body of knowledge acquired over generations of direct experience and hypothesis testing within a bioregion—knowledge that often makes the difference between an adequate diet and starvation. Because of its intergenerational nature, organic science is interwoven with the cultural group's understanding of interdependent relationships – which makes it part of the group's moral code." C.A. Bowers, *Educating for Eco-justice and Community* (Athens: University of Georgia Press, 2001), 42. See also Stephen A. Marglin, "Farmers, Seedmen, and Scientists: Systems of Agriculture and Systems of Knowledge," in *Decolonizing Knowledge: From Development to Dialogue*, ed. Frédérique Apffel-Marglin and Stephen A. Marglin, 142–82 (Oxford: Clarendon, 1996).

28 Charlie Angus and Brit Griffin, *We Lived a Life and Then Some: The Life, Death, and Life of a Mining Town* (Toronto: Between the Lines, 1996), 8.

29 Trevor Herriot, *River in a Dry Land: A Prairie Passage* (Toronto: Stoddard, 2000), 2.

30 Herriot, *River in a Dry Land*, 3.

31 Dan Flores, "Place: Thinking about Bioregional History," in *Bioregionalism*, ed. Michael Vincent McGinnis (London: Routledge, 1999), 46.

32 Jonathan Bordo, "Jack Pine: Wilderness Sublime or the Erasure of the Aboriginal Presence from the Landscape," *Journal of Canadian Studies* 27, no. 4 (1993): 120.

33 Bordo, "Jack Pine," 120.

34 Simon Schama, *Landscape and Memory* (New York: Knopf, 1995), 18.

35 T.S. Eliot, "Little Gidding," in *Four Quartets* (London: Faber and Faber, 1995), 43.

36 Ontario Society for Environmental Education (OSEE), "Information about OSEE," 1995, OSEE, www.osee.org.

37 Environmental Education Ontario (EEON), *Greening the Way Ontario Learns: A Public Strategic Plan for Environmental and Sustainability Education—Summary* (Toronto: EEON, 2003), 18, www.eeon.org/pdf/greeningsummaryint.pdf.

38 EEON, *Greening the Way Ontario Learns*, 12.

39 EEON, *Greening the Way Ontario Learns*, 15–18.

40 EEON, *Greening the Way Ontario Learns*, 9.

41 Chet A. Bowers, *Let Them Eat Data: How Computers Affect Education, Cultural Diversity, and the Prospects of Ecological Sustainability* (Athens: University of Georgia Press, 2000), 167.

42 Ontario, Working Group on Environmental Education, *Shaping Our Schools, Shaping Our Future: Environmental Education in Ontario Schools*, Chair Roberta Bondar (Toronto: Working Group on Environmental Education, 2007), 6, www.edu.gov.on.ca/curriculumcouncil/shapingSchools.pdf. The report explains, "Environmental education is education about the environment, for the environment, and in the environment that promotes an understanding of, rich and active experience in, and an appreciation for the dynamic interactions of:

- The Earth's physical and biological systems
- The dependency of our social and economic systems on these natural systems
- The scientific and human dimensions of environmental issues
- The positive and negative consequences, both intended and unintended, of the interactions between human-created and natural systems."

43 Environmental Education Ontario (EEON), "About EEON," 2007, accessed 12 April 2007, www.eeon.org/about.html, but no longer available.

44 Ontario Ministry of Education, *Acting Today, Shaping Tomorrow: A Policy Framework for Environmental Education in Ontario Schools* (Toronto: Queen's Printer, 2009), www.edu.gov.on.ca/curriculumcouncil/ShapeTomorrow.pdf; Ontario Ministry of Education, *Environmental Education: Scope and Sequence of Expectations* (Toronto: Queen's Printer, 2011), www.edu.gov.on.ca/eng/curriculum/elementary/environ18curr.pdf.

45 Ontario, Working Group on Environmental Education, *Shaping Our Schools*, 16. The recommendations referenced here are numbered 22, 23, 25, 26, 28, 29, 30, and 31.

46 Winona LaDuke, *All Our Relations: Native Struggles for Land and Life* (Cambridge, MA: South End, 1999), 200. Emphasis in original.
47 Bowers, *Let Them Eat Data*, 159.
48 Bowers, *Let Them Eat Data*, 164.
49 EEON, *Greening the Way Ontario Learns*, 21.
50 Transformative Learning Centre, OISE/UT, "The TLC Approach to Transformative Learning: Grounded Hope," OISE/UT, http://tlc.oise.utoronto.ca/About.html.
51 Lanigan, "Aboriginal Pedagogy," 107.
52 Lanigan, "Aboriginal Pedagogy," 108–11.
53 Lanigan, "Aboriginal Pedagogy," 112.
54 Laurent A. Parks Daloz, "Transformative Learning for Bioregional Citizenship," in *Learning Toward an Ecological Conciousness: Selected Transformative Practices*, ed. Edmund O'Sullivan and Marilyn Taylor (Hampshire, UK: Palgrave Macmillan, 2004), 36. Emphasis in original.
55 David Orr, *Ecological Literacy: Education and the Transition to a Postmodern World* (Albany: State University of New York Press, 1992), 146.
56 Orr, *Ecological Literacy*, 146.
57 Herriot, *River in a Dry Land*, 331.
58 Joe Osawabine, "Artistic Statement," Debajehmujig Theatre Group, 2006, http://www.debaj.ca/content/Artistic-Director?q=content/About-Company-Artistic-Statement.

CHAPTER 5

Bridging Academia and Indigenous Environmental Science: Is It Too Late?

Brian Rice

Introduction

During the period of colonization, empires tend to reinforce their knowledge systems over Indigenous peoples. In North America, they did this through policy, residential schools, and what Marie Battiste refers to as cognitive imperialism: "This educational process is called cognitive imperialism, the last stage of imperialism wherein the imperialist seeks to whitewash the tribal mind and soul and to create doubt."[1] In the past, this occurred in more overt ways such as residential schools; and it is now taking place in more subtle ways within academic institutions and in some Native studies programs and programming.

During the 1970s when Indigenous activism was on the rise, Native studies programs (now being referred to as either Aboriginal or Indigenous studies) were developed as a response to the militant activist agendas of groups such as the American Indian Movement. The hope was that students would learn not only about the struggles of Indigenous peoples in protecting their lands, as was happening at places like Wounded Knee, but also about Indigenous philosophies and world views, which would teach students how to protect their own lands and cultures. Like African American programs in the United States where African Americans are at the forefront of the discipline, such schools would be run by Indigenous scholars, elders, and activists who would impart an Indigenous world view to their students. Such a program would require unique, Indigenous-focused approaches to learning. By learning Indigenous nature-based and environmentally sustaining philosophies from the elders, both Indigenous and non-Indigenous students would be trained in non-violent activism, in defending the pristine environments that Indigenous peoples live in, including the watersheds of the Great Lakes. The concept was best expressed as a "basic call to consciousness."[2]

Over the years, some Native/Aboriginal/Indigenous studies programs have veered away from teaching Indigenous environmental philosophies, and have moved towards teaching Euro-Western law as it applies to Indigenous peoples, band management as opposed to self-government and self-determination, the utilization of anthropological research methodologies instead of traditional Indigenous research methodologies, and now, Euro-Western development theory instead of stewardship of Indigenous lands. In some academic institutions, especially in the United States, anthropology has co-opted the discipline of Native studies and thus the philosophies that make up Indigenous environmental science are no longer the focus of these programs. This has given anthropologists who cannot find academic positions in their field of study another venue to teach in. Meanwhile, Indigenous scholars trained in the area of Indigenous environmental science are omitted from positions in Native/Aboriginal/Indigenous studies programs. Indigenous scholars who are making contributions in Indigenous knowledge usually do, if they are lucky, find work in other academic programs, such as history, education, and continuing education. Still other Native/Aboriginal/Indigenous studies programs are now dominated by non-Indigenous scholars whose focus of research is still based on Euro-Western methodologies. This poses several questions that will be the focus of this paper. Are academic institutions and Native/Aboriginal/Indigenous studies programs becoming infiltrated by an imperialist mindset that Battiste referred to as cognitive imperialism? Why is it important that the environmentally sustaining philosophies of Indigenous peoples remain central to the learning in Indigenous studies programs? In this paper, I will include some of my own experiences in and out of Native/Aboriginal/Indigenous studies programs while concentrating the rest on both the difficulty and necessity of maintaining Indigenous environmental science as a focus of these programs.

What Is the Importance of Indigenous Environmental Science in Fighting Imperialism?

Indigenous peoples have a different way of viewing nature, one that does not see it as a part of a hostile empire in need of dominance. Indigenous environmental science is appreciative of the ways Indigenous peoples have come to understand and utilize the natural world in which they live. It is a holistic approach that integrates the natural surroundings into a particular world view with which Indigenous peoples from around the globe can identify. Having been with Indigenous peoples from many parts of the globe, I have discovered that we have a common discourse about the environments we come from in spite of our cultural differences. There exists both a spiritual and physical attachment to place, which is articulated through our stories of origin. Elaborating on this holistic approach, Apela (Pam) Colorado, Oneida/French founder and director of several doctoral programs centred on Indigenous environmental science, and founder of the Indigenous Science Network, writes, "Indigenous Science synthesizes information from the mental, physical, social and cultural/historical realms."[3] She adds that "Indigenous science must be articulated in contemporary terms to permit scholarly exchange."[4] This is one of the tasks that academics from an Indigenous background such as Colorado have tried to achieve. Hopefully this paper is one example of that exchange, as both Colorado and I are bridges between both knowledge systems and both societies. Both of us come from an Indigenous background of mixed heritage and have made our living as academics whose research is focused on Indigenous knowledge systems. The fact that much knowledge of Indigenous science comes from peoples who are from an oral tradition rather than a written tradition means that innovative approaches must be created in order to synchronize the two traditions in academia. However, in order for Native/Aboriginal/Indigenous studies to remain viable in academic institutions, it is important that these institutions remain centred on teaching about Indigenous environmental science. In the United States and in Canada, it is now common for universities to amalgamate any courses with Indigenous content and refer to the result as a Native/Aboriginal/Indigenous studies program.

Psychologist Jurgen Kremer, who helped Apela Colorado oversee a Ph.D. program called Recovery of Indigenous Mind, asks the question, "Is there a way that Indigenous knowledge can be welcomed into academic discourse?"[5] Unfortunately, as a direct result of Euro-Western ideas dominating the realm of science, much of Indigenous science has been relegated to the position of mythology or folklore. Both Colorado and Kremer believe that it is essential to find a means that leads to understanding of Indigenous peoples, their knowledge systems, and what Indigenous environmental science can offer the world in general. We are living in a time when resources are being used up at a dramatic pace and when nations are standing idly by while environmental destruction increases.

Today Indigenous scholars who have been exposed to traditional knowledge are trying to relay to their students information about the plight of the world and offer alternatives to eco-management; they offer information based on years of accumulated knowledge while living in particular natural environments and learning from Indigenous elders. We are running out of time as Indigenous peoples become more and more co-opted into Euro-Western business and corporate practices instead of their traditional knowledge systems and thus become a burden to their own ecosystems.

This transition also has an effect on the direction of Indigenous programs in academia. Having taught in a Native studies program for six years with a master's degree, and after receiving my Ph.D. in traditional knowledge, I have found it impossible to find work in the field that I am trained in, Native/Aboriginal/Indigenous studies. I have since learned that there are Indigenous scholars like myself in both Canada and the United States struggling with this same issue. I am a tenured professor teaching about Indigenous issues in a mainstream education program and am one of the few professors with a terminal degree with an Indigenous-focused doctorate. However, even in the institution I work at, which has several Indigenous programs including one in the Faculty of Education where I am an associate professor, I do not teach in a specifically Indigenous program; yet my peer-reviewed book, *Seeing the World with Aboriginal Eyes*, written originally for a Native studies program, is used by several academic institutions and has sold around four thousand copies. Two other Indigenous scholars in our Faculty of Education, including our most senior Aboriginal member with 23 years of experience at the university, have faced the same dilemma as I: not being allowed to teach in our Aboriginal teachers program.

As a result of globalization and global markets, many Indigenous peoples' lands and resources are coveted by multinational corporations from the West. These practices are replicated throughout the world. As Indigenous peoples lose their lands to corporations, they begin to lose their traditional knowledge and are forced to adapt by replicating the very economic systems that have destroyed their way of life. In the Americas, Indigenous peoples have been and still are seen as impediments to resource extraction and have therefore been removed from many of their traditional lands and confined to reserves or reservations. This is also being replicated in other parts of the globe, including Africa and Asia. When this occurs, the wisdom that Indigenous peoples have about the environments they come from is lost forever.

We in academia are also running out of time as some of the last elders and teachers in North America who lived a subsistence way of life have now passed on into the afterlife. Rather than develop new models of teaching based on traditional concepts about Indigenous environmental science, we have sometimes replicated the same Western models. Our histories, languages, cultures, and ways of being should be the primary focus of all of our Native/Aboriginal/Indigenous courses if we believe that these programs are to become a unique discipline onto themselves.

Ojibwa scholar Melissa Nelson, a former editor of the *Eco-psychology Newsletter*, believes that in order to maintain the health of the earth, our minds must also be in tune with an Indigenous understanding of the world and the knowledge that pollution is tied to a way a society thinks; therefore, it is essential that the world be brought back into healthy balance by bringing society's ways of thinking into balance.[6] Indigenous knowledge is based on the premise of balance among all the components that make up the environment in which we live. This balance may be described in different terms by different Indigenous societies: Hawaiian Elder Lyons Kapi'ioho Naone III, a teacher in the former Traditional Knowledge/Recovery of Indigenous Mind Doctoral Programs in Hawaii, refers to being in balance as *Pono*, Oneida elder Apela Colorado calls it *Skana:kowa*, and Ojibwa Elder (and my former colleague in Native studies) Jim Dumont calls it *Pimatiisiiwin*. Despite their use of different terms, they share a common understanding of what a balanced world and a balanced person signify. In all these cases, there is a different understanding of the environment than a Euro-Western scientific or educational framework offers.

Colorado uses the image of a tree to explain how Indigenous environmental science works: "Like a tree the roots of Indigenous Science goes deep into the history, body and blood of this land."[7] She goes on to say "that the power of Indigenous Science lies in the reasons behind the tree's existence."[8] In other words, in order for this understanding to occur, one must be a participant in a relationship with the tree. The Dakota express this concept best by saying, "Mitakuye Oyasin" (We are all related). This contrasts with Euro-Western notions of science where one does not participate in the science but rather practises science. Morris Berman, who did his doctoral dissertation on the philosophy of Euro-Western science, writes, "Western science is inherently a distancing methodology; it's non-participatory by its very nature."[9] It is this non-participation that has resulted in the objectification of nature and destruction of our ecosystems by logging firms, pollution, nuclear waste, radiation fallout, commercial fishing, and so forth.

As Indigenous programs in academia help develop the future leaders of our societies, should they immerse students in Indigenous knowledge systems or prepare them to integrate into the development models of the Euro-Western world? This is a question that is being asked today in academia. Right now we are in a precarious position as the latter models are taking precedence over the former. Invitees to Indigenous conferences on Indigenous knowledge are often those with degrees outside of the context of those very systems our elders sought to protect when developing the original Native studies programs. Indigenous knowledge in academia can be sometimes used as a façade to hide and protect those with corporate interests.

Indigenous environmental science is based on relationships formed between Indigenous peoples and the environment in order to keep relationships with the natural world healthy and not deplete them. Kaokwa:haka (Cayuga) elder, professor, friend, and teacher, the late Jacob Thomas would tell us that we must look seven generations ahead when extracting anything from mother earth. Even then, the taking of resources must be only for self-sufficiency and not for accumulated wealth. In order for one to have this kind of philosophy, one must come from a tradition that understands the laws of nature. Indigenous environmental science can be practised only when a society is enough in tune with nature to understand its natural laws. For many Indigenous peoples, that means knowing the songs that come from nature and not simply the sound of a bulldozer.

These natural laws include the understanding that all living things have a duty to perform, based on original instructions as given to each species in the process of creation. Each society, human and non-human, has its own instructions that suggest to its members how to conduct their lives on earth in order to keep in balance. As mentioned, the Ojibwa refer to this as *Pimatiisiiwin*, meaning "life to the fullest," or "living the good life." An important part of these instructions is the idea that each person becomes a caretaker of other living things. This is the philosophy that needs to be taught in academia.

How Did Indigenous Ways of Knowing Come to Be Viewed as a Science?

To begin, it is important to note that when we refer to Indigenous ways of knowing as science, we are using Euro-Western terminology as there is no equivalent word in any Indigenous language for science per se. What is meant by this sense of science is how we come to understand and know something. In Euro-Western science, this often means knowledge acquired through observation and experimentation. Indigenous environmental science requires an even deeper understanding. It is this deeper understanding, which has not always been validated by Euro-Western institutions, that led Colorado to take up the cause of making sure that Indigenous ways of knowing are accepted as a legitimate form of science before it is too late. At stake is not only the survival of Indigenous knowledge systems but the people themselves. Lindon (1991) gives us the following example: in the Amazon forests alone, over 90 different nations of people have disappeared in the past 50 years.[10] This is not taking into account the many other Indigenous nations that once existed in the Americas. As these knowledge-rich people disappear, so too do the knowledge systems that may solve some of our contemporary medical problems.

This loss of knowledge is now filtering into academic institutions. Where academic institutions were the depositories of some forms of Indigenous knowledge during the 1970s with elders like Thomas and Dumont, Indigenous programming has often since been co-opted by the very disciplines Indigenous programming was trying to remove itself from.

Colorado related the following story to her traditional knowledge students while at the California Institute of Integral Studies as to the importance of Indigenous knowledge being recognized as its own discipline. Sitting in her dormitory at Harvard University, Colorado was perplexed that the work that she was trying to do was not being validated by Euro-western academic institutions. It seemed that the academics running the institutions were not allowing her to express her ideas in the way that she best understood, a way based on her Oneida cultural belief systems. In despair one evening, the answer came to her. The problem was partially to do with the terminology or lack of it in the Euro-Western world for Indigenous ways of understanding. These ways of understanding could not be defined as discretely or separately as Euro-Western ones can. Indigenous knowledge systems were holistic in their methodology, while Euro-Western scientific methodologies involved categorization into separate disciplines. Regardless, Indigenous methodologies were just as scientific as Euro-Western methodologies if one took into account the fact that they reflected a particular cultural world view.

The reason that Indigenous knowledge systems were not viewed as science was that they were not seen as objective systems in their approach to knowledge. This is related to the fact that they were based on a cultural world view. Western knowledge systems such as science are regarded as objective because they are said to be transcultural and based on experimentation that can hold up under any conditions. However, Berman points out that Thomas Kuhn, who wrote *The Structure of Scientific Revolutions,* and Karl Mannheim, who wrote *Ideology and Utopia,* held different views of Western science. Kuhn believed that scientific revolutions were completely irrational in nature and that they were based more on majority rule than scientific objectivity. Mannheim, in contrast, believed that Euro-Western science reflected the social and economic conditions of the day.[11] African writer Marimba Ani, in her work *Yurugu: An African Centered Critique of European Cultural Thought and Behavior,* observes that Euro-Western methodologies of understanding are defined by European cultural understandings. She offers a review of the finer points of how these ways of knowing developed in European cultures and how they have affected African peoples today.[12]

Indigenous theologian Vine Deloria, Jr., in his book *Red Earth, White Lies,* suggests that Euro-Western science is not always objective. He furthermore states that Euro-Western science has been used as a tool to subjugate and dispossess the Indigenous peoples of the Americas from their land and knowledge systems.[13] It is important to note that Euro-Western science is conditional on the cultural understandings of those professing its objectivity. This is not to say that everything that Euro-Western science offers has not been good. Many of the technological advancements due to Euro-Western science currently benefit the world in important ways. The problem is that these advancements are sometimes bound by cultural notions about nature that have resulted in the idea that nature is something to be objectified and therefore subdued. Until Euro-Western science begins to practice a form of *Pono,* we are on a collision course with nature. As a species, humankind cannot hope to win—and we as Indigenous academics who believe in our traditional knowledge systems are beginning to lose.

How Is Indigenous Environmental Science Understood by Euro-Western Science?

Unlike the Euro-Western scientific framework that separates science into different categories that may have no relationship to one another, Indigenous environmental science is based on the idea of relationship. Each facet of Indigenous environmental science affects every other facet. There is another important difference between Indigenous environmental science and Euro-Western science. In Euro-Western terms, this component is referred to as the spiritual. For Indigenous peoples, the concept of spirituality as something separate and distinct is unknown. Instead, what is regarded as spiritual is in fact for Indigenous peoples a part of the natural process. Dumont (1976), a retired Ojibwa professor of Native Studies at the University of Sudbury and a cultural elder for the Midiwewin lodge, describes Indigenous ways of knowing as encompassing a 360-degree approach rather than a 180-degree approach.[14] Along the same lines, world-renowned physicist David Peat (1994) makes the important point that Indigenous ways of understanding should not be measured by Euro-Western methods of understanding as each has something to offer; each is culturally based. He explains that the Euro-Western concept of nature is based on an evolutionary model while the Indigenous one is not.[15] This contrasts with Frances Widdowson and Albert Howard's (2008) perspective: neither is a scientist, but both believe that Euro-Western science is non-cultural and that true science is based on an evolutionary model with Indigenous peoples and their knowledge systems being on a lower scale of the evolutionary ladder and thus inferior.[16] In contrast, psychologist Jurgen Kremer (1994) explains, "Knowledge exchange among Indigenous people continues to this day in a ceremonial context, a different type of discourse."[17] He also notes that this lived knowledge is scientific.

Kremer and Peat thus agree that Euro-Western thinkers have consistently regarded Indigenous knowledge systems as less important than their own. As Indigenous writer Jose O. Quintana (1992) points out, much of the root of technological advancement in the Euro-western world relates to knowledge acquired in warfare, allowing European nations to dominate much of the rest of the world. He states that only after a period of time is this knowledge applied to civil life.[18] Although technological advancement has benefited European peoples living in the West, it has had less and sometimes little or no impact on improving the lives of Indigenous peoples, who have seen their lands expropriated and their knowledge systems marginalized. Peat notes that Indigenous peoples are believed not to possess any real science as science is said to be a recent development of the European-dominated Western hemisphere,[19] which at one time was solely inhabited by Indigenous peoples.

Deloria (1995) states "that in the European dominated west we are trained to believe that scientists search for, examine, and articulate truths about the natural world and about ourselves."[20] However, few scientists at a personal level know much about living in the natural world. He furthermore explains that in many cases Euro-Western truth is not the truth and that the Euro-Western scientific community desires to protect its own doctrine. The result is that scientific theories, such as Darwin's theory of evolution and selected special species, became pretexts for racism. Indigenous peoples with their less advanced military apparatus were categorized at a lower rung of cultural development on the evolutionary scale. This world view also resulted in others, who were perceived to be more advanced, developing and invoking racist ideas like the doctrine of discovery in order to usurp the lands of Indigenous peoples. This, in turn, has resulted in either a disregard for Indigenous knowledge systems or in some cases the theft of Indigenous knowledge by regarding it as having a non-Indigenous foundation: for example, the Peruvian malarial medicine quinine's properties were said to be discovered by

Dr. Robert Burns Woodward, a Nobel Prize–winning chemist. Even today, in Canada and the United States, when the general population is asked what it knows about the Indigenous peoples who inhabit these lands, the response is often simple stereotypes. These stereotypes include the belief that Indigenous peoples were nomads, hunters, and gatherers, and as Widdowson and Howard (2008) believe, living in either a paleolithic or neolithic state;[21] these categories have no meaning for Indigenous peoples, or much of the world, for that matter. Little time is given to understanding Indigenous knowledge. However, as more and more Indigenous people are displaced from their lands and knowledge systems, the stereotypic arguments become self-fulfilling, although for different reasons. Mostly from the inability of Indigenous peoples to utilize their knowledge, as governments and corporations covet their lands and disrupt their environmentally sustainable systems. Indigenous peoples are thus left with few alternatives but to integrate themselves into the system that has tried to destroy them and hopefully get the best deal that they can through treaties, resource-sharing agreements, and land claims; thus, many end up themselves becoming a burden to the environments in which they live. Such developments have even usurped Indigenous knowledge in academic institutions, allowing non-Indigenous scholars or those trained in Euro-Western knowledge such as business administration to dominate the discourse in Native/Aboriginal/Indigenous studies programs. There is nothing wrong with Indigenous students learning these skills as they are needed; however, they should not be the focus of but rather an appendage to Native/Aboriginal/Indigenous programs.

These issues are not restricted to the Indigenous peoples of America. They pertain to Indigenous people all over the globe. In fact, one must remember that there are still around 300,000,000 Indigenous people in the world and that some of them still possess important accumulated knowledge. One can only imagine the valuable knowledge that is being lost as these people become exposed to societies where values are based on capitalism, profit, material wealth, and self-interest at the expense of self-sufficiency, communal distribution, and subsistence living. As academics, are we contributing to the preservation or loss of that knowledge? It is by better understanding our philosophies pertaining to Indigenous environmental science that we may contribute to the former rather than the latter.

Where Did Indigenous Philosophies about Indigenous Environmental Science Derive From?

Indigenous environmental sciences evolved from natural, everyday processes that Indigenous peoples have observed and calculated as occurring at particular times of the cyclical calendar year. These processes are sometimes referred to as natural law, the laws that make up the functions within nature. Indigenous understandings about nature have often been perceived as esoteric and have been referred to by some as being animistic (that is, the worship of nature). However, Indigenous understandings of the environment are the result of the close relationship that Indigenous peoples have from living with nature. Rather than the worship of nature, it is in fact the gratitude that Indigenous peoples have for what nature provides that is the core of our belief systems.

All living things that exist follow a natural cycle of life. When bird relations migrate south in the winter and then return in the summer, they are following their cycle of life. When the bear relation enters its abode and hibernates for the winter, it is following its cycle of life. When Indigenous people perform their ceremonies following their cyclical calendar year, they are participating in their cycle of life. From birth to death is another cycle of life. When the different constellations appear in the sky during certain times of the year, they are following their cycle of life. The seasons, as well as night and day and the rising and setting of the sun and moon, are also cyclical in their functions. Indigenous ways of knowing are based on understanding these cycles, and thus Indigenous peoples' livelihoods are dependent on this knowledge. Indigenous peoples studied the movements of all things relevant to their lives and based their life-sustaining activities, such as hunting, fishing, farming, and migrations on these cycles within their own environments. Through studying these cycles, they came to understand the actions of the other human and non-human beings of creation.

In order to truly understand the practice of Indigenous environmental science, one has to understand the workings of these cycles. These cycles determine all the life-sustaining activities that Indigenous peoples perform. This means that they must be in balance with the rhythms of nature. One of my teachers in the Traditional Knowledge/Recovery of Indigenous Mind Program in Mexico, Mayan Elder Humbatzman, taught us that everything has a particular energy and that without that energy matter could not exist. Through this energy, everything from the smallest particles to the largest components of nature is given movement. The name of the Mayan creator of all things, Hunab'ku, means both movement and measure. The Mayans believed that they could, by way of measurement through mathematics, measure some of the more complex cycles of renewal in the world. They thus were able to determine events in the future, such as natural disasters that would occur. Another important aspect of Mayan indigenous environmental science is the understanding that all things are integrated in this cyclical process that evolved out of Hunab'ku.

Another of our teachers while in Mexico, Aztec traditionalist and musician Mazatl Galindo, who was for a time the Indigenous cultural ambassador of Mexico, told us a story about when he was in the Andes Mountains with some of the Indigenous people of that region. He was walking up a mountain road with an elder. All of sudden, the elder stopped. They waited for about twenty minutes before the elder proceeded with their journey. Mazatl asked him, "Why did we stop just then?" The elder turned around and said, "Out of respect for the wind. I was waiting for it to pass." It is this respect for both human and non-human aspects of nature that is integral to the philosophy of Indigenous environmental science. By understanding the cycles of nature and our place in these cycles, we become in tune with the rhythms of both human and non-human beings that inhabit the world we live in. For students living around the Great Lakes watershed, their curriculum should include traditional knowledge about this important water system. Somewhat influential about this was a paper I wrote for *Native Voices in Research* called "A Methodology Based on Rotinonshonni Traditions" (Rice, 2003) which described a 700-mile walk I did through Rotinonshonni traditional territory before writing my dissertation.[22] This would later result in me helping to facilitate journeys with members of Six Nations back to our traditional homeland. After reading my paper, one of my former Ojibwa students began to organize walks around the Great Lakes Watershed as a form of healing for both the lake and their personal lives. As academics, it is important that our work, upon completion, have meaning to others in our community.

Mayan Elder Humbatzman explained that everything in the world has an energy force that can be tapped into. Some of the Ojibwa, Cree, and Algonquin peoples of Quebec, Ontario, Manitoba, Wisconsin, Minnesota, and elsewhere refer to this as *Manito,* while the overall energy of all beings is *Kitchi Manito*. The Rotinonshonni refer to it as *Kenéren* or *Orentà*. These energies are embodied with a force, and, like an electrical battery, have both positive and negative aspects to them. Only individuals of strong moral conviction are able to tap into the positive and not be swayed by the negative energies within. Like a conductor, one then focuses these energies on tasks such as curing illness and finding lost love ones. Those who tap into the negative energies for personal gain would also be affected by eventually having that energy turn on them. Cause and effect is also a part of the cyclical process of renewal. The Ojibwa refer to it as *Onjiná*. However, it is through the ceremonial process that we maintain our relationship with the cycles of life. It is up to Indigenous academics who teach in Indigenous studies programs to not only understand the philosophy behind Indigenous environmental science, but to be able to teach it.

What Is the Purpose of Ceremonies in Indigenous Environmental Science?

Often we do not have time to reflect on our surroundings, although sometimes, for a few minutes, we may stop and take in a beautiful sunset. More often than not, however, we live our days as non-participants in the activities of the other human and non-human aspects of creation that inhabit the world with us. In part, this happens because in Euro-Western society, we are taught that we have little say in the functions of the natural world except to exploit it. Indigenous peoples have a different view. We believe that all things have a direct impact on our lives and are imbued with all of the qualities, both physical and non-physical, that humans have. These qualities do not necessarily imply the same amount of intelligence. When we refer to non-physical qualities, we mean an essence that can be tapped into through ceremony. This essence is in the earth, the water, the sun, the moon, animals, plants, and human beings. Indigenous peoples believe that we have a responsibility to acknowledge all components of creation and to thank these components for providing us with the necessities of life. Not to do so would endanger our existence in the world.

The Rotinonshonni believe that, upon rising in the morning, a man should give words of thanks to our elder brother the sun for providing warmth. In the evening, the clan mothers would give thanks to the rising grandmother moon. This would ensure that the sun and moon would continue to provide light and, in the case of the sun, heat. The Rotinonshonni furthermore say to this day that if the people stop performing their obligations through ceremony, the sun and moon will one day stop fulfilling their duties and not rise in the morning and evening. By way of their oral traditions, the Rotinonshonni remember a time when the sun no longer shone brightly and it became very cold. All of the creatures known to them on earth were forced to live in caves. Today we refer to this time as the ice age. When the sun did return and the ice melted, the Rotinonshonni said that they would always give thanks to it for bringing back the warmth. It is this respect for the power inherent in nature that shaped the world view of Indigenous people.

One of the ways that Indigenous peoples in the Americas come in touch with the essences of other human and non-human beings is through tobacco and the sacred pipe. When tobacco is put into a pipe and it is lit by way of the sacred fire and then smoked, thanks is given to all forms of life, thereby acknowledging their contributions to the world. In this way, communication takes place between the one bestowed with the pipe and that which received the tobacco smoke. A relationship built on mutual respect thus exists between the two. When Indigenous environmental science is practised, such acts are done with the deepest understanding and moral conviction one can have. This way there is assurance that exploitation does not occur. In other words, to practise Indigenous environmental science, one has to believe in the relationships that exist among all human and non-human beings. Ojibwa storyteller Basil Johnston explains this idea: "For whatever reason the act was performed, it was always done with reverence and holiness."[23] Indigenous environmental science takes place when one creates the right conditions. My own pipe was earned after dancing for several years out west with the Dakota eagle society at the White Buffalo Calf Sundance. This Sundance was in commemoration of the White Buffalo Calf named Miracle, born in 1994 in Jainsville, Wisconsin, and involved members from nations from the four directions.

Among some Indigenous societies, ceremonies still take place during the monthly lunar cycles. The Rotinonshonni, for instance, had as many as fifteen ceremonies during a thirteen lunar cycle calendar of the year, although today fewer are practised. These ceremonies include midwinter, dead feast, tobacco burning, maple ceremony, thunder dance, medicine mask, seed-planting, strawberry, raspberry, beans, green corn, harvest, thunder dance, and end of season. Each ceremony was a time when the Rotinonshonni practised some aspect of Indigenous environmental science whether it was astronomy, agriculture (planting corn, beans, and squash), or psychology and healing through the dreaming and mask societies. Today these ceremonies continue in the Longhouse. The Rotinonshonni have learned to preserve their culture through adapting it in new forms. As Indigenous academics, we have an obligation to do so as well by teaching about Indigenous environmental science—especially in Indigenous studies programs.

The Midewiwin society of the Ojibwa also follow a calendar cycle when they perform their ceremonies. The term *midewiwin* means "the good-hearted ones." According to Johnston (1982), the term *midewiwin* can be translated in the following way: *mino* meaning "good," *dewewin* meaning "hearted," and *midewe* meaning "sound."[24] This society utilizes a drum sometimes referred to as the Little Boy Drum. Jim Dumont, an elder in the society and former colleague, says the sound that emanates from it represents the sound that was first heard when the universe was created.[25] The Midewiwin ceremonies include the Weekindiwin (Ceremony of induction); Onauminah Midewiwin (Ceremony of medicine); Cheeby Midewiwin (Ceremony of the Dead); Kinebik Midewiwin (Ceremony of the Serpent); Autissokaewininiwuk Midewiwin (Ceremony of Attendants); and Gee / ossae Midewiwin (Ceremony of Hunting).[26]

By participating in these ceremonies, a person is following the natural cycles. By being in tune with the cycles through ceremony, one remains in balance with nature. By being in balance, one can participate in the natural order and become an integral part of keeping the world a stable place to live in. For Indigenous academics, understanding the purpose of ceremony rather than teaching the ceremonies themselves will ensure that students who leave the institution will understand their responsibility to creation.

How Does Indigenous Environmental Science Compare to Euro-Western Science?

There are some areas where Indigenous environmental science may be compared to some areas of Euro-Western science. For example, in terms of observation of data, Indigenous people have been as methodical as Euro-Western scientists. Sometimes they have been even more so. Take, for instance, the area of knowledge of the cosmology. For thousands of years Indigenous peoples have studied the movements of the stars, have collected this knowledge, and have passed it on to others. This has been done for other forms of Indigenous knowledge as well.

Where Indigenous and Euro-Western sciences differ mostly is in the interpretation of knowledge. Colorado believes that Euro-Western science is looking for a new paradigm in order to interpret its ever-growing body of data.[27] There has been some speculation that Euro-Western science is reaching its limits in terms of information about the universe. Others, like Peat, believe that there are areas where Indigenous environmental science can enhance new fields such as quantum physics.[28] This new science considers nature as a whole, much as Indigenous science does. Thus, in the 1990s, the Fetzer Institute brought Euro-Western trained physicists and Indigenous scientists (elders) together to create a better understanding of the concepts of quantum theory. Given that Indigenous languages are holistic and that language often reflects a specific world view, Western scientists like Peat must work hard to tap into the Indigenous world view. Difficulty arises because these scientists are grasping at concepts that noun-based European languages cannot easily define. Indigenous languages may incorporate several concepts at one time. One word, for instance, may include both an idea and description—both of which reflect a particular world view.

Indigenous peoples—whether they are Indigenous peoples from Canada or Pakoyah of Thailand—have a common understanding about the natural environments they live in, although there are cultural differences.[29] They all have knowledge systems that can be of a benefit to the world if the world is ready to receive them. Indigenous environmental science and Euro-Western science must one day meet each other and develop more common understandings. The Fetzer Institute was a beginning and was considered a success by both physicists and Indigenous elders, fulfilling Apela Colorado's dream of a dialogue where both world views would stand on equal footing. As an Indigenous scholar who graduated from a traditional knowledge program and then could not find a position in Indigenous studies, I can say that we have a long way to go.

As individuals, we must realize that Indigenous environmental science can help maintain the balance in our advancing technological society. In North America, as some of the last Indigenous elders to live a subsistence or semi-subsistence lifestyle began to pass away during the last three decades of the twentieth century, this has become harder to achieve. Even in academic institutions, most Indigenous studies programs set up to better understand Indigenous environmental science have steered away from Indigenous knowledge systems in favour of Euro-Western law and business practices as they apply to Indigenous people. We must realize that Indigenous knowledge can help maintain the balance in our advancing technological society and is the root of all Indigenous studies programming in academia. It can offer solutions to contemporary problems if we are willing to take the time to look seven generations ahead.

Notes

This chapter evolved from a manual on Indigenous Science that I wrote for Cambrian College, Sudbury, Ontario, in 1996.

1 Marie Battiste, "Micmac Literacy and Cognitive Assimilation," in *Indian Education in Canada*, vol. 1, *The Legacy*, ed. Jean Barman, Yvonne Hébert, and Don McCaskill (Vancouver: University of British Columbia Press, 1989), 37.

2 Akwesasne Notes, ed., *Basic Call to Consciousness* (Rooseveltown, NY: Mohawk Nation, 1978; rpt. Summertown, TN: Native Voices, 2005).
3 P. Colorado, "Bridging Native Science and Western Science," *Convergence* 21, no. 2–3 (1988): 50.
4 Colorado, "Bridging Native Science and Western Science," 49.
5 Jurgen Kremer, "Indigenous Science: Introduction," *ReVision* 18, no. 3 (Winter 1995): 2.
6 Melissa Nelson, "Reclaiming an Indigenous Mind." *Ecopsychology Newsletter*, Fall 1994, 1–3.
7 Colorado, "Bridging Native Science and Western Science," 50.
8 Colorado, "Bridging Native Science and Western Science," 50.
9 Morris Berman, "Science after Deconstruction: A Second Look at the Sociology of Knowledge [transcript]," paper presented at "Emerging Approaches to Inquiry" conference, Hawkwood College, Stroud, UK (1994), 2.
10 E. Lindon, "Lost Tribes, Lost Knowledge," *Time*, 23 Sept. 1991, 44–56.
11 Berman, "Science after Deconstruction."
12 Marimba Ani, *Yurugu: An African Centered Critique of European Cultural Thought and Behavior* (Trenton, NJ: African World Press, 1994), 30–44.
13 Vine Deloria, Jr., *Red Earth, White Lies* (New York: Scribner, 1995), 17.
14 James Dumont, "Journey to Daylight-land: Through Ojibwa Eyes," in *The First Ones: Reading in Indian/Native Studies*, ed. David R. Miller, Carl Beal, James Dempsey, and R. Wesley Heber (Craven, SK: Saskatchewan Indian Federated College, 1992), 75–80.
15 David Peat, *Lighting the Seventh Fire* (New York: Birch Lane Press, 1994.
16 Frances Widdowson and Albert Howard, *Disrobing the Aboriginal Industry* (Montreal: McGill-Queen's University Press, 2008).
17 Kremer, "Indigenous Science," 2.
18 Jorge Quintana, "American Indian Systems for Natural Resource Management," *Akwekon* 9, no. 2 (Summer 1992): 92–97.
19 Peat, *Lighting the Seventh Fire*, xii.
20 Vine Deloria, Jr., *Red Earth, White Lies* (New York: Scribner, 1995), 17.
21 Widdowson and Howard, 52–63.
22 Brian Rice, "A Methodology Based on Rotinonshonni Traditions," in *Native Voices in Research*, ed. Jill Elizabeth Oakes, Rick Riewe, Alison Edmunds, Alison Dubois, and Kimberley Wilde (Winnipeg: Aboriginal Issues Press, 1994), 171–82.
23 Basil Johnston, *Ojibwa Ceremonies* (Toronto: McClelland and Stewart, 1982), 33.
24 Basil Johnston, *Ojibway Ceremonies*, 95.
25 Dumont, 1976, 75–88.
26 Johnston, *Ojibway Ceremonies*, 108.

27 Colorado, "Bridging Native Science and Western Science," 50.
28 Peat, *Lighting the Seventh Fire*, xii.
29 I spent a couple of summers visiting the Pakoyah.

CHAPTER 6

Empire Revisited: The Covenant Chain of Silver, Land Policy, and the Proclamation of 1763 in the Great Lakes Region, 1760–1800

Karen J. Travers

The Two-Row Wampum Belt, or Gus-wen-tah, exchanged in 1764 between the Native peoples of the Great Lakes region and Sir William Johnson, renewed a diplomatic relationship that had been ongoing for more than one hundred years. The two rows of white beads on a background of purple symbolized two polities who, although inhabiting the same lands, agreed to respect the customs, laws, and ways of the other (see Figure 1).[1] Intending to maintain the peace and friendship of Aboriginal peoples, Great Britain had only a year before issued a Royal Proclamation to protect "Indian lands" from the encroachment of non-Native settlement. In the years that followed, however, once the British perceived the Great Lakes region as securely under their jurisdiction, the original intent of the Two-Row Wampum and the promise of peace, friendship, and respect were forgotten. The ambiguous wording of the Proclamation, open to fraud and abuse, along with historical circumstances that allowed and often encouraged such behaviour, left title to the bulk of traditional Aboriginal lands in the hands of others.

The Two-Row Wampum is also a fitting symbol of the disconnection that has occurred between Aboriginal peoples, the British Empire, and its successor, the Canadian state. Like the two rows of purple beads, the Canadian legal tradition has evolved along a path separate from the historical experience of First Nations, yet, unlike the separation symbolized by the parallel rows, the laws of Canada attempt to regulate Native peoples' environment and their lives. In his book *The Empire of Nature: Hunting, Conservation and British Imperialism*, John MacKenzie traces the evolution of the "hunting code,"[2] and its development and use as an instrument of Empire. The transformation of hunting from an Indigenous food source to a regulated and profitable sport of the elite came to deny Aboriginal peoples access to the hunt even for their own subsistence. Instead of respecting Indigenous custom, he notes that "ideas about the natural world" were informed by colonial attitudes and facilitated the spread of empire by interfering with and restricting Aboriginal access to resources.[3]

While MacKenzie writes that in terms of the hunt—"the club's rules became national laws"[4]—one could draw striking parallels with what might similarly be called a "land code." Despite guarantees contained in the Proclamation of 1763, the commodification and classification of land gradually resulted in piecemeal transfers of the traditional territories of Aboriginal peoples to colonial elites who then deemed them "wastelands" of the Crown.[5] The meaning of land changed so that oral agreements to share resources became supplanted by paper deeds, location tickets, and leases. Moreover, elite landowners increasingly viewed Native people, squatters, and others who did not "improve" the land with contempt. Despite the fact that grand estates and other lands were often fenced off, devoted to extravagant floral gardens, stripped of resources, or simply held for speculative purposes, colonial elites were confident nonetheless that only they made appropriate use of the land. Thus, in the years following the Proclamation, the philosophy behind colonial policy changed from one that recognized the coexistence of two polities, to one that dogmatically believed in the inherent right of one to dominate the other. Land both facilitated and financed this endeavour.

In a modern context, however, this does not mean that the spirit behind Canada's Indigenous policies cannot change again. Edward Benton-Banai has written that, according to the Seven Fires of the Ojibwa, we are indeed in a time of change. The Seventh Prophet stated that in the time of the Seventh Fire we as Canadians would "be given a choice between two roads." By choosing the "right road," we choose a world in which "the Seventh Fire will light the Eighth and Final Fire—an eternal Fire of peace, love, brotherhood and sisterhood."[6] The loss of a sustainable resource base in the Great Lakes and the resultant struggles for the recognition of Aboriginal land and treaty rights are some of the most important and complex issues facing First Nations in Ontario today. The choices Canadians make in the future are important ones, and they must be informed by our collective pasts.

Despite prohibitions contained in the Proclamation of 1763, officials in the employ of the British government privately obtained deeds of land from the Anishinabe and Haudenosaunee[7] in and around the Great Lakes. There is no doubt that this region fell well within the area reserved in the Royal Proclamation of 1763 as Indian Territory and as such these transactions were illegal, null, and void.[8] By proceeding to sell and settle portions of these lands, Sir William Johnson, George Croghan, Alexander McKee, and others in the British Indian Department eventually came to contribute to the very problems they were entrusted to manage and prevent.

The Proclamation of 1763 acknowledged and immortalized the "great Frauds and Abuses" perpetuated against Native peoples by the continual encroachments of settlers on their lands.[9] The problem, however, was endemic before the Proclamation, and it continued afterwards with even greater abandon. Great Britain used the Proclamation to divest itself of responsibility for the welfare of its Aboriginal allies in North America and subsequently embarked on a policy of severe fiscal restrictions. A handful of colonial governors and officers were left with the impossible task of implementing and enforcing the provisions of the Proclamation without sufficient resources to do so. Though they possessed immense power on paper, these officials often suffered a humiliating inability to fulfill their Covenant Chain obligations.

It would be a mistake however, to judge the Proclamation of 1763 itself as a wholesale failure. Conceived in an era when peace, friendship, and coexistence with Aboriginal peoples was not only desired but necessary for the very survival of Britain in North America, this "landmark in North American history," according to Gregory Evans Dowd, is "a testament to the imperial understanding of the Indians' constitutional status."[10] While the Proclamation recognized Aboriginal sovereignty and territorial rights in the spirit of the Covenant Chain, it was also the mechanism of surrender that enabled enterprising colonials to evade restrictions and dismantle protections piecemeal through "continual exceptions and allowances."[11] The only cessions legally permitted under the Proclamation were to take place at public meetings between those willing to sell their land and the governors or commanders-in-chief of the colonies.[12] This, nevertheless, gave way to what essentially became private dealings conducted by well-connected individuals in the colonial administration.[13]

Unable to stop illegal settlement on their own, yet obligated to do so by the terms of the Proclamation, Indian agents came upon a "happy coincidence"[14] of sorts. By obtaining Native lands through gift or purchase, officials believed they could solve many of the problems related to Native peoples' territories in the Great Lakes region and bypass the often delayed and complicated process of obtaining explicit approval of the Crown. By placing their lands in trust to British officials, Anishinabe and Haudenosaunee people were offered protection from squatters, which the Proclamation could not provide. Indian agents could eject squatters from lands deeded to them, settle lots with carefully chosen people, and leave vast tracts open for the traditional use of Native peoples. Furthermore, agents could broker sales of individual tracts to people they trusted, who would in turn "pay" both parties with money or goods.[15] Possessing lands in trust for Aboriginal peoples enabled officers like Sir William Johnson to enter the ranks of the landed gentry and earn incomes they felt entitled to but were denied under Britain's cost-cutting measures. Furthermore, by securing ongoing supplies of goods and cash, agents could fulfill their gift-giving and provisioning obligations under the Covenant Chain despite British cutbacks.

The ability to exact a measure of control (albeit limited and temporary) enabled Indian agents to secure some of the traditional lands guaranteed by the Proclamation of 1763. Oral histories are consistent with the idea that the Anishinabe and Haudenosaunee were quite willing to share their land with Europeans so long as they were compensated and the principles of the Two-Row Wampum were respected. Despite the nature of empire envisioned by policy-makers on the Board of Trade far off in England, these land transactions instead occurred as a result of intimate relations between First Nations and the newcomers they encountered in the colonies on a daily basis—they were never intended to be permanent, large-scale cessions. Those in the colonial power structure, subscribing to Enlightenment theories of the times[16] and blinded by the potential to profit from the land themselves, chose to disregard this. But Aboriginal cultures did not assimilate and slowly die out, leaving the land in the hands of their colonial benefactors. On the contrary, they have not only survived but thrived, and as a result, these deeds have altered their landscape forever.

The Covenant Chain and European-Indigenous Relations, 1700–63

Following the fall of New France in 1760, Great Britain assumed its representatives would march into newly conquered territories and dictate both economic and diplomatic relations with their new subjects.[17] Colonial governors and officers already active in Indian Affairs, particularly in the Thirteen Colonies, knew such a policy would never come to fruition. They had been participants in an elaborate system of Aboriginal diplomacy known among the Six Nations in the Thirteen Colonies and later Anishinabe and Western nations in the Great Lakes region as the Covenant Chain.[18]

The protocol of the Covenant Chain evolved as a result of trade agreements between the Dutch and Mohawk in the middle of the seventeenth cen-

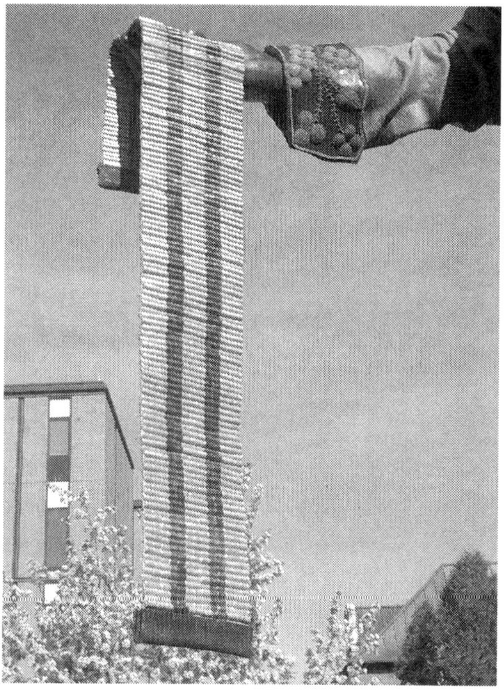

Figure 6.1. The Two-Row Wampum or Gus-wen-tah. Detail of the bronze sculpture *The Emergence of the Chief*, by David McGary, on the Loyola Campus of Concordia University. Photo by Karl S. Hele.

tury, although there is evidence suggesting a much earlier origin.[19] Throughout the colonial period, symbolic representations of the alliance gradually became stronger, appearing in the historical record first as a rope but evolving in later decades into an "iron chain" and finally manifesting itself as the Gus-wen-tah or Covenant Chain of Silver.[20] Corresponding sacred ceremonies performed in countless councils between representatives of the British Crown, Six Nations, and Anishinabe were confirmed with the exchange of elaborate wampum belts. The Two-Row Wampum is one of many that chronicle the history of this diplomatic relationship.[21] Figures joined hand in hand, linked together by the "Chain" or, in the case of the Gus-wen-tah, two rows of purple beads, symbolize the polities (Native and European) who while inhabiting the same lands, agreed to respect the customs, laws and ways of the other.[22]

The Covenant Chain therefore represented two fundamental principles. It was an enduring record of the alliance first made between the Dutch and Mohawk, and later between Great Britain and Aboriginal peoples in the Great Lakes, but it was also a statement and recognition of Aboriginal sovereignty on the part of the British. At a conference at Johnson Hall in 1762, a

Mohawk sachem rose to discuss the importance of the Covenant Chain with Sir William Johnson: "Brother: This Belt, or Covenant Chain, was given to Us several years ago by Nine governments hereon represented, and His Majesty King George at the Top, assuring Us, that the Great King wou'd remain our Friends.... This Belt we only shew you, to let you know that we constantly look at it, and repeat the purport of it to our old and young, so as never to forget the Promises you then made, as We are determin'd inviolably to abide by those made on Our side."[23] The speech intended to impress on Johnson not only the importance of the Chain, but of wampum. It was a subtle reminder that although the Mohawk lacked written records, they would not forget the promises made to them by the British, nor would they suffer to be cheated or misled. Wampum and other mnemonic devices have preserved the understanding of these meetings orally for generations, becoming in effect Native versions of documents, and their interpretations have remained unchanged throughout the colonial period into the present.[24] In these councils, both sides clearly understood the protocol of the belts and recognized that through them, they were pledging their mutual support as allied nations.

Following the conquest, then, an elaborate system of diplomacy evolved, largely of Indigenous invention, that facilitated and mediated differences between Natives and non-Natives in the Thirteen Colonies and later in the region around the Great Lakes. It was clear both militarily and from a numerical perspective that while Great Britain claimed jurisdiction over what was for the most part Aboriginal territory, actually imposing its will on the residents within, was an entirely different matter.

Britain's Indian officers were drawn into the world of Aboriginal diplomacy not only as witnesses but also as active participants. This extended into the social realm, as nearly all the Indian officers married into influential Native families, lived in Indigenous communities for extensive periods of time, or were of Aboriginal ancestry themselves.[25] Others, like interpreter Andrew Montour, were employed specifically for their bicultural backgrounds as messengers, translators, and intermediaries.[26] These men took Native wives and their sons often joined the Indian Department as well. Thus the principles of the Covenant Chain were not only observed for diplomatic purposes, but they also united families. The individual and the position he held in colonial society were readily interchangeable. Indian agents were always on the job; they were representatives of the Crown personally and professionally, and violations of protocol in either circumstance could place them in peril.

Many employed in the Indian Department also built grand houses that in many instances were viewed by the local Aboriginal communities as places of refuge. Descriptions of the homes of Johnson in particular but also those of McKee and Croghan include what can only be described as a motley group of Aboriginal friends, families, servants, and hangers-on coming and going on a daily basis.[27] These agents differed from their counterparts in the British military and government establishment in that they immersed themselves in Aboriginal culture. They maintained the trappings of British aristocracy yet were equally comfortable in Mohawk councils.[28] Outright racism and discrimination based on class did come into play at times, particularly during interactions with non-allied Natives and when Aboriginal and European world views clashed.[29] Aboriginal peoples were also not above exacting their own kind of influence to get a point across when necessary. One particularly ingenious strategy involved plotting to assassinate particular Indian officers. These rumours were almost endemic throughout the eighteenth century, and Johnson wrote several times that he feared for his safety. At one point, Deputy William Claus informed him that Indians allied to the French had bragged "it would be nothing at all to Scale the Walls of ... [Johnson's] house and Kill everybody in it without firing a Gun."[30] Rumour could be quite an effective diplomatic tactic to influence British policy, particularly when the king's representatives became too forgetful or neglectful of their Covenant Chain obligations.[31]

So what are we to make of these men who risked their lives and careers not only to defend the interests of Native people but also to amass for themselves thousands of acres of their land? Sir William Johnson was quite certain that he could balance "the publik good" with his "own private interest."[32] Hindsight nevertheless gives the modern reader the advantage of knowing the outcome, that there would never be enough land to satisfy everyone—a concept arguably beyond the understanding of Europeans living in the eighteenth century. Because of their intimate connection with the land and its resources, what survives in the historical record indicates that at a very early date, the Six Nations did recognize that there would not be enough land. As early as 1755, Hendrick told Johnson, "You desire us to unite & live together ... but we shall have no land left either for ourselves or them, for your People when they buy a small piece of land of us ... they make it large."[33] Europeans could or would not entertain the ramifications of their unbridled settlement and expansion, and summarily dismissed these concerns as nonsense. In their world, they were reserving for themselves but a tiny piece of an entire continent.

As a consequence of these fears, Aboriginal peoples began to cede their land to others in trust for protection. The first and largest of these agreements occurred in 1701 when the Mohawk signed a document for the protection of their hunting grounds entitled "A Deed in Trust to the King of England."[34] Johnson referred to this agreement in council at Mount Johnson in 1755, recorded as "a Covenant of Brotherly Love and Mutual Friendship."[35] In this council, both sides recognized that neither sovereignty nor ownership was surrendered but rather, as a last resort, the Mohawk had realized that they were unable to defend the land themselves and asked for the assistance of the British Crown.[36] Frustrated both by the continual encroachments of settlers on their lands and fraudulent attempts by others to obtain deeds, the Six Nations deeded as gifts several large parcels of land to Indian agents in addition to their hunting grounds.[37] As time wore on, agents themselves took the initiative and negotiated private land sales with the Native people around them.

Many of these early deeds of gift were to Sir William Johnson. Much of this land was within Mohawk territory, and there was an inference that the sachems wished him to reside with them. Johnson settled some of the lands; however, by his own estimates, he seldom had more than one hundred families whom he outfitted with agricultural implements at his own expense and his home was indeed among them.[38] While it is difficult to determine with any real precision the extent of the landholdings of these agents, most held what could be considered enormous but sparsely settled tracts of land.

To say that Johnson, Croghan, and others simply tricked or defrauded the Six Nations into deeding their lands to them denies the intelligence and experience made abundantly clear in the historical record and displayed by Native peoples countless times in councils with the British. Teedyuscung, a prominent Delaware chief, made the British provide him with a clerk to keep his records,[39] and he along with most other Aboriginal peoples in the 1750s understood the concepts of land speculation and profit. They knew who had deeds, and who obtained them by fraud, by "tricks of the compass" and who had not given compensation in return.[40] The Mohawk knew a squatter when they saw one, and their hatred for several men who underhandedly attempted to get their land indicates that they in no way thought the land acquisitions of Indian officers were a threat to their way of life. At Mount Johnson, an Oneida sachem said of the trader Lÿdius, "That man sitting there ... is a Devil, and has stole our Lands, he takes Indians slyly by the Blanket one at a time, and when they are drunk, puts some money in their Bosoms, and perswades them to sign deeds for our lands."[41] Indigenous peoples willingly deeded portions of their land to some and vigorously denied it others for good reason. Johnson and many others were obviously trusted and, for both social and military reasons, could not have afforded to violate that trust. These leases, deeds, and trusts, therefore, must have been mutually beneficial agreements and as such, historical inquiry must look beyond the surviving written documents to find the "talk in the bushes."[42]

Power, Politics, and Instability, 1763–74

By the end of the Seven Years War, Great Britain faced a war debt in excess of £135 million.[43] The colonies were thus forced to deal with policies that not only imposed severe cost-cutting measures on various departments but also demanded that the colonies absorb many costs themselves. Aboriginal peoples suffered especially hard and ultimately resisted in 1763 as a result of their connections to two departments that experienced severe cutbacks—the Military and the Indian departments.

While the imperial government superficially professed its support for its Aboriginal allies, it undermined the efforts of Indian agents at every turn both financially and philosophically. Agents were forced to defy their superiors not only to continue their Covenant Chain obligations but to simply survive in a growing climate of unrest. The Proclamation of 1763, issued in the midst of this crisis, clarified nothing. As Aboriginal peoples incorporated their understanding of the document into the existing Covenant Chain they would soon discover that the King's sacred promises were empty.

Sir William Johnson and other members of the British Indian department did not differ with the Board of Trade so much philosophically as in their sense of timing.[44] Both believed Europeans were simply biding their time until war, disease, and alcohol took their natural course and the remnants of once-powerful Indigenous populations assimilated or quietly died out.[45] Johnson, however, could not understand those who felt the urgent need to displace Indigenous peoples en masse at the expense of social justice.[46] He and other agents found their philosophies in daily social and political interactions with Native people around them, some of whom were family. While these agents were not optimistic about the continued survival of Aboriginal peoples as nations, they saw no reason to hurry the process along. The officers were, however, up against opposing opinions held by many in the Board of Trade and among military officers like Jeffery Amherst and Henry Gladwin, who acted in ignorance and often espoused a hatred of Natives peoples.[47] Amherst "radiated contempt for Indians" and called them dogs while his soldiers at the posts "demeaned and insulted" them.[48] He refused to "purchas[e] the good behavior, either of Indians, or any others" and noted that "When Men of What race soever, behave ill they must be punished but not bribed."[49] Amherst cut off the distribution of presents to allied Natives in 1762, a key aspect of British obligations in the alliance and went so far as to ban all trade and gifts of ammunition[50] in an attempt to disarm them. By 1763, hunters desperate to get ammunition from the forts were dying on their journeys as they could not hunt for food along the way.[51] Agents in the meantime made up the difference, sometimes out of their own pockets.[52] Amherst would never understand the volatility of European–Indigenous relations in 1763. He dismissed information the Indian agents supplied in the early 1760s as "of little consequence" since he believed "it is not in their power to hurt us."[53]

George Croghan later estimated that in the four months Pontiac and the allied nations resisted the oppressive policies of the British, they had killed and captured two thousand people, doomed thousands more to poverty, damaged or destroyed nine forts and plundered about £100 000 in goods and provisions.[54] Aboriginal peoples may have instigated the peace process but were not defeated in battles with British forces.[55] They did succeed in sending the message that they would not suffer to be treated in such a manner nor sit idly by while their lands were taken without their consent.[56]

The Board of Trade responded with a Proclamation on October 7, 1763, guaranteeing Aboriginal peoples lands that were currently in their possession both inside and outside of existing colonies and restricting the initial purchase of their lands to the Crown.[57] Both Natives and Indian agents initially welcomed this document and several important councils with the Anishinabe and Haudenosaunee were arranged soon after. During the Treaty of Niagara, peace following the uprising was settled in conjunction with an explanation of the Proclamation. An elaborate wampum belt bearing the date "1764" was solemnly given to the Western Confederacy by Johnson, promising the protection both of Aboriginal lands and of Aborignal sovereignty upon them.[58] Of course, the Proclamation contained no provisions for enforcement, no increased funding or manpower, and no method for punishing those who chose to violate the law.

As settlers increasingly encroached on Indian lands, Native people resorted to violence. Lacking funds to amend violations of Indigenous protocol with customary payments of presents,[59] the military forces to forcibly remove the settlers, or legal recourse to punish offenders, Indian officers resorted to methods of their own devise to prevent what threatened to become an all-out war. Once intent on peaceful coexistence, Johnson, Croghan, McKee, and others began to resign themselves to the fact that

Aboriginal peoples would have to set aside a territory for themselves well away from current settlements and any possibility of encroachment, before all their lands were lost.[60] The most notorious manifestation of this philosophy was the Treaty of Fort Stanwix, negotiated by Johnson in 1768. Raising the Proclamation line to the Ohio River, Johnson grossly exceeded his authority and the treaty was a disaster despite the fact that he truly believed he had found the perfect solution for all concerned, including himself. The issue of who was going to participate in and profit from the expansion of European settlement was a large component of the controversy surrounding Stanwix. It reeked of self-interest, was ill-considered, and improper, and it would never have happened had Great Britain not allowed the conditions in the colonies to deteriorate to such a degree. Worst of all though, the Treaty of Stanwix opened the door to commercial interests who eagerly financed colonization schemes but who had no intention of taking into account the needs of Native peoples once they acquired the land. No one disputes the fact that agents financially benefited from these deals, and that land fell into the wrong hands as a result; however, the officers were also forced to balance the needs of Aboriginal peoples against the demands of those who, like Amherst, were diametrically opposed to Aboriginal peoples having any benefit at all.

The growing incidences of individual initiative on the part of Indian officers, as well as their intimate knowledge and relationships with Aboriginal peoples, brought them into conflict with many colonial elites and members of the Board of Trade. Employees of the Indian Department were often erroneously perceived as having power *over* Aboriginal peoples—or in the very least the power to command and manipulate their opinions and allegiances. On the one hand this influence was viewed as absolutely crucial to British interests in North America and was encouraged; on the other had, however, it was also something to be suspicious of and therefore was secretly resented. Conflict, moreover, was not just limited to the Military and Indian departments. In her article on the elements of Iroquoian treaty protocol, Mary Druke notes that many departments, elites, and officials seemed to believe the Indian Department worked exclusively for them and to advance their interests.[61] That the department should represent and further the interests of Native peoples when these goals were at odds was never considered—in fact, it was viewed as disloyal.

Those who earned their fortunes as a result of the Indian trade were also often pitted against landed gentry from Britain, who both possessed a finely honed sense of entitlement and were accustomed to deference. Civil and military elites like Amherst, General Edward Braddock, and Frederick Haldimand were condescending in their behaviour to officers in the department who they perceived as having undeserved authority as well as social and racial backgrounds beneath them.[62] Johnson himself was often torn between obligations to his social peers and those of his kin and comrades.[63] Larry L. Nelson theorizes that McKee and other agents of mixed ancestry faced considerable prejudice not only from their contemporaries but also from historians who later portrayed them as "lured to white society in a self-interested quest to acquire wealth and prestige."[64] Despite the fact that modern scholarship has begun to see the mediative abilities of those of bicultural ancestry, it is easier to criticize the actions of these agents where they appear in the world of Europeans than to examine aspects of their less documented lives behind the scenes in Aboriginal villages.

A further blow to the department and to Aboriginal relations that bears mention in this period was the death of Sir William Johnson in 1774. Johnson himself was one of those mediatory personalities who bridged the divide between Great Britain and Aboriginal affairs in the colonies. Although his dispatches often fell on deaf ears, he was a primary broker of information nonetheless.[65] Perhaps the greatest loss was his knowledge of, and participation in the diplomatic relationship governed by the Covenant Chain. With Johnson died much of the context, at least from the agents' point of view, of many of these agreements both on and off the record. It is not surprising then that, following his death, several treaties including those of Detroit and Ontario went missing and were virtually unknown by department officials at the turn of the century.[66] Over time, this had a tremendous effect on Aboriginal peoples as more agents died and, with them, the oral promises and unwritten agreements governing the shared use of the land. The documented versions, though, would speak forever.[67]

The Covenant Chain in the Detroit Settlement, 1765–1800

The principles of the Covenant Chain were ever-evolving, and the fact that they endured so long was precisely because of this adaptable nature. This period was one of reconstruction in which both Aboriginals and Europeans "picked up the pieces and set about rebuilding their world. They saved what they could from the old and used what they could that was new."[68] On the eve of the American Revolution and as a result of their kinship ties to Natives of the Ohio valley, Indian agents and Native peoples reconstructed the Covenant Chain in Detroit. South of the Great Lakes they had tried to implement the provisions contained in the Proclamation of 1763 to protect Aboriginal lands using both legal and illegal means, and they would continue to do so on the other side of an emerging yet undetermined border. These agreements would not be new, but based on the historic and largely unwritten relationship in evolution since the 1600s.

Like the 1701 deed entrusting Mohawk hunting grounds to the king, a series of deeds were signed between chiefs of the Ojibwa, Potawatomi, Odawa, and Wyandot, and the residents of Detroit between 1765 and the turn of the century. They ranged from several small grants of a few acres to the early French inhabitants to larger grants made to Indian agents, merchants, military officers, and traders. These agreements were ultimately illegal under the Proclamation. Although many were roughly surveyed, most were not properly registered and some changed hands frequently. The fact that most of the gifts of land were deeded out of respect for "love and affection" or "love and friendship" suggests a harkening back to the Covenant Chain of Friendship.[69] The orations of Hendrick and Nickus, and speeches in councils with Sir William Johnson from Albany in the 1750s and right back to the earliest non-aggression pacts between the Six Nations and the Dutch spoke of the same values. In them, Europeans and Native peoples were allied and united in peace, friendship, and respect. They referred to each other as "Brethren" and throughout the colonial period agreed to fight against common foes. Most importantly though, Indian agents had secured with wampum promises that they would protect Aboriginal lands. Great Britain, in contrast, had only been consistent in its neglect of its Aboriginal allies.[70] What evolved between the Ohio Valley Nations and Indian agents was largely a subculture of people who had shared a way of life and were threatened in similar ways by the values of a settler-dominated and elite-governed society.

Inevitably, a somewhat muted yet still pervasive squatting problem had also taken root in Canada. When settlers were not purposefully inciting the Anishinabe by abusing and harassing them, their invasive manner of living indirectly destroyed the game, fisheries and berry patches. Moreover, the free movement of Native peoples declined in proportion with timber cutting, the enclosure of fields and erection of houses and mills.[71] Interaction between European and Indigenous societies and a shared use of the land were part of the Covenant Chain, the Proclamation of 1763, and later agreements between the Crown and First Nations, but at no time was wholesale title to their lands ceded or their sovereignty upon it relinquished.[72]

In this spirit, then, the compact nature of the Indian agents' settlement near Fort Malden indicates that it was designed to be protective yet also inclusive and welcoming to Native peoples. The lands directly across from Bois Blanc (Boblo Island) were granted by deeds from the Wyandot, Ottawa, and Chippewa Chiefs, unofficially in 1784 and by treaty in 1786 and subsequently settled by McKee, Caldwell, Elliott and other officers of the Indian Department. Moravian refugees and Delaware converts who fled the massacre at Gnadenhutten in 1782 stayed on the Elliot and McKee properties before securing their settlement at Fairfield, Ontario.[73] Large numbers of Aboriginal people were described as living near the agent's settlements and working on the farms, and in a report on the state of improvements of the lands in 1794, Colonel Alex McKee's property is the only one described as being improved by Indians.[74] Evidence suggests that, unlike the properties of other settlers, these fields were not enclosed and Native peoples were actively using parts of them for their mutual benefit.

Deeds between the local Aboriginal peoples (Ojibwa, Odawa, Potawatomi, and Wyandot) and minor Indian agents, traders, merchants, and government officials also specified that the grantors retained the right to continue traditional activities such as trading, fishing, and hunting.[75] Several from the 1780s specifically mentioned that the "said chiefs their heirs and respective tribes" retained "the privilege of ... fowling, planting corn, building huts and making sugar" but other forms of remuneration and "reciprocal obligations" were described in the text of the deeds.[76] Some contain one-time payments of standard trade goods such as rum, vermillion, tobacco, rifles, skins, ammunition, and wampum; others are slightly more complicated and contain *ongoing* financial payments in the form of currency, goods, or provisions. Descriptions such as "credit" with merchants, "good offices," unidentified merchandise that had already been received, "services," and "diverse other good causes" point to the fact that there was a large underground economy involving Indian lands and oral promises. They also indicate the Anishinabe and Wyandot were well aware they could be financially compensated for lands no longer in "use" as several of the deeds refer to the lands as abandoned or former village sites.[77]

John Borrows suggests that, in order to analyze the Aboriginal understanding of European documents, the historian must examine speeches, symbols, and conduct.[78] If we do so, it becomes clear that there is a consistent oral history confirming not only that Aboriginal people expected to be compensated for the use of their land but that they negotiated usage agreements rather than cessions to protect them. This is the Aboriginal understanding of the surrender provisions contained in the Proclamation of 1763 and a source of misunderstanding and frustration that continues to this day. Even if the surrender procedures were followed to the letter (which they rarely were), from an Indigenous perspective, no one person or group owned the land:

hence there was nothing to cede. At these public meetings, which were most often initiated by officials, Aboriginal people were negotiating coexistence—how both groups could mutually benefit by sharing access to resources. For instance, George Croghan recorded a speech in council with the chiefs of the Ottawa, Chippewa, and Potawatomi in which Pontiac stated that although the French had settled part of their lands, it had never been sold. Rather, he said that "their Country was very large and they were willing to give up such part of it ... provided they were paid for it and a sufficient part of the Country left them to hunt on."[79] Pontiac was confident that there was land enough for everyone, so in neither the French nor English periods was the land ever permanently alienated; it was shared. This particular speech is significant because it links the Anishinabe point of view regarding their traditional territories and European settlement in two distinct time periods; it illustrates the unwavering consistency of Anishinabe opinion concerning the land and their interpretation of the Proclamation of 1763.

The oral history of the region's Anishinabe residents has also remained consistent with the spirit of these agreements. In 1766, during negotiations at the Treaty of Lake Ontario, Sir William Johnson and other Indian agents assured Pontiac and the Ottawa chiefs that not only would they remain independent with their own customs and laws, but they would also be provided "with the Crown's official representatives to reside *within* ... the Aboriginal Nation's Territories."[80] In council with Indian agent William Jones in 1830, elders recounted a speech made by McKee in which he guaranteed the lands were theirs to manage as they saw fit. According to the elders, McKee had assured them that the land was not to be taken from them but that "this land should forever belong to the three tribes ... keep it ... and never part with it."[81] Again in 1839, elders told Samuel Jarvis, then head of Indian Affairs that "[s]ome of our Chiefs unmindful of the warning of the White Elk [McKee], deaf to the voice of our fathers have given away our land and with it our happiness.... This land is ours.'"[82]

The deeds worked only for a time, however, and gradually the repercussions of the failed Proclamation caught up to the small community in the wilderness. Once the intrusion of British institutions gained a foothold, the deeds caused increasing confusion. The creation of the Land Board in what was then known as the District of Hesse in 1789 suddenly bureaucratized what had been an informal and mutually profitable venture.[83] The board not only provided an avenue for personal promotion and advancement through the office itself, but it also commodified the land in the region by inviting the possibility that Indian deeds could eventually become legitimate sources of title. The Land Boards were part of an aggressive settlement program favoured by Lieutenant John Graves Simcoe, intended to distribute alienated Indian lands to Loyalist settlers, militiamen, soldiers, and sailors.[84] The Indian agents, who held a bloc of what was considered to be the best land in the area, and the Anishinabe with unceded lands of their own came under increasing pressure by the colonial government to move out of the way of settlement. The board accused the agents and other holders of Indian deeds of retaining them for speculative purposes. However, perhaps alternative explanations can be posited.

According to nineteenth-century concepts of land use, speculators accumulated and held large tracts of land without the intention of developing them.[85] If the goal of Aboriginal peoples was to remain undisturbed in their lands and they deeded specific tracts of land in trust to various non-Indian residents of Detroit, then these deed-holders by virtue of leaving large areas undeveloped for Aboriginal usage would by default be deemed speculators. In fact, most of the Indian agents who held these deeds have been historically defined as speculators precisely because they did not "improve" the land.[86] It is not surprising, then, that the bulk of the complaints from various interests throughout the 1780s and onward concerning the holders of Indian deeds centres not on the fact that they were making vast sums of money from their holdings but that *they were preventing others from doing so and the lands were going to waste.* While conclusive proof that the Indian agents were not holding the land for speculation is not yet found, they certainly did not act against the interests of Aboriginal peoples; in fact, by retarding settlement in the area, they actively assisted such interests. If agents were making agreements with the Anishinabe to allow, limit, or prevent settlement on Aboriginal lands, then the wholesale development of the region would have indeed been difficult, resulting in the complaints. As the Detroit settlement illustrates, the assumption based on European philosophies of land use that one not actively improving the land must be holding it for speculative purposes may not be historically accurate in all circumstances where Native lands were deeded to non-Aboriginals. Given long-standing and consistent oral traditions that dispute the intent to permanently alienate the land, other options such as trusts and shared-use agreements must also be considered.

The underlying problem with land deeded to others outside the Indian Department is that, like the Treaty of Stanwix, multiple transactions allowed land to fall into the hands of genuine speculators: those who were either not expressly aware of the oral promises or who simply refused to honour them. John Askin, for example, became indebted to Isaac Todd, James McGill, and other Montreal merchants, and was forced to sell significant parts of his holdings to people outside of the settlement.[87] According to John Clarke, it was these merchants who eventually came to own many of the Indian deeds and their scattered nature proves that they were acquired piecemeal.[88] Additionally, lands that were originally deeded in protective blocs but later sold individually became more susceptible to squatting and aggressive resource extraction like timber cutting. The acceptance of deeds as payment for goods and the ease with which merchants and traders moved into lucrative civil offices entitling them to advance notice of lots for sale may have contributed to the problem. The security of the deeds and by extension Anishinabe lands came to be threatened by the wheeling and dealing of individual merchants and the fortunes of the commercial interests they represented.

Conclusion

Deeds contracted between Aboriginal peoples of the Great Lakes and officers of the British Indian Department enabled those with access to the colonial power structure to secure compensation for the use of Native lands that otherwise would have been encroached upon and expropriated by those who refused to either abide by or enforce the law.[89] It was, however, the oral component of these agreements that mediated the differences between the rigidity of the law and the flexibility of custom, and so long as people remained aware that there were obligations beyond the written words of the documents, divergent interests could be accommodated. Problems occurred later, when interests promoting settlement chose to accept the validity of the written deeds over the complementary oral history that gave them their true meaning.

The Proclamation of 1763, rather than securing a viable land and resource base for Aboriginal peoples in North America, actually exacerbated an already illegal and immoral system of land acquisition precisely because it was hastily implemented, ill thought out, and deliberately vague in its wording. Imperial Britain did not appreciate the complicated and volatile situations it created in colonial North America. By summarily cutting the very departments necessary to ensure enforcement of the Proclamation, Great Britain abdicated its "imperial responsibility towards Native people"[90] and ensured that successive governments in the colonies would be able to create quasi-official bodies like land boards knowing full well they would pressure Aboriginal peoples to cede their land. Consequently, rather than void the original Indian deeds as required by the Proclamation, the colonial government coerced the Anishinabe into relinquishing what was already occupied in

1789–90. Legitimate titles were thereafter issued to the deed holders[91] and are now at the core of a significant number of specific claims launched against the federal government nearly two hundred years later.

The 1790s in many ways represented the end of an era; William Dummer Powell called the older Indian agents "'left-overs' from the pioneer era before the War of 1812" and as McKee, Caldwell, Elliot, and the other agents died, with them went the last hope that these oral agreements and the spirit of the Covenant Chain would be recognized in Ontario.[92] When Indian agent John Butler, who had been present at many treaties in Southwestern Ontario, died in 1796, Joseph Brant said that he "was the last that remained of those that acted with that great man the late Sir William Johnson, whose steps he followed and our Loss is the greater, as there are none remaining who understand our manners and customs as well as he did."[93]

People like Sir William Johnson, George Croghan, Alexander McKee, and others in the British Indian Department recognized and encountered on a daily basis the functioning of elaborate Indigenous legal, political, and social systems within a culture as sophisticated as that of Europe. They were able to acquire a perspective on Indigenous–European relations unparalleled and unknown among their contemporaries in colonial governments and on the Board of Trade. While they were originally sent to further the interests of Great Britain, they came at times to serve the interests of Native people against those of Britain, and at others to serve their own, to the peril of both.

As MacKenzie writes, "the economic, sociological and natural historical dimensions of hunting, set within a wider cultural context, have perhaps proved dauntingly complex."[94] Colonial social and class hierarchies, and by extension the power possessed by those at the summit, were as evident in the protocol of the hunt as in the fenced and carefully manicured estates and manor houses of Upper Canada. Both reflected and advanced a colonial project that increasingly excluded Aboriginal peoples by design and application. Despite lofty ambitions of empire, the true spirit of the Covenant Chain of Friendship and the agreements made under its guiding principles can only be uncovered by understanding these day-to-day interactions of people who lived it first-hand. If the spirit of the Two Row Wampum tells us anything, it is that we were once on the "right road." Until this rift is reconciled, however, frustration and indeed occasional hostility will continue to overshadow the attempts of the Canadian state and First Nations to find common ground.

Notes

I would like to thank David T. McNab and Carolyn Podruchny for their direction and comments. I would also like to thank Karl Hele, participants, and community members in attendance at the Empire of Nature and Nature of Empires Conference held at Bkejwanong (Walpole Island) in April 2006 for their insight and encouragement. A significant part of this paper was drawn from my Master's Research Paper.

1 John Borrows, "Constitutional Law from a First Nation Perspective: Self-government and the Royal Proclamation," *UBC Law Review* 28 (1994): 24.
2 John Mackenzie, *The Empire of Nature: Hunting, Conservation and British Imperialism* (Manchester: Manchester University, 1988), 43.
3 Mackenzie, *Empire of Nature*, 2.
4 Mackenzie, *Empire of Nature*, 300.
5 Mackenzie, *Empire of Nature*, 23; R.G. Riddell, "A Study of the Land Policy of the Colonial Office, 1763–1865," *Canadian Historical Review* 18 (1937): 385. Mackenzie notes that the hunting code and the restriction on hunting to the upper classes relied upon the classification and ordering of the natural world.
6 Edward Benton-Banai, *The Mishomis Book* (Hayward, WI: Indian Country Communications, 1988), 93.
7 Anishinabe is the collective term for the Ojibwa, Odawa, and Potawatomi peoples; Haudenosaunee refers to the Six Nations or Iroquois. The Ohio or Western Nations referred to are principally the Delaware and Shawnee although George Croghan noted that it became difficult at times to tell all the "tribes" apart as non-Native settlement encroached on their traditional territories and pushed them westward. Nicholas B. Wainwright, *George Croghan: Wilderness Diplomat* (Chapel Hill: University of North Carolina Press, 1959), 40.
8 Thomas Gage, "Letter from Thomas Gage to Captain James Stephenson at Detroit," in "'For Good Will and Affection': The Detroit Indian Deeds and British Land Policy, 1760–1827," by Victor Lytwyn, and Dean Jacobs, *Ontario History* 92, no. 2 (Spring 2000): 17.
9 "Royal Proclamation, October 7, 1763 (Extract)," in Derek G. Smith, ed., *Canadian Indians and the Law: Selected Documents, 1663–1972* (Toronto: McClelland and Stewart, 1975), 2–4.
10 Dorothy V. Jones, *License for Empire: Colonialism by Treaty in Early America* (Chicago: University of Chicago Press, 1982), 48; Gregory Evans Dowd, *War Under Heaven: Pontiac, the Indian Nations, and the British Empire* (Baltimore: Johns Hopkins University Press, 2002), 178.

Jones states that, in the years leading up to and for sometime after the Proclamation of 1763 was conceived, "far from wanting to exterminate the Indians, the British wanted their friendship and sought alliances with them."

11 Darlene Johnston, *The Taking of Indian Lands in Canada: Consent or Coercion?* (Saskatoon: University of Saskatchewan Native Law Centre, 1989), 93.

12 "Royal Proclamation, October 7, 1763," 2–4. The Proclamation states firmly that "if at any Time any of the said Indians should be inclined to dispose of the said Lands, the same shall be Purchased only for Us, in our Name, at some public Meeting or Assembly of the said Indians, to be held for that purpose by the Governor or commander in chief of our Colony respectively within which they shall lie…."

13 Jones, *License for Empire*, 119.

14 Quoted in Jack Stagg, *Anglo-Indian Relations in North America to 1763 and an Analysis of the Royal Proclamation of 1763* (Ottawa: Indian and Northern Affairs Canada, 1981), 361. "The happy coincidence of system" described by Thomas Pownell encapsulated the Proclamation's perceived ability to solve a number of problems at once.

15 Alan Taylor, *The Divided Ground: Indians, Settlers, and the Northern Borderland of the American Revolution* (New York: Vintage Books, 2007), 10.

16 As a result of continual warfare, the introduction of alcohol, and European diseases, the population of North America's Native peoples was at this time in serious decline. It was believed that with the addition of assimilative policies or "gradual civilization," Aboriginal peoples as distinct cultural entities would eventually cease to exist.

17 John Borrows, "Wampum at Niagara: The Royal Proclamation, Canadian Legal History, and Self-Government," in *Aboriginal and Treaty Rights in Canada*, ed. Michael Asch (Vancouver: UBC Press, 1997), 157.

18 Paul Williams, "Oral Tradition on Trial," in *Gin Das Winan: Documenting Aboriginal History in Ontario*, Occasional Papers of the Champlain Society no. 2, ed. Dale Standen and David McNab (Toronto: Champlain Society, 1996), 31. The Six Nations were originally the Five Nations; the Tuscarora became the sixth in the 1720s. The Anishinabe and other Western Nations were thereafter incorporated into these agreements of alliance and resource sharing. One of the most well known was The Dish with One Spoon, an agreement in which the chiefs of both confederacies (the Anishinabe and Haudenosaunee) would "share a bowl of Beaver Tail Stew," a metaphor for peaceful coexistence and resource sharing. See Victor Lytwyn, "A Dish with One Spoon: The Shared Hunting Grounds Agreement in the Great Lakes and St. Lawrence Valley Region," in *Papers of the 28th Algonquian Conference*, David H. Pentland, ed. (Winnipeg: University of Manitoba, 1997): 210–27.

19 Francis Jennings, "Glossary of Figures of Speech in Iroquois Political Rhetoric," in *The History and Culture of Iroquois Diplomacy: An Interdisciplinary Guide to*

the Treaties of the Six Nations and Their League, ed. Francis Jennings (New York: Syracuse, 1995), 116; William N. Fenton, "Structure, Continuity, and Change in the Process of Iroquois Treaty Making," In *The History and Culture of Iroquois Diplomacy: An Interdisciplinary Guide to the Treaties of the Six Nations and Their League*, ed. Francis Jennings (New York: Syracuse, 1995), 16. Fenton notes there is evidence suggesting the Confederacy of Five Nations and subsequent interactions with the Dutch may date to 1635; however specific reference to the Covenant Chain in extant documents begins only in 1677.

20 Jennings, "Glossary," 116; Robert S. Allen, *His Majesty's Indian Allies: British Indian Policy in the Defence of Canada, 1774–1815* (Toronto: Dundurn, 1992), 15.

21 Tehanetorens, *Wampum Belts* (Oshweken, ON: Iroqrafts, 2003); this book was originally published in Onchiota, New York, by the Six Nations Indian Museum in 1972 and gives a brief history of several wampum belts that record significant events in the history of the Haudenosaunee.

22 David T. McNab, "Sovereignty, Treaties and Trade in the Bkejwanong Territory," *Journal of Aboriginal Economic Development* 3, no. 2 (2003): 53.

23 "Proceedings with the Sachems, and great Warriors of the united Six Nations at Johnson Hall ...," 8–10 September 1762, in *The Papers of Sir William Johnson*, vol. 10, ed. Milton W. Hamilton (Albany: University of the State of New York), 506.

24 John Borrows, "A Genealogy of Law: Inherent Sovereignty and First Nations Self-Government," LLM thesis, University of Toronto, 1991, 51–52; Tehanetorens, *Wampum Belts*.

25 See biographies by Milton W. Hamilton (*Sir William Johnson: Colonial American, 1715–1763*), Larry L. Nelson (*A Man of Distinction among Them: Alexander McKee and the Ohio Frontier, 1754–1799*), and Wainwright, *George Croghan*, as well as the following entries in *The Dictionary of Canadian Biography Online*, at Library and Archives Canada, http://www.biographi.ca: L.L Kulisek, "William Caldwell"; Reginald Horsman, "Matthew Elliot"; and Douglas Leighton, "Simon Girty." Sir William Johnson married Joseph Brant's sister Molly, McKee married a daughter of Shawnee Chief Blue Jacket, and George Croghan married the daughter of Mohawk sachem Nickus (Karaghtadie). Billy Caldwell, son of William Caldwell, was also of Native descent, Matthew Elliot had a Shawnee wife and children, and Simon Girty had been a captive of the Seneca for several years in his youth.

26 Wilbur R. Jacobs, *Wilderness Politics and Indian Gifts: The Northern Colonial Frontier 1748–1763* (Lincoln: University of Nebraska Press, 1950), 94.

27 Milton W. Hamilton, *Sir William Johnson: Colonial American, 1715–1763* (New York: Kennikat, 1976), 310–12. George Croghan's estate at Aughwick (Cooper-

stown, NY) was described as having "above twenty cabins about his house, and in them at least two hundred Indians, men, women and children ... [who] frequently come to fetch a meal"; Wainwright, *George Croghan*, 73.

28 Allen, *His Majesty's Indian Allies*, 23.

29 Sir William Johnson, "Journal of Indian Affairs, Jan. 2–31, 1764," in *The Papers of Sir William Johnson*, vol. 11: 26–27. This is most obvious in correspondence following the Pontiac Resistance in 1763.

30 William Claus quoted in Hamilton, *Sir William Johnson, Colonial American, 1715–1763*, 215.

31 Gregory Evans Dowd, "The French King Wakes Up in Detroit: 'Pontiac's War' in Rumor and History" *Ethnohistory* 37, no. 3 (Summer 1990) 254–78. Dowd has argued that persistent rumours of a French return in the 1760s were not in fact spread by France but by Native peoples in an attempt to manipulate France into returning to North America.

32 "Letter to John Pownall, Johnson Hall, 18 April 1762," in Alexander C. Flick, ed., *Papers of Sir William Johnson*, vol. 3: 90.

33 "Minutes of a Council Meeting at Fort Johnson, July 3, 1755," Library and Archives Canada (LAC), Indian Affairs, RG 10, Series 2, Vol. 4, Reel 1221, p. 66.

34 This is also known as the Nanfan Treaty. In 1701, Haudenosaunee leaders asked John Nanfan, the Governor of the New York colony, for a legal instrument signed by the King that would protect their beaver-hunting grounds. Drawn up and executed in 1726, the deed covers portions of modern-day southern Ontario, Michigan, Illinois, Indiana, and Ohio. See council and "Deed from the Five Nations to the King of their Beaver Hunting Ground," in E.B. O'Callaghan, ed., *Documents Relative to the Colonial History of the State of New York*, Vol. 4 (Albany: Weed and Parsons, 1853), 907–11, and Vol. 5 (Albany: Weed and Parsons, 1853), 800–01.

35 "Brethren, Sachems & Warriors of the Confederate Nations here Represent," n.d., LAC, RG 10, Indian Affairs, Series 2, Vol. 4, Reel 1221, pp. 35–39. Johnson also professed that they would all eventually become "one Body, one Blood & one People" united against a common enemy (the French). He reminded their youth to remember that their lands had been placed "under the Protection & Dominion of the Great King of England ... by a solemn Deed in writing signed by your Great Men."

36 Allen, *His Majesty's Indian Allies*, 18

37 See "Letter to John Pownall, Johnson Hall 18 Apr. 1763," *The Papers of Sir William Johnson*, 4: 89–91, for the description of one Mohawk gift of land to Sir William Johnson.

38 Johnson, "Letter to John Pownall," 4: 89–91.

39 Anthony F. Wallace, *King of the Delawares: Teedyuscung, 1700–1763* (Syracuse, NY: Syracuse University Press, 1990), 157.
40 W.R. Jacobs, *Wilderness Politics and Indian Gifts*, 171.
41 "Early Meeting at Mount Johnson, 15 May 1755," LAC, RG 10, Indian Affairs, Series 2, Vol. 4, C-1221, pp. 66–67.
42 Jennings, *History and Culture of Iroquois Diplomacy*, 27. "Talk in the bushes" is an Iroquoian metaphor for agreements and discussions made outside of or prior to the commencement of official treaty councils.
43 Ian K. Steele, *Warpaths: Invasions of North America* (New York: Oxford University Press, 1994), 225.
44 Richard White, *The Middle Ground: Indians, Empires and Republics in the Great Lakes Region, 1650–1815* (Cambridge: University of Cambridge Press, 1991), 259.
45 White, *Middle Ground*, 260.
46 White, *Middle Ground*, 260; Johnson, "Letter to John Penn 20 Jan. 1764," *Papers of Sir William Johnson*, 11: 18. Johnson wrote that unrestricted and advancing settlement unnecessarily threatened trade and endangered homesteaders. He maintained that a simple policy of peace and fairness would have gradually led to the same objective without bloodshed.
47 C.P. Stacey, "Jeffery Amherst," *Dictionary of Canadian Biography Online*. Amherst's views were probably shared by the majority of people in this time period who, either out of fear or ignorance, did not associate with Native people. He is most often cited simply because his venomous writings have survived.
48 Dowd, *War Under Heaven*, 65–66.
49 Quoted in C.P. Stacey "Jeffery Amherst," *Dictionary of Canadian Biography Online*.
50 McNab, "Sovereignty, Treaties and Trade," 54.
51 Peter S. Schmaltz, *The Ojibwa of Southern Ontario* (Toronto: University of Toronto Press, 1991), 70.
52 Wainwright, *George Croghan*, 76, 78.
53 Quoted by Wainwright, *George Croghan*, 194.
54 Wainwright, *George Croghan*, 199.
55 McNab, "Sovereignty, Treaties and Trade," 55.
56 Borrows, "Genealogy of Law," 46.
57 "Royal Proclamation, October 7, 1763 (Extract)," in Derek G. Smith, ed., *Canadian Indians and the Law: Selected Documents*, 2–4. The Proclamation did not protect these lands in perpetuity and contained a somewhat confusing method of purchase for those nations who wished to cede all or parts of their land. As noted, this was to take place at a public meeting or assembly called specifically for the sale by the governor or the commander-in-chief. All private sales were prohibited.

58 Borrows, "Wampum at Niagara," 163; McNab, "Sovereignty, Treaties and Trade," 55.
59 White, *Middle Ground*, 320.
60 Wainwright, *George Croghan*, 246.
61 Mary A. Druke, "Iroquois Treaties: Common Forms, Varying Interpretations," in *The History and Culture of Iroquois Diplomacy*, ed. Francis Jennings (New York: Syracuse, 1995), 95.
62 Hamilton, *Sir William Johnson*, 179. During military campaigns Indian officers were given rank and command of Aboriginal allies. This often conflicted with military superiors who acquired their positions not through experience but as a result of wealth and privilege.
63 Hamilton, *Sir William Johnson*, 179; Julian Gwyn, "Sir William Johnson," *Dictionary of Canadian Biography Online*.
64 Larry L. Nelson, *A Man of Distinction among Them: Alexander McKee and the Ohio Frontier, 1754–1799* (Kent, OH: Kent State University Press, 1999), xiii.
65 Allen, *His Majesty's Indian Allies*, 23; Nelson, *Man of Distinction*, 30.
66 McNab, "Sovereignty, Treaties and Trade," 57.
67 Druke, "Iroquois Treaties," 91. The Seneca told Samuel Kirkland in 1765 that "some of the Indians were afraid of *writing* any *letters* because those letters would *speak* for a great many years afterwards."
68 Colin Calloway, *New Worlds For All: Indians, Europeans and the Remaking of Early America* (Baltimore: Johns Hopkins University Press, 1997), xiii.
69 See Victor Lytwyn and Dean Jacobs, "'For Good Will and Affection': The Detroit Indian Deeds and British Land Policy, 1760–1827," *Ontario History* 92, no. 2 (Spring 2000): 9–29.
70 Great Britain ceded the Ohio Valley to the US by the Treaty of Paris (1783), agreed to a border dividing the Great Lakes by the Jay Treaty (1794), and evacuated the Western posts (1796), all without the input or even knowledge of its Aboriginal allies.
71 Sheila Van Wyck, "Harvests Yet to Reap: History, Identity and Agriculture in a Canadian Indian Community," Ph.D. thesis, University of Toronto, 1992, 161.
72 Borrows, "Genealogy of Law," 52–54.
73 Ernest J. Lajeunesse, *The Windsor Border Region: Canada's Southernmost Frontier: A Collection of Documents*, Ontario Series, 4th ed. (Toronto: Champlain Society, 1960), 156–58, 163, 165.
74 Leighton, "Simon Girty"; Fred Coyne Hamil, *The Valley of the Lower Thames, 1640–1850* (Toronto: University of Toronto Press, 1951), 335.
75 "Potawatomi and Ottawa deed to Antoine Beaubien, Jean Marie Beaubien at River Raisin," Register of Deeds, Wayne County [microfilm reel no. P8], 200–201.

76 "Copy of Indenture Made between Chippewa Chiefs and James A. May, Jacob Bogart and Bernarbus Harson, 1797-02-04," Michigan Pioneer and Historical Collections, vol. 8, 498–500; Victor Lytwyn and Dean Jacobs, "'For Good Will and Affection': The Detroit Indian Deeds and British Land Policy, 1760–1827," *Ontario History* 92, no. 2 (Spring 2000): 24.

77 I am indebted to Victor Lytwyn for providing me with the text of these deeds, which have been located in various repositories in both the United States and Canada.

78 Borrows, "Wampum at Niagara," 156.

79 Pontiac to George Croghan, quoted in Lytwyn and Jacobs, "'For Good Will and Affection,'" 15.

80 David T. McNab, "Sovereignty, Treaties and Trade," 57; italics mine.

81 Quoted in Dean Jacobs, "Introduction," in Dale Standen and David McNab, eds., *Gin Das Winan: Documenting Aboriginal History in Ontario*, Occasional Papers of the Champlain Society no. 2 (Toronto: Champlain Society, 1996), 4.

82 Ibid., Jacobs in Standen and McNab, eds., *Gin Das Winan*, 5.

83 The process is studied on the other side of the border in Lawrence B.A. Hatter, "The Transformation of the Detroit Land Market and the Formation of the Anglo-American Border, 1783–1796," *Michigan Historical Review* 34, no. 1 (Spring 2008): 83–99.

84 John Clarke, *Land, Power and Economics on the Frontier of Upper Canada* (Montreal: McGill-Queen's University Press, 2001), 195.

85 John Clarke, "Geographical Aspects of Land Speculation in Essex County to 1825: The Strategy of Particular Individuals" in *Historical Essays on Upper Canada: New Perspectives*, ed. J.K Johnston and Bruce G. Wilson (Ottawa: Carleton University Press, 1991), 83.

86 John C. Weaver, "Concepts of Economic Improvement and the Social Construction of Property Rights: Highlights from the English Speaking World," in *Despotic Dominion: Property Rights in British Settler Societies*, ed. John McLaren et al. (Vancouver: University of British Columbia Press, 2005), 88. "Improvement," or the difference between the use of a tract of land and its perceived potential, was used to justify the appropriation of Aboriginal hunting territories by European agriculturalists. It was commonly believed that Aboriginal peoples "wasted the land" by leaving it wild whereas the latter made better "use" of it by clearing it and planting crops.

87 "Land Holdings of John Askin," in *The John Askin Papers*, ed. Milo M. Quaife (Detroit: Detroit Library Commission, 1928), 2: 16. These are described as lands he had "to dispose of," and Isaac Todd was given authorization to sell them.

88 "Land Holdings of John Askin," 16. Most of the merchants, except Jacques Baby, were severely indebted to each other at one time or another. At one point, John Askin was forced to sell several of his properties to repay debts owing. Clarke notes that D.W. Smith, John Pownall, Alexander Grant, Leith, and Louvigny, as well as James Baby, Arent DePeyster, and Thomas Williams, held enormous numbers of deeds, but that their scattered nature indicates that they were acquired through debtors or lost through the merchant's own indebtedness. John Clarke, "Geographical Aspects of Land Speculation," 94, and John Clarke, *Land, Power and Economics*, 135, 151.

89 Sidney L. Harring, *White Man's Law: Native People in Nineteenth-Century Canadian Jurisprudence* (Toronto: University of Toronto Press, 1998), 27.

90 Allen, *His Majesty's Indian Allies*, 37.

91 Robert J. Surtees, "Land Cessions, 1763–1830" in *Aboriginal Ontario: Historical Perspectives on the First Nations*, ed. Edward S. Rogers and Donald B. Smith (Toronto: Dundurn, 1994), 111–12. The lands known as the McKee purchase were ceded for £1200 in goods.

92 Robert E. Saunders, "What Was the Family Compact?" *Ontario History* 49, no. 4 (1957): 167. Most of the Indian agents, traders, and military officials who had intimate knowledge of the colonial period prior to the Revolution died in the late 1790s and early 1800s.

93 Quoted in R. Arthur Bowler and Bruce G. Wilson, "John Butler," *Dictionary of Canadian Biography Online.*

94 Mackenzie, *Empire of Nature*, 7. The influence and effect of the land in colonial society bears a striking similarity to Mackenzie's conclusions regarding hunting. He writes, "it is known too that hunting developed sociological significance, became subjected to rules and rights, at a very early period."

CHAPTER 7

Lines on the Land: Surveying Townships after the 1790 Treaty

Rhonda Telford

The starting point for this paper is the unclear textual and cartographical identification of the northwest angle in Treaty 2 of 19 May 1790, and subsequent surveying difficulties that arose in running the 1790 treaty line—one of two land-based lines defining the affected area. In a wider context, treaties and surveys were among the tools used by foreign authorities to garner legitimacy vis-à-vis lands and resources and their disposition. This was especially the case in "Ontario" both before and after it became known as Upper Canada in 1790. Legitimate or not, treaties and surveys were an integral part of the dominion that Britain sought to establish over Indigenous property. As we shall see, however, this road to empire was neither smooth nor speedy.

This chapter is more concerned with the surveys following Treaty 2 than with negotiations leading to the treaty. Treaty 2 was concluded between members of the Chippewa, Ottawa, Pottawatomi, and Huron nations, and local representatives of the king on 22 June 1790. The Crown believed that this treaty severed all rights and interests of the Indigenous population in the subject area, whereas the Chippewa, Ottawa, Pottawatomi, and Huron nations believed that they had shared the subject area with the Crown. This treaty generally involved land south of the Thames River to the border of Lake Erie, east to Catfish Creek, and west to Lake St Clair.[1] Looking at the external boundaries of the treaty, it is clear that except for the north–south line at Catfish Creek, the only other to be drawn on land was the west–east line from the Chenail[2] Ecarte to the Thames River. This chapter is primarily concerned with the latter boundary. This northwest angle of Treaty 2, also known as the "Chenail Ecarte" Tract, was not identified until 1796 during the council meetings for Treaty 7 of 7 September 1796, between the Chippewa and representatives of the king. The location of the northwest angle was apparently established by Deputy Superintendent General Alexander McKee, and drawn on the accompanying map by surveyor Thomas Abraham Iredell. McKee had been present as the Indian agent at the 1790 Treaty. The southern boundary of the 1796 Treaty was part of the northern boundary of the 1790 Treaty.[3] Still, the line was not run. Survey instructions and field notes dealing with the production of the 1790 northern land boundary show that it was not surveyed until early in the following century. The westernmost part of the line continued to be revisited and/or altered into the 1820s. This paper also examines the surveyors' township field-note books and plans as sources that locate Aboriginal presence on the ground. These sources provide a wealth of information about the location of old and/or abandoned cornfields, clearings, campgrounds, sugar bushes, and other marks of Aboriginal occupation on the territory.

Problems Defining the 1790 Treaty Line

The problem of the northwest angle of Treaty 2 rests squarely in the treaty document and accompanying map. The document describes the tract, starting from Catfish Creek, running west along the "border" of Lake Erie, and "up the Streight to the mouth of the Chenail Ecarte and up the main branch ... to the first fork on the south side, then ... due east until it intersects" the Thames, and up the Thames to the northwest corner of the 1784 Treaty, following its western boundary south to the mouth of Catfish Creek. This description cannot be reconciled with the map, which does not show the islands in the delta, including Walpole Island and St. Anne's Island in their correct positions. The Chenail Ecarte was also positioned incorrectly, thus making the depiction of the "first fork on the south side" incorrect.[4]

Although the 1790 Treaty did not require an immediate survey, this was an important issue for the Crown, which planned to open the area to an expected influx of American and other settlers.[5] Furthermore, the Moravian missionaries and their Delaware converts had established a community north of the Thames River in 1792 on the strength of previous promises of a land grant. The Moravians and the Delaware met with Lieutenant Governor John Simcoe early in 1793, as he was travelling from Niagara to Detroit. On his return trip, Simcoe assured them that their village was in the clear. He approved for them a larger area, which was to extend "northward to the purchase line."[6]

Nevertheless, as late as the fall of 1793, the location of the northern boundary was unknown, and the exact limits of the treaty remained unclear on the ground. David Smith, the acting surveyor general, instructed Lieutenant Colonel England, president of the Land Board of Kent and Essex, that Lieutenant Governor Simcoe wanted the boundary settled. Smith observed that Simcoe,

> being anxious, that the Boundary of the last purchase made from the Indians should be run, I am to request you would be pleased to direct the Surveyor of your district to execute this Service, *and as this office is not furnished with sufficient Information as to the exact Limits of the purchase, or the Course it takes from Chenal Ecarte to the River La Tranche*—I request you would have the goodness to collect the necessary Information from your Register and direct the Business to be carried into Execution....
>
> As this office has very few Documents of Survey from your District, the Council has desired, that Plans of the several Townships, on separate Pieces, and a Plan of the District be prepared.[7]

Subsequent correspondence indicated that England's District Office similarly had no information about the 1790 Treaty.

The motivation for this sudden determination to survey the northern line appears to have been agitation from the Moravian missionaries who could not obtain a Crown deed for their grant unless the line was run showing that their land was not on that still retained by the Chippewa.[8] In addition, there were problems with squatters along the Thames River, and a plethora of Indian land deeds granted to settlers along the Detroit River and elsewhere.[9]

Not until 17 November 1793 did David Smith inform Lieutenant Colonel England that he had found a draft report of the Land Board, including the text of the 1790 Treaty, which provided a description of the area purchased. Smith advised England that it would be preferable to run the northern treaty line not from this information but from the deed, which neither he nor the Land Board had in hand:

> *On turning over almost every paper I have, I at length found one* indorsed [*sic*] "No. 41 Draft Report from the Land Board for the District of Hesse 1st June 1790—Entered Register No. 2 folio 238—DWL" dated "Detroit 1st June 1790" addressed "My Lord"—I find therein that the Board "did by minute of 7th Decem. last recommend to Mr. McKee the Deputy Agent to treat with the Indians for the purchase of a Tract of Land from the End of the last purchase

> from the Mississaugas commencing at the mouth of the Riviere au Chaudiere or Kettle Creek, *running around the north side of Lake Erie, and up the straight to the mouth of Chenal Ecarte, and up the said Chenal Ecarte, to the first south fork, then a due East Line until it intersects the River la Tranche,* and up the River La Tranche to the Boundary of the purchase from the six Nations, and following the direction of which a due South Course to the mouth of the said Kettle Creek."
>
> By his letter of 21st May the Conclusion of that Business is announced to the Board. We have directed an early Report of the Survey of the Front of the Tract purchased....
>
> *The course from Channel Ecarte to the River la Tranche is mentioned in the foregoing part of this Letter. This Survey should be connected from the mouth of the la Tranche along the Shore of Lake St. Clair to Channel Ecarte, up that River as described, and then till it strikes the la Tranche again by the course mentioned. I wish, however, if possible, the Deed should be had recourse to,* for the boundaries of the purchase from the Indians which will prevent any mistakes.[10]

By August 1794, however, the 1790 northern boundary had still not been run. Smith informed surveyor Patrick McNiff that he wanted the treaty Line from the Chenail Ecarte to the Thames run as soon as possible because "the Boundary Lines of the several Townships [were to be] projected on the District plan" before they were surveyed. Smith was particularly concerned about problems that would arise in Sandwich Township where the lines were "very irregular."[11] McNiff, however, did not run this line as instructed, writing in response that it would be impossible to do so unless in the dead of winter because of marshy, swampy terrain. Shortly thereafter, McNiff was terminated and absconded to the States.[12]

The notation on a sketch from the Crown Land Department to surveyor Abraham Iredell, dated 1795, stated, "It is supposed that the boundary of the purchase line will run here abouts."[13] Nevertheless, Iredell did not run such a line in 1795. He was, however, present the following year on 7 September 1796 at the negotiation and signing of Treaty 7, between the Chippewa and local representatives of the king, involving a small area north of the unsurveyed northern treaty line at its most western end. This area was also known as the Chenail Ecarte Tract. Also present at this Treaty was Alexander McKee, identified in the document as the deputy superintendent general of Indian Affairs.[14] In 1790, McKee had been the Indian agent present at Treaty 2. The southern boundary of Treaty 7 was the northern boundary of Treaty 2. The southwest angle of Treaty 7 was the northwest angle of Treaty 2. Consequently, the location of this spot was of some immediate importance. The treaty document described the area as follows:

> all that parcel or tract of land lying on and near to the said River Chenail Ecarte, which river is known in the Indian names as follows (that is to say) from the River St Clair to the first fork on the south side Pakeitchewanse and from the said fork on the north side Wapissejunkissycawpowa, *beginning at the said first fork where the Ottawa Village now stands and where the east line of the lands purchased of us and other Indian Nations by the Crown in the year [1790] commences* and following the several windings of the said river up the stream to the River St Clair; thence up the said River St Clair following the several windings thereof to a hickory tree marked with a broad arrow, fifty links above a small run being twelve miles and a half on a direct north course from the said fork; thence east nine hundred and twenty three Gunter's chains; thence south until it intersects the east line of the said land purchased as aforesaid, in the year [1790]; thence west following the said east line to the said fork, being the place of beginning.[15]

This was the first time the location of the northwest angle of Treaty 2 had been identified. The treaty text and map may have been produced on the spot by McKee and Iredell respectively. This was the first map to show the northwest angle of the 1790 Treaty on the Chenail Ecarte in line with the Ottawa Village as noted in Treaty 7.[16] The treaty text and map are remarkable for their improvement in geographical understanding of the location of St Anne's and Walpole islands, as well as the course of the Chenail Ecarte and its forks, including the Chippewa names for the forks on the river. Furthermore, the map was signed by the Chippewa signatories to the treaty. Iredell's map was only theoretical, he did not actually run the 1790 treaty line at that time. A "rough sketch" of the area around Lake St Clair (bearing McNiff's name, and therefore likely compiled from his prior work)[17] does not show the 1790 "Indian Purchase" line having been run.

Seven years later, in 1803, Joint Commissioners of Crown Lands William Chewett and Thomas Rideout, instructed surveyor Abraham Iredell to "proceed to the Boundary Line Between the Townships of Camden & Chatham and continue the same on a course north 45 [degrees] west until you intersect the northern boundary or [1790 Indian] purchase Line which you are supposed to have already run."[18] Iredell, it seemed, had only run a small portion of that line, namely 208 chains east from the Ottawa village.[19] Next, he was to lay out the line between Chatham and Dover townships, however, it was clear from his instructions that the Crown Land Department was not familiar with the waters and islands around Walpole Island and adjacent to those townships.

In December 1803, Iredell was told to survey the remaining parts of Dover and Chatham, proceeding to the division between Chatham and Dover, and to continue on the same northwest course until he intersected the northern boundary or Chenail Ecarte. Iredell was directed to be cautious and take "care not to cross any waters, so as to carry your Survey into any Island or Islands, as we have reason to [conjecture?] that the Chenal Ecarte forms more than one Island, although their position and extent are unknown to us."[20] Following Iredell's survey of the 1790 line, it was discovered that Simcoe's assurances to the Moravian missionaries had been in vain and that the Moravian Reserve was located on land not included in the treaty. The village was rebuilt on the south side of the Thames in 1815.

Iredell's survey lines, particularly those pertaining to Sombra Township, stood until 1819, when Surveyor General Thomas Rideout instructed Thomas Smith to re-run them. This instruction must have indicated that Iredell's lines, including Sombra's southern township line or the "Indian Purchase" line of 1790, were deficient in some way. Smith's re-survey was difficult, plagued with unhealthy and incompetent assistants whose work he had to redo. To "reimburse himself" for his trouble, Smith suggested that in addition to his regular pay, His Excellency allow him to choose an unstated quantity of land from the best lands in Sombra Township. Identified among the various lots from which he would choose, amounting to some 4,445 acres, was the "Head of St Anne's Island," part of the protected and unceded Walpole Island Reserve.[21]

All of Iredell's Sombra boundaries were to be re-run. Thomas Rideout instructed Thomas Smith to "resurvey the Northern and Eastern shore of the Chenal Ecarte and River St Clair from the first Forks at the Ottawa Village to a Hickory Tree marked with a broad arrow on two sides, half a chain above the mouth of a small stream on the East bank of said river about 12½ miles distant, in a North direction, and then to reopen, reblaze and to correct the Northern Boundary Line of Said Township."[22] Thus, Smith was to start at the southwest angle of the township, or at the point where the "Indian Purchase" line of 1790 intersected the Chenail Ecarte and re-examine the shoreline up to the northern boundary. Following the correction of the northern boundary line, Smith was instructed to: "proceed in the same manner with the Eastern Boundary Line ... and the Southern Boundary Line ... [back] to the 1st station at the Fork at the Ottawa Village, noting the difference on the said courses by your Needle and that of Mr Iredells."[23] Whether the re-running of all the township lines, but especially the southern line, affected the easternmost projection of the 1790 northern treaty line (that is, the location where it intersected the Thames River), remains unknown.

Smith was further directed to run concession lines, lots, and roads to "form a double Front for Settlement," noting all swamps, rivers, creeks, springs, mill seats, lakes and minerals, as well as improvements. Smith did not comment on the mineral potential of the area, but did note a number of improvements, some of which were Aboriginal.[24] These are discussed below.

When Roswell Mount surveyed Moore Township in 1829, he asserted that the line between Moore and Sombra was incorrectly situated. Mount recorded a short history of this line, noting that it had been surveyed in 1820 by Mr. Hanchett, who was Thomas Smith's deputy surveyor. According to Mount, "It is a very careless and badly run line. In order to find the true course of it I produced a line from the rear of these townships to this place"[25] This line was north of the 1790 northern treaty line, running parallel to it. Similar to Smith, Mount noted a number of improvements, some of which were Aboriginal. These are also discussed below.

Thus, the divergent textual and cartographical information regarding the northern boundary of Treaty 2 in 1790 was not cleared up until 1796 when Treaty 7 was written down. The map produced for Treaty 7 indicated an improved understanding of the islands in the delta and the location of the Chenail Ecarte and its forks. Although Treaty 7 identified the Ottawa Village as the northwest angle of Treaty 2, this did not lead to the running of the northern boundary of Treaty 2. Seven years later, in 1803, the lines for Sombra Township were run, the southern boundary of which was the same as part of the northern boundary of Treaty 2. These lines, including the southern boundary of Sombra (therefore, part of the northern boundary of Treaty 2) continued to be adjusted. At the same time that surveyors' field-note books and plans allow us to trace the history of government lines on the land, however, they also allow us to trace the history of Aboriginal control of the land.

Aboriginal Presence on the Ground

Since at least 1791, surveyors in the Western District were aware of an old Indian village on the south side of the Thames River in present-day Tilbury Township. According to McNiff, this village was south and west of a tract originally deeded to Aboriginal trader Sally Ainse in 1780 by two Chippewa chiefs.[26]

Other old Aboriginal settlements existed near the southern shores of Lake St Clair and on its interior rivers. In 1799, surveyors noted the presence of a "small settlement of French and Indians" about six miles down the Ruscum River in present-day Rochester Township.[27] Shown on an undated, unsigned "Schedule of the lots on this [Sandwich Tp] side of the River [Detroit River]" were the locations of several Ottawa and Huron settlements. On the Sandwich mainland, in the vicinity of Peach and Hogg Islands, a large Ottawa village and Ottawa burying place had existed. Further south a Huron village and fields had existed.[28] Still further south, Abraham Iredell's 1796 map of the Huron Reserve, in the area which came to be called the 'Petite Cote,' on the north side of the River Canard there had been another Huron settlement. Of this place Iredell asserted in a marginal notation that French settlers had been driven out by the Huron.[29] There was also an Aboriginal sugar camp at the southeast corner of lot 1, concession 6, behind the front lots.[30]

At the 11th concession on the base line between Dover and Chatham, Smith recorded the presence of "Indian Cabbins [*sic*] & Sugar Camps."[31] At lot 7 along Baldoon Street, he noted an old sugar camp near a small creek. Smith noted the location of a sugar camp in the 4th concession along Little Bear Line. On Cul de Sac Line along the 8th concession near a small creek, he observed evidence of an old sugar camp.[32] Smith's field notes show the location of another "old Indian sugar camp" between two creeks at the 11th concession. At the 12th concession, he recorded an "Indian Cabbin [*sic*] & Sugar Camp," at the 13th, he emphasized two additional "Indian Cabbin[s] and Sugar Camp[s]," and at the 14th line, he saw "an Indian Path along the north border of [Little Bear] Creek" and close by an "old Indian Sugar Camp."[33]

In dealing with the concession lines running southwest from Little Bear Line, Smith saw "old Indian corn fields" at the 14th line in lot 13. At the 12th concession in lot 15, he noted an "old Indian Sugar Camp."[34] Two additional "old Indian Sugar Camp[s]" existed along the 11th concession in lot 16 and along the 4th concession line in lot 13.[35]

While laying out lots in Dover West, a triangular area at the southern end of Dover Township, Smith did not mention an Aboriginal presence. However, an earlier map showing land and rivers along the southeast and south shores of Lake St. Clair clearly indicated an important Chippewa presence in that area. A notation on the map, in what became Dover West, states, "In the side of this Knole there are great Quantities of human bones: a battle is said to have been fought near it between the Chippewas and Seneka contending for the Dominion of this Country, when the latter was put to flight with great slaughter and drove across the River at Niagara."[36]

Smith's 1819 field notes identify several Aboriginal clearings and villages along the shoreline, banks, and the interior of Sombra Township. Smith noted an "Indian clearing" and an "Indian field" near the northwest angle of Sombra Township. Both were adjacent to the "Meanders of [the] Chenal Ecarte."[37] Additionally, Iredell noted a Chippewa village on the American side near Clay Creek.[38]

According to Smith, Charles Fisher, a member of the Walpole Island Band, had an unidentified "improvement" along the bank of the Chenail Ecarte, as did his wife. Smith noted "the old Ottawa village" at the forks of the Chenail Ecarte on the mainland across from the head of St Anne Island.[39] In Concession 3 at lot 12 he recorded the presence of an "Indian Field," and drew attention to another "old village" behind a marsh in lot E of the 5th Concession. There was an "Indian field" and/or an "old Indian Corn field" in lot E, Concession 9.[40] Lastly, at the northern boundary of Dover and Chatham, Smith mentioned an "old Indian fort on the left on the border of a swail or thoroughfare."[41]

Roswell Mount's 1829 field notes noted a number of improvements, but did not always state whether they were Aboriginal. He described the presence of old American Fort St. Clair on the American side, and further north, the remnant of a number of signs of Aboriginal occupation on Stag Island in the River St. Clair adjacent to Moore Township: "An Indian camp upon the Island near the Margin of a Marsh at the edge of the River.... Another Indian Camp which stands about the same distance from the water's edge. A third Indian camp which stands about 1 c [one chain?] from the water's edge."[42]

Surveyors' field-note books and plans for a number of townships in the Western District[43] are not only sources of points for the location of external treaty boundaries, but also sources that can be used to pinpoint the location of old and abandoned Chippewa cornfields, clearings, campgrounds, sugar bushes, and other occupations. The same books and maps that the Crown relied on to detail and depict its physical manifestation of empire on the ground, preliminary to its disposal of that same ground for agricultural and other uses, also provided evidence of previous Indigenous dominion on the ground and a similar agenda of agricultural and other uses.

In Conclusion

Treaty 2 and the following surveys represented the Crown's desire to establish dominion over land that was owned, occupied, and fully utilized by an Indigenous population, which considered themselves to be independent masters of their own domain. From the Crown's perspective, Treaty 2 allowed it to extend its empire and claim ownership of someone else's land. In contrast, the Chippewa, Ottawa, Pottawatomi, and Huron nations believed they were sharing the land with the Crown and those whom the Crown would place on the land.

The subsequent surveys might be viewed as representative of Crown dominion on the land, carving it up into smaller more manageable pieces for agricultural, settlement, and security purposes. However, the surveying books and maps that were produced and subsequently relied upon by the Crown also provide evidence of Indigenous dominion and mastery over the land, and its resources and waters. The Crown only saw that the treaty and the surveys created a legal context for its plan to turn land and resources into part of its empire. The road to empire, however, was messy and slow.

Although taken in 1790, the northern boundary of Treaty 2 was not surveyed for 13 years. Significantly, the contradictory information presented in its written and cartographical components was once and for all clarified in 1796 when Treaty 7 was written down, likely by McKee on the spot. Similarly, Iredell's map, also likely produced on the spot, advanced a vastly improved depiction of the situation of islands in the delta and the location of the Chenail Ecarte and its forks. This treaty was the first instrument to provide a reference point (the Ottawa Village) for the origin of the north west angle of the 1790 Treaty. Even so, the conclusion of the 1796 Treaty did not lead to the actual production of the 1790 line. This took another seven years: Abraham Iredell was instructed to run the Sombra Township lines in 1803, the southern boundary of which was part of the 1790 Treaty line. Subsequently, these lines, including the southern boundary, were revisited and re-run by Thomas Smith. To date, it has not been determined whether Smith's refiguring affected some part or parts of the east–west southern Sombra line or, more significantly, whether it changed the course of the line from its northwest angle, which would have meant that it intersected the Thames River at a different location. This remains an area for further research.

Of equal significance are the township survey field notes in this period for pinpointing at least a portion of Aboriginal activity on the ground. Ironically, the surveyors were at once identifying and preserving, but also precipitating the demise of these old and/or abandoned sites, as they ran their lot and concession lines in the townships, which settlers would soon fill and alter forever. The preserved information showing Aboriginal command over their territory is of much practical use to the historian, anthropologist, and archaeologist interested in gathering information pertaining to seasonal rounds, harvesting and residential activity, use of waterways, and site location.

Aboriginal people in the area used their waterways, shores, islands, and mainland for many activities integral to their survival. The rich and varied resources harvested by the Chippewa, Ottawa, and Pottawatomi from their many fields, sugar camps, orchards, fisheries and hunting grounds were the foundation for a wide and extensive trade between themselves, French and English military establishments, traders, and settlers. Clearly what was about to unfold in the treaty areas, with their straight line boundaries, lots, and concessions, was at variance and in opposition to long-standing Aboriginal mastery of their territory.

Notes

1 Nin.Da.Waab.Jig, Walpole Island First Nation, *Walpole Island: The Soul of Indian Territory*, (Walpole Island, ON: Nin.Da.Waab.Jig, 1987), map facing page 28.
2 Spelling varies in the original documents. My quotations reflect this, but in the text I use "Chenail."
3 Nin.Da.Waab.Jig, *Walpole Island*, map facing page 28.
4 Canada, *Indian Treaties and Surrenders*, Vol. 1, (Saskatoon: Fifth House, 1992), Surrender #2, 1–5, and map opposite page 26.
5 See, for example, Nin.Da.Waab.Jig, *Walpole Island*, map facing page 17–24.
6 Linda Sabathy-Judd, *Moravians in Upper Canada: The Diary of the Indian Mission of Fairfield on the Thames, 1792–1813*, transl. and ed. Linda Sabathy-Judd (Toronto: Champlain Society, 1999), xxvii.
7 D.W. Smith, Acting Surveyor General, to Lieut. Col. England, President, the Gentlemen composing the Land Board of Kent and Essex, 1 September 1793, in *Instructions to Land Surveyors, Ontario, Crown Surveys*, 16 October 1792–7 May 1796, Vol. 2., pp. 62–64, Survey Branch, Ministry of Natural Resources (MNR). Emphasis added.
8 Sabathy-Judd, *Moravians in Upper Canada*, xxviii.
9 John Clarke, *Land, Power, and Economics on the Frontier of Upper Canada* (Montreal: McGill-Queen's University Press, 2001), 121–26.
10 D.W. Smith, Acting Sur. Genl. to Colonel England ..., in *Instructions to Land Surveyors, Ontario, Crown Surveys*, 16 October 1792–7 May 1796, Vol. 2, MNR Surveys Branch, 68–70.
11 David Smith to Patrick McNiff, 3 August 1794, in *Instructions to Land Surveyors, Ontario, Crown Surveys*, 16 October 1792–7 May 1796, Vol. 2, pp. 121–22, Survey Branch, Ministry of Natural Resources (MNR).
12 Patrick McNiff to Lt. Col. England, 26 September 1793, Archives of Ontario, RG 1, A-I-1, Vol. 3, p. 68.
13 Land Department, "A sketch of Part of the Western District for A.T. Iredell, London office, Newark, 2 August 1795. D.W. Smith, Act. Surv. Gen., No. 15." AO, B-39.

14 Canada, *Indian Treaties and Surrenders*, Vol. 1, Surrender #7, 19–22.
15 Canada, *Indian Treaties and Surrenders*, Vol. 1, Surrender #7, 20; or for representative area of treaty, see Nin.Da.Waab.Jig, *Walpole Island*, map facing page 28. Emphasis added.
16 Canada, *Indian Treaties and Surrenders*, Vol. 1, see sketch accompanying Surrender #7, third foldout map (on inside of fold), opposite page 26.
17 Patrick McNiff, Lake St. Clair and Vicinity (photostat), 1797, AO, B-67.
18 Chewett and Rideout, Joint Commissioners of Crown Lands, to Thomas Abraham Iredell, 15 December 1803, in *Instructions to Land Surveyors, Ontario, Crown Surveys*, 1 June 1796 to 6 December 1819, Vol. 3, p. 149, Surveys Branch, MNR.
19 Iredell's line stopped on the south side of the present-day Sydenham River; it had not been run through the Baldoon settlement or across the Chenail Ecarte and over the head of St. Anne Island. See Iredell, 6 March 1805, MNR Surveys Branch, 904 D10; Iredell to Chewett & Rideout, 12 June 1804, AO, RG 1, A-1-6, MS 30/5, Vol. 27, No. 220. Iredell also ran other external township lines for Sombra. These were erroneous, and in 1819 Thomas Smith was commissioned to re-run all of Iredell's Sombra lines. The Ottawa Village referred to was noted on an earlier plan by Iredell, where its size was described as "large"; the village was shown on the head of St. Anne Island and extended onto the mainland across the forks of the River St. Clair and the Chenail Ecarte. See A. Iredell, "Sombra, formerly Shawanese W.D. [Western District]," 9 July 1800, AO, RG 1-470-0-0-324 Shawanee (Sombra Tp), [N-2290].
20 Chewett and Rideout to Iredell, 15 December 1803, 149–50. Iredell's "Diary for the Western District, commencing 1 January and ending the 30 of June 1798," highlights some of his problems in the field. While running lines for Chatham Township, some of Iredell's party sold their clothes to procure liquor, the consumption of which led to a brawl and the demise of Iredell's glass surveying instrument. Later, while working in Sandwich, Iredell's boat was stolen. See MNR, Surveys Branch, *Fieldnotes Transcribed from Original Books*, Vol. 3, pp. 92–94.
21 Thomas Smith, Survey, 1820 and letters of instruction and fieldnotes, in *Field Notes Transcribed from Original Books*, Vol. 10, 585–94, MNR, Surveys Branch.
22 Thomas Smith, Survey, 1820, *Field Notes Transcribed from Original Books*, Vol. 10, p. 585.
23 Thomas Smith, Survey, 1820, *Field Notes Transcribed from Original Books*, Vol. 10, p. 586.
24 Thomas Smith, Survey, 1820, *Field Notes Transcribed from Original Books*, Vol. 10, p. 586.
25 Roswell Mount, Survey of Moore Township, Field Note Book 537, pp. 22–22A, MNR, Surveys Branch.

26 Patrick McNiff, "Plan of River La Trenche from the Entrance up to the end of the first Township or to entrance of the Branch unknown Clark's Mills are build from actual Surveys made April 1791," 5 December 1793, Tilbury West 91245 Y51-15, MNR, Surveys Branch; Patrick McNiff, "Survey of the River Thames formerly River La Tranch from its Entrance or confluence with Lake St. Clair to the upper Delaware Village from the Entrance to the 12th lot of the 3rd Township was Surveyed Two years since from the 12 lot of the 3rd Township to the upper village. Surveyed in April and May 1793," 25 June 1793, Tilbury West 7089 0 18-7, MNR, Surveys Branch.

27 "St. Clair Lake from Belle River to River La Tranche. (Partial)," Rochester 2492 K19, MNR, Surveys Branch; and Rochester 1989 C8 [no title], [1799 as noted on the twin Maidstone map to this one (both are identified as A24), signed by Iredell, 24 January 1799], MNR, Surveys Branch.

28 Untitled document showing "A schedule of all the lots on this [U.S.] side of the River [Detroit River]" and "Schedule of the lots on this [Sandwich Tp] side of the River [Detroit River]," n.d., AO, F47-5-1-0-44.2.

29 Abraham Iredell, "Plan of a Tract of Land called the Huron Reserve, situate on the River Detroit, Western District and Province of Upper Canada, containing Twenty-three thousand six hundred and forty acres," Sandwich 2425 K18, 20 February 1796, MNR, Surveys Branch. Notation reads: "French settlers drove off by the Huron Indians."

30 Thomas Smith, Sandwich 2034 D14, 1807, MNR, Surveys Branch.

31 Thomas Smith, "Field Notes of East & West Dover in the Western District Surveyed by Mr. Thomas Smith Deputy Surveyor," 1809, *Field Notes Transcribed from Original Books*, Vol. 13, p. 354, MNR, Surveys Branch.

32 Smith, "Field Notes of East & West Dover," *Field Notes Transcribed from Original Books*, Vol. 13, 358, 359, 361.

33 Smith, "Field Notes of East & West Dover," *Field Notes Transcribed from Original Books*, Vol. 13, 365–66.

34 Smith, "Field Notes of East & West Dover," *Field Notes Transcribed from Original Books*, Vol. 13, 369–70.

35 Smith, "Field Notes of East & West Dover," *Field Notes Transcribed from Original Books*, Vol. 13, 371, 377.

36 "St. Clair Lake from Belle River to River La Tranche. (Partial)," Rochester 2492 K19.

37 Smith, Survey, 1820, *Field Notes Transcribed from Original Books*, Vol. 10, pp. 596, 614–15; Thomas Smith, "The Shawnese Township Western District, Surveyed by Order—March 1820. Thos. Smith, D.S," B-17.

38 Iredell, "Sombra, formerly Shawanese W.D.," [N-2290], 9 July 1800.

39 Smith, Survey, 1820, *Field Notes Transcribed from Original Books*, Vol. 10, pp. 597, 598, 601, 603. Note also, as we have seen above, this village was identified by Iredell in 1800: AO, RG1-470-0-0-324 Shawanee (Sombra Tp) [N-2290]; "Sombra, formerly Shawanese W.D." [Western District], A. Iredell, 9 July 1800.

40 Smith, Survey, 1820, *Field Notes Transcribed from Original Books*, Vol. 10, p. 607.

41 Smith, Survey, 1820, *Field Notes Transcribed from Original Books*, Vol. 10, p. 616.

42 Russell Mount, 1829 Field notes, Field Note Book 537, p. 117A, MNR, Surveys Branch. These three camps are mentioned on several other occasions from different perspectives, see pages 113A, 119, 123A, and 124.

43 For a representation of the location of the various townships in the Western District, please consult the frontispiece map in Fred Coyne Hamil, *The Valley of the Lower Thames, 1640–1850* (Toronto: University of Toronto Press, 1951).

CHAPTER 8

Poisoning the Serpent: The Effects of the Uranium Industry on the Serpent River First Nation, 1953–1988

Lianne C. Leddy

A boy went on a fast on the North Shore of Lake Huron on his thirteenth birthday. He wanted to return home, but his mother forced him to stay and continue his vision quest. When she returned for him, he had vanished, but nearby hunters described an extraordinary sight: a giant horned serpent had risen above the waters and the boy was seen clinging to the creature's back. After that, others began to disappear and quiet nights were disrupted by terrible noises.[1] The Serpent was angry. The Anishinaabek believe that the Serpent, a being with cat-like features, lurks beneath the water and has a den where the mouth of the Serpent River meets Lake Huron. The creature-spirit is said to be responsible for minerals and water resources, and to steal from it will result in death and destruction.[2] This warning found in Anishinaabe oral tradition has, in recent decades, become pertinent to discussions about environmental justice, resource exploitation on and near Aboriginal communities in Canada, and the role of First Nations in those processes.

The Serpent's den and waters have been disturbed and polluted, as minerals have been exploited in the interests of financial gain. This chapter examines the historical role of empire—partially defined in this collection of essays as the Canadian state and its economic interests—in shaping a colonial legacy of environmental damage. Indigenous–settler relations in this area have been shaped by uranium mining, the establishment of a sulphuric acid plant, and First Nations politicization. In 1953, the "Back Door Staking Bee" led to several uranium claims in a Z-formation near what is now Elliot Lake, approximately thirty-five kilometres northwest of the Serpent River First Nation. In the 1950s, the Serpent River, a source of water for the community as well as for the animals and fish on which they relied, was polluted by the waste resulting from uranium extraction at Elliot Lake. This problem was compounded by the Department of Indian Affairs' (DIA)[3] encouragement of the establishment of an acid plant in the community in the name of economic development; this proved disastrous for the community's land and water resources. DIA mishandled the very project they sought to establish on the reserve and did not protect the interests they were mandated to oversee. The federal government was partially responsible for this environmental degradation, as it was directly involved in contracts with the United States for uranium export and encouraged development at Elliot Lake.[4] Furthermore, the Government of Canada, through DIA, facilitated the establishment of the acid plant on the Serpent River First Nation and failed to provide the proper opportunities to mitigate environmental damage in a timely fashion, leading to disastrous consequences for the community.

While the unique power of DIA is evident, at the same time, the chief, council, and residents of the First Nation were not passive in this paternalistic relationship; they were often vocal in their complaints about the ways in which their resources were affected by uranium extraction and processing. Aboriginal resistance has become the subject of historical study, particularly as more historians have explored the relationship between Aboriginal peoples and DIA.[5] Environmental issues on reserves in Canada have also been central to the framing of this study, the best example being the mercury pollution of the river system near Grassy Narrows in Northern Ontario.[6] At the Serpent River First Nation, responses to governmental inaction and its impact on their natural resources changed over time. In the 1960s, Chief William Meawasige publicized his concerns locally in the media and passed band council resolutions to attempt to address water problems in the community.[7] By the 1980s especially, band members and their elected representatives sought to find more radical solutions to the environmental problems they faced as a result of industrial and governmental intervention in their affairs.

The Serpent River Indian Reserve (now First Nation) was established after Chief Windawtegawinini signed the Robinson-Huron Treaty on 9 September 1850. The land was ceded to the Crown with the promise that hunting and fishing rights would be protected, along with the best interests of the Aboriginal people in the area, whose remaining territory would be divided into seventeen reserves scattered throughout what are now parts of central and northern Ontario. Genaabaajing is situated on a peninsula between the north shore of Lake Huron and the Serpent River, which flows south from the Elliot Lake area.[8]

As with other Aboriginal communities in the area, the Serpent River First Nation has a strong history of fur trading and forestry in the eighteenth and nineteenth centuries. However, by the 1950s, a new natural resource was sought for weapons and later, energy: uranium. The Serpent River First Nation and Elliot Lake are connected by the Serpent River water system, which led to the pollution of the Serpent River by waste resulting from uranium mining at Elliot Lake. This environmental concern was compounded by a lease negotiated between the Indian Affairs branch of the Department of Citizenship and Immigration and Noranda Mines for the establishment of a sulphuric acid plant on the Serpent River First Nation to service Elliot Lake's uranium industry.[9]

Elliot Lake was established in the 1950s solely for the extraction of the unprecedented deposits of uranium staked in 1953.[10] Once the staked claims were processed, twelve mines began operating in the Elliot Lake area, and in 1957 the federal government entered into a $1.6 billion contract with the Atomic Energy Commission in the United States.[11] By this time, a permanent townsite had been established to accommodate the influx of miners and later their families.[12] By the end of the decade, more than 10,500 people were employed in mining the 320 million tons of uranium ore estimated to be deposited in the region.[13] Between 1955 and 1961, uranium extraction was extremely profitable; however, this came at a cost for the Serpent River First Nation.

The Serpent River is connected through a series of rivers and lakes to Quirke Lake, which was used as a dump site for waste from nearby mines in the early days of uranium extraction at Elliot Lake.[14] Reports suggest that the water from the wells located near the river was contaminated, and indeed there have been several water problems in the community dating back to the 1950s. The river system has long been known to have been contaminated by chemical waste and other harmful mining by-products, especially in the earlier days of mining in the 1950s, when "there was far less public concern and indeed, less available technology on such matters."[15] In 1983, the Ministry of Natural Resources had to reintroduce pickerel and trout into the Serpent River system because of earlier damage. Once the environmental impacts of uranium extraction and processing became a greater public concern, policies and technologies were put in place to control seepage, and the ministry was hopeful that water quality conditions would improve to a sufficient level to support a healthy fish population once again.[16]

However, residents of the Serpent River First Nation claim that the environmental concern came far too late: "All our fish are gone. Our rivers are never ever going to come back to what they was. Never. I mean, I used to be able to go fishing down the Serpent River down by the highway over there and catch all kinds of fish. Every time you'd put the line in the water. It's nothing now."[17] A man identified as Junior told this story in a meeting of elders on the Serpent River First Nation. He was not the only one to mention the dangers in the river. John Souliere talked about the change in the water over the years due to its contamination from mining: "I think we did experience a lot of contamination of our water, because most of our water from the Serpent River comes from the Elliot Lake area. Whichever way it was contaminated, we drank most of that water because actually, before the mines came, you could look right down in that water, the sand looked like jewels down there. But now, a couple years later, that sand grain is scum."[18] The environmental change brought about by the uranium industry occurred only over a relatively short time. However, the results have affected the community members of the Serpent River First Nation in many ways, particularly in having to find other sources of water. Terry Jacobs made it clear that the residents are well aware of the hazards of the river: "we don't drink the water from the Serpent River anymore, of course."[19]

Although clean water is a necessity for any community, it has not been the only thing lost to the Serpent River reserve. As in any ecosystem, elements of an environment depend on each other. For instance, the wildlife that depended on the river system has also suffered, which has become particularly dangerous for those who hunt and fish in the area. Junior recalled that the quality of moose was questioned by the Ministry of Natural Resources, and that there was "something about the kidneys and the livers they wanted for a while there because they were contaminated ... what about the rest of it, the whole body?"[20] Indeed, if the livers and kidneys, the cleansing organs of a mammal are contaminated, it is fairly clear that the rest of the animal most likely is not safe for human consumption. For a community with historical and economic ties to hunting and fishing, this is certainly detrimental to the traditional way of life for its residents.

Terry Jacobs mentioned the contamination of beaver, which is enjoyed by many elders:

> My wife used to make—she still does, actually—we used to eat a lot of beaver. [She was] born and raised around here. Now what, five or six years ago, she got colon cancer. Now where did she get that? I tell you what she does. She did like to eat the beaver tail, because it's very rich, very tasty, and then all of a sudden she ended up with this colon cancer. Now, I never did associate that thing

> with beaver. I kind of let that go until recently, you know, I almost lost my wife because of it ... the vegetation, too. The beaver eats the vegetation, drinks the water.[21]

The ingestion of beaver was no longer safe because of the contamination of its habitat, the Serpent River watershed. The levels of contaminants in moose became more troublesome, and beaver were also affected by the pollution in the Serpent River system. Not only was the river water itself a concern for band members, but so too was the quality of the food on which they depended. Water and wildlife contamination was such a concern that in 1976 federal officials agreed to test trappers, as well as nearby wells and river water, for unsafe levels of radioactivity.[22]

Community members voiced their concerns repeatedly and went so far as to initiate, along with neighbouring Mississauga and Sagamok First Nations, a study to evaluate their changing environments in the context of nearby resource exploitation. A progress report was submitted by the Institute of Environmental Research, the organization overseeing this study, to the Serpent River First Nation in April 1984. It outlined community members' concerns that fishing and hunting had worsened in the preceding five years, and suggested that "local resource developments ha[d] affected environmental conditions on the reserve."[23] The uranium industry was responsible for the detrimental environmental effects it had on the Serpent River First Nation's natural resources, but the federal government's interest in uranium extraction trumped its responsibility for the well-being of Aboriginal peoples.

The residents of the community were not the only ones to notice the contamination. Indeed, it made front-page news in the *Globe and Mail* on several occasions throughout the 1960s, especially as public knowledge about the negative effects of the uranium industry grew. In 1964, a front-page article entitled, "Facts Secret Two Years: Elliot Lake Contaminated by Radioactive Waste" broke the news about the negative effects of uranium waste on the environment, and charged that the Ontario government had known about it since 1962. Ontario Premier John Robarts claimed he had no concern about the drinking water for the residents of Elliot Lake and surrounding communities, but he nevertheless ordered an investigation. The Ontario Water Resources Commission found that ten picocuries per litre was an acceptable concentration of radioactivity, but that "nearby Quirke Lake water [had] been measured at 40 to 100 picocuries and plankton in the lake at thousands of picocuries."[24] Curies are units that measure radiation levels, and a picocurie is "a millionth of a millionth of a curie."[25] According to Health Canada, the

United States currently measures radon in picocuries per litre (pCi/L), and this was the unit of measurement used in determining radiation levels in the Serpent River watershed in a 1976 study entitled, "Status Report: Water Pollution in the Serpent River Basin."[26] Since Quirke Lake is connected to the Serpent River system, the higher measurements of picocuries described in the article did not bode well for the organisms dependent on it, including the residents of the Serpent River First Nation, who ate the fish and wildlife in the area; some also drew water from the river.

Although the report looked like a promising step toward responsible environmental policy, the release of its conclusions was delayed by the tourism industry, whose representatives requested that findings of radioactive waste not ruin the upcoming summer season in 1965. It was further delayed by the 1965 federal election; according to a statement made by the premier's aide, it was not "gentlemanly" to release the report during an election, as it could blame the federal government for not having more stringent environmental concerns.[27] Since the incumbent prime minister, Lester B. Pearson, was also the member of Parliament for the Algoma riding (in which both Elliot Lake and the Serpent River are located), another dimension was added to the political effects of the report. The incident highlights an essential point about jurisdiction: while the federal government had a vested interest in the uranium industry because of international trade and defence in the context of the Cold War, natural resources are a provincial matter. Aboriginal affairs are under the jurisdiction of the federal government, and this split between responsibilities made it more difficult to ascertain exactly which level of government was responsible for the quality of water for the residents of the Serpent River First Nation.

This tension between governments had particular relevance in 1976, when a meeting was held by community and National Indian Brotherhood leaders, as well as provincial and federal officials.[28] Water test results from the Serpent River where it runs through the reserve revealed a level of 6.2 picocuries per litre of water.[29] While this level fell below the standard set by the federal government, it was more than double the province's accepted concentration at the time. Lloyd Tataryn, who was the research director for the National Indian Brotherhood, was furious with the double standard:[30] the water was not safe for provincial residents, but it was deemed acceptable for First Nations residents in the same area because it was administered under a different governmental structure.

The inaction of Indian Affairs and the federal government was also to blame for the complete lack of access to water for some homes located near the Noranda acid plant. Chief William Meawasige was impatient for results from DIA, and in a 1969 interview with a reporter from the *Standard* he stated, "They have not even given the band permission to go ahead with plans of its own to bring water to the dwellings. If they don't want to do it why don't they tell me?"[31] Chief and council had approved a $3,000 budget from band funds to alleviate the problem, but were not given DIA approval to carry out their plans.[32] While Chief Meawasige waited for approval, residents in that area of the reserve were forced to gather water from a creek and a spring. However, the creek water was discoloured, and Meawasige believed it could have been contaminated by the sulphur from the acid plant nearby. With the long-term problem a severe threat to the well-being of the residents who were without water, the chief's frustrations were apparent: "All I want to know is whether or not the department will put in the water and if they won't whether we can do something ourselves."[33] The strained relationship between DIA and the local band government structure was apparent in the chief's plea for answers. He was prepared to take action at the band level if the government was not prepared to help, but even that required DIA approval, resulting in long delays and unanswered questions while some reserve homes were left completely without access to clean, safe water. Through this interview, Meawasige was able to use the media to showcase the problem to residents in the area and embarrass DIA by demonstrating the department's unresponsiveness to both the band's concerns and the questions he asked as the band's elected leader.

While Meawasige continued to voice his concerns about the community's water supply, by 1970, the state of the river system itself was not improving. A *Globe and Mail* article appearing on 10 June of that year exposed the findings of a study of the watershed that had been conducted by Nels Conroy on behalf of the Ontario Water Resources Commission. The study found that "plant and fish life in the Serpent River basin near Elliot Lake has been affected by pollution from uranium mine tailings" and that "chemical waste from mine tailings have sharply reduced plankton communities and decimated the basin's walleye population," as well as those of other species.[34] A few months later, the *Globe and Mail* lamented that "the Serpent River basin up by Elliot Lake, and Quirke and Whiskey and Precors Lakes, are not yet recovered to safe drinking state from the uranium pollution discovered some four years back."[35] The concept of economic and industrial progress was questioned in the light of its environmental costs to humans and other organisms. However, this realization happened too late for the band members of the Serpent River First Nation.

Indeed, by 1970, yet another study had been released concerning the water problems in the community. The "Potable Water Study, Serpent River Reserve" was released in late 1970 by Health Canada. Chief Peter Johnston, who had succeeded Chief Meawasige, and the band council were working to ameliorate their water situation. At a band council meeting on 16 March 1971, the following resolution was passed:

> That the Dept. of Indian Affairs provide the necessary funds to institute the recommendations of the Dept. of National Health and Welfare in regard to provision of potable water for the members of our Band contained in the report, "Potable Water Study, Serpent River Reserve" dated December 1, 1970; and that a permanent Construction supervisor, in addition to one now under jurisdiction of the Sudbury office, be posted to the Sault Ste. Marie Agency office. The need for such a position is evident in the fact that a similar report about potable water exists concerning the Spanish River Indian Band [nearby Sagamok First Nation]. It has been pointed out that Bands in the Sault Ste. Marie agency are not at this time administering as many programs as Bands on Manitoulin Island and it is the opinion of this council that the appointment of a construction supervisor to the Sault Ste. Marie Agency office would be of great help to those Bands considering greater responsibility for their own affairs.[36]

This council resolution, passed by Chief Johnston and endorsed by councillors Doreen Pine and Lawrence Lewis, is just one way that Aboriginal community leaders attempted to improve the quality of water on-reserve. They recognized the difference in treatment from one Indian agency to the next, and voiced their concerns about the uneven development on the Serpent River First Nation compared to other reserves in neighbouring agencies that did have the funds to hire staff and implement quality of life improvement programs. While the hiring of a single construction supervisor would be insufficient to solve all of the problems in the community, this situation was a powerful example of the potential inequality between First Nations communities, and demonstrated the extent to which Serpent River First Nation was dependent on the will of DIA. The band council resolution was, in effect, a significant demand for action and a signal of the community's desire to have greater control over band matters.

For instance, once the resolution was passed, something had to be done at the level of the Indian Agency. Correspondence from Indian Affairs files exposes the many levels of approval that taking action on the resolution would require. A memorandum dated 22 March 1971 was sent from A.D. Cameron, the superintendent of the Sault Ste. Marie Indian Agency, to the regional director, William McKim, in Toronto. It expressed familiarity with the long-standing problem at Serpent River First Nation:

> Attached please find copies of *unsolicited* Band Council Resolution No. 13 for your information and guidance. It is assumed that this is a follow up of Chief Johnston's request at a meeting held last June at Garden River with the Union of Ontario Indians and our Minister. I understand that a position is recommended under the Regional Engineer's five year forecast, but until it is approved by Ottawa, no further action is expected by this office. May we be advised of any current or new developments on the above to enable us to reply to Chief and Council.[37]

The memo reveals a great deal about the agency superintendent and his dealings with the community. Cameron was not blind to the fact that the Union of Ontario Indians had become a political organization through which chiefs in the province could address DIA policies and paternalism. He acknowledged that there had been a problem with water and that Chief Johnston had been outspoken about it the preceding year. He was also aware of the hierarchy within which he had to operate. He would not take a stand on the resolution until the expenses required were approved by Ottawa, nor had he responded to chief and council without first contacting the regional director. He would not deal with the band as a partner in their band administration, but instead asked permission from the Toronto office to move ahead with improvement plans.

A separate letter was sent from the member of Parliament for the District of Algoma, Dr. Maurice Foster, to McKim asking for his consideration in the matter of hiring a construction supervisor, stating "it seems quite logical to me that, as the Band Council's resolution points out, they would be able to take on additional programmes if there was a construction supervisor attached to the Sault Ste. Marie Agency."[38] Not only were chief and council involved in lobbying DIA for the improvement of the water system on-reserve, but the local member of Parliament saw fit to support their claim.

What is interesting about Foster's involvement is the letter he received in response from McKim almost a month later:

> With reference to the report, "POTABLE WATER SUPPLY, SERPENT RIVER RESERVE", Mr. Cameron, Superintendent, Sault Ste. Marie Indian Agency, and Mr. Mulligan ... have begun to take action to implement the recommendations of this report. Sufficient funds have not been provided for the appointment of a Construction Supervisor for the Sault Ste. Marie Indian Agency for the present fiscal year, but such an appointment will certainly be considered for the fiscal year, 1972–73.[39]

Note that the action being taken by Cameron and Mulligan was not specified, and that no promises were being made about the likelihood of actually hiring a construction supervisor in 1972–73 (three years after the water study was released), although it was to be taken under consideration.

A letter addressed to Chief Peter Johnston, dated 14 April 1971 (a week prior to that written to Foster) from J.G. McGilp, the director of the Community Affairs Branch of DIA, stated that

> Mr. McKim, our Regional Director, has informed the Agency Superintendent, Mr. A. Cameron, that the Recommendations in the "Potable Water Study, Serpent River Reserve" report dated December 1, 1970, are being implemented. Of the $65,000 in the Sault Ste. Marie Agency budget for 1971–72, $20,000 has been allocated for new wells and repairs to old wells on your Reserve. Funds for the provision of a Construction Supervisor in the Sault Ste. Marie Agency have been included in the Estimates for the 1972–73 fiscal year. Mr. Cameron will be informing you of the Regional Director's decision on this Resolution, if he has not already done so.[40]

The action being taken by Indian Affairs on behalf of the community looks to be more substantial than the letter to Foster a week later suggests. The construction supervisor was to be hired in 1972 or 1973, years after the study came out with recommendations for improvement of the reserve's water supply, and decades after the first complaints of water problems reached the DIA bureaucracy. Certainly, the funding that was allocated for well improvements looked promising, but it was unfortunate that it took so long for the community's concerns to be addressed. In the early 1970s, the work of the band council to lobby for improvements to their community was not over yet.

By 1976, in the context of another uranium boom, two mining companies in Elliot Lake were looking to expand their industrial output. The proposed expansions of Rio Algom and Denison were the subjects of public debate and inquiry into the environmental ramifications of the plan, which was one of the first in the province.[41] The knowledge about radioactivity and chemical contaminates in the water was already relatively common, as residents of the First Nation had already been told by Environment Canada in 1974 to avoid drinking the water from the river or from certain wells that had unsafe levels of radioactivity.[42]

The Serpent River First Nation was not silent in this debate. Chief Peter Johnston, who later went on to become the band manager, stated that he did not want the mines to expand until the community was compensated for the loss of its water sources through the contamination of the Serpent River and for the heavy expense of having to dig wells. Chief Johnston drew attention to the loss of the community's land and water resources that occurred as a result of the acid plant's operations on the reserve in the 1950s and early 1960s.[43] Gertrude Lewis recalled her involvement in the debate: "I was one of them that fought against the expansion of the uranium mines in Elliot Lake in the '70s, and I didn't want to see that happen until they found a safe way to dispose of their waste. But we weren't listened to. Of course, we were looked on as sort of, how you say, just trouble makers or something like that. But that wasn't the reason. We wanted a safe disposal of the waste."[44] This struggle would foreshadow the efforts of the Serpent River First Nation to redress contamination on their land and in their water for the next decade.

The contamination of the Serpent River and lack of access to water were not the only environmental problems facing the Serpent River band as a result of the uranium industry in Elliot Lake. Noranda Mines established the acid plant at Cutler in 1956[45] (the same year Elliot Lake was recognized as a development site) with the understanding that several Serpent River First Nation members would be employed there. Leslie Roberts, in his book *Noranda*, argued that the location of the acid plant was practical because it was close to water, rail, and the Trans-Canada Highway.[46] The Serpent River First Nation would be an ideal location for the plant, because it would be an opportunity for economic development and employment for the reserve's band members. In this case, a booming but poisonous industry was found to keep reserve members employed, but mostly, to facilitate uranium extraction and processing.

The *Globe and Mail* reported that C.W. Clark, the director for Research and Development, met with Indian agent Laurence and Chief William Albert Owl in order to negotiate a lease of 125 acres of reserve land. The article also gave a brief outline of the company's plans and the way in which the community could accommodate them: "the Indians will direct a resolution to the Department of Indian Affairs in Ottawa requesting that they be given permission to lease this land to Noranda Mines for 99 years" and that the plant would have "a production capacity of 500 tonnes of acid per day."[47] However, according to one newspaper article in the *Standard*, the local Elliot Lake and North Shore newspaper, a deal was struck between Indian Affairs and Noranda with little involvement of band representatives: "back in 1955 Noranda mines approached Indian Affairs about leasing land next to the

Indian village of Cutler. The land was leased and Noranda started operations in 1956. In 1962, the plants were sold to Canadian Industries Limited (CIL) which abandoned the factories and waste in 1963."[48]

The question of whether or not chief and council of the Serpent River First Nation had a great deal of say in the negotiations between Indian Affairs and Noranda Mines is debatable. The plant brought promise of long-term employment, but more importantly, it would have also been an important side-process in the uranium industry, which was immensely important to the Canadian economy at the time. Therefore, it was seen as an ideal situation for all those involved: Noranda Mines had the opportunity to be a key player in the uranium mining industry, community residents would have steady, full-time employment, and the Indian agent would no longer have to worry about the economic and social future of the reserve. Perhaps the involvement of band council representatives was insignificant anyway, as historian R. Jarvis Brownlie argues,

> In certain situations, band councils were able to exercise some power vis-à-vis the Indian Agent and/or the DIA, though they needed the united support of the rest of the band to do so. This could occur when a DIA official wanted to pursue a particular project and required the council's consent. A united band and council could successfully thwart official plans, as long as they could sustain their unity. Steadfast refusal to approve a DIA proposal would bring down official displeasure, but the department was unlikely to act against the united will of a band. Nonetheless, it was often difficult to maintain the necessary unity, especially given the divisions colonialism had created or exacerbated within First Nations societies. When an agent stubbornly pursued a project, marshalling his own allies and utilizing the people's economic vulnerability, he stood an excellent chance of eventually obtaining Aboriginal consent.[49]

Although chief and council were elected by the community, the Indian agent still wielded a great deal of power in terms of the management of band resources and policies, particularly as they pertained to economic development schemes.

In fact, the roles of chief and council were not modelled on traditional forms of government, but were instead the products of colonial policy. In his study of the history of Indian Affairs policy toward Aboriginal Peoples in Canada, John L. Tobias argues that "the elected band council was a means to destroy the last vestige of the old tribal system, the traditional political system. The reserve system, other sections of the Indian Act, and missionaries were thought to have dealt effectively with all other aspects of traditional Indian values."[50] The imposition of a municipal-style governing structure by the Indian Act was just as important to the "civilization" program for First Nations peoples as Christianization and Western education. These efforts were particularly important when seen in the context of the presence of the Indian agent: although communities were expected to operate without a trace of their traditional government structures, and were, on paper, given powers to make their own decisions as long as they followed the format set out by DIA, they were still monitored closely by the Indian agent. He also still had a great deal of power in band council decisions. Given the colonial aims of the band structure, it is hardly surprising that if Chief William Owl was present at the negotiations, he would have had in reality little power to demand the band's independent legal representation in the deal in any material way. The agreement would have also been framed as being in the best economic interest of the band, although it would later prove to be extremely costly to the finances, environment, water, and health of the Serpent River First Nation.

While the plant was in operation, the sulphur had negative effects on the residents. Gertrude Lewis talked about the dangers of having open windows in their homes because of the sulphur plant: "our throats would be really dry and burning from the sulphur fumes. And even when we hung out our clothes out on the clothesline—now this is being laughed about, but it really happened—when I'd hang my clothes out on the line they'd have little weeny, tiny holes in them."[51] The acid plant affected the whole community, and had health implications for them.

If breathing conditions seemed bad at home, then one can only imagine the effects of working in the plant. Terry Jacobs worked at the plant from 1957 to 1962 and suffered the effects of sulphur: "It had an effect on my throat more than once. Any thunderstorm, you'd get stuck in there. There were times you couldn't wear the gas masks in there. The diaphragms would freeze up and you'd choke yourself. You didn't get anything else. About 175 people worked there."[52] The lack of proper safety equipment, or its disintegration due to extensive exposure to sulphur, as well as insufficient protocols in an environment like a sulphur roaster plant, had several health implications for the employees. Although the plant provided jobs for band members, they came at a high cost.

The Institute of Environmental Research report submitted to chief and council in April 1984 found that exposure to the acid plant led to "ill health" in 75% of men over 45 years old, and that "there ... appears to be an elevated rate of unexplained fetal deaths and abnormalities in live born offspring for acid plant workers, relative to the non-exposed males over 45 years of age."[53] The report went so far as to state that "the costs may well outweigh any benefits derived from nearby resource developments" and further claimed that the residents of the Serpent River First Nation were twice as likely to suffer from chronic diseases than were members of two neighbouring reserves, the Mississauga and Sagamok First Nations.[54] Occupational exposure to uranium and the acid plant was found to be a significant factor in the health of Serpent River band members and their offspring.

Although on-reserve employment opportunities were created through the establishment of the acid plant, the seemingly benevolent actions of DIA were undermined by minutes from meetings of the Privy Council in 1960, which point to a catering to the mining industry over the interests of band members. In a 10 June 1960 meeting, David James Walker, the minister of Public Works, stated, "Noranda Mines Ltd. would consider constructing a fertilizer plant, at an estimated cost of $10 million, at Cutler, Ont., about 16 miles from Elliot Lake, provided the Department of Public Works built a wharf there. The plant would utilize sulphuric acid from the existing plant at Cutler which *was built solely to meet requirements for Elliot Lake mining operations*."[55] Little mention was made about the other reason for the potential establishment of the fertilizer plant: employment for the community members of the Serpent River First Nation. Although there was a promise that building the new fertilizer plant would increase employment, this was not an opportunity aimed at First Nations peoples. In fact, the federal minister of Citizenship and Immigration (the department responsible for Status Indians at this time), Ellen Fairclough, said nothing in the meeting about the situation or the proposal. Decisions were to be made about industry in a First Nations community without representation from the people who lived there. Presumably a new plant would have required additional land, which would involve the Department of Citizenship and Immigration directly in a new land surrender or lease. However, no comments came from the minister, although she was present at the meeting.

What is more, Fairclough did speak at a 30 June 1960 meeting when she outlined the plan of the Industrial Commissioner at Elliot Lake to make a National Film Board project to entice the relocation of various industries to Elliot Lake.[56] The one person in government with jurisdiction over Aboriginal affairs had nothing to say about the proposed wharf project, or the increase in industry at Serpent River First Nation and how that might affect its inhabitants. She did, however, propose that further industry be brought to

Elliot Lake, suggesting that the federal government was far more concerned with the uranium industry as a whole and the town of Elliot Lake than it was with the Aboriginal people affected by it. Thus, employment on-reserve was of little significance in discussions surrounding the potential establishment of the plant, while the accommodation of the uranium industry was the primary focus. In any case, the wharf project was not approved due to cost-sharing disagreements between Noranda Mines, and the federal and provincial governments;[57] Aboriginal people did not enter into the discussion.

Cabinet meeting minutes that highlight the dispute over the financing of the wharf foreshadow Noranda's reluctance to invest in a long-term project at Cutler. It is therefore not surprising that it sold the plant to Canadian Industries Limited soon after the following synopsis was announced in Noranda's 1961 annual business report: "The Cutler acid plant was lower at 344 tonnes of acid per day, about 35% of capacity, due to reduced demand for acid from the uranium mines. Some 85,000 tons of pyrite concentrate was burned to yield 125,500 tons of acid and 57,000 tons of iron calcine."[58] When compared to the production of the plant in 1959, when it operated at close to capacity,[59] the 1961 results were disappointing, and directly tied to the "bust" period of Elliot Lake and the uranium industry in the early 1960s.

Canadian Industries Limited closed the plant in 1963 after operating it for only eleven months. The abandoned buildings were problematic for both the Serpent River Anishinaabek and the North Shore tourism industry, as the "scabrous look of deserted and derelict buildings"[60] was an eyesore for anyone driving through the reserve on the Trans-Canada highway. Chief Meawasige wanted to be able to use the land for a practical purpose, such as a home for elders. However, CIL, the last owners of the plant, refused to co-operate with plans for demolition, and DIA was also unresponsive. The band could not finance such a project independently, so letters to the prime minister had been written by the chief.[61]

Finally, a solution was found: "in 1969, the buildings were destroyed in a military exercise conducted by the Department of National Defence and the waste was spread over the site."[62] The diffusion of toxic materials during the demolition resulted in dangerous waste: "pyrite was the major raw product used to supply industrial grade sulphuric acid to the Elliot Lake uranium mines for refining operations. The Cutler acid site was built in 1956 and the plant ceased operations in 1963.... In the waste was calcine, which is a solid waste product produced by high temperature roasting of pyrite, which was discharged to a settling pond and marsh area at the western end of the site.[63] These chemical by-products were then mixed in with the concrete, and poisonous dust filled the air as a result of the Department of National Defence demolition. The environmental mismanagement of DIA, whose representatives failed to ensure that there was a clean-up clause in the lease agreement they made with Noranda Mines,[64] compounded by the "improvement" exercise carried out by Department of National Defence, ensured that the cost of decontaminating the site decades later would prove to be extremely high.

The decommissioning process was complicated by the paternalistic nature of the lease agreement that Noranda had negotiated with Indian Affairs, and this was highlighted in the *Standard* article "Serpent River Band Tells a History of Complaint." Band members claim the community was not permitted to hire its own lawyers and that DIA told them that their interests would be protected by government lawyers.[65] However, the DIA lawyers did not take the effects of the plant's closure into consideration, and after the plant was abandoned, residents of the First Nation were left to "inhale the fumes from the 130,000 cubic metres of sulphur" and cope with unemployment.[66] The community was assured that DIA lawyers would protect their interests, and yet sulphur continued to contaminate their lands for decades after the plant's closure.

This occurred despite complaints made by Chief William Meawasige and other band members. Calls to clean up the acid plant area on the reserve came as soon as it closed in 1963; however, by the 1980s, the land was still contaminated by sulphur and health problems were being studied by the Institute of Public Health.[67] In 1986, Chief Earl Commanda chose a new tactic and threatened to block the highway with burning sulphur and debris. To this end, "the band council passed a resolution in January stating if we don't get a meeting with the minister that the possibility of this type of action will exist. We've talked about this type of action as a protest against the lack of response from Indian Affairs."[68] Although Commanda wanted to negotiate with the ministry and the two companies that leased the plant grounds, DIA wanted to find out who was more responsible for the clean-up. Commanda charged that DIA could lose the most out of a potential deal, as they were "in breach of trust by allowing the plant to be built" in the community, particularly when the leases for each company did not include agreements about demolition or responsible environmental policies.[69]

By 16 February 1986, one week after the threat of a highway blockade was published, Chief Commanda had his meeting with Minister of Indian Affairs David Crombie.[70] He also promised to call a meeting with Environment minister Tom McMillan and Health minister Jake Epp before 31 May of that year.[71] Although the problem was publicly recognized by DIA, there were no promises of action. By October 1986, steps had still not been taken to improve the situation, and Chief Commanda and band planner Keith Lewis threatened that the band would use its finances to transport the waste to the highway in order to block it. This would have had crippling effects for the uranium industry, and it would have impeded travel access for others using the highway. At the time, Keith Lewis stated, "quiet negotiation has brought us along to where we are now. It's getting us nowhere and we're forced to consider other options."[72] Clearly, the impatience felt by Chief Bill Meawasige in the 1960s had reached a boiling point after two decades of government inaction. While the community waited for answers about a potential plan for contamination clean-up, "spontaneous sulphur fires threatened reserve property and occasionally the Trans-Canada highway and acid run-off affected local waters."[73] The frustration of a First Nations community and its leaders had reached a point where they made very public demands of the federal government and resorted to more open forms of resistance to colonialism.

By July 1988, negotiations had taken place between DIA and community leaders. This time, the band had its own legal counsel, and Indian Affairs administrators were waiting on budget approval from the treasury board to begin the clean-up that summer.[74] The community was relieved and overjoyed when the project was approved and the waste removal process began in August 1988.[75] The clean-up and subsequent replacement of contaminated soil with new top soil cost more than $5 million, which was covered by the federal government.[76] CIL, the last company to operate the plant, settled with the band, giving them $106,500 in compensation. Noranda retracted their $50,000 offer in November 1988, even though the company negotiated the lease with Indian Affairs and operated it for more than five years.[77]

Although the clean-up was successfully negotiated, there are charges that the process was insufficient. The land was not used for an elders' home, but was used as the powwow grounds for the annual community celebrations in August. Unfortunately, the legacy of the sulphur plant is still very apparent in the area, and in recent years, the powwow grounds had to be moved because of continued contamination. Even though one would never guess that the grounds were once covered in concrete, pyrite, and sulphur, the rocks leading down to the water are reddish orange from the waste, and there is still the strong and unmistakable smell of sulphur in several places.[78] The acid plant is still talked about by many elders in the community, as they or their spouses worked there or were affected by the quality of air in the region.

The Serpent was respected by the Serpent River Anishinaabek, who understood the precarious balance of their environmental surroundings and the destructive consequences that would result from upsetting that balance. The territory of the Serpent River First Nation has been seriously harmed in the name of economic development, and its community members have suffered significant detrimental effects. The legacy of the paternalistic relationship between the Department of Indian Affairs and the Serpent River First Nation is still present in the day-to-day lives of community members, as is the detrimental effect of uranium big business on the natural resources and wildlife on the traditional territory of the Anishinaabek. The acid plant's destructive environmental effects on the First Nation are still felt today, and the damage demonstrates how the larger interest at stake was that of the uranium industry and not that of the community, pointing to the failure on the part of DIA and the federal government to fulfill their fiduciary responsibilities toward the Serpent River Anishinaabek, as well as their failure to allow First Nations peoples to enact their own solutions to community issues. When the Robinson-Huron Treaty was signed in 1850, this was hardly what Chief Windawtegawinini had envisioned for the people he represented when the agreement he signed promised them reserves "for their own use and benefit."[79]

The community's subsequent chiefs have found ways to resist the governmental and economic intrusions that have left a legacy of health and environmental suffering. Chief Meawasige turned to the media when his concerns were not sufficiently addressed by Indian Affairs. He used his position as chief to gain authority, and tried—independently of Indian Affairs as much as possible—to rectify water problems and the eyesore that was the abandoned acid plant. When it became apparent decades later that neither the Canadian government nor Noranda Mines were going to assist the band to clean up the acid site, Chief Commanda again went to the media, this time with a threat to close the Trans-Canada highway by blocking it with burning sulphur. He was not alone in his action. Community members rallied to protest government inaction, and eventually, a more effective clean-up was arranged and paid for after more than two decades of unanswered concerns. Although the area was decommissioned in 1988, more needs to be done to reclaim the land as contamination from the plant continues to render the site unusable. The Serpent River First Nation's participation in the National Day of Protest in 2007 and 2008 publicized the issue of the acid plant contamination and growing concerns about the prospect of reopening uranium mines in the Elliot Lake area.[80] Citizens of the First Nation continue to act as stewards of the river and the Serpent for which the community is named.

Notes

Funding for this research was provided by both a Master's and a Ph.D. Canadian Graduate Scholarship administered by the Social Sciences and Humanities Research Council (SSHRC). The author wishes to thank Drs. Karl Hele, Roger Hall, Susan Neylan, and Mark Humphries, as well as the anonymous reviewers of this edited collection for their comments on earlier drafts.

1 Tom Haddow, "Serpent River Home of Giant Reptile: Ojibway," *Standard* (Elliot Lake), 29 March 1983. Many thanks to Ray Ethelston and the staff at the *Standard* for their assistance in accessing some of these articles.

2 Theresa S. Smith, *The Island of the Anishnaabeg: Thunderers and Water Monsters in the Traditional Ojibwe Life-World* (Idaho: University of Idaho Press, 1995), 112.

3 In 1950, Indian Affairs fell under the jurisdiction of the Department of Citizenship and Immigration, and was moved several times to different departments in the time period studied here. For the sake of simplicity and clarity, it will be referred to as the Department of Indian Affairs or DIA throughout this chapter.

4 The Province of Ontario and mining companies are also implicated in this process, though their involvement in planning the townsite at Elliot Lake.

5 David T. McNab's *Circles of Time: Aboriginal Land Rights and Resistance in Ontario* (Waterloo: Wilfrid Laurier University Press, 1999) examines disputes between Aboriginal peoples and governments that have resulted in reserves being forced into lengthy and often unfruitful negotiations, leading to protests and blockades. McNab returns to this theme with Bruce W. Hodgins and Ute Lischke in *Blockades and Resistance: Studies in Actions of Peace and the Temagami Blockades of 1988–89* (Waterloo: Wilfrid Laurier University Press, 2003). A recent study in the complexities of colonial relations with reserves is Robin Jarvis Brownlie's *A Fatherly Eye: Indian Agents, Government Power, and Aboriginal Resistance in Ontario, 1918–1939* (Don Mills: Oxford University Press, 2003). Brownlie examines the roles of the Indian agents and their paternalistic relationships with the band members they encountered. She argues that there were instances of resistance; however, it was very difficult to attain the band membership unity needed to confront the will of the Indian agent. Janet E. Chute's study of the Garden River First Nation, and specifically the leadership of Shingwaukonse, adds nuance to the view of First Nations political structure. Chute follows Shingwaukonse's life as chief until his death in 1854, as well as his legacy of leadership initiatives, and claims that his success stemmed in part from his use of political power to protect Ojibwa culture and interests. Chute, "Pursuing the Great Spirit's Plan: Nineteenth-Century Ojibwa Attitudes

Towards the Future of Logging and Mining on Unsurrendered Indian Lands North of Lakes Huron and Superior," in *Social Relations in Resource Hinterlands: Papers from the 27th Annual Meeting of the Western Association of Sociology and Anthropology*, ed. Thomas W. Dunk (Thunder Bay: Lakehead University Centre for Northern and Regional Studies, 1991), 173–203.

6 See George Hutchison and Dick Wallace, *Grassy Narrows* (Toronto: Van Nostrand Reinhold Ltd., 1977); Anastasia M. Shkilnyk, *A Poison Stronger Than Love: The Destruction of an Ojibwa Community* (New Haven: Yale University Press, 1985); Christopher Vecsey, "Grassy Narrows Reserve: Mercury Pollution, Social Disruption, and Natural Resources: A Question of Autonomy," *American Indian Quarterly* 11, no. 4 (Autumn, 1987): 287–314; Connie Deiter, *Human Security and Aboriginal Women in Canada* (Ottawa: Status of Women Canada, Policy Research, 2005).

7 Meawasige was chief from 1941 to 1953 and then again from 1957 to 1969, according to "Previous Chiefs and Councils," a document is held at the Serpent River First Nation Library.

8 The Serpent River First Nation is also referred to as Genaabaajing, as well as Cutler, as a village by the latter name was present very near the reserve until the 1930s. For details about the people's remaining territory, see "Copy of the Robinson Treaty Made in the Year 1850 with the Ojibewa Indians of Lake Huron Conveying Certain Lands to the Crown," *Aboriginal Affairs and Northern Development Canada*, www.aadnc-aandc.gc.ca/eng/1100100028984.

9 Serpent River First Nation Chief Earl Commanda and Council Member Keith Lewis, "What You Are Losing Is Forever," in *This Is My Homeland: Stories of the Effects of Nuclear Industries by People of the Serpent River First Nation and the North Shore of Lake Huron*, ed. Lorraine Reckmans, Keith Lewis, and Anabel Dwyer (Cutler: Serpent River First Nation, 2003), 2–3. This work is a history of the effects of the acid plant and uranium on the community, told in the words of the people who live there.

10 Catharine Dixon, *The Power and The Promise: The Elliot Lake Story* (Elliot Lake, ON: Gillidix, 1996), xv.

11 Dixon, *Power and The Promise*, 20; Shawn Heard, "The City of Elliot Lake to 1991: Before the Roof Fell In," in *Boom Town Blues Elliot Lake: Collapse and Revival in a Single-Industry Community*, ed. Anne-Marie Mawhiney and Jane Pitblado (Toronto: Dundurn, 1999), 22.

12 Rudolf A. Helling, *Elliot Lake ... Beginning* (Windsor: Assumption University of Windsor, 1960), 4.

13 Helling, *Elliot Lake*, 2–3.

14 Gilbert Oskaboose, "The Serpent Doesn't Live Here Anymore," *Indian News*, December 1977.

15 "Serpent River Plan Interesting," *Sudbury Star*, 23 March 1983.

16 "Serpent River Plan Interesting."

17 Serpent River First Nation elders, uranium miners, and sulphuric-acid-plant workers Leo Day, Junior, Orville Commanda, John Souliere, Terrence Jacobs, Gertrude Lewis, and Frank Lewis, "We Don't Drink the Water from the Serpent River Anymore," in *This Is My Homeland*, 33.

18 Serpent River First Nation elders, "We Don't Drink the Water," 41.

19 Serpent River First Nation elders, "We Don't Drink the Water," 41.

20 Serpent River First Nation elders, "We Don't Drink the Water," 41.

21 Serpent River First Nation elders, "We Don't Drink the Water," 42.

22 "Poisons Pile Up in the Serpent River; Double Standard Angers Indians," *Globe and Mail*, 16 December 1976, 11.

23 Institute of Environmental Research (IER), Inc., "Environmental Impact Protection Program (Summary Progress Report)," 3 April 1984, 20. I am extremely grateful to Gertrude Lewis for her help in locating this report. The program was initiated by the Sagamok, Mississaugi, and Serpent River First Nations working in partnership together, along with the Jesuit Centre and the IER, to evaluate and protect traditional territory.

24 Barrie Zwicker, "Facts Secret Two Years: Elliot Lake Contaminated by Radioactive Waste," *Globe and Mail*, 13 November 1964, 1.

25 Zwicker, "Facts Secret Two Years," 1.

26 Health Canada, "Radon Frequently Asked Questions," *Environmental and Workplace Health*, http://www.hc-sc.gc.ca/ewh-semt/radiation/radon/faq_fq-eng.php#dbequerel. According to Health Canada, "on average, 10% of lung cancers are attributable to radon exposure worldwide. In 2006, an estimated 1,900 lung cancer deaths in Canada were due to radon exposure. Radon is the 2nd leading cause of lung cancer, after smoking." See also Ministry of the Environment, "Status Report: Water Pollution in the Serpent River Basin," Toronto, 1976, 9–11.

27 Barrie Zwicker, "Hold-Up Report on A-Pollution until After Vote," *Globe and Mail*, 2 November 1965, 1.

28 "Poisons Pile Up in Serpent River," 11. The National Indian Brotherhood is now known as the Assembly of First Nations.

29 "Poisons Pile Up in Serpent River," 11.

30 "Poisons Pile Up in Serpent River," 11.

31 "Water Everywhere but Must Be Hauled to Cutler Homes," *The Standard*, 24 July 1969, 10.

32 "Water Everywhere," 10.
33 "Water Everywhere," 10.
34 "River Basin Is Polluted by Uranium," *Globe and Mail*, 10 June 1970, 1. See also Report on Business Excerpt, "Canada," *The Globe and Mail*, 10 June 1970, B01.
35 "The Other Side of Progress," *Globe and Mail*, 3 August 1970, 6.
36 Serpent River First Nation, "Band Council Resolution #13," 16 March 1971, Library and Archives Canada (LAC), RG 10: Indian Affairs, Vol. 10300, File 493,8-2-7-7, Reel T-7577.
37 "Memorandum from Cameron to Regional Director," 22 March 1971, LAC, RG 10, Vol. 10300, File 493,8-2-7-7, Reel T-7577.
38 Maurice Foster, MP, to William McKim, 31 March 1971, LAC, RG 10, Vol. 10300, File 493,8-2-7-7, Reel T-7577.
39 William McKim to Maurice Foster, 20 April 1971, LAC, RG 10; Vol. 10300, File 493,8-2-7-7, Reel T-7577.
40 J.G. McGilp to Chief Peter Johnston, 14 April 1971, LAC, RG 10, Vol. 10300, File 493,8-2-7-7, Reel T-7577.
41 Peter Whelan, "Peril in Expanded Uranium Mining to Be Probed," *Globe and Mail*, 24 September 1976, 4.
42 Mick Lowe, "Ontario Government Accused of Indifference to 20 Years of Pollution in Serpent River," *Globe and Mail*, 30 September, 1976, 10; Whelan, "Peril in Expanded Uranium Mining," 4.
43 "Indians Oppose Mines' Growth," *Globe and Mail*, 2 August 1979, 4.
44 Serpent River First Nation elders, "We Don't Drink the Water," 51.
45 "Two Contractors Want Cutler Waste Job," *Standard*, 17 July 1988, 1.
46 Leslie Roberts, *Noranda* (Toronto: Clarke Irwin, 1956), 199.
47 "Sulphuric Acid Plant in Algoma," *Globe and Mail*, 8 June 1955, 28.
48 "Serpent River Band Tells a History of Complaint," *Standard*, 29 June 1988, 1.
49 Brownlie, *Fatherly Eye*, 61.
50 John L. Tobias, "Protection, Civilization, Assimilation: An Outline History of Canada's Indian Policy" in *As Long as the Sun Shines and the Water Flows: A Reader in Canadian Native Studies*, ed. Ian A.L. Getty and Antoine S. Lussier (Vancouver: University of British Columbia Press, 1983), 46.
51 Serpent River First Nation elders, "We Don't Drink the Water," 45.
52 Serpent River First Nation elders, "We Don't Drink the Water," 46.
53 IER, "Environmental Impact," 11.
54 IER, "Environmental Impact," 19.
55 "Cabinet Conclusions," 10 June 1960, LAC, RG 2: Privy Council Office, Vol. 2746, File C. 17 May–30 June, 3. Emphasis added.

56 "Cabinet Conclusions," 30 June 1960, LAC, RG 2, Vol. 2746, File C. 17 May–30 June, 4.
57 "Cabinet Conclusions," 30 June 1960.
58 Noranda Mines, *A Report on Progress: Noranda Mines, Limited, 1961*, LAC, RG 20: Industry, Trade, and Commerce, Vol. 775, File 23-100-N17.
59 Noranda Mines, *A Report on Progress: Noranda Mines, Limited, 1959*, LAC, RG 20, Vol. 775, File 23-100-N17.
60 "'Like Stalingrad After the Siege': Ojibway Chief Doesn't Have Solution" *Standard*, 2 February 1967, 5.
61 "Like Stalingrad After the Siege," 5.
62 Jeff Wilkinson, "Chemical Company Compensating Band," *Standard*, 18 December 1988, 1.
63 "Two Contractors," 1.
64 "Cutler Acid Waste Going ..." *Standard*, 20 July 1988.
65 "Serpent River Band Tells a History of Complaint," 1.
66 "Serpent River Band Tells a History of Complaint," 1.
67 "Band Could Block Highway," *Standard*, 9 February 1986, 1.
68 "Band Could Block Highway," 1.
69 "Band Could Block Highway," 1.
70 "Band Chief More Hopeful, but No Clean-up Promised," *Standard*, 16 February 1986, 1.
71 "Band Chief More Hopeful," 1.
72 "Leaders' Threat: Reserve Will Take Its Own Steps Unless Government Moves on Acid," *Standard*, 1 October 1986, 1.
73 "Leaders' Threat," 1.
74 "Sulphur Waste: Still Waiting for Funding," *Standard*, 3 July 1988, 1.
75 "Waste Removal Starts," *Standard*, 14 August 1988, 1.
76 "CIL 'Overjoyed' with Cutler Deal," *Standard*, 21 December 1988, 1.
77 "Noranda Won't Help with Cutler Clean-up," *Standard*, 23 November 1988, 1.
78 The author's personal observations.
79 "Copy of the Robinson Treaty."
80 See, for instance, Pele Mountain Resources, http://www.pelemountain.com/.

CHAPTER 9

Divided Spaces, Divided Stories: Animal Control Programs in Canada's Northern Indigenous Communities

Maureen Riche

In the introduction to his comprehensive overview of indigenous dogs in Canada, *First Nations, First Dogs,* Bryan Cummins theorized that a lack of scholarly interest in canine subjects to date was due to the liminal theoretical space the animal occupies. "Perhaps," Cummins wrote, this lack of research activity is rooted in ambiguity, in that the dog is neither "fully '*culture*'—the raison d'être of anthropology and anthropologists—nor fully '*nature*.'" Rather, he posits, "man's best friend ... straddles the world between" the two poles.[1] It seems a simple enough proposition. Dogs, as Cummins points out, are essentially wolves; they are of the natural world, not just in the sense of being descended from a wild ancestor, but also in the sense that, in terms of their current DNA structure, they are distinct from the wolf by only a fraction of mitochondrial modification. Likewise, the dog is obviously a product of culture. Human beings have domesticated them, used them for their own ends—from survival to companionship to entertainment—and laid out ethical rules for their care. There seems to be little room for dispute here: the dog is indeed a bipolar being. The question, however, remains: who has the right, the privilege or the power to decide exactly where the line between nature and culture is to be drawn? Who determines where nature should end and where culture should begin? Who authorizes the boundaries that delineate this inbetweenness embodied by the canine species? Of course, the spectre of empire necessarily raises its head here, for what is the imposition of a culture onto a natural entity—such as the dog—if not an act (or potential act) of imperialism?

In February 2006, as a Master's student at Laurentian University in Sudbury, Ontario, I was offered the opportunity to travel to Kashechewan First Nation with the Ontario Society for the Prevention of Cruelty to Animals (OSPCA).[2] That winter, I was completing the practicum requirement for my degree, a fourteen-week fieldwork project at a community organization of my choice—the Sudbury OSPCA pet adoption centre. At the same time, the regional inspector headquartered there was gearing up to bring a sophomore version of her Spay North program to the troubled Cree community on the Albany River. Spay North is a mobile clinic specifically designed to deliver veterinary services to remote communities in Northern Ontario that have no such resources available. Previously piloted in Moose Factory and Moosonee, the OSPCA-led initiative involved the transport of an eight-member team of veterinary and humane education professionals to Kashechewan, where they would set up a temporary operating room and perform a breathless blitz of sterilizations, de-wormings, vaccinations, and miscellaneous emergency surgeries, all free of charge. All animals were tagged and photographed, and files were created; many animals were taken out of the community for adoption in larger centres down south. One of the goals of such a project is to help communities avoid resorting to their usual method of animal control—dog shoot days, which the OSPCA considers inhumane—and to encourage them instead to sterilize their animals and, ultimately, enact animal control by-laws. While it was not a planned component of my practicum agenda, I eagerly jumped at the chance to take the last available seat on the King Air A100 that would transport the Spay North team to the frozen Kashechewan airstrip. I traded my services as chief surgical instrument washer and sanitizer (the only job I was remotely qualified to do) for five days in a place most Canadians only ever see on newscasts depicting the social, health, and environmental woes that have plagued the community in recent years. I also reasoned that my time in Kashechewan, however brief, might offer me some insight into cross-cultural differences in animal–human relations, a burgeoning area of research interest at the time.

My experience in Kashechewan exceeded my personal and scholarly expectations, so much so that over two years later, I have yet to completely work through everything I saw and did in those few cold days in February 2006. To be honest, I had put my field notes and photos of Spay North on the proverbial shelf, unsure of how to approach the mixed memories, emotions, and meanings the trip north had engendered. Then in September 2007, as a PhD student at York University, I found myself in a graduate course on Indigenous knowledge and public memory with Dr. David McNab, where

I began researching allegations about an Royal Canadian Mounted Police (RCMP)–led dog slaughter in Nunavut and Northern Quebec in the fifties, sixties, and seventies. What was at stake in the Nunavut project was the untangling of a knot of issues and themes, among them contested memories of white and Indigenous history, the privileging of written over oral records, cultural appropriation and control, assimilation, and, at its core, a series of crisscrossing chasms between the Indigenous view of animals and the white view, between North and South, nature and culture, past and present. Many of these thematic nodes, emerging from my study of textual production surrounding the Nunavut dog slaughter, helped me to reframe and re-engage in my experience in Kashechewan First Nation with the Spay North program. Further, as part of the same graduate coursework, Professor McNab assigned us the daunting task of writing our own autobiography. As I worked to unravel the threads of my own past, I began to reveal a possible mixed European and Indigenous ancestry that compelled me even more deliberately towards a return to my work with the dogs of Kashechewan. I am originally from suburban Newfoundland, Irish on my mother's side and, perhaps most relevant for this paper, a typical Western dog owner with a decidedly sentimental attachment to companion animals. My father's family is from Labrador, however, and my grandfather kept sled dogs according to the traditional Indigenous ways of the North; they were working animals, not pets, their use and care defined by an altogether different way of life from the one I knew as a middle-class suburbanite. My return to the North—literally to Kashechewan and figuratively to Nunavut—thus became part of my own personal journey as well.

This chapter, then, is a consideration of two distinct stories, from two distinct places and times, both concerning the delivery of animal control programs in Indigenous communities. One is a story of past tragedy, contested memory, and trauma that continues to resonate today. The other is a present-day story of animal welfare activism and the ongoing negotiation of acceptance and resistance it continues to generate inside a growing movement of northern dog initiatives nationwide. Spay North is not the only such program currently in operation in Canada; but it is the one I find myself—as a white, educated, southern Canadian—personally implicated in. As I tune in to the voices of pride and pain echoing across the decades from Nunavut and Northern Quebec, I know I must reconsider my role in (an arguably) similar initiative and how such contemporary control mechanisms impact Indigenous knowledge in the present day. It is my hope that, as a preliminary exploration of the intersections between these two stories, this chapter will lead us towards important lessons on the implementation of Indigenous animal welfare initiatives specifically and of the fostering of white–Indigenous relations in general. This chapter is about boundaries—what happens when we cross them and when we create them.

Spay North in Kashechewan

The Spay North team touched down on the airstrip in Kashechewan First Nation on Monday, 13 February, at 4:30 p.m. This was the group's second trip north; the program was piloted in Moose Factory and Moosonee in 2004, at which time the team spayed and neutered 54 animals. In Kashechewan, we would complete 104 surgeries, performing a spay or neuter operation every twenty minutes for three and a half days. This productive team included the OSPCA regional inspector/team leader; a veterinarian and his assistant from Newmarket; two SPCA veterinary technicians, one from Newmarket, one from Midland; a humane society manager from St. Catharines; a college student/humane educator; and myself, an observer and volunteer with roots in both (European) Newfoundland and (Indigenous) Labrador. The program was funded by the OSPCA, the International Fund for Animal Welfare, the World Society for the Protection of Animals, and Sir Sandford Fleming Community College. Material support, such as animal crates and leashes, came from the Lincoln County and Kitchener–Waterloo Humane Societies. The project had the support of the local band council, especially the deputy chief at the time, who was concerned about her own animals and hoped to keep them without producing endless litters of pups. The attitude of the team was positive, excited and respectful as we set about unloading our gear, hitching rides into the community and piecing together our mobile clinic. As time went on, however, it became apparent that there was resistance and resentment in the community regarding our activities, and the "us/them" divide grew exponentially as the week wore on. This divide was made manifest in a series of racial and spatial boundaries.

To begin, the entire Spay North team was visibly marked as white. We were all from distant southern towns and cities, and as a unit, we stood out in the sea of Cree faces. We had no Indigenous representation on the team whatsoever. The main point of contact for Spay North "on the ground" was a local elementary teacher in Kashechewan who, like many teachers in such communities, was an outsider: a white woman originally from New Brunswick. An energetic animal welfare advocate, she had been instrumental in caring for the dogs of Kashechewan while the majority of residents had been evacuated during the water crisis of October 2005, and she was instrumental in working with residents and the local band council to bring Spay North to the community. Even though we had an ally within the community, and someone with access to the local band council, that someone was still white, and we were immediately aligned with "the other." Further, our clinic was originally housed in the Kashechewan Nursing Station and team members were accommodated in the teachers' houses, which were vacant at the time because the local school was closed due to fire damage. Both sets of buildings are connected with professionals coming into the community from the outside. The nursing station, for instance, features an apartment complex for the on-site staff and visiting personnel, such as the dentist from Timmins who flies in once a month, primarily to perform extractions. There were few alternatives available to us for either our clinic or our housing requirements; I doubt we could have been billeted with locals when most tiny bungalows already support more than one family. The school, another public space, was also unavailable until the fire damage could be assessed and repaired. Nonetheless, it is significant to note that our sequestration in the nursing station and the teachers' homes further aligned us with the outside world. Racially marked as white, we had already been separate. The message subsequently sent by the spaces we came to occupy was that the Spay North team was more closely allied with educated, professional, non-local elements, and not a part of the community itself.

Spatially, the divide deepened as the week unfolded. Initially, our clinic had an open-concept arrangement so that nothing was hidden from the view of the community residents. We took over one room of the nursing station, and the entire space was used to house a reception area, operating room, and recovery room for the animals. There were no walls, no boundaries, no space off limits. The large room had two doors, one near the front entrance of the station and one closer to the human medical clinic, and people could walk freely through our mobile vet hospital at their leisure, and view the surgeries in action. This was by design: the team wanted to put people at ease about the surgical procedures the veterinarian would be performing. Many curious onlookers dropped in to check us out, and the infusion of Cree faces was assuring. It was a well-intentioned bit of interior design but, unfortunately, it backfired. On the first night of the clinic, one local decided she did not like what she saw, and although she had planned to bring her dog in the following day to be spayed, she changed her mind after viewing the surgery up close. Our team leader then made the decision to physically separate our reception area from our surgery, and the nursing station security guard provided us with a large orange curtain to this end, which we hung to divide the room in half and prevent clients from seeing the surgeries as they waited. The drape served to create another division between the local clients (dogs and owners) and the visiting experts (veterinarians and vet techs). If the concept of performing a surgery to remove the sex organs of a dog baffled some locals before, the veiling of the operating room did little to demystify the process.

Nonetheless, the first full day of clinic operations had a very nice community feel. Our teacher–co-ordinator had scheduled three full days of appointments, and at her urging, many of the local people did indeed keep their appointments this first day. Kids came in and out, asking questions, calling us by name, getting candy and other treats. We talked easily with Kashechewan residents, and met many of their wonderful animals. We were free to walk back and forth from our area to the nursing station proper, to ask for items needed for our clinic: water, a mop, extra chairs. All our requests were graciously accommodated. As the security guard said to me, "We work as a team here." By the second day, something shifted. The community did not seem as enthusiastic. Appointments were not being kept, and the teacher would set out door-to-door convincing, sometimes begging or bribing, people to bring their animals in. If they allowed her, she brought them in on her own. We saw fewer and fewer local faces, and what's worse, we were getting word that the nursing staff was fielding an increasing number of complaints from people who felt the noise and smell of our operations were offensive. By early afternoon, our team leader was called to an emergency meeting to deal with the mounting complaints.

As a short-term solution, the maintenance staff sealed us off from the station waiting area with a big blue tarpaulin stretched across the doorway, and positioned two fans there to direct offensive animal and surgical odours away: another physical divider was in place. People could no longer wander in; we could no longer pop out to ask for items we needed. By the supper hour, the head nurse and a security guard came in to tell us that someone in the community had phoned Health Canada, who said we were not permitted to perform animal surgeries in the same building where human patients were being seen. By this time, the local member of Parliament was involved in the schism; the northern CTV affiliate was filing regular reports on what was going on. Disheartened, we finished the remaining surgeries, broke down our mobile clinic that night and moved it in several small truckloads to the teacher's living room. This is where we conducted the remainder of the work: segregated, no longer in a public place, but in a private (white) residence, completely isolated from the community we intended to serve.

This brief study in the material reality of Spay North 2006—the division in space from the orange curtain to the blue tarp to the teacher's living room—represents for me the "us/them" divide that existed between the veterinary team and Kashechewan First Nation. Differentiated by the markers of race from the outset, and subsequently cloistered in spaces already separate from the community proper, we quickly found ourselves further and further distanced by a succession of symbolic barriers. It was disheartening; and, indeed, nothing seemed to affect the morale of our group more than the proverbial "final curtain," the blue tarpaulin that came to represent the groundswell of resistance and resentment towards our presence. This division was the culmination of a growing chorus of complaints from Kashechewan residents; it was instigated by the community and is the most telling evidence I have of opposition to efforts such as the one carried out that February by the OSPCA. There is an opportunity here to carry out further ethnographic work in Kashechewan, and collect the views of local residents in their own words about this difficult week in 2006; unfortunately such data collection was not a part of my practicum mandate. Within the northern dog movement in general, similar teams have reported encountering what they feel are "misconceptions such as do-gooder attitudes [and] neo-colonial influences," and I cannot help but think that these are some of the same attitudes that underpinned our reception in Kash.[3] Resistance is a reality in this sort of work. In 1999, for example, efforts of the Montreal SPCA to stop a dog shoot in an Inuit village were met with a powerful act of resistance, even defiance: after the Montreal group airlifted six dogs out of the community to "rescue" them from a planned dog shoot, the residents shot the remaining dogs anyway, "a move seen as a [deliberate] snub to southern sentimentality" according to one media report.[4] The report goes on to explain that the Inuit were "alternately amused and annoyed by the outside interference of animal lovers."[5] When representatives from our team met with the local band council in Kashechewan, there certainly was snickering. One of the contacts I have maintained since that time tells me there was joking among residents about our work, as well as annoyance and outright anger. Some, she reported, were simply not pleased that, in their view, the animals were getting better health care treatment than their own children usually receive.

The Nunavut Dog Slaughter

In 2006, when I was asked to join the Spay North team as they took their mobile spay/neuter clinic to Kashechewan, the invitation came with a warning that we might not be met with the warmest of welcomes by all members in the community. I was not surprised to learn that a remote Indigenous community might be skeptical of the motives of a team of white outsiders. They certainly have every right to be. What I was surprised to hear was that the history of Canada includes a chapter of aggressive, systematic control initiatives specifically targeted at northern Indigenous dogs. At the time, and perhaps like most white Canadians, I knew nothing about the alleged dog slaughter that took place in Nunavut and Northern Quebec in the fifties, sixties, and seventies. The team leader for Spay North mentioned it specifically in her caveat to me, I think, as a way of promoting a philosophy of caution and respect among her team as we prepared to enter Kashechewan at a particularly turbulent time, on the heels of the water crisis and evacuation, and in the face of another spring flood. The dog slaughter was offered up as a cautionary tale of how such programs can go terribly wrong. However, it was not until November 2006, more than a year after my return from Kashechewan, that I would understand the depth of pain and resentment potentially associated with white animal control programs in Indigenous communities. That month marked the release of the *Final Report of the RCMP Review of Allegations Concerning Inuit Sled Dogs*, the culmination of an investigation into the alleged dog slaughter. Much of the discursive framework surrounding this review proved to be unsettlingly familiar to me in the wake of my Spay North experience. While I cannot say with any certainty that the people of Kashechewan have any awareness of the Nunavut affair, the parallels between the two stories are unmistakable, and so I offer it here as a cautionary tale to future northern dog programs. The Nunavut dog slaughter is a story of division as well; but the divide in this story was, and is, a narrative one. Perhaps not surprisingly, the Inuit elders and the RCMP each tell a markedly different story about the events in question.

The Inuit of Nunavut and Northern Quebec claim that in the fifties, sixties, and seventies, local RCMP officers, acting on orders from government, systematically shot and killed up to 20,000 sled dogs. This was done, the Inuit are certain, in a bid to force them to end their nomadic lifestyle and to further assimilate them into the white way of life. In the late 1990s, the Inuit decided to collect their memories of this massive, government-initiated dog slaughter and deliver them to the highest levels of government. Their petition got nowhere; the governments said any records from that time had been destroyed and the matter could not be investigated. Then, in 2005, an Inuit-produced documentary film called *Echo of the Last Howl*, featuring heartbreaking stories of slaughter recounted by Inuit elders, renewed interest in the matter and threatened to make the accusations made by the Inuit communities more widely known. As a result, representatives from the communities were invited to speak before Ottawa's Standing Committee on Aboriginal Affairs and Northern Development in March 2005. Among those who stood to speak at that time was elder Mr. Joanasie Maniapik, who recalled,

> Back in 1965 my dogs were killed around March 13—I'm not sure of the exact date. I had gone to buy supplies using my dog team. My wife was back at camp, and I was going to go back to camp the next day. Because I was going to leave the next day, I went to buy supplies right away. As I was buying supplies, someone approached me and told me my dogs were being shot. I went to see what was happening and I saw two police officers. There was an officer and an assistant, and all my dogs were dead.... I was in so much pain. My life was destroyed. I tried taking their harnesses off. As I was trying to take them off, I was crying.[6]

Another elder, Ms. Alisee Joamie told the committee:

> We had already bought our supplies and we were preparing to leave. One of our children, who was eight years old at the time, came running to us to tell us that our dogs were ready to go, and without anyone consulting with us, they were being shot and there were only three left. When that happened, my husband and I went down. There were only a few left. There was an Inuk and a kablunap [white man] who had shot them. Our son was hitting his father's back, crying and telling him to stop them. When all the dogs were shot, everyone outside was crying.[7]

Based on such wrenching testimony, the minister then responsible for the RCMP filed a formal request for the police to begin "a comprehensive review of the RCMP actions regarding sled dogs in the North between 1950 and 1970."[8] As the investigation unfolded, the review team assured government that "all possible sources of information relevant to this matter were located and reviewed objectively."[9] They researched some 42,000 pages of historical documents, and interviewed 120 former Mounties, as well as nurses, clergy, Hudson's Bay Company employees and government officials. Without collecting any input whatsoever from the Inuit elders (who refused to co-operate with an investigation they worried was neither independent nor objective), the RCMP finalized its report on 5 May 2006. It stated that "The RCMP review team did not uncover any evidence to support the allegations, within the large volume of information collected, of an organized mass slaughter of Inuit sled dogs.... The review team did find evidence that sled dogs were destroyed by members of the RCMP, as authorized by law. [This] was undertaken by RCMP members for public health and safety reasons."[10]

The Inuit who testified before the House Standing Committee recall in vivid detail the events surrounding the deaths of their sled dogs. They remember specific dates, locations, and circumstances; they remember who carried out the acts. Some told stories of cowering in their homes as RCMP officers shot the dogs as the animals hid under the house. Some told stories of burying the carcasses themselves as they wept. Some say the Mounties ordered them to take all their animals to the frozen bay one morning, which they did in blind obeisance to the white power figures, only to have their animals executed on the ice. All the narratives they shared captured the confusion, pain, anxiety, and desperation they felt when their sole mode of transportation, and thus their livelihood, was, in their eyes, brutally taken away from them without cause or explanation. The RCMP, for their part, do not necessarily dispute that their northern detachments carried out the deaths of sled dogs in Nunavut and Northern Quebec. In the bureaucratic language of their review paper, they assure readers that the killings were "authorized by law" and were done primarily in an effort to curb overpopulation and canine disease. It's a classic they said/they said situation, an impasse made all the more frustrating by the division between oral and written communications, and their assumed value in White, Western society. A January 2007 article in *Maclean's* magazine, for instance, added insult to injury when it termed the slaughter a "myth," and quoted two Canadian scholars as dismissive of the value of Indigenous history. One, a professor emeritus of history at York University, said that "old men forget and remember selectively. Almost no one can remember dates or facts but they will always be able to tell you they hated so-and-so."[11] The article's author then opines, "This makes oral history a better source for emotions than statistics." A University of British Columbia social work professor further trivialized the oral testimony provided to the Aboriginal Affairs Standing Committee, saying, "There never was a grand conspiracy to kill dogs. I have heard the stories, but there is no other evidence."[12]

The concept of what constitutes valid evidence carves another key divide in the dog slaughter debate, as two temporally and racially separate investigations have yielded (or will yield) two separate bodies of evidence. The pages of written material pored over by RCMP investigators led to the conclusions presented in the *Final Report*: final, as in a closed book. This closure was brought about without any input whatsoever from the wronged party, yet still managed to earn a final stamp of approval from the country's police force. In response, the Qikiqtani Inuit Association has mounted its own investigation in the form of a Truth Commission. Over the course of three years, and at a cost of $2 million, a panel will travel from community to community in Canada's North to collect oral testimony from elders and other interested parties regarding the dog slaughter. The mandate of the commission is to overcome barriers and erase the divide between Inuit and white officials: "The truth and reconciliation process seeks to promote healing for those who suffered wrongdoings, as well as to heal relations between Inuit and the Government by providing an opportunity for uncovering all pertinent facts and allowing for acknowledgement and forgiveness."[13] As the official RCMP file remains firmly closed, however, and as the Inuit embark on their own path towards truth, what we might potentially be left with is further, deeper and more pronounced discursive divisions: two separate investigations, two separate reports, two irresolvable evidentiary solitudes.

Conclusion: Parallels and Lessons from Across the Divide

My work on Indigenous dogs to date has focussed on two distinct stories, drawn from two different culture groups—the James Bay Cree and the Inuit of Nunavut and Northern Quebec. These stories come from two different places and two separate times in Canadian history, and, some might argue, deal with two essentially different outcomes: one can be read as a story of annihilation (the wilful slaughter of animals) and the other as a story of preservation (working to ensure that dogs have a healthy future in Indigenous communities). I do not dispute the differences; but I think it is crucial that we come to understand the similarities. Both are stories of boundaries and barriers, division and disconnect, separation and segregation. The partitions that divided "us and them" during my time in Kashechewan were, literally, material ones: a series of veils and walls that stymied any productive communications between the Spay North team and the community we aimed to serve. The schism that has come to define the controversy surrounding the dog slaughter in Nunavut and Northern Quebec was, and continues to be, a narrative one: the oral testimony of the elders on one side and the written records of the RCMP on the other. Both are examples of a white bias deeply entrenched in the discourse of their respective institutions, a bias that seems to go unquestioned. This naturalized predisposition to white privilege can be seen in the Mounties' decision to move forward on a "comprehensive" investigation and "final" report without the input of the Inuit of Nunavut and Northern Quebec. It can also be seen in Spay North's decision to align itself with the white, outsider, temporary population of Kashechewan First Nation. There are, perhaps, valid reasons for such exclusionary measures: the RCMP maintain that they approached Inuit elders to participate in the investigation, but could find none who believed the allegations of a dog slaughter. Spay North, a non-profit initiative facing a constant funding challenge, takes its support, accommodations, and contacts where it can find them. Notwithstanding, either entity, and the others that follow in their wake, need to be aware of the manner in which they present their projects, lest they inadvertently position themselves as others, even *colonizing* others. For example, much of the media coverage of the Spay North trip, as well as the promotional material produced by the OSPCA, frames the program in the imagery of rescue, often using military discourse. In one SPCA press release, the dog situation in Kash is referred to as a "plight."[14] Another release about the "emergency evacuation" of animals during the spring flood reads, "the Ontario SPCA is *initiating phase one*" of the Spay North program, and that the team has been "*deployed*."[15] Finally, in the official OSPCA magazine, *Animals' Voice*, an article on our trip to Kashechewan was printed in the section titled "Working in the Front Line."[16] Considering such discursive choices, it is difficult to imagine how the program could be seen as anything other than invasive, or even imperialistic.

Of course, at their core, both the Nunavut dog slaughter and the Kashechewan veterinary clinic are stories of animal control programs delivered in Indigenous communities and the problems such programs face. The core problems, as indicated in the analysis above, are problems of division. In reflecting upon my personal experience in Kash, and in considering the reports produced regarding the Nunavut dog slaughter, I further contend that we can distill this array of divisions—material and discursive, textile and textual—into one central issue: a lack of understanding of cross-cultural differences in animal ownership, use and care, and cultural status. Indigenous animals were traditionally not considered as pets in the same manner their more southern, pampered peers are. They were work animals, invaluable to the survival of Indigenous people and a central part of First Nations culture, but workers nonetheless. As such, a different standard of care was in place. In contemporary communities, Indigenous dogs face an identity crisis: no longer proud working animals, but not quite pets, they straddle the gap between their past and present, between nature and culture, between North and South, and between their Indigenous identity and the identity being imposed upon them in post-contact Canada. It is a crisis not unlike the one being faced by their Indigenous *human* counterparts.

This is becoming an increasingly relevant and pressing issue in Canada as programs like Spay North continue to proliferate: a 2007 Northern Dog Conference sponsored by the World Society for the Protection of Animals welcomed delegates from some 50 animal welfare organizations, all of whom deliver animal control programs in Indigenous communities, all promoting the credo of "Responsible Animal Ownership." Questions persist: Who defines responsible? Who defines ownership? The divide endures across the decades. Commenting on Inuit reaction to the RCMP *Final Report*, principal reviewer Staff Sgt. Phil Campbell allowed that elders accurately remembered the deaths of their animals, but that they were "mistaken about the significance."[17] In addition to the tacitly condescending tone to this claim, there is also the suggestion—and a correct one, in my view—of an intrinsic cultural divide when it comes to understanding the role of dogs within a culture, and how they should be used and maintained. The Inuit outlined aspects of this divide in their response to the RCMP report. The RCMP claimed that they shot dogs to curb an outbreak of canine disease; the Inuit counter that they were fully capable of identifying and managing the health of their dogs, as they have been for thousands of years. The RCMP further stated that many dogs were starving; the Inuit disagree with this, but also point out that if there was a famine at the time, it did not make sense to rid the communities of their primary means for hunting food—their dog teams. Finally, the RCMP said that the size of the dog population was out of control, and that the dogs were loose in the communities, acting "primitive" and "aggressive." Each of these justifications hit home particularly hard for me—these were some of the same reasons Spay North had used to prop up its presence in Kashechewan First Nation in 2006. If we consider both stories within the broader narrative of nature and empire, another troubling layer emerges: if animal welfare officials are engaged in efforts to *tame* the "primitive," to *calm* the "aggressive," to *impose* their own cultural standards on the canine nature, then perhaps we need to face the possibility that animal control in Indigenous communities might be something akin to an act of canine colonialism.

Notes

1 Bryan D. Cummins, *First Nations, First Dogs* (Calgary: Detselig: 2002), 11.

2 For more information, see http://www.ospca.ca.

3 Josey Kitson, *Northern Dogs: A Summary of the 2007 Conference* (Toronto: WSPCA Canada, 2008), http://www.wspa.ca/nd/Conference_Summary.pdf.

4 Gloria Galloway, "Expensive Bid to Save Dogs Cuts No Ice among Inuit," *National Post*, 13 February 1999, A1.

5 Galloway, "Expensive Bid," A1.

6 Standing Committee on Aboriginal Affairs and Northern Development, Slaughtering of Inuit Sled Dogs, Meeting 23, 10 March 2005, 11:15 a.m.

7 Standing Committee on Aboriginal Affairs and Northern Development, Slaughtering of Inuit Sled Dogs, Meeting 23, 10 March 2005, 11:35 a.m.

8 Royal Canadian Mounted Police (RCMP), *Final Report: RCMP Review of Allegations Concerning Inuit Sled Dogs*, 30 May 2006, 3, http://www.rcmp-grc.gc.ca/ccaps/sled_dogs_final_e.htm.

9 RCMP, *Final Report*, 6.

10 RCMP, *Final Report*, 23.

11 Quoted in Peter Shawn Taylor, "The Myth of the Sled Dog Killings," *Maclean's*, 1 Jan. 2007, 21.

12 Quoted in Taylor, "The Myth."

13 "The Qikiqtani Inuit Association Soon to Embark on Truth Commission Hearings," *Fan Hitch* 10, no. 1 (2007), http://homepage.mac.com/puggiq/V10N1/V10,N1News.html.

14 OSPCA, "Ontario SPCA Deploys Staff to Kashechewan for Emergency Evacuation of Pets Due to Flooding," *Media Release*, 25 April 2006, http://www.ontariospca.ca/press_releases/2006/2006_apr25.html.

15 OSPCA, "Ontario SPCA Spay North Team Flying to Kashechewan First Nation Community to Spay/Neuter and Offer Additional Veterinary Services," *Media Release*, 9 February 2006, http://www.ontariospca.ca/press_releases/2006/2006_feb09_1.html.

16 "Working in the Front Line: Kashechewan Spay North 2006," *Animals' Voice*, Summer 2006, 16.

17 Chris Windeyer, "Qikiqitani 'Not Satisfied' with Dog Slaughter Report," http://nnsl.com/frames/newspapers/2006-12/dec4_06dg.html.

CHAPTER 10

First Nations Diasporas in Canada: A Case of Recognition

María Cristina Manzano-Munguía

Beginning with colonization, First Nations people in Canada experienced displacement from their homelands and were eventually confined to live "on-reserve."[1] Ward Churchill conceptualizes the displacement of Indigenous peoples from their original land and resources as an Indian diaspora; thus, they should be included in diaspora studies.[2] Moreover, James Clifford argues that tribal people possess diasporic identities through the experience of displacement and dispossession of their land.[3] One way to look at the nature of the British Empire is the forced displacement that Indigenous populations, including First Nations, have experienced from their original territories since colonization.

This chapter explores precisely this political mobilization with two intertwined goals: first, to define First Nations experience in Canada as *diasporic*; second, to propose that the concept of diaspora explains some First Nations experiences in urban centres. The locus for this study is First Nations people who experienced historic and contemporary displacement from different settlements or reserves to the city of London, Ontario. During the course of my fieldwork[4] in London, I built a rapport with its First Nations community. Archival research and interviews[5] with First Nations people formed the methodology employed for data collection. Drawing from my qualitative data, I will give force and saliency to my argument that First Nations are, indeed, diasporic. This is a qualitative study and as Regna Darnell suggests, data analysis will "explore the storied experience relevant to the domain of explanation."[6] It is the pattern of personal experiences that explains and corroborates our theoretical concepts. The first part of this paper will provide a theoretical framework and historical background of First Nations people as diasporic. In the second section, theoretical constructs are tested against ethnographic examples in order to explain how First Nations experience urban areas as spaces of diaspora. This chapter contributes significantly to the ongoing discourse on First Nations urban experience.[7]

First Nations Diasporas: Grounding Remarks

During the past few decades, social science and humanities scholars have failed to clarify what the "field" of diaspora or refugee studies means. Thus, one can argue that there is an epistemological inconsistency within it.[8] Importantly, Nicholas Van Hear argues that research on forced migration, the displaced, the uprooted and on refugee people must remain an "open" field, rather than one of narrow thinking and dead ends.[9] As such, this study is a vivid example of that "openness," in its call for the inclusion and conceptualization of First Nations peoples as *diasporas*. According to Clifford, diasporas are "dispersed networks of peoples who share common historical experiences of dispossession, displacement, adaptation and so forth.... United by similar claims to 'firstness' on the land and by common histories of decimation and marginality, these alliances often deploy diasporist visions of return to an original place."[10]

First Nations peoples "are unique: neither immigrants nor European founders, they were here first,"[11] and thus they share different historical processes of displacement. At the same time, they resist and negotiate social realities of poverty, violence, racism, lack of services, political isolation, and economic inequalities; it is feasible then to define them as diasporic communities.[12]

The state's ability to "*impose* boundaries, to *limit* who may come and go within specific areas" tends to enforce people's displacements, which may account for the "ongoing project of legibility ... that aims at manipulating society."[13] The conceptualization of a First Nations diaspora must include the fact that these peoples have been subject to states' projects of *legibility*, such as their historical experiences of forced displacement and enforced sedentarization.[14] The state "makes the general population legible to itself" through multiple techniques, such as monitoring, counting, assessing, managing categories, and imposing "simplifications" in order to treat people according to the state's "schemata."[15] If a state knows its legible society then it will increase the probability of implementing successful interventions and planning new social orders such as, changing health practices and employment standards.[16] Another good example is the reserve system created for First Nations in Canada.[17]

If a state lacks knowledge about its legible population, then social engineering projects may have a devastating effect on targeted populations.[18] In other words, if the state incorporates "practical knowledge" about and needs of subaltern groups in its planning, then we will encounter an escalating trend in the successfulness of social engineering projects like health practices, employment and housing.[19] Michel-Rolph Trouillot suggests that the "legibility effect" is the knowledge and language needed for governance and the creation "of theoretical and empirical tools that classify and regulate collectivities."[20] There is also recent interest in how targeted populations experience the legibility effect.[21]

The British and Canadian states forced the displacement and sedentarization (through the reserve system) of First Nations people through policies and legislation.[22] Canadian Indian policy and legislation emerged from the state's interest in making the population legible to itself, as well as dominant group motives and values that historically intertwined with Indians, their families, and communities.[23] Alain Cunningham identifies the traditional era for studying the Indian policy-making in Canada, which included the assimilation and segregation of Indians that culminated with the creation of a Reserve system.[24] Moreover, the laws of a nation are a formal expression of policies that govern various areas of our lives. Early Indian legislation followed a top-down model, where non-Indian state officials and their advisors designed the legislation that, in principle, governed the lives of Indians who were "protected" and "subordinated" by these laws.[25] The legislation created by the British and Canadian authorities for governing "Indians" is multiple and contradictory.[26] In order to fully comprehend the historical displacement and dispossession of First Nations, we must look at the traditional Indian policy-making era in conjunction with the legislation that gave force and saliency to those policies.

Indian Policy and Indian Displacement in the Traditional Indian-Policy Era

The Royal Proclamation of 1763 represents the basis of Britain's paternalistic Indian policy where Indians were treated as infants (children) in need of protection. This proclamation established a boundary line between "Indian" and European lands while establishing and legitimizing the Crown's right to purchase such lands. At the same time, the Crown legitimized the acquisition, sale, and purchase of First Nations lands by non-Natives, which reinforced a pervasive and "fraudulent" way of acquiring Indian lands that had taken place since the earliest encounters.[27] Thus, the Royal Proclamation created new avenues of fraud and frictions between the state, its representatives, Indians, and settlers. These frauds were confirmed by the special Sub-Committee of the Aborigines Protection Society, who clearly outlined in its 1839 report "the unjust and improvident manner in which the land of the Indians has been dealt with by us [British government],—their insecurity of title,—and their actual removal from it in late remarkable cases under an oppressive and fraudulent treaty,—and by unjust contract."[28]

In 1791, the British Parliament passed the Constitutional Act, which divided the territory known as New France into two regions: Upper Canada, located west of the Saint Lawrence River, currently known as the Province of Ontario; and Lower Canada, currently known as the Province of Quebec. The Indian Department also experienced administrative changes that pertained to those controlling the department's affairs in Upper and Lower Canada. Emphasis will be placed on Upper Canada given that the City of London falls within the limits of this geographical area. In Upper Canada, overall control was under the lieutenant governor, while the military secretary remained in charge of the Indian Department in Lower Canada.[29] Under these individuals were a series of superintendents who controlled and implemented state policies; the London region falls under the jurisdiction of the Western District.[30]

At the end of the eighteenth century and the beginning of the nineteenth century, an advocacy group known as the Humanitarians supported activities (e.g., agriculture, Christianity) that protected and civilized Indigenous people in the new colonies.[31] This initiative was soon embraced by British governments that objected to the high costs of the annual "presents" to the Indigenous population to maintain relationships and more easily acquire their lands. By 1830, this British policy of "Indian Friendship" became a "Civilization policy." It was unofficially implemented by missionaries (Methodists, Anglicans, Baptists, Roman Catholics, and Moravians), teachers, instructors, and officially appointed agents who targeted Indigenous people in a project to make them "full members of the society" and wards of the government.[32]

In 1828, General Darling (Indian agent) reported to Earl Dalhousie, Secretary of State:

> The Mississaquas of Rice Lake, consisting of 317 souls and the Mohawks of Bay of Quinti, do not exceed 319 souls.—Of these the Mississaquas of Bay of Quinti and the rice Lake have recently been converted to Christianity by the Methodist society, who have introduced missionaries among the Indians here and in part of Upper Canada.... It is undoubted they have done some good, by influencing the Indians to embrace Christianity, and have inculcated the first

> principles of civilization, particularly in the tribes now under consideration, which shows itself in the desire which they have recently expressed to be collected in a village, and have lands allotted them for cultivation.
>
> Chippawas under the Chief Yellow Head—These Indians amount upon an average to 550 souls; they occupy the lands about Lake Simcoe, Holland River, and the unsettled county in the rear of York. They have expressed a strong desire to be admitted to Christianity, and to adopt the habits of civilized life...
>
> Mohawks of the Six Nations.—Under 2,000 souls are settled on the banks the Ouse, or Grand River, a fine and fertile tract of country which was purchase from the Chippawas (the Aborigines) exclusively from them when they were brought to this country from the Mohawk River, in the state of New York, at the termination of the revolutionary American war.... Their knowledge of farming is exceedingly limited, being chiefly confined to the cultivation of Indian corn, beans and potatoes; but those of more industrious habits follow the example of their white neighbours, and have separate farms, on which they raise most kind of English grain.
>
> Mississaquas of the Credit.—The present state of this tribe, amounting to 180 souls, who were lately notorious for drunkenness and debauchery, affords in my humble opinion the strongest encouragement to extend to the other tribes now exposed to Christianity and civilization the experiment that has been tried by his Excellency Sir Peregrine Maitland.... They are now settled in a delightful spot on the banks of the Credit [River], about 16 miles from York, in a village consisting of 20 substantial log huts, 18 feet by 24, having an upper story or garret to each. They have a school-house for the boys (in which is combined decent arrangement for the performance of the divine service, which is regularly attended,) and another for the girls.... They have two enclosures of about seven acres of wheat, and a field on the banks of the river, containing about 35 acres of Indian corn, in a promising state of cultivation.[33]

In Upper Canada, Lieutenant Governor Peregrine Maitland encouraged Methodist projects directing Indigenous settlements towards agriculture, where the people were "civilized" and Christianized. Thus, settled Indigenous people received instruction in agriculture, husbandry, and Christianity; they also received rations of seeds, agricultural tools, and assistance in building houses.[34] In 1830, Sir John Colborne, Indian agent, followed a similar course of action as he described in his report to Sir George Murray, Secretary of State: "I have directed houses to be built for them on detached lots, and they are now clearing ground sufficient to establish farms at each station for their immediate support ... experienced farmers have been engaged to instruct them, and school masters appointed to educate their children."[35] He further mentions that in the area of the Thames and Lake St. Clair, "similar measures are on trial at the Indian stations."[36] These settlements became the basis of the reserve system in Canada and a "social laboratory where the Indian could be prepared for coping with the European," which in turn also meant that the First Nations population was in the process of becoming legible to its rulers.[37]

Despite the claims of Indian agents and superintendents about the success of Indian farming settlements and civilization programs, Sir Francis Bond Head, the lieutenant governor of Upper Canada from 1836 to 1838, was convinced of quite the opposite: the failure of the civilization policy.[38] He promoted his own program of "removal" and segregation of Indigenous peoples to specific and isolated territories, such as the Manitoulin Island chain along the North Shore of Lake Huron and Georgian Bay.[39] There Indigenous people, according to Head, were able to fish, hunt, shoot birds, and gather fruit without the presence of white people. Moreover, they had to surrender their "vast and fertile" lands that were greatly needed by the colonists and "hailed with joy by the whole Province."[40] Head arranged land cessions from Ojibwa and Ottawa leaders from Manitoulin Island, as well as from the Saugeen Ojibwas of the Bruce Peninsula, and other Ojibwa tribes who fell under his jurisdiction.[41] However, the findings of the Sub-Committee of the Aborigines Protection Society's stated that the First Nations people "accept the elements of civilization at our [British] hands, as well to be gradually incorporated with the colonists."[42] Thus, the British Parliament rejected Bond Head's scheme of removal but not the idea of land cessions through treaties.[43] Nevertheless, the allegedly successful Christianization, civilization, and settlement of the "Indians"[44] encountered resistance. Not only did First Nations people resist moving to the new territories but some colonists also expressed indifference, hostility, and obstruction.[45]

The policy of removal was not only a social engineering project forcing displacement of First Nations people from their original hunting and gathering territories to live on villages and later, reserves; but it was also a contributing factor in the development of assimilationist policies that continued throughout the twentieth century.[46] By the 1850s, a new version of "smaller reserves for individual bands located next to or near European–Canadian communities"[47] was enforced through legislation in Canada.

Indian Legislation Pertaining to Land Displacement and Indian Civilization

In 1850, the *Act for the protection of the Indians in Upper Canada from imposition, and the property occupied or enjoyed by them from trespass and injury* was enacted to protect First Nations and their property. These acts not only "protected" their lands from scheming whites, but also prohibited taxation on the land occupied by "Indians" or persons married to them:

> No taxes shall be levied or assessed ... for or in respect of any of the said Indian lands, nor shall any taxes or assessments whatsoever be levied or imposed upon any Indian or any person inter-married with any Indian so long as he, she or they shall reside on Indian lands not ceded to the Crown, or which having been ceded may have been again set apart by the Crown for the occupation of Indians.[48]

Furthermore, the government undertook to encourage "civilizing pursuits" among First Nations peoples through multiple strategies such as the practice of agriculture.[49] The "civilization" of First Nations was specifically addressed and legislated in the 1857 legislation entitled the *Act to encourage the gradual Civilization of the Indian Tribes in this Province, and to amend the Laws respecting Indians*. The ultimate goal of "civilization" was to remove all legal distinctions between "Indians" and "non-Indians" and to integrate the former into mainstream society. The term "enfranchised" was introduced in this act:

> The Visiting Superintendent of each Tribe of Indians, for the time being, the Missionary to such Tribe for the time being, and such other person as the Governor shall appoint from time to time for that purpose, shall be Commissioners of examining Indians, being members of such Tribe, who may desire to avail themselves of this Act ... and such Commissioners shall meet for the said purposes at such places and times as the Superintendent General of Indian affairs shall from time to time to time direct, and shall have full power to make such examination and inquiry: and if such Commissioners shall report in writing to the Governor that any such Indian of the male sex, and not under twenty-one years of age, is able to speak, read and write either the [E]nglish or the [F]rench language readily and well, and is sufficiently advanced in the elementary branches of education and is of good moral character and free from debt, then it shall be competent to the Governor to cause notice to be given in the Official Gazette of the Province, that such *Indian is enfranchised* under this Act.[50]

Thus, First Nations men aged between twenty-one and forty, with good morals, free of debts, "of sober and industrious habits," and able to speak English or French were eligible to relinquish their Status Indian identity and to embrace their new "Christian" names and lands allotted to them. These pieces of legislation gave force and saliency to early Indian policy that pertained to protection, confinement, assimilation, and civilization of First Nations people.[51] However, as time progressed, not many chose to enfranchise, forcing the federal government to create other pieces of legislation that better ensured and enforced their enfranchisement.[52] With minor revisions, the concept of enfranchisement remained a key component of Indian policy until 1985, when Bill C-31 abolished it and many, but not all, First Nations people regained their Status and band membership, including the right to hold property and live on-reserve.[53]

Established in 1867, the Dominion of Canada included the following provinces Ontario, Quebec, New Brunswick and Nova Scotia. The federal government of Canada continued the Indian policy inherited from Britain and its former colonies. In 1868 Canada enacted the first piece of National legislation: *An Act providing for the organisation of the Department of the Secretary of State of Canada, and for the management of Indian and Ordenance Lands.* This act "merely incorporated the earlier colonial legislation concerning Indian lands ... the only definitions of who was an Indian and the penalties imposed for trespass on Indian lands."[54]

In 1876, the first *Indian Act* consolidated previous legislation and served as the mechanism to distinguish between "Indians" and "non-Indians" and to make "Indians" become legible to the state by promoting and enforcing settlement.[55] The state agent, the minister of the Interior, controlled and managed everything pertaining to them and their lands. The task of defining who was and who was not an Indian (Status), land tenure, on-reserve governance, taxes, health, and government fiduciary responsibilities were consolidated across time through the various *Indian Acts*.[56]

Darnell, however, suggests that First Nations people in Canada have been neither sedentary nor assimilated.[57] Instead, they move from reserves to urban centres and vice-versa. It is questionable whether the "permanence of residence is an appropriate index of the strategies people actually use to decide where they will live at a given moment."[58] Simply put, some First Nations people who live in urban centres do not cease to be "Native" or "Indian," and it is precisely their decision-making strategies for subsistence (e.g., poverty, employment, education, health, skills development) that trigger the persistence of their diasporic culture regardless of the place in which they dwell. Thus, my argument is that some contemporary First Nations people dwelling in the cities are "diasporas within the states."[59] One of Jonathan Boyarin and Daniel Boyarin's major theoretical contributions to understanding diaspora is the inclusion of "cultural dynamics" and the persistence of "specific identities."[60] Thus, I argue that urban First Nations people not only carry a historical sense of displacement from their original territories, but these populations also identify themselves according to their First Nation, which might be a reserve near London or one across Canada. Moreover, they cherish the hope, or at least there is a desire, to return to their "home" or reserve at some point in time. It is the particulars of this argument that need to be further discussed by looking at the urban First Nations people dwelling in the City of London.

The Faces of London

The Urban Presence of First Nations People

The 2006 census data shows that 72.1% of the off-reserve Aboriginal population lives in urban centres, compared to 26.3% who live on reserves. Statistics Canada also reports a total of 12,028,895 inhabitants in the Province of Ontario; 2%, or 242,495 reported having at least some Aboriginal ancestry, an increase of 1.29% from the 2001 census.[61]

The research area is the City of London, which is an urban centre located in southwestern Ontario, midway between Toronto and Windsor, and the seat of the Middlesex County. This is the thirteenth-largest city in Canada and the fifth-largest in Ontario with a total population of 452,575 habitants; the Aboriginal population represents 1.37% (n=6,195) although this is dramatically underestimated since "historically, Aboriginal people have been reluctant participants in the census for a variety of reasons."[62] As Joseph stated, "we [referring to Natives] are more than that."[63]

London is one of the major cities to which First Nations people migrate from reserves and from other cities across Canada; their presence permeates different spaces within the urban spectrum, including, but not limited to, non-government Native organizations, shopping centres, coffee places, university, college, shelters, libraries, health centres, neighbourhoods, and parks. This city also represents a unique site for conducting research among the First Nations population given the proximity of First Nations communities like Walpole Island, the Oneida Nation of the Thames, Chippewas of Sarnia, Chippewas of Kettle and Stony Point, Moravian of the Thames, Six Nations of the Grand River, Chippewa of the Thames, Mississaugas of New Credit, Muncey, and Caldwell Nation. This is not to say that First Nations people living in London exclusively belong to those reserves but rather to quantify the constant mobility occurring from reserves or settlements to urban centres, and vice versa.[64]

In a twelve-month period, 22% of Aboriginal people moved, compared with only 14% of the non-Aboriginal population.[65] The 2006 census emphasizes the high mobility of the Aboriginal population in Ontario: 50% First Nations people did not live at the same address 5 years prior to the census.[66] Thus, we cannot think of Aboriginal populations as residing "permanently" in London or any other city since their residential patterns are complex and may last from a couple of months to decades.[67]

The presence of First Nations peoples in London is not a recent social phenomenon. It is part of the social fabric of this place since before colonization. The continuing migration of First Nations people to urban areas is indeed, a "reality" documented and recognized by the Canadian government, the media, research firms, and scholars.[68] This is an important acknowledgement that First Nations people have neither been assimilated nor eliminated in spite of the myriad attempts exerted by the Canadian government through various policies, programs, projects, and institutions such as the disenfranchisement of Indians and the elimination of their political institutions.[69] This is London, a city of contrasts and extremes, the place where my research began in the summer of 2003.

Encountering the City

The bus route along Richmond and Dundas was part of my journey for five years—the buildings, stores, houses, green areas, and parking lots seem familiar. The heart of London is the downtown area with its intersecting streets, like the corner of Dundas and Richmond or King and Dundas. These are places where people "hang around" and experience the city in a way that can be called the "art of straying."[70] In other words, people lose themselves and seem not "to find [their] way in the city" and, at the same time the conflicting fact is that the city discloses itself to us the "walkers."[71]

A similar experience accounted for my innermost thoughts during my first months of fieldwork in the downtown area, walking the streets back and forth, looking at the homeless, those stranded with drugs and alcohol, the drug dealers, and those who are, in increasing numbers, young smokers, parents, and loiterers with different cultural backgrounds and skin colours. Then I look again and there is the other scenery: the business or casual dress, the suit properly fitted, the expensive cars driving through, the look of success rather than hopelessness. This is the look from the street. My fieldwork notes cannot reflect the full reality; this is just a partial view, a partial exploration of the city. What is a city? Perhaps it is a place where such extremes meet.

Michel de Certeau might have fruitful and illuminating responses to my query. He explored the practices of every day life and conceptualizes cities as "migrational or metaphorical" spatial practices.[72] The planned and readable city is a mere chimera, an imaginary totalization. The streets are places where the extremes collide: "extremes of ambition and degradation, brutal oppositions of races and styles, contrasts between yesterday's buildings, already transformed into trash cans, and today's urban irruptions that block out its space."[73]

My first exploration of London occurred in the summer of 2003. Since then, I have been conducting fieldwork and building rapport with the Aboriginal community while working as a research assistant for Dr. Regna Darnell in a project related to operationalizing the "accordion model of Algonquian social organization."[74] This research experience honed my interviewing skills in the field and proved to be fruitful and illuminating during my second phase of fieldwork in 2006.

First Nations People and London

For the past two centuries, First Nations histories have been presented by academic authorities who did not have to give up their own land, ideals, dreams, culture, history, and freedom. Since the last quarter of the twentieth century, Native and non-Native scholars' "battle for truth" remains central in presenting an ethnographic and historical account of the primitive or colonized from a questionable standpoint of cultural relativism.[75] It must be remembered that anthropological research "begins with immersion in local experience and local knowledge."[76] Ethnographic research is one way to achieve "face-to-face interaction with particular individuals and communities over a substantial period of time" and through this process the researcher might come to understand and interpret larger political economic and cultural contexts of "local" populations.[77]

Fieldwork encompasses "deep hanging out" and listening to the stories First Nations people tell about the people who are part of their lives, to gossip, and to tales of their experiences, places, surroundings.[78] The community experience provides a template for that of the individual.[79] From 2006 to 2007 I conducted open-ended interviews (n=20) with members of the Aboriginal community.[80] This section encompasses the interviews conducted with ten individuals from 2004 to 2007 (see Table 10.1). My interviews focused on First Nations peoples' experiences within the city, such as the reasons they left their "home" place (or reserve) and moved to the city (n=10) their home base was a reserve), and their struggles to access the programs and services available to them through Native non-government organizations.[81] The collection and analysis of qualitative data is extremely complex and not convertible into standard measurable units of objects seen and heard.[82] Qualitative data vary at the level of abstraction, frequency of occurrence, and source.[83] For the goals envisioned in this case study, sampling was irrelevant to my qualitative research design. In addition to the qualitative data, my collaborators responded to some questions pertaining to demographics, such as age, gender, living arrangements, and dwelling accommodations. Table 10.1 summarizes the findings.

Fifty percent of the population fell between 45 and 60 years of age. Their gender is almost equally distributed, considering that 60% were women. Over half of the First Nations population interviewed is either single or divorced/separated (n=6). Another 40% reported to be either married or living in common-law relationships. Family size varies: 40% have one to two children; 20% reported three to four children; and 20% reported no children at all. Family composition in urban centres may include single parents with one or two children dwelling in the household. Almost half of the First Nations population lives alone. Only 20% live with extended family like aunts or cousins. These findings create a dialogue with the resonant discourse surrounding urban First Nations people, suggesting that they practise living arrangements and household composition like "back home" or "back on the rez" where "people tend to have more children than does the average mainstream society [which has 1–2]."[84] Future research needs to explore these new lines of inquiry. The challenge will be to identify and collect demographic data from First Nation families dwelling in urban centres.

The majority of Aboriginal people dwell in apartments (60%) compared to 40% who live in houses; only 20% are owners. Affordable housing is one of the major challenges that many residents in London face. The City of London has recognized this problem, and in 2005 launched an Affordable Housing Strategy for the City of London, targeting the main housing needs, including those of the Aboriginal population.[85] To date this problem remains: a good number of bureaucratic meetings have taken place but no action or solution has altered the status quo of Native housing or co-ops.

All of my collaborators emphasized their desire to go "home" or "back to the rez," despite their continued displacement to other cities, some of them outside the Province of Ontario. While some said that London represented the first city in which they lived off-reserve (n=3). For others London was

Table 10.1 Demographics of First Nations People Interviewed in London

Study Variable (n=10)	Percent
Age	
Under 25 years of age	10
25-45 years of age	40
45-60 years of age	50
Female Gender	60
Current Marital Status	
Single/divorced/separated	60
Married	20
Common law	20
Number of Children	
None	20
One or two	40
Three or four	20
Five	10
Nine	10
Type of Dwelling	
House	40
Apartment	60
Own or Rent Dwelling	
Rent	80
Own	20
Living Arrangements	
Living by yourself	50
Living with your child or children	30
Living with your aunts/cousins	20
Return to your "home" (Reserve)	
Yes	100

just another city added to their list (n=7). Additionally "neither the Reserve nor the city represents a permanent residence for Indians who struggle to subsist in both worlds."[86] What we are witnessing is a "reified nomadic pattern" that has been continuously practised by First Nations people despite their forced displacement and the sedentary policies in place by the Canadian government. Within this framework, I now turn to discuss the experiences of Aboriginal people residing temporarily in London.

Neither from Here nor from There: Moving to the City

For some First Nations people, London represents their site of birth but was not their place of residence until they left their reserve, which is usually located a short distance from the city. Others may move from reserves located in other provinces or from the United States. In addition to First Nation people, Métis and Inuit also dwell in this city. There is no single factor that may trigger the migration of Aboriginal people to urban areas, but rather these are "moments of decision-making" where multiple, complex, and intertwined crises prompt individuals to leave their "home" and relocate.[87] Rene's account provides a glimpse of the kind of crises that First Nations people encounter at home:

> My Dad decided ... wanted me to leave ... because it was social and less healthy on reserve ... ahhh ... there was drinking ... lots of drinking involved and he knew there was going to be problem so he did not want me to be part of that. So just before Christmas, he told me to leave gave me some money and I left the reserve. I was about 16 maybe 17 at that time when I left and I left with my brother who was working in a small town.
>
> We didn't understand the reserve in my path. My Mom will go up to the trap line ... from the fall right to the winter and then in the spring. During the summer my Dad will guide the Americans ... the fishermen will come in the summer and then in the fall and they will come back to the reserve and buy the supplies for the winter. [He will] go back all over the trap line [and] we did that. But we were taken to residential school when I was seven so we were in residential school from the end of August to June. We will come back by the end of June we stayed for the summer and then go back again ... We did that through elementary school and then through high school ... and ... most of the summers we spent with my Mom and Dad and then most of the falls through the spring I was in residential school. And so while I was in residential school ... in grade ten when they all started dropping off ... my support system my brothers dropped out of school, my cousins dropped out of school, and then friends started dropping out of school and I was the only one that was left at the high school. I didn't make it after that ...
>
> So I left, it was spring so I guess it was my grade ten and then I went back up north with my Mother and Father and did a little trapping with them. And I went in the summer with them and did more trapping. That's when my Dad told me again he says: "you know trapping isn't a life anymore." Because I didn't have the skills perhaps in trapping ... because I was in school all this time. I didn't have the skills to survive on the wilderness. So I went back to

> school (in a city located in the northern part of Ontario) got my high school degree, then I went took a couple of courses. It was hard for me to go back ... I kind of adjust to. I got my grade 12 but then I decided to do something better. I went back to school and took more credits ... and went back again to get more credits to get a job in teaching.[88]

Rene's father envisioned the challenges and accommodations that his son and his people would need to make in order to survive in an off-reserve environment. Neither trapping nor any other traditional mode of subsistence meant "survival" in the first half of the twentieth century. This scenario has not changed on reserves in the present day: "there is nothing, there are no jobs the unemployment rate is sky high and with all the alcohol down there [referring to the reserve]."[89] In other words, the vast majority of reserves in Canada are poverty-stricken.[90]

Sami, a 2006 resident of London, moved from one place to another due to her parents' work and better living:

> I was born here in London, in Victoria Hospital. My family move out of the reserve in 1959 he and my Mom decided to live their life for God and he went to bible school in Minnesota for some years. We were out reserve for about 7 years maybe.... We were seven of us, we all move back in 1969 but then my two older brothers decided they didn't like it and move back to Canada. They were older 14 or 15 maybe. All my relatives live on reserve, except for my mom and my dad [both deceased]. I have two brothers and a younger sister living there.
>
> We lived in Wisconsin and North Dakota so my Dad moved around because of his job [preacher] ... we didn't lived on reserve we lived in a little town next to the reserves, right ... It was like one of the town because I didn't know that I was different, I didn't know I was brown, I didn't know that I was a living [name of reserve]. You know, because the people that we lived with, they all welcomed my parents and embraced my whole family. So I didn't know any colours, I did not know any differences in Aboriginals. I have no idea that I was one ... I didn't even know that.
>
> I was four when we moved [to her home reserve] and I didn't even know like nobody, not even my own family when we moved eh ... So coming back and moving forward was really, really different.[91]

When Sami returned to her reserve she felt alienated, but after a few years she identified with her community and people. Again, given the lack of opportunities and poverty after living ten years on-reserve she had to move to London. "It is difficult to leave home and more difficult to find your way in the city," as Joe said while he ate his burger and fries at the Covent Market. Joe came by himself and the only person he knew was his cousin who was living in London at that time:

> She helped me ... you know, I didn't have a place to stay, no food, no clothes, no money ... just myself. Thinking that maybe I will make money here and there, perhaps meet someone and start a family. I didn't know what to do or where to go. I called her from the street ... someone gave me a ride [I mistakenly asked him if he took the bus].... Holy shit, there are no buses on reserve, you get your own car, pay for the trip or get a ride. I got a ride but that's it.
>
> Still remember the first time I called Lisa, it was over there [pointing to Dundas and Richmond] and it was really stressful but I did it.[92]

Many First Nations people need only "one contact" who will provide help and shelter while the newcomer gets used to the dynamics of the city. As Carol stated, "I lived with my auntie, I took the bus and get off Dundas. I walked to Nokee Kwe [Native Non-government organization providing employment and training services] for my training and I know a few people there."[93]

Some urban First Nations do not cease to be "Indians" and moving away from poverty (e.g., lack of employment, education, housing) and the revival of their Indian identity in urban centres is what actually triggers the persistence of their diasporic culture regardless of the place in which they dwell at any given moment.[94] Moreover, the majority of the First Nations people interviewed (n=10) expressed their desired to return to their "home" or reserve at some point in time. Thus Joe, who left his reserve ten years ago, cherishes the hope to go back to "home" and retire when "the time has come to go back."[95]

First Nations people dwelling in the cities are a diaspora not only because they carry a historical sense of displacement from their original territories but also because these populations find themselves separated from their on-reserve territories. Today being a member of the First Nations diaspora is primarily related to First Nations' claim as original peoples to land and territories that go "beyond" the national frontiers.

Conclusion

This chapter represents an effort to stimulate a discussion that will lead to further rethinking of First Nations as a diaspora in Canada. The histories, complexities, realities, and premises posed in this paper about urban First Nations people are an example of how the academia should question and rethink theoretical constructs closely intertwined with social practices. Social actors may challenge and/or contribute to our understanding of them, and I hope that this study will represent a major substantive contribution to the comparative study of diaspora in Canada, to the diversity of the First Nation experience in cities, and to the nature of empires.

First Nations people dwelling in urban centres are a diaspora because they carry a historical sense of displacement from their original territories and some continue to experience a continual dispersal from their on-reserve territories to urban areas across Canada. There is a strong desire to "go back home" or "back to the rez," even if this place might represent an imagined sense of community. Arjun Appadurai states that "displacement and exile, migration and terror create powerful attachments to ideas of homeland that seem more deeply territorial than ever"; thus the challenge will be for the nation-state to work with and tolerate this diversity and, at the same time, making this diverse population legible to the state.[96]

The present study has some limitations. Future studies need to explore the experiences of other First Nations people living in other urban centres. In addition, a longitudinal and comparative study of the experiences of on- and off-reserve First Nations peoples might bring fruitful contributions that will broaden our understanding of diaspora not only within Canada but across the borderland (with the United States and Mexico). As well, we need to examine the dynamics that are in place at the local and national level. Even though my study was mostly centred at the local level, a macro analysis of the economic, political, and cultural dynamics that are in place may suggest productive action paths for First Nations communities, government, and non-government stakeholders.

Notes

An earlier version of this chapter was presented at the Mobility and Insecurity: Diasporas, Democracy, and Canada Workshop, York Centre for International and Security Studies (YCISS), at York University, Toronto. Funding for this research was awarded by the Democracy, Diasporas, and Canadian Security in International Perspective Research Award (2007–2008) and the YCISS. I would like to thank the anonymous reviewers and Karl Hele for their insightful comments and recommendations. Needless to say, I am responsible for the views and interpretations expressed in this chapter.

1 The term *First Nations people* refers to registered band member "Indians"; see *Indian Act 1985*: c. I-5 s. 10; Ward Churchill, *Acts of Rebellion: The Ward Churchill Reader* (New York: Routledge, 2003); Elizabeth Colson, "Forced Migration and the Anthropological Response," *Journal of Refugee Studies* 11 (2003): 1–18;

Peter Schmalz, *The Ojibwa of Southern Ontario* (Toronto: University of Toronto Press, 1991); John Steckley, *Full Circle Canada's First Nations* (Toronto: Prentice Hall, 2001).

2 Churchill, *Acts of Rebellion*, 141–42.

3 James Clifford, *Routes: Travel and Transformation in the Late Twentieth Century* (Cambridge: Harvard University Press, 1997), 253.

4 This chapter encompasses a section of the findings related to my doctoral dissertation research. I conducted fieldwork in London, Ontario, Canada (2003–2007) and used three kinds of field methods for data collection: open-ended interviews and life histories with Aboriginal peoples, Aboriginal leaders and Native non-government organizations (NNGOS) workers (twenty individuals); archival research; and participant observation within NNGOs and at community events. See María C. Manzano-Munguía, "Mediating Aboriginal–State Relations through Native Non-Governmental Organizations and Aboriginal Leaders: An Alternative Model," Ph.D. thesis, University of Western Ontario, 2009.

5 I conducted interviews in London, Ontario, with ten individuals from 2004 to 2007.

6 Regna Darnell, "Qualitative Demographics of Aboriginal Urban–Rural Migration: The Persistence of Nomadic Habits," Paper presented at the Canadian Anthropology Society, Halifax, 2003: 24–25.

7 For details on the diversity of First Nations experience in Canadian cities, see Environics Institute, *Urban Aboriginal Peoples Study, 2010* (Scarborough: Environics Institute, 2010), http://uaps.ca/wp-content/uploads/2010/03/UAPS-Main-Report_Dec.pdf, 2010; Heather Howard and Craig Proulx, eds., *Aboriginal Peoples in Canadian Cities: Transformations and Continuities* (Waterloo: Wilfrid Laurier University Press, 2011); David Newhouse, "Urban Life: Reflections of a Middle-Class Indian," in *Aboriginal Peoples in Canadian Cities: Transformations and Continuities*, ed. Heather Howard and Craig Proulx (Waterloo: Wilfrid Laurier University Press, 2011), 23–38; Evelyn Peters. "Emerging Themes in Academic Research in Urban Aboriginal Identities in Canada 1996–2010," *Aboriginal Policy Studies* 1, no. 1 (2011): 78–105; Craig Proulx, *Reclaiming Aboriginal Justice, Identity and Community* (Saskatoon: Purich, 2003) and "Aboriginal Identification in North American Cities," *Canadian Journal of Native Studies* 26, no. 2 (2005): 405–38.

8 See for details Jana Evans Braziel and Manita Mannur, eds., *Theorizing Diaspora* (Oxford: Blackwell Publishing, 2003); Robin Cohen, "Diaspora and the nation-state," *International Affairs* 72.3 (1996): 507–20; Gabriel Sheffer, *Diaspora Politics: At Home Abroad* (Cambridge: Cambridge University Press, 2003), 8–9. For details on the "black Atlantic" diasporic paths see Paul Gilroy, "The

Black Atlantic as a Counterculture of Modernity," in *Theorizing Diaspora:* eds. Jana Evans Braziel and Manita Mannur (Oxford: Blackwell Publishing, 2003), 49–80.

9 Van Hear, Editorial Introduction, *Journal of Refugee Studies,* Special Issue, 11 (1998): 341–49.

10 Clifford, *Routes,* 253.

11 Regna Darnell, "Canadian Anthropologists, the First Nations and Canada's Self-Image at the Millennium," *Anthropologica* 42 (2000): 165.

12 Clifford, *Routes,* 261.

13 James Scott, *Seeing Like a State: How Certain Schemes to Improve the Human Condition Have Failed* (New Haven: Yale University Press, 1998), 80.

14 Scott, *Seeing Like a State;* Michel-Rolph Trouillot,"The Anthropology of the State in the Age of Globalization: Close Encounters of the Deceptive Kind," *Current Anthropology* 42, no. 1 (2001): 125–38; see also María C. Manzano-Munguía, "Indian Policy and Legislation: Aboriginal Identity Survival in Canada," *Journal of Studies in Ethnicity and Nationalism* 11, no. 3 (2011): 404–26.

15 Trouillot, "Anthropology of the State," 126; Scott, *Seeing Like a State,* 82.

16 Scott, *Seeing Like a State,* 78.

17 John Tobias, "Protection, Civilization, Assimilation: An Outline History of Canada's Indian Policy," in *As Long as the Sun Shines and Water Flows: A Reader in Canadian Native Studies,* ed. Ian Getty and Antoine Lussier (Vancouver: University of British Columbia Press, 1983), 39–55.

18 Scott, *Seeing Like a State.*

19 Scott, *Seeing Like a State,* 78; Antonio Gramsci, *Selections from the Prison Notebooks,* ed. and transl. Quintin Hoare and Geoffrey Nowell Smith (New York: International, 1971), 57.

20 Trouillot, "Anthropology of the State," 126.

21 Veena Das and Deborah Poole, "State and Its Margins: Comparative Ethnographies," in *Anthropology in the Margins of the State,* ed. Veena Das and Deborah Poole (Santa Fe: School of American Research Press, 2004), 16; and more generally the other papers in this edited collection.

22 See *An Act for the gradual enfranchisement of Indians, the better management of Indian affairs, and to extend the provisions of the Act 31st Victoria,* Statutes of Canada 1869, c. 6 (32 Vict.); *An Act to encourage the gradual Civilization of the Indian Tribes in this Province,* 1857, 22 Vict., c. 26; Aborigines Protection Society, *Report on the Indians of Upper Canada* (London: William Ball, Arnold, 1839); and *Indian Act,* Statutes of Canada 1876, c. 18.

23 Scott, *Seeing Like a State,* 80; see also Menno Boldt, *Surviving as Indians* (Toronto: University of Toronto Press, 1993); Leroy Little Bear, Menno Boldt, and

J. Anthony Long, eds., *Pathways to Self-determination: Canadian Indians and the Canadian State* (Toronto: University of Toronto Press, 1984); Rick Pointing and Roger Gibbins, *Out of Irrelevance: A Socio-political Introduction to Indian Affairs in Canada* (Toronto: Butterworths, 1980); and Sally Weaver, *Making Canadian Indian Policy: The Hidden Agenda, 1968–1970* (Toronto: University of Toronto Press, 1981).

24 See also Alain Cunningham, *Canadian Indian Policy and Development Planning Theory* (New York: Garland, 1999), 3; 31. Tobias, "Protection, Civilization, Assimilation," 41.

25 See Menno Boldt and Anthony Long, "Native Indian Self-Government: Instrument of Autonomy or Assimilation?" in *Governments in Conflict? Provinces and Indian Nations in Canada*, ed. Anthony Long, Menno Boldt, and Leroy Little Bear (Toronto: University of Toronto Press, 1988), 38–56; and Thomas Isaac, *Aboriginal Law: Commentary, Cases and Materials* (Saskatoon: Purich, 2004).

26 See Isaac, *Aboriginal Law*; Delia Opekokew, *The Political and Legal Inequities among Aboriginal Peoples in Canada* (Kingston: Institute of Intergovernmental Relations, 1987); and Joe Sawchuk, "Negotiating an Identity: Métis Political Organizations, the Canadian Government, and Competing Concepts of Aboriginality," *American Indian Quarterly* 25, no. 1 (2001): 73–84.

27 Tobias, "Protection, Civilization, Assimilation," 40.

28 Aborigines Protection Society, *Report on the Indians of Upper Canada*, 4.

29 Tobias, "Protection, Civilization, Assimilation."

30 See George Stanley, "As Long as the Sun Shines and Water Flows: An Historical Comment," in *As Long as the Sun Shines and Water Flows: A Reader in Canadian Native Studies*, ed. Ian Getty and Antoine Lussier (Vancouver: University of British Columbia Press, 1983): 1–26.

31 Tobias, "Protection, Civilization, Assimilation," 41.

32 Robert Surtees, "Canadian Indian Policies," in *Handbook of North American Indians: History of Indian–White Relations*, ed. William Sturtevant and Wilcomb Washburn (Washington: Smithsonian Institution, 1998), 88; see also Stanley, "As Long the Sun Shines"; Edward Rogers, "The Algonquian Farmers of Southern Ontario, 1830–1945," in *Aboriginal Ontario: Historical Perspectives on the First Nations*, ed. Edward S. Rogers and Donald B. Smith (Toronto: Durdurn Press, 1994), 122–66; and Tobias "Protection, Civilization, Assimilation."

33 General Darling to Earl Dalhousie, in *Report on the Indians of Upper Canada*, Aborigines Protection Society, 6–7.

34 Rogers, "Algonquian Farmers," 125; and Surtees, "Canadian Indian Policies," 88.

35 Sir John Colborne to Sir George Murray, in *Report on the Indians of Upper Canada*, Aborigines Protection Society, 15.

36 John Colborne to Sir George Murray, in *Report on the Indians of Upper Canada*, Aborigines Protection Society, 15.

37 Surtees, "Canadian Indian Policies, 88; Tobias, "Protection, Civilization, Assimilation," 41.

38 Rogers, "The Algonquian Farmers," 127; and Roger Nichols, *Indians in the United States and Canada: A Comparative History* (Lincoln: University of Nebraska Press, 1998), 190.

39 Nichols, *Indians in the United States and Canada*, 190; and Olive Patricia Dickason, *Canada's First Nations: A History of Founding Peoples from Earliest Times* (Oxford: Oxford University Press, 2002), 213.

40 Sir Francis Bond Head to Lord Glenelg, in *Report on the Indians of Upper Canada*, Aborigines Protection Society, 17–18. Italics in original.

41 Rogers, "Algonquian Farmers."

42 Aborigines Protection Society, *Report on the Indians of Upper Canada*, 5

43 Rogers, "Algonquian Farmers," 128.

44 Aborigines Protection Society, *Report on the Indians of Upper Canada*, 19.

45 Aborigines Protection Society, *Report on the Indians of Upper Canada*, 47; Stanley, "As Long as the Sun Shines," 9; and Surtees, "Canadian Indian Policies," 88–89.

46 See Surtees, "Canadian Indian Policies."

47 Tobias, "Protection, Civilization, Assimilation," 42.

48 *Act for the protection of the Indians in Upper Canada from imposition, and the property occupied or enjoyed by them from trespass and injury*, Statutes of the Province of Canada, 1850, c. 74, s. 4.

49 *Act for the protection of the Indians in Upper Canada.*

50 *Act to encourage the gradual Civilization of the Indian Tribes in this Province, and to amend the Laws respecting Indians, Statutes of the Province of Canada*, 1857, c. 26 s. III. Emphasis added.

51 See Tobias, "Protection, Civilization, Assimilation," 43; and Wayne Warry, *Ending Denial: Understanding Aboriginal Issues* (Toronto: Broadview, 2007).

52 See *An Act for the gradual enfranchisement of Indians, the better management of Indian affairs*, 1869; and *Indian Act*, 1876.

53 Bill C-31 retained the Euro-Canadian preference for male lineage as applied to Indian Status prior to 1985. The "second generation cut-off rule" applies one generation earlier for female Indians than their male counterparts who married and had children with non-Indians prior to 1985. This gender inequity was challenged by Sharon McIvor, a member of the Lower Nicola First Nation, in British Columbia's Supreme Court (see *McIvor v. Canada, Registrar of Indian and Northern Affairs*, 2007 BCSC 827). Bill C-3, *An Act to Promote Gender Equity*

in Indian Registration (short title: *Gender Equity in Indian Registration Act*) responded to the Court of Appeal for British Columbia decision in *McIvor v. Canada* and came into force on 5 April 2010. See for details Bill C-3, http://www.parl.gc.ca/HousePublications/Publication.aspx?Language=E&Mode=1&DocId=4901865; Parliament of Canada, http://www.parl.gc.ca/About/Parliament/LegislativeSummaries/bills_ls.asp?Language=E&ls=C3&Mode=1&Parl=40&Ses=3&source=library_prb; and the Canadian Bar Association, *Bill C-3: Gender Equity in Indian Registration Act,* http://www.nwac.ca/sites/default/files/imce/WEBSITES/201105-06/Bill%20C-3-eng1.pdf.

54 Tobias, "Protection, Civilization, Assimilation," 4.

55 *Indian Act*, 1876.

56 The current legislation is the *Indian Act 1985*. See Dickason, *Canada's First Nations*, for details on the *Indian Act* and its numerous amendments.

57 For a recent study involving Aboriginal people dwelling in urban centres, see Environics Institute, *Urban Aboriginal Peoples Study*.

58 Regna Darnell, "Qualitative Demographics of Aboriginal Urban–Rural Migration: The Persistence of Nomadic Habits," *Proceedings of the 35th Algonquian Conference*, ed. H. Wolfart (Winnipeg: University of Manitoba, 2004), 7.

59 Jonathan Boyarin and Daniel Boyarin, *Powers of Diaspora: Two Essays on the Relevance of Jewish Culture* (Minneapolis: University of Minnesota Press, 2002), 22.

60 Boyarin and Boyarin, *Powers of Diaspora*, 23. In contrast, Ramirez's term Native diaspora refers to "landless Natives' imagining and maintaining connections with their tribal nations ... to the development of intertribal networks and connections within and across different nation-states"; see Renya Ramirez, *Native Hubs: Culture, Community, and Belonging in Silicon Valley and Beyond* (London: Duke University Press, 2007), 11.

61 Aboriginal people include Indian, Inuit, and Métis as defined by the *Constitution Act 1982*, s. 35, and the Canadian Charter of Rights and Freedoms 1982, s. 25, part 1. See Statistics Canada, "Aboriginal Identity Population by Age Group, Median Age and Sex, 2006 counts, for Canada, Provinces and Territories," 6 October 2010, www12.statcan.ca/census-recensement/2006/dp-pd/hlt/97-558/pages/page.cfm?Lang=E&Geo=PR&Code=01&Table=1&Data=Count&Sex=1&Age=1&StartRec=1&Sort=2&Display=Page.

62 Statistics Canada, "Aboriginal Identity"; Canadian Press, "Number of Aboriginal People Living in Toronto Continues to Grow," *CBC News*, 15 January 2008, www.cbc.ca/canada/toronto/story/2008/01/15/tto-census.html/

63 Personal communication, 2004.

64 Regna Darnell, "Rethinking Band and Tribe Community and Nation: An Accordion Model of Nomadic Native North American Social Organization," *Papers of the 29th Algonquian Conference*, ed. David Pentland (Winnipeg: University of Manitoba, 1998), 98–105.

65 Statistics Canada, "Aboriginal Peoples of Canada in Census 2001," www12.statcan.ca/english/census01/products/analytic/companion/abor/canada.cfm#2.

66 Statistics Canada, "Aboriginal Identity," 2006.

67 Regna Darnell and María C. Manzano-Munguía, "Nomadic Legacies and Urban Algonquian Residence," *Papers of the 36th Algonquian Conference*, ed. H.C. Wolfart (Winnipeg: University of Manitoba, 2005), 173–86.

68 Royal Commission on Aboriginal Peoples, "Urban Perspectives," in *Report*, vol. 4, *Perspectives and Realities* (Ottawa: Canada Communication, 1996): 519–612; Tara Brautigam, "2006 Census: Aboriginal Profile: Dying Too Young," *London Free Press*, 18 January 2008, A3; Canadian Press, "Number of Aboriginal People"; and, Jennifer O'Brien, "Aboriginal Numbers Grow Quickly," *London Free Press*, 18 January 2008, A1–A3; Ekos Research Associates and Anishinabek Consultants Incorporation, *Survey of First Nations People Living Off-reserve, Metis and Inuit: Final Report to the Indian and Northern Affairs Canada* (Ottawa: Ekos Research Associates Incorporation, 2006); Environics Institute, *Urban Aboriginal Peoples Study*; Darnell, "Qualitative Demographics"; Darnell and Manzano-Munguía, "Nomadic Legacies"; Donald Fixico, *The Urban Indian Experience in America* (Alburqueque: University of New Mexico Press, 2000); Heather Howard and Craig Proulx, eds., *Aboriginal Peoples in Canadian Cities: Transformations and Continuities*; Bonita Lawrence, *Real Indians and Others Mixed-Blood Urban Native Peoples and Indigenous Nationhood* (London: University of Nebraska Press, 2004); David Newhouse, "Urban Life: Reflections of a Middle-Class Indian"; Evelyn Peters, "First Nations and Métis People and Diversity in Canadian Cities" (Montreal: Institute for Research on Public Policy. 2006), http://www.irpp.org/books/archive/AOTS3/peters.pdf); and Craig Proulx, *Reclaiming Aboriginal Justice, Identity and Community*, and "Aboriginal Identification in North American Cities."

69 See *An Act for the gradual enfranchisement of Indians*, 1869; and Little Bear, Boldt, and Long, *Pathways to Self-determination*.

70 Walter Benjamin, "A Berlin Chronicle," in *Selected Writings: Walter Benjamin*, ed. Marcus Bullock and Michael W. Jennings (Cambridge: Belknap, 1996), 598.

71 Benjamin, "A Berlin Chronicle," 598; Michel de Certeau, *The Practice of Everyday Life* (Los Angeles: University of California Press, 1984): 93.

72 de Certeau, Practice of Everyday Life, 93.

73 de Certeau, *Practice of Everyday Life*, 91.

74 Darnell, "Rethinking Band and Tribe" and "Qualitative Demographics"; and Darnell and Manzano-Munguía, "Nomadic Legacies."

75 Michael Foucault, "An Interview with Michel Foucault, October 25th, 1982," in *Technologies of the Self: A Seminar with Michel Foucault*, ed. L.H. Martin, H. Gutman, and P. Hutton (London: Tavistock, 1998), 531. See also Churchill, *Acts of Rebellion*; Vine Deloria, *Custer Died for Your Sins: An Indian Manifesto* (New York: Macmillan, 1969); "Conclusion: Anthros, Indians and Planetary Reality," in *Indians and Anthropologists*, ed. Vine Deloria Jr. (Arizona: University of Arizona Press, 1997), 209–21; Arturo Escobar, "The Making and Unmaking of the Third World Through Development," in *The Post-Development Reader*, ed. Majid Rahnema and Victoria Bawtree (Halifax: Fernwood, 1997), 85–93; Gustavo Esteva, "Basta! Mexican Indians say 'Enough!'" in *The Post-Development Reader*, ed. Majid Rahnema and Victoria Bawtree (Halifax: Fernwood, 1997): 302–6.

76 Eric Wolf, *Pathways of Power: Building an Anthropology of the Modern World* (Berkeley: University of California Press, 2001), 51.

77 Darnell, "Qualitative Demographics"; Stephen Schensul, Jean Schensul, and Margaret LeCompte, *Essential Ethnographic Methods: Observations, Interviews, and Questionnaires* (London: Altamira, 1999), 5. Some limitations to this method relate to time requirements for conducting the study and the process of "selecting" and conducting open-ended interviews (it could take months or years rather than a few hours or days); the impossibility to replicate ethnographic research given the conditions in which it is unfolded (natural setting and fieldwork connotations); and finally the small number of participants in a small-scale environment (for further details see James Clifford, "Notes on (Field)notes," in *Fieldnotes: The Makings of Anthropology*, ed. Roger Sanjek (Ithaca: Cornell University Press, 1990), 47–70; David Fetterman, *Ethnography: Step by Step; Applied Social Research Methods*, vol. 17 (London: Sage, 1998); and Nigel Rapport and Joanna Overing, *Social and Cultural Anthropology: The Key Concepts* (New York: Routledge, 2000).

78 Renato Rosaldo, *Culture and Truth* (Boston: Beacon, 1989).

79 Julie Cruikshank, *Life Lived Like a Story* (Lincoln: University of Nebraska Press, 1990); and Keith Basso, *Wisdom Sits in Places* (New Mexico: University of New Mexico Press, 1996).

80 Manzano-Munguía, "Mediating Aboriginal–State Relations." Collaborators who attended, visited, worked, accessed services, and/ or volunteered at Native non-governmental organizations were invited to participate in the study.

81 See Maria Manzano-Munguía, "Conceptualizing Native Non-Government Organizations in Canada: An Ethnographic Approach," *International Journal of Interdisciplinary Social Sciences* 2, no. 1 (2007): 449–59.
82 Norman Denzin and Yvonna Lincoln, *Handbook of Qualitative Research* (London: Sage, 1994).
83 Katherine Marshall, and Gretchen Rossman, *Designing Qualitative Research*, 2nd ed. (London: Sage, 1995), 112.
84 Chester Langille, quoted in Jennifer O'Brien, "Aboriginal Numbers Grow Quickly," *London Free Press*, 18 January 2008, section A.
85 London, *An Affordable Housing Strategy for the City of London* (London: London City Hall, 2005), 35.
86 Darnell and Manzano-Munguía, "Nomadic Legacies," 185.
87 Darnell and Manzano-Munguía, "Nomadic Legacies," 181.
88 Manzano-Munguía, interview with Rene 2006.
89 Manzano-Munguía, interview with Liliana 2007.
90 See Canada, First Nations and Inuit Health. Health Canada, http://www.hc-sc.gc.ca/fniah-spnia/pubs/aborig-autoch/index-eng.php; Peter Kulchyski, Don McCaskill and David Newhouse, eds., *In the Words of Elders: Aboriginal Cultures in Transition* (Toronto: University of Toronto Press, 2003); and Statistics Canada, "Aboriginal Identity."
91 Manzano-Munguía, interview with Sami 2006.
92 Manzano-Munguía, interview with Joe 2007.
93 Manzano-Munguía, interview with Carol 2006.
94 See Manzano-Munguía, "Mediating Aboriginal–State Relations."
95 Manzano-Munguía, interview with Joe 2007.
96 Arjun Appadurai, *Modernity at Large: Cultural Dimensions of Globalization* (Minneapolis: University of Minnesota Press, 1996): 176–77.

CHAPTER 11

Assessing Environmental Health Risks through Collaborative Research and Oral Histories: The Water Quality Issue at Walpole Island First Nation

Christianne V. Stephens and Regna Darnell

In his opening remarks to *Imperialism and the Natural World* (1990), historian John M. MacKenzie describes the divergent theoretical approaches applied to the study of imperial history in the late nineteenth century. These include those who viewed imperial rule as "natural, inevitable, and beneficial" and their critics, who saw it as "corrupting, immoral, and dangerous."[1] He uses a rather dramatic metaphor to describe ensuing trends in the field of imperial history: "In the era of decolonization, the search was on for explanations of imperialism as an aberrant phenomenon, a fever in human affairs with a complex epidemiology requiring close aetiological scrutiny. In each case, a fog of powerful emotions obscured scholarly clarity."[2] Ostensibly, the comparison of imperialism to sickness reads as a critique against the more zealous knee-jerk approaches to deconstructing imperial history and serves as a cautionary tale of inquiry based on emotion (rather than reason). Beneath the surface, however, the loaded metaphor is an indexical reminder of a more literal state of affairs—the biological impacts of imperialism on "the colonized," a subject that represents a highly politicized area of research in the sphere of Indigenous studies.

To Native[3] elders who endured trauma and disease in residential schools, and to successive generations residing in reserve communities struggling with disproportionately high rates of infectious and chronic diseases, substance abuse, and mental health issues, Aboriginal health outcomes are incontestably viewed as flowing from historical, social, and economic contingencies instigated by imperial rule and colonial policies. For historians and medical anthropologists studying the "pathogenicity and virulence of empire,"[4] the subject of empire and disease is not broached without first giving due consideration to the larger epistemological questions that the topic encompasses. Quantifying the health impacts of colonization on Indigenous populations evokes a maelstrom of intellectual debate and public emotion and opens up a veritable Pandora's box of theoretical, methodological, and ethical issues.

Few First Peoples or academics would deny the fact that social determinants significantly impact the health status of individuals and entire communities. Researchers and community members alike are cognizant of the many variables that contribute to disease outbreaks. They recognize that gaining a clear understanding of historical and present-day epidemiological trends requires simultaneous analysis of the contemporaneous ideologies, policies, and political courses of action that laid the foundations of imperial expansion in the Americas and fostered the changes in social and natural environments that facilitated the emergence of specific disease ecologies. Epidemiological models have illuminated the fundamental components of the relationship (where environment refers to both physical and social factors). Studies by leading scholars in historical demography have clearly demonstrated how colonization affected Native populations in North America in different places, at different time periods, and under a diverse set of circumstances.[5] A common feature of these studies is the dynamic, biocultural frameworks employed to distinguish factors that contributed to the varied impacts of imperial expansion among different Aboriginal groups. The parallel histories of colonization and epidemiological transitions are framed as evolving in a complex biosocial matrix, where diverse ideologies, economies, political structures, and cultures converge: the product of this synergy materializes as a punctuated equilibrium of historical moments marked by a broad spectrum of epidemiological events.[6]

Scholars dedicated to unravelling the "machine of imperialism" are fine-tuning their theories and methods, which in turn are challenging preconceived notions of the extent and magnitude of the social and biological after-effects experienced by Aboriginal populations during the post-contact period. "Apocalyptic" approaches to environmental history have given way to neo-whiggish interpretations and more recently, to models that reframe European imperialism as a short period in history that is no greater in significance than the recurrence of difficulties that appear to have been endemic in the pre-colonial past.[7] This new ethos has led to a major re-assessment of imperial histories. Broad-based studies on the influence of intercultural exchange on Indigenous populations popularized by Alfred W. Crosby (1972, 1986, 1994) and Jared Diamond (1997) are giving way to more fine-grained research that treats imperialism neither as an "ideological monolith" and "supremely effective system" nor as uniquely transforming and peculiarly destructive.[8] Recent studies envision imperialism as "but one phase in much longer cycles of environmental ups and downs" and are dedicated to revealing how "environmental propaganda" and "our modern anxieties about environmental threat have coloured the past, and not least the imperial past."[9]

Theorizing historical events in a more politically, economically, and culturally informed interpretive framework helps us to better contextualize and interrogate visions of equilibrium and disruption, notions of short-range transformation and degradations and long-term cycles between the construction of humans as dominating and destructive figures or what Alfred Crosby has called "passive and distracted participants."[10] The new environmental histories refrain from labelling "environmental heroes and villains" and are wary of predictions of extreme threat. This new paradigm includes "not demean[ing] people by viewing them as helpless victims of economic and environmental behaviour promoted by systems of elites."[11]

The pursuit of less homogenizing interpretations of imperialism heralds an exciting phase of research—one that grants us the opportunity to view history in a new light. Strides to improve the interpretive power of existing theories and the rigour of methodologies are of great import to the value and credibility of academic work. However, for researchers who work with marginalized and disenfranchised populations, the very act of theorizing health can be a source of cognitive dissonance. As scholars, we walk a very fine line, at once dedicated to fulfilling our scholarly responsibilities, which include refining our conceptual toolkits and honing our interpretive skills, while at the same time maintaining our moral obligations to those we work on behalf of, and alongside, as allies. The yearning to do justice to our data should be tempered by an equal desire to do justice to the memories, lived experiences, and histories of the countless individuals who bear the physical, emotional, mental and spiritual traumas of *structural violence* that sadly, are often not documented in the official historical record.[12] Evidence from archaeological and archival sources, together with oral histories, has persuasively shown that European newcomers left their indelible marks not only on the territories they carved out, but on the bodies of Indigenous populations that endured the inequitable and exploitative dimensions of forced acculturation. Although analyses based purely on "blind emotion" do not a good researcher make, adopting a strictly neutral stance devoid of empathy and compassion toward the social, psychological, and biological consequences of imperialism's dark legacies equally hinders attempts to gain a complete understanding of events that have transpired. Those who are intimately engaged in research in Aboriginal communities and who have witnessed first-hand the legacy of centuries of socio-economic marginalization, disempowerment, and systemic racism clearly recognize that "maintaining objectivity" does not mean telescoping one's standpoint by physically or emotionally distancing oneself from those whom one studies. In the field of anthropology, a thorough analysis of the origins and manifestations of biological and socio-cultural phenomena entails adopting a more grounded view by embedding oneself in the study community; this standpoint is made possible through long-term, intensive interactions with informants through participatory observation, participatory action, and collaborative research.

Our rather lengthy preamble is meant to contextualize some of the issues that complicate research on Aboriginal health. In our experience, environmental health issues in Native communities embody and encapsulate many of the intellectual and ethical problems that confound health studies and fuel the Pyrrhonian crises that trouble researchers. The contested domain of environmental health, embattled by arguments about evidence and validity, the perceived collusion between industry and Western science, and the media sensationalization of ecological issues, takes on an even more contentious form in Native communities, where corporate greed and bureaucratic complacency have come to be viewed as cogs in the wheels that have propelled the machines of empire in the twentieth and twenty-first centuries. In many ways, environmental illnesses have become the new plagues—air, water, and sediment pollution represent the contemporary smallpox blankets that threaten the health and survival of the world's Indigenous peoples.[13]

The environmental discourses of the First Peoples speak powerfully to the changes brought on by modernization and industrialization: climate change, the proliferation of invasive plant and animal species, declining animal and plant populations, and high human morbidity and mortality from diseases uncommon among Indigenous populations in earlier times are recurring themes. Fears of contamination and the spectre of environmental illness influence decisions about subsistence choices and, by extension, affect the traditional consumption and harvesting practices that are central to maintaining Indigenous economies, social cohesion, and cultural identity.[14]

Stories are an integral part of the cosmology and epistemology of Aboriginal peoples.[15] The life histories, lived experiences, and traditional ecological knowledges preserved through oral tradition offer important insights into indigenous value systems, modes of adaptation, conservation practices, and responses to colonization.[16] As anthropologists who are actively involved in collaborative, interdisciplinary research with colleagues in the natural and medical sciences, we recognize the utility of narrative as a vehicle for navigating the very elements that distinguish Native and non-Native metaphysics and epistemologies—the fundamental ways of "being," "knowing," and "doing" in the world that ultimately inform and reinforce divergent standpoints on environmental philosophy and praxis.

Against this broader and more textured epistemological backdrop, this chapter explores the various dimensions of environmental health research at the Walpole Island First Nation, a Southwestern Ontario Native community that has been combating an array of environmental challenges for several decades. The goals of our chapter are threefold: (1) to provide a brief summary of the impact of colonial policy on Aboriginal health in Canada; (2) to discuss the specific environmental challenges faced by the Walpole Island community and how the community has responded to these threats; and (3) to illuminate how current research being conducted by the Walpole Island First Nation in collaboration with the University of Western Ontario's Ecosystem Health Research Team is forging a more integrated, inclusive, participatory community health research model for the purpose of gaining a more nuanced understanding of local health concerns, while at the same time respecting and adhering to community research standards and cultural protocols. Findings derived from our recent research on environmental health issues in the Walpole Island community are used as a foil for navigating a plethora of interrelated conceptual and methodological issues in the spheres of Aboriginal and environmental health. Taken as a whole, our chapter highlights two important workshop themes: the role of collaboration between First Nations and academic institutions to decolonize attitudes that have historically been Eurocentric in nature[17] and the range of contemporary environmental health issues that continue to threaten First Nations communities in the Great Lakes region.

Background: Aboriginal Health in Historical Context

The processes and historical contingencies that underlie the spectrum of health problems in Aboriginal communities are complex and multifactoral. For centuries, Indigenous groups around the world have experienced major changes to their lands, economies, lifeways, and cultures as a direct result of imperial expansion and postcolonial processes. Understanding the history, nature, and scope of contemporary First Nations health issues (including environmental health issues), requires analysis of Aboriginal health and wellness within the context of the legacy of colonialism. The Royal Commission on Aboriginal Peoples (RCAP) estimates that during the first two hundred years of colonization and settlement, Aboriginal populations declined between fifty and ninety percent as a result of warfare, loss of land, famine, and disease. Epidemics of smallpox, influenza, measles, polio, and diphtheria had devastating political, economic, and cultural consequences for Aboriginal nations.[18] The rapidly growing settler population and shift from fur-trade economy to agricultural settlements in eastern North America during the 1800s led to an increased demand for land. Establishment of the reserve system in Canada was accompanied and implemented by long-standing assimilation policies. The consolidation of all existing legislation on "Indians" into one statute, the Indian Act of 1876 (and its subsequent revisions) was designed to control virtually every aspect of the lives of Aboriginal peoples.[19] The Indian Act stringently undermined or outlawed long-standing Indigenous social systems, values, and spiritual practices.[20] Traditional forms of government were rendered illegal and were replaced, often violently, by the chief and council electoral system. Church missionaries denounced Native spirituality and practices as witchcraft and idolatrous, while traditional ceremonies and rituals were banned.[21]

The health threat posed to Euro-Canadians by rampant outbreaks of tuberculosis in Native communities and residential schools spurred the Canadian government to create a much needed health-care program for Inuit and First Nations peoples. Beginning in the 1950s, medical care was provided to Aboriginal communities in the form of on-reserve nursing stations. Although these initiatives helped to improve the poor health status of Natives living on reserves, they also came at a great cost.[22] Aboriginal people lost control over their own health and health care. Western medical practitioners had little knowledge of, or respect for Aboriginal traditions, values, and health world views.[23] The legacy of these policies continues to be felt in Native communities, where high rates of infectious and chronic diseases, suicide, and substance abuse persist.[24]

For many First peoples, industrialization and globalization represent modern manifestations of imperialism.[25] Like the pathogens and plagues that accompanied the first colonization of the Americas, modern development has introduced its own form of health hazards—ecological degradation and environmental pollution. Dioxins, polychlorinated biphenyls (PCBs), heavy metals, and mercury are just some of the industrial by-products that pose a serious threat to ecosystem integrity. A number of health outcomes have been associated with exposure to toxic substances. Chemicals that might interfere with human neonatal development (referred to as endocrine disruptors) include PCBs, dioxins, methylmercury, chlorinated insecticides such as chlordane, and metabolites of DDT, including DDE.[26] Recent studies have revealed a positive correlation between low birth weight, birth defects (especially in male infants), and neurocognitive development and exposure to PCBs.[27] Consumption of fish contaminated with high levels of mercury can cause severe neurodevelopment deficiencies in newborns. Diabetes, hypothyroidism, and cerebral palsy have also been identified as negative health outcomes that may be associated with exposure to PCBs and methylmercury. Although air, water, and sediment pollution affect everyone, there is an unequal distribution of environmental health risks within populations. A growing body of research has shown that "race," ethnicity, and income are important determinants of degree of toxic exposure. Industrial complexes and waste disposal sites are more likely to be built in neighbourhoods and areas occupied by visible minorities, the poor, and the disenfranchised, representing the most stark and blatant forms of environmental racism.[28]

In 1953, widespread mercury poisoning among residents of the town of Minamata, Japan, brought international attention to the issue of chemical contamination.[29] In Canada, environmental health threats are an enduring problem for First Nations and Inuit communities. Poor sanitation and waste management, unsafe water supplies, and lack of community resources represent physical conditions that jeopardize the health of Aboriginal peoples.[30] Robinson and Moffatt (1985) describe a particularly devastating outbreak of gastro-intestinal disease in a James Bay Cree community caused by the *E. coli* bacterium.[31] In 2005, residents of the Kashechewan reserve in Northern Ontario were evacuated from their community after *E. coli* was found in their water supply system. Chlorine levels had to be increased to "shock" levels, which led to a worsening of common skin problems, such as scabies and impetigo.[32]

There are several factors that place Indigenous populations at a higher risk of exposure to environmental contaminants. Aboriginal populations have a higher risk of ingesting contaminated food sources because of their traditionally high consumption of local fish and wildlife. As toxins accumulate in body tissues in aquatic animals, they become magnified through the food chain. In the 1970s, high levels of mercury in fish from the English-Wabigoon River system in Northern Ontario had serious health consequences for members of the Grassy Narrows and White Dog reserves in the Kenora region. A large number of residents were diagnosed with Minamata disease, a suite of clinical symptoms associated with mercury poisoning.[33] Community members were also diagnosed with a broad spectrum of negative psychological, social, and behavioural outcomes as a consequence of actual or perceived contamination.[34] Clinical studies on PCB contamination at the Akwesasne Mohawk Nation reserve (which borders the St. Lawrence River in northern New York State, Ontario, and Quebec) have revealed a statistically significant inverse relationship between growth in youth and levels of PCBs.[35]

The effects of pollutants on human health are varied and far-reaching. Studies in environmental psychology have revealed how stress from what is referred to in the medical literature as *chemophobia*[36] influences both mental health and physical well-being. Local perceptions of environmental health risks have serious social, cultural, and psychological consequences for individuals, particularly those living in "high risk" areas. Because the adverse effects of environmental contamination go beyond environmental pathology (measured as pollution-induced trauma manifesting at the biological level), assessing the social and cultural impacts of environmental threats is a fundamental component of health risk assessment. For example, Michael Edelstein and Janet Fichten have brought attention to the emotional and psychological impacts of living in a high risk, contaminated area, while anthropological studies of Superfund sites have documented community grassroots initiatives to address environmental health threats.[37] Christine Egan's 1999 study of cultural perceptions of pollution provides an important gendered and culture-based analysis of the different meanings ascribed to pollution by the scientific community and Inuit women.[38] Studies in epidemiology and culture have provided important insights into how different world views shape the risk perceptions of different populations.[39]

Environmental Health Concerns at Walpole Island

Known as Bkejwanong, which means "where the waters divide" in Ojibwa, Walpole Island First Nation lies at the heart of Lake St. Clair.[40] This First Nation is world-renowned for its wetlands, tall-grass prairies, and ecological diversity, and is home to many species of endangered plants and wildlife. It also supports a profitable sports fishing and hunting economy.

The traditional territory of Walpole Island First Nation is situated in a region with a long industrial history. Canada's oil industry began in Lambton County in and around Oil Springs and Petrolia, areas rich in oil seeps and asphalt beds. By 1863, Petrolia was the major supplier of crude petroleum products in Canada. The establishment of synthetic rubber manufacturing plants in Sarnia during the Second World War bolstered the city's status as a major petrochemical industrial centre. Today, Sarnia is the "chemical capital of Canada"; "40% of Canada's petrochemical industry is located in the city's immediate vicinity."[41] Walpole Island First Nation is located downstream from Sarnia's "Chemical Valley" and downwind from the core of the industrialized American midwest. Over several decades, chemical industries and industrial waste sites in the region have released large quantities of effluent containing both organic (solid waste) and inorganic substances (chemicals) into the river in the form of accidental spills and daily discharges; the latter permitted under certificates of approval issued by the Ontario Ministry of the Environment. Between 1974 and 1986, it is estimated that a total of thirty-two major spills, as well as hundreds of minor ones, were responsible for the discharge of more than ten tons of pollutants into the St. Clair River.[42] In 1996, Imperial Chemical Industries released 3.4 billion litres of treated industrial pond water into the river despite local concerns over the toxicity of the effluent and its potential impacts on the local environment. Recent spills continue to heighten public fears. A chemical spill at Royal Polymer Industries on 4 August 2003 resulted in the discharge of over 5 million litres of vinyl chloride into the St. Clair River. On 1 February 2004, the Imperial Oil Refinery reported a spill of 157,000 litres of industrial solvents (methyl ethyl ketone and methyl isobutyl ketone) into the river.[43] In addition to toxic chemicals and municipal sewage, pollution also enters the St. Clair River as agricultural run-off. Lake St. Clair is the tile bed for much of southwestern Ontario's farmlands and agricultural pesticides drain into the lake via the Thames Valley watershed. Dredging and the lake's use as a commercial shipping route have historically contributed to the degradation of water quality. High winds and the passage of commercial shipping vessels re-suspend chemical sediments that have settled at the bottom of the St. Clair River.[44]

The Canada–U.S. International Joint Commission, a bi-national independent organization established under the Boundary Water Treaty of 1909, has identified Lake St. Clair as one of 43 Areas of Concern.[45] Areas of Concern are severely degraded geographic areas within the Great Lakes Basin. They are defined by the U.S.–Canada Great Lakes Water Quality Agreement (Annex 2 of the 1987 Protocol) as "geographic areas that fail to meet the general or specific objectives of the agreement where such failure has caused or is likely to cause impairment of beneficial use of the area's ability to support aquatic life."[46] Persistent organic chemicals and heavy metals are two of the greatest problems facing the Great Lakes and surrounding regions. In the 1970s, water birds in the Great Lakes were among the most highly contaminated in the world. Many organic chemicals mimic hormones, interfering with reproductive and immune systems. Tumours, malformations, and reproductive problems continue to be identified in Great Lakes freshwater fish species. Segments of the human population who consume large amounts of fish and wildlife, particularly Indigenous populations, have higher than average levels of several persistent chemical contaminants.[47] The Lake St. Clair water system is the main water supply for Walpole Island First Nation residents and a significant source of subsistence, sports fishing, and recreational activities. Measurement of pollution-induced injury in diverse Walpole Island animal species provides evidence of the serious effects of exposure to persistent toxic substances like PCBs and dioxins.[48] Preliminary results from environmental health assessments conducted at Walpole Island and other First Nations communities located in the Great Lakes Basin have identified a heightened risk of exposure to methylmercury in certain segments of the population. Findings from the E.A.G.L.E Project identify three sensitive or high-risk groups for mercury poisoning: (1) people with high mercury hair levels; (2) high consumers of fish and wild meats; and (3) mothers and nursing children.[49] These data highlight some of the ways in which water pollutants threaten community health. Many Walpole Island residents believe the community's food supply (local plant, fish, and wildlife species) and drinking water are seriously threatened by industrial pollution. Beach closures, water intake shutdowns following chemical spills, and the construction of a new water treatment plant attest to community concerns over water quality and fears of toxic exposure.

In response to longstanding community concerns, the Nin Da Waab Jig Walpole Island Heritage Centre, in co-operation with the community's health centre, contracted a group of specialists from the University of Western Ontario's Schulich School of Medicine and Dentistry to begin investigating the Walpole Island community's risk of exposure to environmental contaminants.[50] The ecosystem health team is a multidisciplinary group of clinical doctors, toxicologists, epidemiologists, statisticians, and cultural anthropologists with expertise in the area of environmental health. In 2005, the team conducted a feasibility study to ascertain whether there is enough clinical and scientific data and community support to proceed with a full-scale epidemiological study to examine potential health effects resulting from exposure to contaminants in the local ecosystem. The research project was funded by the National First Nations Environmental Contaminants Program.[51]

Ecosystem Health Discourses: Pilot Interviews

As the anthropologists on the ecosystem health research team, we were responsible for investigating local perceptions of environmental health risks and the social, cultural, and economic implications of environmental degradation and pollution in the community.[52] Specifically, our study focused on how community discourses on environmental contamination reveal environmental risk perceptions, water quality concerns, the conceptualization of community health, and the strategies individuals and/or respective groups employ to respond to or actively seek to change stressful environmental situations. An important component of the research project involved examining how oral histories conveying Indigenous knowledge(s) in general, and traditional ecological knowledge in particular, are able to complement conventional epidemiological research rooted in Western science. To explore these interrelated issues, we conducted a series of pilot interviews in the community. Discourses on ecological themes and environmental health were collected and analyzed.

Research methodology informed by linguistic and socio-cultural anthropology (open-ended interviews, focus groups, and participant observation) was used to explore a range of perspectives in the community regarding environment and health (and the inseparability of these variables) and explore health-seeking behaviours (e.g., the use of biomedical and traditional healing treatment strategies). Qualitative research aims to develop a more contextualized understanding of a problem by developing objective knowledge about subjects' understandings (*emic view*) rather than focusing solely on statistically significant associations between researcher-defined variables.[53] In the context of ethnographic fieldwork, this unique perspective can be gained by placing the researcher in close association with the subjects through participant observation, participatory action, ongoing conversations, and interviews.[54] Interviews are foundational to social research and many scholarly texts have been written describing the use of this specific research tool.[55] In the tradition of naturalistic inquiry, pilot interviews were conducted in the Walpole Island community.[56] Interview subjects were selected to reveal multiple standpoints, degrees of expertise, and levels of awareness with respect to environmental health issues. Just as contaminants discourses are contextual and based upon a speaker's knowledge of or interest in the topic of discussion,[57] constructions and perceptions of risk are also socially mediated. People's risk perceptions are influenced by the accumulation and assimilation of personal experiences over a lifetime, as well as by interpersonal communication in a variety of domains and networks.[58] Interviews with community members allowed us to explore how cultural understandings of water contamination issues as they relate to human health and perceptions of health risk are "constructions which can take on different meanings to different people, depending on the context of the discourse."[59]

Methods

Several methods were employed to encourage community consultation and participation in the study. Flyers describing the feasibility study were distributed in the community and various presentations and information sessions were held at different community venues. A booth was set up at the local powwow where information on the study was distributed, and a call for interview participants was made. A feast for elders hosted by the Heritage Centre provided an opportunity to conduct group interviews. A list of potential interview participants was compiled by the project's community team leaders. The selection of participants was based on their knowledge of local history, particularly events relating to environmental and ecological changes (such as dredging in the area), and their knowledge or recollection of specific environmentally significant events (such as the dates of major chemical spills). Interview subjects were also selected through the non-probability sampling technique of "snowball" or "chain sampling."[60] Major interview subgroups included elders, hunters and fishermen, health-care workers, expectant mothers and mothers of young children, community environmental technologists, and local environmental activists.

Approximately twenty semi-structured interviews were conducted in May 2005.[61] An interview questionnaire was used as a guide for the interviews but was not distributed to informants. Rather, interview questions were used as a tool to facilitate discussion of major themes relating to the topics of health and water quality in the community. The data collected were analyzed according to the principles of *grounded theory*. First developed by Glaser and Strauss (1967) and more recently refined by Strauss and Corbin (1990; 1997), grounded theory is largely based on an iterative process of data analysis. In this model, data are first coded using open (as opposed to predetermined) categories. Categories are determined as having reached the level of "saturation" when additional data yield no new categories. Similarities and differences between categories are then examined. After the formulation of preliminary hypotheses, a second level of coding (axial coding) is conducted, during which time connections between categories are made. The repetition or iteration of components leads to the development of a theoretical scheme, which is then tested against the data. This approach is particularly useful in qualitative research, as it aids in "developing the best method to address research questions that may be evolving, in order to best serve the overall purpose of the research."[62] By using this thematic process, concerns are contextualized and then linked to the way people experience everyday life.

Results

Community narratives revealed a number of issues relating to ecosystem health, water quality, and pollution. The following is a summary of some of the major themes that emerged during interviews with Walpole residents.

Water Pollution as a Problem in the Walpole Island First Nation

All of the informants interviewed identified water quality and water contamination as primary concerns in the community. Human health outcomes associated with exposure to contaminated water ranked as the most critical concern for residents, followed by the detrimental effects of pollutants on the variety of wildlife and natural resources at Walpole Island.

Knowledge of Water Pollution in the Community

Interview subjects were well informed on the issue of water contamination in their community. There is widespread awareness that Walpole Island's geographical proximity to "Chemical Valley" and the designation of Lake St. Clair as an Area of Concern heighten residents' risk of exposure to environmental contaminants. Scientific discourses disseminated through the popular media, in public spill notifications, and by word of mouth were identified as the primary sources of information on local environmental health issues. Many of those interviewed cited first-hand observations of cumulative changes in the local ecosystem throughout their lifetime and identified specific changes to water quality following major chemical spills (e.g., changes in water clarity, smell, and taste). Most community members have a good understanding of the types of chemicals they may be exposed to and the dangers associated with these toxins.

Perceived Effects of Environmental Degradation on Human Health

Although a formal epidemiological study has yet to be conducted in the community, there is a widespread belief that a large proportion of community members suffer from varied acute and chronic diseases. Elders who were interviewed felt that community health has drastically degenerated through the years, and many explicitly attributed this decline to changes in the environment. The increased prevalence of allergies, respiratory ailments, diabetes, heart disease, cancers, and other health conditions (that were non-existent or rarely experienced in previous generations) was a common theme in the elders' discourses. Many informants also discussed what they perceived to be unusually high levels of morbidity and mortality in the community. In many cases, elevated frequencies in chronic and degenerative diseases were attributed to high levels of air and water pollution. Informants cited particular examples as evidence.

Perceived Effects of Environmental Degradation on the Health of the Island's Flora and Fauna

Environmental pollutants were perceived as adversely affecting the health of the flora and fauna that constitute Bkejwanong's ecosystem and provide the local food supply. The growth of many of the island's rare and endangered plant species are actively monitored through community-based initiatives like the *Species at Risk Project.*[63] Many interview participants believe that water and air pollution have caused specific changes to plant and animal populations on the island. Major ecological themes included decreased biodiversity, reduced plant size, shorter growing seasons, scarcity of previously common medicinal plants, reduced animal populations, and the prevalence of malformed and "sick" fish and wild game. Many of those interviewed recognize that cyclical changes in climate and floral and faunal populations are indeed common; what is of concern, however, is the extent to which rapid development, changing land use patterns, and industrial pollution represent a dangerous acceleration of human-induced changes that interact with climatic and other natural cycles to produce irreparable or irreversible damage to the planet—a matter that has also been pondered by environmental historians.[64]

Several elders discussed how methods for acquiring water have changed through time. In earlier years (and prior to the establishment of water distribution infrastructure in the community), water was hauled directly from the river, underground springs, or private wells. Water clarity, taste, and overall "purity" were criteria used by residents to describe the state of the community's drinking water. Elders described how the water was clear, clean, and "safe" to drink prior to the establishment of industrialization in the area. Many commented on the present cloudy colour of the water and its strong, unpleasant smell. Almost all of those interviewed said that they avoid drinking tap water because of the bad taste and concerns over whether the water is contaminated with chemicals. Most people reported that they purchase bottled water, although this option is economically prohibitive for a number of those interviewed. Fear of exposure to contaminated water also affected the lifestyles, behaviours, and food choices of residents. Some informants disclosed that they forbid their children to swim or play in the lake or river. Although fish and wild game are staples of the traditional diet, fear of contamination has led a number of Walpole Island First Nation residents to reduce their consumption of these local food sources.

Psychosocial Stress Associated with Fear of Toxic Exposure

The interviews revealed varying degrees of psychosocial stress over the issue of water quality, and this stress manifested in several different ways. Most of the community members interviewed worried about the effects of contaminants on the health of children. There was also concern over the added economic burden of purchasing filtered or bottled water. Many people are anxious over the possibility of a *Valdez*-type disaster occurring, given the high traffic of ocean-going freighters in local waters. A majority of interview participants feel that Walpole Island residents are not alerted of chemical spills in a timely fashion. The absence of independent scientific evidence on the reliability of spill reports has made residents wary and distrustful of the information that is disseminated. Moreover, many feel that residents of nearby Wallaceburg and Sarnia are provided more expedient and accurate information on the nature, timing, and severity of chemical spills than Walpole residents.

Cultural Significance of Water

The centrality of the natural world to the Anishinaabeg is a prevalent theme. The Indigenous world view of nature is one that emphasizes balance and the interconnectedness and interrelatedness of all living things. The Natural Laws foundational to Native lifeways and spirituality are based on respecting the relationship between the lives of humans, animals and plants, and maintaining and preserving nature's equilibrium.[65] In accordance with these laws, Walpole Island residents recognize their important role as stewards of the earth. They recognize that the impacts of environmental pollution go beyond loss of biodiversity and natural resources. Environmental degradation and the destruction of the earth and its waters are viewed as severing the connection between humans, "nature," and a "higher spiritual being." Losing the ability to "live off the land" is viewed not only in economic terms but as a loss of identity and well-being, a way of life that is best captured by Naomi Adelson's description of the Cree concept of *miyupimaatisiiun* or (as Adelson translates in English) "being alive well."[66]

Symbolically, water is viewed as the blood of the Earth Mother; the rivers, streams, and groundwater are viewed as the Earth Mother's veins, which carry nourishment to all her living parts, and which sustain her. The women's environmental group Akii Kwe ("Earth Women") explains that, because of its power, water is viewed as sacred and must be kept pure. Female beings are believed to be the corporeal manifestations of the Earth Mother and share many qualities with her, such as spiritual power and the ability to create life. Women are the keepers of the water. This cultural tradition is maintained at Bkejwanong by Akii Kwe. The group works tirelessly to increase knowledge and awareness of environmental issues at the local, national, and international levels. The women's commitment to maintaining and preserving a clean and healthy ecosystem for future generations is a testament to their important contribution to environmental justice.[67]

Economic Impact of Water Contamination

The economy of Walpole Island First Nation is based on activities tied to the land and water. Many informants described how traditional subsistence strategies like fishing and hunting continue to be important economic strategies for island residents. Older fishermen recounted a vivid example of the devastating effects of water contamination. In the 1970s, high levels of methylmercury detected in Lake St. Clair fish were traced to spills from two of Sarnia's DOW Chemical chlor-alkali plants. As a result, commercial fishing in the area was banned for a decade. Many interview participants described how the closure of the Walpole Island fishery affected the community. There was a major loss of revenue from commercial fishing. Fishermen received an extremely small compensation from the government and from DOW Chemical. Many community members feel that the ban was later used by the Government of Ontario as a policy instrument to remove commercial fishing permanently from the lake through the imposition of a strict management regime that was implemented in the 1980s.[68] Though the closure of the fishery ended in 1980, there are still consumption advisories for large fish. The island's sports fishing industry was also affected through the loss of permit revenue and guide income.[69] High unemployment led to an "economic depression" in the community as fishermen were forced to find other lines of work. Men who lost their social and economic role as breadwinners experienced a loss of self-esteem. At the same time, boys and young men missed out on the opportunity to learn the trade of their fathers. Fishing and hunting are not only viable economic strategies but mediums through which the socialization of youth and "passing on" of cultural knowledge take place. The roles of women also changed as they sought out employment as factory workers and domestic help in the United States so that they could contribute to their household income. Another area of the island economy affected by this event was the deposition of mercury-contaminated dredgings on Seaway Island. The health threat posed by these mercury disposal sites has greatly decreased Seaway Island's potential for future development.[70]

Because many Walpole Island First Nations residents did not follow consumption advisories and warnings and continued to eat fish during the 1970s, they were at high risk of exposure to mercury. The Medical Services Branch of Health and Welfare Canada tested several community members for mercury poisoning during the 1970s. Due to inconsistent documentation and a lack of records, specific information regarding test dates and the numbers of individuals tested on each occasion is unclear. Although the summary of the tests provided by the Medical Services Branch states that mercury poisoning in the community was of "no serious concern" and that no obvious Minamata-type symptoms were present at the time of testing, long-term health problems from possible exposure cannot be ruled out because the diagnosis of chronic or "incomplete type" of mercury poisoning is difficult due to the fact that symptoms may take several years to manifest.[71] A 2008 study by Michael Gilbertson has identified cases of Minamata disease in the Great Lakes region.[72] This fact alone warrants further investigation into historical mercury exposure on Walpole Island.

Today, water contamination and ecological degradation continue to threaten the livelihood of Walpole residents. Traditional economies have evolved into multimillion-dollar industries. The value of natural resources is measured economically by employment as hunting club employees and guides, oil and gas sales, groceries, suppliers and outfitters, restaurant meals, lodging, transportation, sales of native crafts, commercial and sports fishing, and trapping. Reliance on natural resources and economies also helps to sustain traditions and cultural continuity.[73] The adverse effects of water and land pollution continue to affect both the economic viability and social cohesion of the Walpole Island community.

Political Dimensions of Water Issues

Another important theme was the inextricable connection between ecosystem health and the political issue of self-government. Many of those interviewed consider self-government to be the only solution for current environmental problems. Effective stewardship and protection of the island's natural resources and wetlands requires Walpole Island First Nation to have power and control over decisions involving its resources.[74] Since the 1870s, the First Nation has actively protected its lands, marshes, and natural resources through the negotiation of various leases, and assertion of rights and title to the waters and marshlands. Throughout its history, Walpole Island First Nation has "resisted the intrusion in its affairs of the Indian agent, and 'Headquarters', the Department of Indian Affairs in Ottawa, and non-Indian users of the marshlands."[75] Walpole Island has taken pioneering steps towards self-government and sustainable development. In addition to research to support land claims, the community has undertaken protests, abatement practices, and advocacy work. These have included lobbying governments and working with Chemical Valley industries to reduce discharges, conducting air-monitoring studies, investigating lead-shot poisoning, experimenting with conventional tilling and low-till farming techniques, and intervening against several development applications by large corporations that would affect either the ecozone or the land claims of the First Nation.[76] A rotary kiln (incinerator) application by Laidlaw, a pipeline project (Interprovincial Pipelines) crossing the bed of the St. Clair River, and a proposed electrical bulk transmission line by Ontario Hydro were all subsequently denied or dropped by the respective corporations due to community protest and intervention.[77] In 2008, the community was a strong voice in the environmental assessment of a proposed expansion of Sarnia's Shell Oil Refinery. Walpole Island's commitment to ecological issues has been recognized by several national and international agencies. The community received a major international award—the United Nations' We the Peoples: 50 Communities Award—in recognition of its commitment to environmental advocacy. Community environmental leaders recognize the importance of enforcing legislation that spells out industries' duty to consult with Aboriginal communities on environmental issues.

Willingness of Walpole Island First Nation Residents to Participate in Future Epidemiological/Clinical Studies

All of the volunteers interviewed expressed a willingness to participate in future studies in the community that would investigate the health effects associated with exposure to environmental contaminants. However, interview participants stressed that research projects must meet certain criteria. Clinical data should only be accessed with the informed consent of community members. Studies must include community input and participation at all stages of the research project and must be sufficiently equipped with mechanisms to effectively disseminate research findings to community members. Most importantly, research must provide tangible benefits to the community.

Ecosystem Health Models and the Integration of Research Projects

Just as the study of disease cannot be reduced to the study of pathogens alone, epidemiological research must look beyond the scope of human health to the health and integrity of the larger ecosystem. The Walpole Island First Nation has long taken a leadership role in bringing public attention to issues of ecosystem health, environmental justice, and sustainable development and the linkages between them. There is a widespread recognition in the community that successful political and social advocacy is based on sound knowledge. This ethos is reflected in the mission statement of the community's research arm, the Nin Da Waab Jig Heritage Centre, which is dedicated to preserving, interpreting, and promoting Bkejwanong's natural and cultural heritage.

In the same spirit, we recognize that successful research is comprised of several key components. It is research that is based on strong and sustained community partnerships, and that is conducted in an ethical, respectful, and culturally sensitive way. Effective research promotes capacity building and skills transfer, and has the potential to improve the quality of life of community members. Good research also builds upon grassroots community initiatives. The ultimate success of any academic research project depends on how well it can address community concerns, elicit community participation, harmonize with existing community projects, and model its theoretical and methodological approaches so that they are commensurable with the community's research paradigm and agenda. Our research on the socio-cultural aspects of environmental threats represents one piece of a larger environmental health research project initiated by the Walpole Island Heritage Centre and Health Centre and the Schulich School of Medicine and Dentistry's Ecosystem Health Research Team. A large body of knowledge has already emerged from studies initiated through this research collaboration. These include an environmental health feasibility study (2005), a mercury exposure through fish consumption study (2006), blood and hair testing for mercury and PCBs (2008), administration of an adult and child-health survey (2008), the digitalization of selected (study volunteer) community health records (2008), and the assessment of clinical records for evidence of health outcomes associated with toxic exposure. Important work has also been done on the health history of the community.[78] Christianne Stephens' dissertation (2009) examines the environmental discourses of young mothers, hunters and fishermen, elders, and community environmental activists and researchers (which she has termed "Toxic Talk") and draws attention to the important role of Indigenous knowledge and environmental narratives for assessing the broader impacts of toxic exposure on the health and well-being of Indigenous peoples and refining the conceptual frameworks and language of risk employed by biomedicine, industries, and regulatory agencies. The research also reveals that although risk perceptions vary according to the age, gender, spiritual practices, and occupation of informants, they are still grounded in shared cultural values.[79] Our research has also dovetailed with community-based projects, most notable is our collaboration with fluent speakers of Anishinaabemwin and members of the Heritage Centre (Clint Jacobs and Dave White) on a *Species at Risk* publication documenting endangered plant and wildlife species at Walpole Island in the Ojibwa language.[80]

The Role of Oral Histories and Traditional Ecological Knowledge in Epidemiological Studies

The benefits of incorporating oral histories into environmental health projects are numerous. Community discourses provide important information on cumulative changes in the environment, historical events, and ecosystem and human health that are typically not captured by conventional clinical statistics or health surveys. These stories powerfully convey local perceptions of environmental risks, health world views, lifestyles, attitudes, and behaviours.[81] Narratives provide a rare view of how environmental concerns and fears are embodied by the local population, and how these anxieties compound and amplify existing social stress and historical trauma, further compromising the mental, spiritual, and emotional well-being of community members.[82]

Ecosystem health discourses also provide an important view of Indigenous understandings of nature that differ from Western paradigms of human–environment interaction. Recognition of and deep respect for the interrelatedness of all living things (captured by the term *all my relations*) and the framing of decisions regarding environmental stewardship and human health within the context of responsibility to seven generations are fundamental cultural teachings that are held in common by most Indigenous peoples. Knowing and appreciating the differences between Native and Western scientific knowledge systems and values is integral to reducing the occurrence of cross-cultural miscommunication in the areas of preventative health, ecological stewardship, and environmental protection and legislation.

Exploring Indigenous knowledges and diverse forms of environmental activism practised by Aboriginal communities (a subject currently being studied by Christianne Stephens at Walpole Island) can help to dispel homogenizing notions of imperial power and its effects on Aboriginal groups.

As John MacKenzie observes, "our greater awareness of indigenous response and resistance, as well as knowledge and collaboration, helps to confirm the difficulty of seeing imperial rule either as an ideological monolith or as a supremely effective system."[83]

Conclusions

Theorizing Aboriginal Environmental Health Issues: Towards a Qualitative Cultural Epidemiology

Our collaboration with the Walpole Island First Nation and the UWO Ecosystem Health Team has brought to view the complex nature of contemporary environmental health issues affecting Native communities. Unpacking the Walpole Island community's water quality problem entails the concurrent unpacking or deconstruction of a number of epistemological "black boxes" that represent the taken-for-granted and often-unexamined assumptions, ideologies, and standards of evidence that constitute our own world view—that is, the ways we, as Western researchers understand and experience the world and reproduce these understandings and experiences in the language, categories, and paradigms we use to design our studies and justify our research findings. From a theoretical standpoint, we recognize why the collection and analysis of scientific and psychosocial data must be preceded by serious critique of divergent world views. In the case of environmental issues in Native communities, this necessitates acknowledging that environmental crises and debates over how to resolve them stem from fundamental differences between Native and non-Native conceptualizations of *nature, risk, evidence,* and *accountability*. Mediating these philosophical "incommensurabilities" is crucial to building strong research partnerships between Indigenous communities and Western academic institutions.

The benefits of community-based, collaborative research are numerous. Drawing on multiple lines of evidence and combining anthropological and epidemiological approaches can help increase awareness of the unique environmental health issues and needs of the Walpole Island First Nation community and bring forth positive outcomes in the areas of health monitoring and risk assessment, preventative care and health care delivery, chemical spills reporting procedures, and remedial action. An emerging *cultural epidemiology,* one that focuses on disease classification, health risk, and behaviour (in addition to social variables such as income, marital status, and occupation)[84] and is grounded in Indigenous teachings and values can clarify the physiological and psychological impacts of environmental health threats and crises. Health research that is participatory, transgressive, constitutive of difference, practical, engaged, emancipatory, interpretive, critical,[85] and that transcends conventional disciplinary boundaries has the capacity to illuminate the intricate and dynamic webs of bio-social interactions that underpin health outcomes in Aboriginal communities. Beyond providing richer data sets, dynamic, integrative health models can empower marginalized communities in their ongoing struggle to attain social and environmental justice.

As scholars, we recognize that the histories of imperialism and disease are as complex as they are mutually imbricated. As consultants and advocates, we strive to strike a delicate balance between our recognition of, and respect for the lived experiences of those we work with, and the intellectual pursuit that supplants sweeping generalizations with more detailed analyses and nuanced interpretations of historical and social phenomena. The new era in ethnohistorical and environmental research has compelled us to learn more about the differential global–local impacts of imperial rule and the scientific dimensions of empires. Our ethnographic fieldwork on environmental issues at Walpole Island represents but a tiny fragment in the rich and colourful mosaic that is Indigenous history. Insights emerging from our collaborative research are forging a useful template for bridging the solitudes of Western science and the knowledge systems of Indigenous peoples. The knowledge gained will go toward further developing an intellectually rigorous and ethically sound framework for community–institutional partnerships in Aboriginal health research. We hope that our continued work with the Walpole Island First Nation will shed new light on the multidimensional aspects of environmental health risks threatening Bkejwanong's rare ecosystems and in the process, improve the health and quality of life of its citizens.

Notes

1 J.M. MacKenzie, *Imperialism and the Natural World* (Manchester: Manchester University Press, 1990), 1.

2 MacKenzie, *Imperialism and the Natural World*, 1.

3 The terms First Nation, Native, Indigenous, and Aboriginal are synonymous in many contexts. *Native American* is used instead of First Nation in the United States. *Indian* is used in only contexts of the *Indian Act* in Canada. Most First Nations groups prefer to be identified by their specific identity (e.g., Walpole Island First Nation). *Anishinaabe* refers to the Algonquian-speaking peoples of the Three Fires Confederacy (Ojibwa, Odawa, Potawatomi) and is sometimes extended to include all Native peoples of North America.

4 C.V. Stephens, "From Scourges and Historical Traumas to Environmental Health Fears: A Multi-temporal Case Study of Discursive (Re)Constructions

of Health and Well-being at the Walpole Island First Nation," paper presented at the Annual Meeting of the American Society for Ethnohistory (7–10 Nov. 2007); and Stephens, "Toxic Talk at Walpole Island First Nation: Narratives of Pollution, Loss, and Resistance," Ph.D. thesis, McMaster University, 2009.

5 C. Carpenter and L. Sattenspiel, "The Design and Use of an Agent-based Model to Simulate the 1918 Influenza Epidemic at Norway House, Manitoba," *American Journal of Human Biology* 21, no. 3 (2009): 290–300, www.3interscience.wiley.com; P. Hackett, *A Very Remarkable Disease: Epidemics in the Petit Nord, 1670 to 1846* (Winnipeg: University of Manitoba Press, 2002); D. Ann Herring, "Toward a Reconsideration of Disease and Contact in the Americas," *Prairie Forum* 17 (1992): 1–13; D. Ann Herring, "'There were young people and old people and babies dying every week': The 1918–19 Influenza Pandemic at Norway House," *Ethnohistory*, 41, no. 1 (1994): 73–105; D. Ann Herring and Robert D. Hoppa, "Endemic Tuberculosis among Nineteenth-Century Cree in the Central Canadian Subarctic," *Perspectives in Human Biology* 4, no. 1 (1999): 189–99; Robert D. Hoppa, "Mortality in a Northern Ontario Fur-trade Community: Moose Factory, 1851–1964." *Canadian Studies in Population* 25, no. 2 (1998): 175–98; J.B. Waldram, D.A. Herring, and T. K. Young, *Aboriginal Health in Canada: Historical, Cultural, and Epidemiological Perspectives*, 2nd ed. (Toronto: University of Toronto Press, 2006).

6 Stephens, "From Scourges and Historical Traumas" and "Toxic Talk at Walpole Island First Nation."

7 John M. MacKenzie identifies three strands in the writing of imperial environmental history: "Apocalyptic refers to the first historical response to the beginning of the green controversies of the 1960s and 1970s. It is a polemic that has remained politically useful to the Green Movement. Neo-whiggish is a longstanding tradition that still has its modern, even recent practitioners. It too is influenced by green politics, to the extent that it sees modern sensibilities as an enlightened form of ecological awareness, the roots of which can be found in the cultural histories of both manners and ideas in the past. The third strand refers to the adoption by scholars of a longer historical perspective, recognizing that the era of European imperialism represents but one brief period in the larger time frame of events in human history." MacKenzie, *Empires of Nature and the Nature of Empires: Imperialism, Scotland and the Environment* (East Linton: Tuckwell Press, 1997), 23.

8 Alfred W. Crosby, *The Columbian Exchange: Biological and Cultural Consequences of 1492*. (Westport, CT: Greenwood Press, 1972; reprinted 2003); Crosby, *Ecological Imperialism: The Biological Expansion of Europe, 900–1900* (New York: Cambridge University Press (1986; reprinted 1993, 2004); Crosby, *Germs, Seeds,*

and Animals: Studies in Ecological History (Armonk, NY: M.E. Sharpe, 1994): Jared Diamond, *Guns, Germs, and Steel: The Fates of Human Societies* (New York: W.W. Norton, 1997).

9 MacKenzie, *Empire of Nature and the Nature of Empires*, xiv, 4, 19.

10 Alfred W. Crosby, "The Past and Present of Environmental History," *American Historical Review* 100, no. 4 (October 1995): 1177–89.

11 MacKenzie, *Empire of Nature and the Nature of Empires*, 80–81.

12 Paul Farmer, *Infections and Inequalities: The Modern Plagues* (Berkeley: University of California Press, 1999); and *Pathologies of Power: Health, Human Rights, and the New War on the Poor* (Berkeley: University of California Press, 2003).

13 Stephens, "From Scourges and Historical Traumas."

14 R. Darnell and C.V. Stephens, "Keepers of the Water, Keepers of the Fire: Building Bridges Between Academic and Indigenous Knowledges in Environmental Health Research," *International Journal of the Humanities* 5, no. 10 (2007): 105–14; C.V. Stephens and R. Darnell "The Interdisciplines of Ecosystem Health: As Revealed in First Nations Collaborations," *International Journal of Interdisciplinary Social Sciences* 3, no. 1 (2008): 147–60.

15 Julie Cruikshank has written extensively about the role of stories among Aboriginal peoples. See J. Cruikshank, *The Social Life of Stories: Narrative and Knowledge in the Yukon Territory* (Lincoln: University of Nebraska Press, 1998); "Oral History, Narrative Strategies, and Native American Historiography: Perspectives from the Yukon Territory, Canada," in *Clearing a Path: Theorizing the Past in Native American Studies*, ed. N. Shoemaker (London: Routledge, 2002): 3–27; and *Do Glaciers Listen? Local Knowledge, Colonial Encounters, and Social Imagination* (Seattle: University of Washington Press, 2005). See also J. Cruikshank, A. Sidney, K. Smith and A. Ned, *Life Lived Like a Story: Life Stories of Three Yukon Elders* (Lincoln: University of Nebraska Press, 1990).

16 Cruikshank, *Do Glaciers Listen?*

17 MacKenzie, *Empire of Nature and the Nature of Empires*; D. McNab, *Earth, Water, Air and Fire: Studies in Canadian Ethnohistory* (Waterloo: Wilfrid Laurier University Press, 1998); Marie Battiste, *Reclaiming Indigenous Voice and Vision* (Vancouver: UBC Press, 2000); Linda Tuhiwai Smith, *Decolonizing Methodologies: Research and Indigenous Peoples* (London: Zed Books, 1999).

18 Royal Commission on Aboriginal Peoples (RCAP), *Report*, vol. 1, *Looking Forward, Looking Back* (Ottawa: Canada Communication Group, 1996), 112–13; Assembly of First Nations, *The E.A.G.L.E Project: The Effects on Aboriginal Peoples from the Great Lakes Environment: Annual Report* (Ottawa: Health Canada, 1995), 7. http://www.chiefs-of-ontario.org/sites/default/files/files/socio-c.pdf.

19 L. Simpson, D. Martin-Hill, P. Driben, and M. Wheatley, "Effects on Aboriginals from the Great Lakes Environment E.A.G.L.E. Project: Sociocultural Pilot Project Technical Report" (Assembly of First Nations/Chiefs of Ontario/Health Canada Partnership, 2001), 5–10; RCAP, *Report*, vol. 1.

20 RCAP, *Report*, vol. 1; RCAP, *Report*, vol. 3, *Gathering Strength* (Ottawa: Canada Communication Group, 1996).

21 Simpson, "Effects on Aboriginals"; RCAP, *Report*, vol. 1.

22 Simpson, "Effects on Aboriginals."

23 RCAP, *Report*, vol. 3, *Gathering Strength.*

24 Simpson, "Effects on Aboriginals"; Waldram et al., *Aboriginal Health in Canada.*

25 C.V. Stephens, "Where the Waters Divide: Water Quality and Human Health at the Walpole Island First Nation—Preliminary Findings." Stephens presented this paper as recipient of the 2006 Richard Salisbury Award at the Canadian Anthropology Society Annual Conference, 9–14 May 2006, Concordia University, Montreal; and Stephens, "Toxic Talk at Walpole Island First Nation."

26 J.R. Bend, B.A. Corbett, R. Darnell, C.P. Herbert, G. Koren, N. Kowal, M.J. Reider, C.V. Stephens, C.G. Trick, *Feasibility of Conducting Epidemiological Studies to Assess the Health Risk of the Walpole Island First Nation Community from Exposure to Environmental Contaminants*, research report (Environmental Contaminants Health Program, First Nations and Inuit Health Branch, 2005); and J.R. Bend, R. Darnell, C. Trick, C. Herbert, N. Kowal, C.V. Stephens, N. Williams, and D. White, *Walpole Island First Nation. Mercury Exposure through Fish Consumption Study, 2005/2006*, research report (Environmental Contaminants Health Program, First Nations and Inuit Health Branch, Health Canada, 2006).

27 Bend et al., *Feasibility of Conducting Epidemiological Studies.*

28 A. McElroy and P.K. Townsend, *Medical Anthropology in Ecological Perspective*, 4th ed. (Boulder, CO: Westview, 2004).

29 In Japan, people were poisoned by eating fish from Minamata Bay (hence the term *Minamata disease*) that had been contaminated by methylmercury discharged as a by-product of the acetaldehyde process of the Chisso Chemical Company. Y. Harada "Congenital Minamata Disease," in *Minamata Disease*, ed. T. Tsubaki and K. Irunkayama (New York: Elsevier Scientific, 1977), 209–39; see also the other essays in this volume.

30 S.S. Anand, S. Yusuf, et al., "Risk Factors, Atherosclerosis, and Cardiovascular Disease among Aboriginal People in Canada: The Study of Health Assessment and Risk Evaluation in Aboriginal Peoples (SHARE-AP)," *Lancet* 358, no. 9288 (2001): 1147; C. Loppie-Reading and F. Wein, *Health Inequalities and Social Determinants of Aboriginal Peoples' Health. Report* (National Collaborating Centre

for Aboriginal Health, 2009), http://www.nccah-ccnsa.ca/docs/social%20 determinates/NCCAH-Loppie-Wien_Report.pdf.

31 E.J. Robinson and M.E. Moffatt, "Outbreak of Rotavirus Gastroenteritis in a James Bay Cree Community," *Canadian Journal of Public Health* 76, no. 1 (1985): 21–24.

32 Anonymous, "Kashechewan: Water Crisis in Northern Ontario," CBC *News*, 9 November 2006, http: www.cbc.ca/news/background/aboriginals/kasheche wan.html.

33 Methylmercury exerts its toxic effects on the central nervous system. Common symptoms of Minamata disease include muscular tremors, sensory impairment, lack of coordination, and emotional disturbance. Continual exposure to mercury affects the highest levels of the brain, resulting in loss of eyesight, hearing, and speech, and a progressive deterioration of the intellect. Methylmercury penetrates the placental barrier, which may lead to accumulation in the fetus, resulting in neurological disorders. S.J. Marchand, *Environmental Impacts on the Lake St. Clair Fishery: A Case Study of Mercury Pollution and Its Effects on Walpole Island Reserve*, occasional paper no. 11 (Walpole Island: Nin Da Waab Jig Heritage Centre, 1986); K. Irukayama, "The Pollution of Minamata Bay and Minamata Disease," in *Mercury in Fish and Fish-Eating Birds Near Sites of Industrial Contamination in Canada*, ed. N. Fimreite, W.N. Holsworth, J.A. Keith, P.A. Pearce, and I.M. Gruchy (1966: reprint, 1985), 211, 220.

34 Psychosocial effects can occur from either real or perceived threats of contamination. An example of psychosocial effects resulting from an actual threat of contamination is illustrated by the case of the Grassy Narrows and White Dog reserves, as described in Anastasia M. Shkilnyk, "A Poison Stronger Than Love: The Destruction of an Ojibwa Community" (New Haven, CT: Yale University Press, 1985). An example of psychosocial stress resulting from a perceived threat is that of Smithsville, Ontario. In 1985, it was discovered that people from this town were exposed to PCB contamination through leakage to groundwater from a nearby PCB transfer station built in 1978. The ensuing effects experienced by residents were attributed to psychosocial stress arising from a perceived risk. Tests conducted in 1992 showed that the chemical exposures were insufficient to cause physical health effects in the population. J. Dunn, S. Taylor, S. Elliot, and S. Walter, "Psychosocial effects of PCB Contamination and Remediation: The Case of Smithsville, Ontario," *Social Science and Medicine* 39, no. 8 (1994): 1093–104.

35 McElroy and Townsend, *Medical Anthropology*; Lawrence M. Schell and Alice Tarbell, "A Partnership Study of PCBs and the Health of Mohawk Youth: Lessons from Our Past and Guidelines for Our Future," *Environmental Health*

Perspectives 106 (Supplement 3): 833–40; Lawrence M. Schell, L. Hubicki, A. DiCaprio, M.V. Gallo, and the Akwesasne Task Force on the Environment, "Polychlorinated Biphenyls (PCBs)and Thyroid Function in Adolescents of the Mohawk Nation at Akwesasne," in *Human Growth from Conception to Maturity*, ed. G. Gilli, L. Benso, and L. Schell (London: Smith-Gordon, 2002), 289–96.

36 Chemophobia is a biomedical term that describes the fear that people experience as a result of confusion or uncertainty regarding the reality of environmental risks and what it means to them and their families. C. Egan, "Inuit Women's Perceptions of Pollution," Ph.D. thesis, University of Manitoba, 1999.

37 Michael Edelstein's study examines the response of Legler residents (a section of Jackson, New Jersey) to groundwater contamination and provides insights into the emotional stress of living near toxic waste sites; Edelstein, *Contaminated Communities: The Social and Psychological Impacts of Residential Toxic Exposure* (Boulder, CO: Westview, 1988). Janet Fichten looks at the meaning of *home* to understand the emotional impact of groundwater contamination experienced by New York communities J.M. Fichten, "When Toxic Chemicals Pollute Residential Environments: The Cultural Meaning of Home and Home Ownership," *Home Organization* 48, no. 4 (1989): 313–24. One of the most publicized accounts of an urban community's exposure to toxic waste is that of New York State's 'Love Canal': L.M. Gibb, *Love Canal: The Story Continues ...* (Stony Creek, CT: New Society, 1998).

38 Egan, "Inuit Women's Perceptions."

39 J.A. Trostle, *Epidemiology and Culture* (New York: Cambridge University Press, 2005).

40 Walpole Island First Nation is located in the province of Ontario, Canada, and borders the state of Michigan, U.S. Bkejwanong territory consists of lands and waters in Lake St. Clair and the St. Clair River. Walpole Island First Nation represents the homelands of Odawa (Ottawa), Anishinaabeg (Ojibwa), and Potawatomi peoples, who together comprise a political alliance (compact) known as the Council of the Three Fires or Three Fires Confederacy. Nin Da Waab Jig, *Minishenhying Anishnaabe-aki: Walpole Island: The Soul of Indian Territory* (Walpole Island: Nin Da Waab Jig Heritage Centre, 1987).

41 Quoted in *The Beloved Community* (2006), a film by Pamela Calvert/Plain Speech, produced in association with Detroit Public Television (Jeff Forster, executive producer). The statistic is listed also in the film's online discussion guide: http://www.newsreel.org/guides/belovedcommunity/bcdiscuss.htm. See also Margaret Wooseter, *Living Waters: Reading the Rivers of the Lower Great Lakes* (Albany: State University Press of New York, 2009), 10.

42 D. Jacobs, "The Great Lakes Today: A View of Bkejwanong," paper presented at Reddin Symposium XI, "The Environment of the Great Lakes," Canadian Studies Centre, Bowling Green State University, 1988.

43 Ontario Ministry of the Environment, *Industrial Spills in Ontario*, May 2005, PIBS 5085e, http://www.ene.gov.on.ca/stdprodconsume/groups/lr/@ene/@resources/documents/resource/std01_079453.pdf.

44 Assembly of First Nations, *The E.A.G.L.E Project: The Effects on Aboriginal Peoples from the Great Lakes Environment; Annual Report* (Ottawa: Health Canada, 1995).

45 Since 1972, the Canadian and the United States governments have been involved in the implementation of the Great Lakes Water Quality Agreement. This agreement is pursuant to the 1909 Boundary Water Treaty. This treaty provided a framework for subsequent cooperation between the United States and Canada on water (especially but not only in the Great Lakes). It created the International Joint Commission, and includes the basic principle that the boundary waters and waters flowing across the boundary shall not be polluted on either side causing the injury of health or property on the other. The Water Quality Board of the International Joint Commission has recognized 43 Areas of Concern in the Great Lakes basin (26 in the U.S. and 17 in Canada). All show biological communities affected by contamination of sediments and most by toxic substances in the water.

46 Great Lakes Information Network (GLIN), *Areas of Concern in the Great Lakes Region*, http://www.great-lakes.net/envt/pollution/aoc.html#overview.

47 T. E. Colborn, A. Davidson, S.N. Green, R.A. Hodge, C.I. Jackson, and R.A. Liroff, *Great Lakes, Great Legacy?* (Harper: Conservation Foundation and the Institute for Research on Public Policy, 1990).

48 G.D. Haffner, V. Glooschenko, C.A. Straughan, C.E. Herbert, and R. Lazar, "Concentrations and distributions of polychlorinated biphenyls, including non-ortho congeners, in mink populations from Southern Ontario," *Journal of Great Lakes Research* 24, no. 4 (1998): 880–88.

49 Walpole Island was one of 15 First Nations communities that participated in the E.A.G.L.E. Project (Effects on Aboriginals from the Great Lakes Environment). The project, initiated in the mid-1990s, looked at the effects of environmental contaminants on First Nation peoples in the Great Lakes Basin. Assembly of First Nations, *E.A.G.L.E Project.*

50 The Nin Da Waab Jib Walpole Island Heritage Centre was officially opened in 1989. The mission statement of Nin Da Waab Jig is to preserve, interpret, and promote the natural and cultural heritage of the Walpole Island First Nation community. This has been achieved through various research projects within

the areas of history, land claims, environmental issues, and cultural heritage, as well as through activities which involve members and non-members of the community.

51 The National First Nations Environmental Contaminants Program was launched in 1999 as a collaborative research program between the Assembly of First Nations (AFN) and Environmental Research Division of the First Nations and Inuit Health Branch, Health Canada. The program's objective is to help First Nations assess the extent of environmental contamination exposure and the potential for associated risk to the health and well-being of First Nations in Canada.

52 C.V. Stephens and R. Darnell, "Water Quality Issues in the WIFN Community," in *Feasibility of Conducting Epidemiological Studies to Assess the Health Risk of the Walpole Island First Nation Community from Exposure to Environmental Contaminants*, ed. J.R. Bend, B.A. Corbett, R. Darnell, C.P. Herbert, G. Koren, N. Kowal, M. J. Rieder, C.V. Stephens, and C.G. Trick (Environmental Contaminants Health Program, First Nations and Inuit Health Branch, 2005).

53 L. Connor, C. Treloar, and N. Higgenbotham, "How to Perform Transdisciplinary Research: Qualitative Study Designs and Methods." In *Health Social Science: A Transdisciplinary and Complexity Perspective*, ed. N. Higgenbotham, G. Albrecht, and L. Connor (Oxford: Oxford University Press, 2001), 228.

54 Connor et al., "How to Perform Transdisciplinary Research: Qualitative Study Designs and Methods," 227–66.

55 For example, J. P. Spradley, *The Ethnographic Interview* (New York: Holt, Reinhart and Winston, 1979); E.R. Babbie, *Survey Research Methods*, 2nd ed. (Belmont: Wadsworth, 1990); A.N. Oppenheim, *Questionnaire Design, Interviewing and Attitude Measurement* (London: St. Martin's, 1992); H.R. Bernard, *Research Methods in Anthropology: Qualitative and Quantitative Approaches* (Thousand Oaks: Sage, 1994).

56 Lincoln and Guba describe naturalistic inquiry as a research method that includes ethnography and other unstructured qualitative research. This approach is used to "contextualize as fully as possible the nature of social relationships in complex research settings" and to study "unfolding social processes and the interaction of many variables in situations of change." Yvonna S. Lincoln and Egon G. Guba, *Naturalistic Inquiry* (Newbury Park, CA: Sage Publications, 1985). See also Byles, Higginbotham, and Heller, "How to Perform Transdisciplinary Research: Epidemiological Study Designs," 206–26.

57 P. Kaufert and J. O'Neil, "Analysis of Dialogue on Risks in Childbirth," in *Knowledge, Power and Practice*, ed. S. Lindenbaum and M. Locke (Berkeley: University of California Press 1993): 32–54; Egan, "Inuit Women's Perceptions."

58 Egan, "Inuit Women's Perceptions."

59 Kaufert and O'Neil, "Analysis of Dialogue on Risks in Childbirth"; and Egan, "Inuit Women's Perceptions," 23.

60 An interview technique in which a list of interview subjects is compiled based on the recommendations of informants who have already been interviewed.

61 Semi-structured interviews allow the researcher to ask about a list of specific topics yet are more flexible than structured interviews, giving interviewees the freedom to use their own words to respond to questions and address issues in order of their preference (Connor et al., *How to Perform Transdisciplinary Research*, 240).

62 Byles et al., "How to Perform Transdisciplinary Research: Epidemiological Study Designs," 247. A. Strauss and J. Corbin, "Grounded Theory Methodology: An Overview," in *Handbook of Qualitative Research*, ed. N.K. Denzin and Y.S. Lincoln (London: Sage Publications, 1994), 1–18; J. Byles, N. Higginbotham, and R. Heller, "How to Perform Transdisciplinary Research: Epidemiological Study Designs," in *Health Social Science: A Transdisciplinary and Complexity Perspective*, ed. N. Higgenbotham, G. Albrecht, and L. Connor (Oxford: Oxford University Press, 2001), 206–26. See also B. Glaser and A. Strauss, *Discovery of Grounded Theory: Strategies for Qualitative Research* (Chicago: Aldine de Gruyter, 1967).

63 Many plants and animals considered rare or at risk in Canada are locally abundant on Walpole Island. In 2002, Walpole Island First Nation published *Species at Risk on the Walpole Island First Nation* (compiled by Helen Roy, J. Summer Sands, Clint Jacobs, Abigail Nahdee [Wallaceburg, ON: Walpole Island Heritage Centre, 2006]), which describes and identifies the current level of "risk" listed for each species (as listed by the Committee on the Status of Endangered Wildlife). A version of the book was translated into Ojibwa was published in 2006. Nin Da Waab Jig Heritage Centre, R. Darnell, and C.V. Stephens, *E-Niizaanaag Wii-ngoshkaag Maampii Bkejwanong: Species at Risk at the Walpole Island Nation (Ojibwe version)* (London: University of Western Ontario, 2006); R. Darnell and C.V. Stephens, "Species at Risk, Language at Risk: Reflections on Biodiversity and Translation at the Walpole Island First Nation," in *Proceedings of the 38th Annual Algonquian Conference*, ed. C. Wolfart (Winnipeg: University of Manitoba Press, 2007): 129–42.

64 MacKenzie, *Empires of Nature and the Nature of Empires*, 23.

65 W. LaDuke, *All Our Relations: Native Struggles for Land and Life* (Cambridge, MA: South End, 1999); Simpson, "Effects on Aboriginals."

66 An excellent example of Indigenous constructions of health is given by Naomi Adelson in her description of *miyupimaatisiiun*, or "being alive well," a health

construct of the Cree of Great Whale River. This construct of health is defined through local beliefs and practices, incorporating references to an idealized past, as well as contemporary ideals and practices of health that are tied to their identity as Cree. A. Adelson, *Being Alive Well: Health and the Politics of Cree Well-Being* (Toronto: University of Toronto Press, 2000).

67 Akii Kwe was formed in 1995 in response to a proposal put forward by Imperial Chemical Industry to discharge waste water into the St. Clair River. The women protested the discharge and have since worked toward bringing attention to local and global environmental issues. The group draws on various cultural teachings and spiritual practices in their work to heal and protect the earth and its waters. Akii Kwe (formerly The Women of Bkejwanong), Minobimaatisiiwin—We Are to Care for Her," position paper (n.d.).

68 S.J. Marchand, *Environmental Impacts on the Lake St. Clair Fishery: A Case Study of Mercury Pollution and Its Effects on the Walpole Island Reserve*, Occasional Paper No. 11 (Walpole Island: Nin Da Waab Jig Heritage Centre, 1986).

69 Nin Da Waab Jig, *Co-Operative Study of Socio-Economic and Environmental Factors in Resource Management on the Walpole Island Reserve—Final Report*, Occasional paper no. 24 (August 1986); Nin Da Waab Jig and Chreod, "*Where the Waters Divide": Bridging Traditional and Modern Approaches to Environmental Management: The Experiences of Walpole Island First Nation*, Technical Report (1997), Walpole Island Heritage Centre and Chreod Ltd.

70 Marchand, *Environmental Impacts*.

71 Marchand, *Environmental Impacts*, 68.

72 Michael Gilbertson, "Injury to Health: A Forensic Audit of the Great Lakes Water Quality Agreement (1972–2005) with Special Reference to Congenital Minamata Disease," Ph.D. thesis, University of Sterling, U.K., 2008.

73 D. Jacobs, Witness Statement, ICI Canada vs. Ontario Consolidated Hearings Board, Transcription of Court Hearing Proceedings 19.1 (1996) (Walpole Island Heritage Centre Archives), 7.

74 Jacobs, Witness Statement, ICI Canada vs. Ontario.

75 McNab, *Earth, Water, Air and Fire*, 55.

76 Jacobs, Witness Statement, ICI Canada vs. Ontario, 6–7.

77 Jacobs, Witness Statement, ICI Canada vs. Ontario, 7.

78 Bend et al., *Feasibility of Conducting Epidemiological Studies*; C.V. Stephens, "A Preliminary Overview of the Nineteenth Century Health History of the Walpole Island First Nation: With Special Focus on the Historical Documents Contained in the Reverend Andrew Jamieson Collection," research report (Hamilton: McMaster University, 2004); Stephens, "'She was weakly for a long time and the consumption set in': Using Parish Records to Explore Disease

Patterns and Causes of Death in a First Nations Community," in *Research in Anthropology and Linguistics (RAL-e) Monograph Series*, ed. J. Littleton, J. Park, A. Herring and T. Farmer (Auckland: Department of Anthropology, University of Auckland, 2008), 134–48; and Stephens, "Syndemics, Structural Violence and The Politics of Health: A Critical Biocultural Approach to the Study of Disease and Tuberculosis Mortality in a Parish Population at Walpole Island (1850–1885)," in *Proceedings of the 39th Annual Algonquian Conference*, ed. Karl S. Hele and Regna Darnell (London: University of Western Ontario, 2008), 581–613.

79 Stephens, "Toxic Talk at Walpole Island First Nation."

80 Nin Da Waab Jig et al., *E-Niizaanaag Wii-ngoshkaag;* Darnell and Stephens, "Species at Risk, Language at Risk."

81 Stephens and Darnell, "The Interdisciplines of Ecosystem Health."

82 C.V. Stephens, "Toxic Talk: Calibrating Divergent Aboriginal and Biomedical Conceptualizations and Understandings of Risk and Environmental Illness in a Contemporary Native Community," paper presented at the Annual Meeting of the American Society for Ethnohistory, 2008; Stephens, "Toxic Talk at Walpole Island First Nation."

83 MacKenzie, *Empires of Nature and the Nature of Empires*, 79.

84 J.A. Trostle, *Epidemiology and Culture* (New York: Cambridge University Press, 2005), 41.

85 N.J. Fox, *Beyond Health: Postmodernism and Embodiment* (London: Free Association, 1999).

CHAPTER 12

Landscape and Mindscape Conjoined: The Empire of Nature and the Nature of Empire in the Journals of Ezhaaswe (William A. Elias) (c. 1848–1929)

David T. McNab

John MacKenzie has written that "local knowledge should never be underestimated: top-down policies have time-and-again shown themselves to be inadequate and the bottom-up perspective is always a necessary corrective. Nor should we demean people by viewing them as helpless victims of economic and environmental behaviour promoted by systems or elites."[1] This chapter explores local knowledge from a community perspective from the bottom-up by offering some reflections on the empire of nature and the nature of empires in William A. Elias's journals. The focus will be an analytical and original study of the two worlds of the life and the writings of William A. Elias. Elias worked as a medicine person, teacher, and Methodist missionary on both sides of the line drawn upon the waters, also known as the international border.

The finding of Elias's journals (in the fall of 2003) offers an unusual, if not unique, opportunity to reflect on this theme of environmental history. Elias's journals came to me in 2003 through my community-based research at Shawanaga First Nation and by the First Nations' oral traditions that are embedded in their family histories. They were given by his daughter, Mrs. George Sharkey, to her friend, Lucy Adelaide Clark, who taught at the Shawanaga School at the end of World War Two. Clarke's daughter sent them to the Shawanaga First Nation in the summer of 2003. It is significant to note that Elias was never a member of the Shawanaga First Nation and did not reside on their reserves. These twenty-five journals cover various years for the time period from 1884 to 1928 and consist of more than four thousand pages of journal entries. Some of them bear the marks of living in the bush for many years, having porcupine teeth marks on the margins. They begin when Elias was at Victoria College in Cobourg in the mid-to-late 1880s. They provide a fascinating glimpse of what an Indigenous person thought about college life and his training as a Methodist minister. They also provide information about the individuals who were then teaching at the college. The following chapter will be told in seven stories.

The *Compact Oxford English Dictionary* defines *Nature* as "the physical world, including plants, animals, the landscape, and natural phenomena, as opposed to humans or human creations."[2] For Indigenous people, *nature* includes human beings as well as the physical and the spirit worlds. Perhaps George Blondin, the Dene elder, said it best when he observed that the proper relationship between the Dene and the rest of creation seems to be governed more by the spiritual than by the laws of man. Indeed, "with regard to medicine power, it is attached to mother earth and all the animals, birds, fish, the air, the weather, and so on."

> When I say everything was based on medicine power, it was just that. That's the way the Indigenous people of the north governed themselves.... To them [the Dene, for he only speaks out of his own experience] the land represents a creation of the creator, that is why they have a lot of spiritual culture. That is why some elders pray to the sun, because it is a creation of the creator. That is why some elders carry a drum at all times because it is used to pray with.... They would say that the creation of the land by the creator represents a mother feeding her children, so our mother land is feeding us. We should thank the creator for that favour. Some elders would thank the creator for other benefits, and so on. They had a lot of spiritual and cultural attachments to the land.... They thanked the creator for everything they got.... In time the land became part of their minds.[3]

Nature is landscape and mindscape conjoined.

Who Was Ezhaaswe (William A. Elias)?

Ezhaaswe was a significant figure in late-nineteenth-century Indigenous history. His English name comes from a variation of the name of the Hebrew prophet Elijah. Elijah was a "troubler" who went to places and did things that no one had ever done before and always took the longest way. An Odawa/Ojibwa, likely of the Bear Clan, his father Medweskug (Jonas Elias) had come to Walpole Island from the Grand Traverse Bay community of Ottawa in present-day Michigan in the early nineteenth century.[4] William Elias was also the grandnephew of the hereditary chief of the Bkejwanong First Nations (Chief Peterwegeschick [In Between Dawn; c. 1817–c. 1926]) at the Walpole Island Unceded Reserve in present-day Southwestern Ontario.[5] An uncle of Elias was Ash qua geezhig (Esquageeshig, known as James Elgin) (c. 1831–c. 1910), also a prominent islander, who was appointed secretary and interpreter for the Walpole Island Council on 25 August 1882.[6] A teacher, interpreter, and Wesleyan Methodist missionary, Elias was one of the first Indigenous people educated at Victoria College, Cobourg (which subsequently moved to Toronto and became Victoria University, University of Toronto); there he was educated and ordained in 1889 as a Wesleyan Methodist minister. His younger brother, Waldron, was a teacher, interpreter, and secretary to the council at the Saugeen Reserve for many years in the early 20th century.[7]

William Elias married Eleanor A. Madwayosh, daughter of the hereditary Chief Madwayosh from the Saugeen Reserve, in Saugeen Township on 22 August 1876.[8] They met when both were students at the Mount Elgin Institute, a residential school founded in 1849,[9] and were married thereafter. They had four daughters: Dorothea Florence (b. 1884?), who perhaps died in childbirth; Lizzie (b. 1885); Beatrice (b. 1891); and Elias's adopted daughter Mildred G. (1917–82). Mildred married Emerson Sands (1912–91) of Walpole Island, and they had twelve children. There are many descendants on the island today.[10]

There is a wonderful story about Elias's relationship with his wife in his journal of 1885. In August 1885, while residing at the Christian Island Reserve, William asked Eleanor whether he could go to Parry Sound for two weeks. At first he recorded that she did not reply to him. When he asked again he got an earful. This was, he said, the first harsh word that she had ever spoken to him since they had been married. He did not write down the swear word or words, likely in the English language, that she had used. He confessed that he was at fault and that he hoped that their perfect union in the eyes of God would be restored. The next day, he wrote that they had reconciled. On 25 August 1885, he wrote that the local Ojibwa midwives, Mrs. George Monague and the "Widow Ka de ge gwan" had come to their place, and that all was ready for the birth of his second child, Elizabeth (Lizzie), who was born at 9 a.m. the next day. I am not sure what the moral of this lesson was for Elias, although it certainly appears that he learned it the hard way.

William Elias's career included working as a teacher and a missionary at the Parry Island mission, which included Cape Croker (1878–87), Henvey Inlet, French River and Grumbling Point (Point Grondine) (July 1876–84), Christian Island (1884–85), Victoria College, Cobourg (1884–90), Walpole

Island (1888–99), Mount Pleasant, Michigan (1899–1903), Petowsky (1903–1908), and Parry Sound and Shawanaga (1908–29), where he passed away in July 1929. Elias was also educated by his mother in the traditional way as a medicine person beginning in 1871. There are no diaries for the war years and, since he was far too old to serve in the Canadian armed forces (he was likely 66 in 1914), this may have been the time he began to practise full-time as a medicine person. He also played a significant and pivotal role in the Methodist Church in Ontario and at the national level, and helped to bring the Church into its union as the United Church of Canada at its key meeting in Sundridge, Ontario, in 1925.[11]

Elias's English name reflects the meaning of his Ojibwa name, "Never gone there." In his life, he always went where others had "never gone there" before. His English name comes from the nineteenth-century Christian tradition of the Wesleyan Methodist Church: Elias is an English version of the Old Testament name for Elijah the prophet. Elijah was also known as a "troubler" who continually told truths that no one wanted to hear.[12] His prophecies came true. In his own life, William Elias was also a "troubler" in a political sense since he was the first Indigenous person to request enfranchisement under Duncan Campbell Scott's revised Indian Act of 1921. He raised issues of integration and modernism by the very actions of his life. He became enfranchised in 1923. Thereafter the Department of Indian Affairs took monies from the Walpole Island trust fund accounts and paid him his share. They also gave him his lot on the reserve without first making a treaty, thereby seemingly creating an artificial black hole in part of the reserve.[13]

Above all, these journals contain a plethora of detail about these First Nation communities. Elias was a good storyteller and had a keen eye for detail, and his almost daily entries give us an insider's portrait of these communities on such topics as politics, the landscape, the weather, and above all, the names—both English and Ojibwa—of the community members. The entries are not humdrum meaningless observations. They describe the people and the land and the stories that came from the land. Since he knew English as a second language well, Elias acted as the recording secretary for the chief and council, and he often clashed with the Indian agents who consistently manipulated the written records sent to Ottawa. Sometimes the journals contain the only written record of what happened during these meetings.

Stories of the Nature of Empires

Story 1: The British Empire: Queen Victoria

Elias was born in the mid-nineteenth century in the Victorian Age during the height of the British Empire. That was the fundamental political framework of Canada during the late nineteenth and the early twentieth centuries. At that time, Indigenous people were seemingly disappearing from the face of what became Ontario. Imperial commentators such as Herman Merivale (1806–1874) could write that "the hunting tribes which first became known to Europeans were the mere fragments of a great family of the human species, losing, in every successive generation, something of the qualities which had distinguished their predecessors, diminishing in numbers and resources, and on their way toward extinction; and there are some who hold the same opinion respecting all the races commonly called savage."[14] Contrary to this view, Merivale argued that the Chippewa people were still in their places and thriving in spite of their encounters with Europeans:

> ... a painful, and I am sure an unnecessary task. The general features of the subject are by this time sufficiently known, and perhaps regarded with sufficient abhorrence: it remains for us now to act; and with a view to that purpose, it is perhaps desirable that we should not cease to dwell so exclusively on the dark side of the picture, as many have hitherto done; still more, that we should not rest contented with vague and general desires of good, or imagine that the evil influences at work are to be counteracted by great undirected efforts—by proclaiming principles—by organizing societies—by pouring forth the lavish contributions of national generosity, without examining for ourselves the channels into which they are to flow. All this is little better than idle philanthropy; or, it should rather be said, than the mere fulfilment of certain ceremonies, by which the mind relieves itself of the sense of a debt.[15]

This was the British imperial intellectual conversation in which Elias was raised. The Anishinabe tradition put forward by his great-uncle of seeing with two eyes—one forward into the future with European learning and the other back to Anishinabe traditions—taught him how to resist this imperial ethos and in the end to survive into the twentieth century (and it is of course relevant to survival in the early twenty-first century as well). At the same time, however, Elias appears to have been invisible in the historical record.

Other than his recently discovered journals, Elias left behind only a brief reminiscence of his life, which is in the United Church Archives in Toronto. He is not referred to in any of the standard studies of the history of Methodism in Canada.[16] Nor is there any reference to him, much less any separate biography, in the most recently published volume of the *Dictionary of Canadian Biography*, in which he would have appeared since he passed on in 1929. Neil Semple in his official history of the Methodist Church states incorrectly that Indigenous people disappeared as ministers of the Methodist church in the 1860s; such was clearly not the case.

Elias grew up under the aegis of the British empire. His journal entry for Tuesday, 26 May 1925, provides his views on this subject:

> It was a chilling north wind that kept everybody so much in delicate bones aching and made the creatures suffering keen sense of pain and could not much realize the joy of the Victoria celebration: that stampeded by the young people in their exultation over the ball games the Adults and the children that have been combined to play together in the celebration of the Victoria Day[.] Greatest Day of all the celebrated Holidays and all Nations in the World rejoice in this day because The Queen Victoria was a true Christian in its reality no other Sovereign was and is. will never be as true Christian as she was. She was honored in all the whole world among all Nations.

While paying honour to Queen Victoria, Elias syncretically was celebrating a "Christian" holiday that was the occasion in 1925 of Queen Victoria's birthday.

Story 2: Protecting the Land from the Canadian Empire: From Christian Island to Toronto and Ottawa, Winter 1886

After the seeming demise of the British Empire in the Canadian nationalist context, a "new" one took its place in 1867 with the Canadian Confederation, constructed on the basis of the Two-Row Wampum, which was a treaty framework. This was the assumption in which Elias operated in 1886, just months after the 1885 Métis resistance movement and the hanging of Louis Riel. Elias clearly knew highly prominent persons in the late nineteenth century who ran the Canadian empire with British imperial and colonial ideology intact.

Early in January 1886, Elias was asked by then-chief Noah Assance to go with the Christian Island chief and council to Toronto to investigate their land rights issues where they called on their newly hired lawyer, George Ritchie (of the Toronto firm of Gilroy and Ritchie); they went with him on 6 January to the Crown Lands Department where they copied the "map of the surrenders." They then went to dinner and soon after they started off for the Education Office, but Dr. Hodgins, then the Ontario Minister of Education, "being not in the office they had to visit him at his mansion—they were cordially received, and were conducted into the drawing room, where they were entertained by Dr Hodgins personally and soon they left for the museum and at once proceeded to the office of Dr Sutherland," who was then the Mission Secretary of the Methodist Church, had a long interview with him.[17] This effort was followed up by another trip to Toronto on 8 and 9 March. Here they met Dr. Orientikha, Sutherland, and Dr. Burwash of the Methodist Church. Elias was told that a branch residential school of the Shingwauk School in Sault Ste. Marie was proposed by E.F. Wilson, the "Church of England Priest." It was to be opened on the Rama Reserve at Lake Simcoe. Elias noted that he was "fully objecting [to] the scheme." On the same trip, they also went to Ottawa in March 1886, where they arranged to meet with officials of the Department of Indian Affairs and the prime minister, Sir John A. Macdonald, who was then also the minister of Indian Affairs. On 11 March, Elias recorded that he and Chief Noah Assance went with Ritchie to Ottawa by train, where they met Allen Salt of Roseneath and William Beatty of Parry Sound and "made some arrangement to meet in the House of Commons at the precise hour of ten." In Ottawa, they

> met some members of Parliament. H.H. Cook M.P. was the first one to take them around through the Parliament Buildings and then they were led to Mr. Obrien M.P. who also took special interest in conducting them to the office of Deputy of the [Supt. Genl.] of Indian Affairs. who received them kindly and given them permission to see all the papers containing the surrenders of the different periods. at twelve oclock they left for the Parliament Buildings to fill the engagement of dining or rather lunching with Col. W.E. Obrien M.P. in the private lunch rooms of members of Parliament. they had so good a lunch, but the colonel ordering the [grog] called the port, rendered the unpleasantness of the occasion which made the Lawyer who had the weakness to take it, unbalanced his eyes to the uneasiness of Mr. Elias. soon after lunch they went in the Indian offices again. They got through at three oclock p.m. and started off for the Parliament Buildings from the Indian Office to hear the debating in the House. which was packed to the doors. But H.H Cook M.P enables them to be ushered into the crowded gallery. where they had a chance of seeing Sir Jno. A. McDonald the Premier of Canadian Government. he was sitting in a graceful style an innocent figure. but who can tell "where the responsibility of the North West Rebellion will rest" mind you reader the eight millions of dollars had been expended on that memorable target of Indian huts, which had been better to devote it ($8,000,000) in civilizing

> them by the gospel of Jesus Christ and freely circulating the Holy Bible. those poor half breeds would have learned to be loyal to their Sovereign the Queen Victoria. by first being taught to be loyal to their highest Sovereign Our Lord and [Saviour] Jesus Christ. may every man be careful to what he is doing for the sake of earthly [honour]. May all serve God with the humbleness of heart- Friday March 12th Mr. Elias early in the morning went to meet Mr. Ritchie at Russels and arranged to interview with Sir John at 3 p.m. Mr. Elias had an interview [with] L. Van Koughnet about the school management fund, to aid him attending the College of Bellville—Mr. Van Koughnet thought the band of Walpole Island might aid him for one hundred dollars $100.00 at least. providing that Mr. Elias be willing to have his shares deducted to replace the amount thus taken out of the principal money—they met Sir Hector Langevin instead of Sir John A. who favourably received then and made a promise that the should consider their 'case' in Government hands—After which they attended the debate in the House of Commons, at 11 oclock p.m. they started for their House.[18]

Elias was harshly critical of Macdonald and the Canadian imperial policy in what became part of Western Canada.

He also felt the operation of this imperial policy through the federal Indian Act of 1876 and its successors, legislation which is still with us today. The monies for Elias's education should not have been taken out of the Walpole Island First Nation trust funds by the federal Department of Indian Affairs, and a specific claim should be filed today with the federal government regarding this transaction. Other than Elias's subsequent education at Victoria College, it is not precisely known what immediately came from these visits to Toronto and Ottawa regarding land and treaty rights. However, it does appear that these early initiatives led eventually to the validation by the federal government of these land rights and then the unfortunate failure of the Williams Treaties of 1923, and to the still ongoing efforts to restore Indigenous land and treaty rights.[19] It was at this meeting in Toronto on 6 January 1886 that Elias was able to arrange for his education at Victoria College, which would lead to his ordination as a Wesleyan Methodist minister. This was not a free ride since the monies to pay for it came out of his own annuity payments.[20]

The journals also provide commentary on the various spiritual practices—Christian or otherwise—of community members. Although the journal is primarily written in English, some of Elias's sermons are written in Ojibwa; the journal also contains some of his drawings of the places in which he resided, such as at Bay Mills when he first visited that place in 1903. Elias was fluent in Ojibwa and preached his sermons in his own language. The journals will be of great interest to the current members of these communities because of the loving portraits of the individuals in them as written by Elias, such as his portrait of his great-uncle, the hereditary Chief "Petwekeshig" at Walpole Island, who is one of the best sources for both the oral and the written history of the community in the nineteenth century. Elias's journal entry of Tuesday, 20 October 1891, is particularly striking, especially since the former chief was then ninety years old:

> The storm is a good sized one[.] [O]n returning home I called on grand uncle Petwekeshig who was at home. He was glad to see me once more in his old fashioned shanty[.] [A] wooden chimney at the one end of the house, a bright fire was before him, a big wooden pipe in his left hand and a piece of sliffer (sliver) in his right hand reaching down to the fire apparently to the interest of lighting his pipe. When I commended his piece of workmanship on that rustic chimney of his a bright happy smile lit his sallowed face. [T]o describe his furniture would not be much. [B]ut would readily be understood by those who have visited the poor Indian home with a careful eye[.] [O]n the right hand side of the shanty two logs laid cross-wise on which some planks are resting almost reaching the whole height of that home, constituting a bed on which five or six blankets were lying strewn in every shape to suit the careless living[.] [S]ome cooking utensils were carelessly laid on a place near the fire, left there apparently in readiness for their use—On the left hand corner near the door a board was fastly nailed diagonally, so into that enclosure, three or four different kinds of apples, which holds about five or six bushels, were stored, ready for their consumption. [A] square little box was pointed to me for a seat on which I gladly rested to begin a good old chat. This aged friend was one time a great man of the island—who was head chief of the place for a long time—and was the wealthiest Indian of the place. But my dear reader what brought him into this most dismal little home? [I]t was, I will answer the question through that demon drink of alcohol, which dragged this poor old soul to such sad circumstances.[21]

Now, while we should not deny the seeming impact of alcoholism, it is a bit too much to make such moral judgements about a person more than ninety years old, who went on to live well over one hundred years. Elias did have biased Wesleyan Methodist blinkers about intemperance, even when he was in the presence of greatness.

Story 3: Walpole Island in the 1890s: The American Empire

Closer to home, Canada collaborated with the American empire to bring changes to Elias's homeland. Fraud, white speculators, and corrupt Indian agents were the everyday order of things, and Elias was not exaggerating since his comments have been borne out by ongoing treaty and land rights research over the last four decades.[22] On 7 January 1898, he recorded the following portrait of the state of affairs on Walpole Island at the end of the nineteenth century:

> While in the state of stupor by the influence of liquor the yoke of oxen they had and domestic fowls were all carried away by these freebooters [pirates or terrorists] over to the American side[.] [T]his freebooting took place before the [William (1843–1901), twenty-fifth president of the United States] McKinley Bill [the high tariff of 1890] was introduced on the United States when cattle and horses were entering ["into" stroked out] the States without any fee[.] [S]uch traders, freebooters, or poachers as they might be characterized would bring liquor and the Indians would indulge collectively drinking carousals when it would often be dangerous ["al," stroked out] to go along the river shore[.] [C]ertain locations infested by these freebooters or poachers for [pillaging] was going on, chickens, ducks, geese, and turkeys and some time the pigs will be minus in the possession of the Indian families without any one to protect the community. I was at this time worried that my life was in danger if I persisted to use my influence against wicked acts at one time when remonstrating against the selling of liquor to the Indians. That those freebooters would shoot me like a dog, but I was not to be frightened by such threats.[23]

However, Elias was removed from Walpole Island by the Methodist Church (likely for his own safety) early in the twentieth century to Michigan, replacing the Reverend John Jacobs at Petoskey. His homeland was no longer secure and he moved to another part of Anishinabeg Territory.

Story 4: Land and Treaty Rights in Michigan: The American Empire Again

The American empire had also attempted to "conquer" the Odawa homeland of William Elias's father in the early nineteenth century. After being driven out of "Canada," Elias moved to central Michigan. In the spring of 1905 he became involved in the struggle for land and treaty rights in Michigan, undoubtedly connecting to issues from his Odawa father's past in Grand Traverse Bay. The Odawas (Ottawas) had never signed the early Treaties which covered Michigan in the early and mid-nineteenth century. He recorded that

> Charlevoix, [18 March] 1905
>
> Yesterday I met A.C. Ames Esq. he told me if I could see Mrs. Penassy he was willing to give me fifty dollars $50.00 and give her chance to the use of the farm for one summer. I was glad to find that he was not anxious about his money just then I owe him $7.00 on the rent. together with the new applicants for some researchers have been my lot to look into. I am convinced that I shall use the United States for my claims. Simon Kezhegobenasse received a communication from the Chester Howe of Washington. Senator Burrows was to bring the Bill pass through the Senate.

On 13 April 1905, Elias wrote in his journal that they had made a trip to Grand Rapids relating to the land and treaty rights of the Chippewa and Odawa communities of central and northern Michigan:

> We arrived this morning at the Union Depot we did not see Bro. Robert D. Agosa and at once went to a Hotel where we had out breakfast and while we partook it, our Bro. Agosa passed the the [*sic*] street going towards our station. When we were about to step out of this Hotel we met our friend. Finding we had some time to spare, before the hour of 10.oclock a.m. had arrived which was set apart for our interview with Wm Alders Smith (Congressman), went around to view the City. We had a good time. The hour soon came when we had to go into Wm Alders Smith's office, we found him ready to receive us. he accorded us a royal welcome.
>
> We got our interrogations answered satisfactorily and put us on the right course for the persue [pursuance] for the filing of our claims before the court of claims. We left the City 1.50 p.m....
>
> Petoskey Ap.19, 1905
>
> at 8 oclock Bros. Agosa and Wm Petoskey came into my place, went into the office of Pailthorp (*Lawyer*)[.] A Power of Attorney was prepared for us, and determined to act for the Indians, I met a quite number of Indians today. some women from Cross Village selling fancy bark work. I remained at home all day, engaged in reading....

> Petoskey Ap. 20, 1905
>
> Indians early this morning flocked into the office of Pailthorp. the blank forms of power of attorney came out at 9 oclock and they were duly signed by many Indians, who were Ottawas. In the afternoon I came to Susan Lake or Charlevoix stayed over night at Mrs. Susan Walkers and then came Benjamin Willis' where I am staying.... [24]

Elias kept alive these land claims, which were beginning to be resolved in the early twentieth century within the American empire.

In 1910, Elias seems to have left the Methodist Church for at least a decade. It may have been because he had reached retirement age. For Elias, the church by then was a religious empire in its own right. At least until the 1920s, Elias's occupation of "hunting for souls" seems to have been replaced by residing on his farm adjacent to the Shawanaga Reserve near Georgian Bay and his practice of traditional medicine—Indian doctoring, as it was then known.

The Empire of Nature

Story 5: Drawings of Bay Mills, 5 October 1903

Elias also drew the landscape when he first visited the Bay Mills community on 5 October 1903. These drawings have survived in his journals for more than 100 years. Like any good story, they have a spirit in them, and they were returned to this community in April 2005. This was significant because Elias's drawings were the only ones existing that show what the Bay Mills community looked like in 1903. His drawings are now part of their stories and the history of this community. In these drawings of Bay Mills, landscape and mindscape are conjoined and become again a circle of time.[25]

Story 6: Central Lake, Michigan, 14 November 1904

Mindscape can evoke landscape as well. In this sense, Elias's writings in his journals are also like drawings—"just like tracks" as Louise Erdrich describes them in her children's book *The Birchbark House* (1999).[26] The Michigan peninsula on the west side is a very beautiful place. Below is Elias's description of this part of the empire of nature on 14 November 1904:

> I brought my ticket to Petoskey, but could only get as far as Central Lake, I was glad to find this train soon steaming its way into the station of Central Lake, a fine little town it is, considering its surroundings. I went around to several places and to the bridge which crosses the Central River on the east side of the

> town, then I came back to the station to jot down what I have got to record in my journal. I first we went to the town to buy a pencil for I had broken my pencil just when I tried to sharpen it. anon, it is 1.15 p.m.—I bought a pencil and began to jot down the incidents noted on the way here and then I went around some through the town which the citizens were having their dinners and had seen much of it. I was very glad to have had the opportunity in looking around the town. The Lake to look at it from the town bridge was something took me at once to my fancy nothing could exceed its beauty and loveliness considering it situation from the interior stand point of views. [A]ll other places will have their respective beauty on their situation with the largest Lakes. [B]ut this one ranging from one half mile to one mile wide was it five or six miles long, fish according to the story goes, they are abounding. the scenery around this town was just grand. Farther away you or a person goes from the town east and west heavier the land is found[.][27]

I visited this place in the first week of April 2006, and the landscape is still conjoined with mindscape. Many of the Indian Methodist churches in which Elias preached have been preserved by the Anishinabe and are still there today.

Story 7: The Farm at Shawanaga

Elias's farm was located adjacent to the Shawanaga Reserve on the Shawanaga River on lot 100, concessions 5 and 6, Shawanaga Township. Shawanaga means "the place of sand at the bottom of the bay." Elias said that he was going to rest and acquired a licence of occupation from the Ontario government for a farm and built a log cabin on it. He lived there for almost two decades. However, it was not his "home." He went home to Bkejwanong and passed away early in July 1929. Below are some of his observations from his journal from his second home adjacent to the Shawanaga Reserve. This landscape became his mindscape. The seasons drew him in to the empire of nature:

> Monday, July 6, 1925
>
> The sun came out with such a brilliancy that a heat emitted from it had it pronounced the day was going to be excessively hot: and I had the pleasure of knowing that some good may be expected this excessive heat it is to drive the people out of the southern States to the shores of Georgian Bay; and cool off here to recruit of the loss of health due from the excessive heat that produces unwholesome air and ague feeling in head, a sense of heaviness over comes

the strength of action. I was very glad and thankful to realize such life of joy in breathing the wholesome breeze fresh from the lake. I started for the farm alone and did some hoing [*sic*] corn and writing. It rained in after-noon and nearly the whole night. lot of rain we had last night, and could not do any thing till after the rain: I sat down and watched the flaring light of the tremendous thundering: It shook the house freely for the concussion of the air was tremendously great by the incessant thundering.

Shawanaga, Thursday,—Oct. 6, 1910.—Again a rainy morning that has done so much to ["change," stroked out] hasten the change of the fall weather that the hues so illuminating to mark the Autumn season generally striking in a pleasing appearance making the contrast the blooming season of the Spring, both are the seasons to be glad in. I am every body feels happy the thought to see another Autumn season: when the grains are harvested and many other things come to consumination that the visitors once more doth come: for many people dread the winter to think of the chilling air that they think the people in majority at this time who are more or less invalids: must needs pass away because of cold blasts of the winter frost which bites so briskly as to the very ones of the suffering one: in this vise the ghastly death is so much dreaded of: but one who implicitly trust the Almighty God. will never think about the death but thinks simply ["thinks," stroked out] of the glorious transfer that will be consummated of this particular period even though it comes when it may....

Friday:—Oct. 7, 1910 Excessively cold morning. but one of the pleasant features of the day was. it was clear bright to a perfection: the stillness of the ["air," added] was some thing marvellous, not a breeze to move a leaf which is hued with a most lovely exquisite tinge as the autumn atmosphere colors the nature of the leaves.

Friday.—Nov. 11, 1910. Snowy morning once more not milder that the storm had only just begun and according to the version of the old man James Pawis that the winter had settled down for good: because there were no snow during the time that the leaves were yet attached to the tops and branches. This is the old Indian signification that a long winter was coming and the snowing time would not cease till a plenty of snow have fallen on the ground. then the wintry weather may slack for some time again.

January 18th, 1911

snowing today and some thing more may be done to make the roads nice and productive ["much," stroked out] of much good. Not snowing any great deal just flurries: like the play of swallows upon the air chasing one of another: that we may look for the good time in the winter season, for it is said that snow is the greatest fertilizer. that man who works on farm could wish to strew on his fields but this is by kindness or merciful kindness of God. for a man. that the work is done for him instead of strewing fertilizer it is done by his creator. This is the merciful kindness of God.

Thursday, 26 March, and Friday, 27 March, 1925

Thursday
This is a real spring weather. I saw four blackbirds sitting on the tree: just come from the south. Yes the full time for sugar making has come after all.

Friday
A thunder storm did stir the atmosphere last night and had much of the service to rot and rend the ice and snow off the ground and waters; The air is full of mist almost like a fog the heaviness of the air seem to weigh the very skies: I am satisfied to think that the winter is about really over; O there may some days in store for real cool weathers to follow this unusual very mild weather: it generally does....[28]

The time of sugar-making is described in great detail. This aspect of spring is one of the most beautiful in the landscape and in the mindscape of the Anishinabe people. And so it was for Elias.

Retrospect: The Empire of Nature and the Nature of Empires

Indigenous knowledge comes from the land. The Elias journals, the drawings, and the stories in them come from the land. Since the landscape and mindscape in these journals are conjoined, they are being gifted and going back to the land. Elias fought constantly against both the Canadian and American empires protecting the land—sometimes successfully, sometimes not. There is no doubt that he saw the empire of nature around him as something animate and very powerful—he deeply appreciated its beauty and its many gifts of knowledge. The empire of nature is the essence of the Indigenous knowledge and the stories in William A. Elias's journals. He was able to bridge the borders of knowledge between oral traditions of First Nations, including the empire of nature, and the Imperial world of the Euro/American knowledge systems embedded in pen and ink and was able to go to many places where others have never gone before.

The last word on nature should be best left to Elias's poetry, from his journal entry of 26 March 1925, entitled "An Enrapt Spring":

The spring cometh out of sun's rays.
Sooner desolveth the snow by-ways:
The birds do come with joy in sight.
Crows made their plaintive growling sigh;

The children can turn to rapture,
O'er the return of joyful 'stir:
Their voices are mingled streamlets,
As they ripple through furro'ed grass.

The rocky bluffs, with snow daubing,
Mingled with fur scrub contrasting,
Creates a scene, incomparable:
No artist painter can compare.[29]

Notes

1 John M. MacKenzie, *Empires of Nature and the Nature of Empires, Imperialism, Scotland and the Environment* (East Linton: Tuckwell, 1997), 81.

2 *The Compact Oxford Dictionary*, 2nd ed., ed. Catherine Soanes (Oxford: Oxford University Press, 2003), 750.

3 George Blondin, "My Life in the Sahtu," Submission to Royal Commission on Indigenous Peoples, June 1993, 8–9. I am indebted to David McLaren for this reference.

4 At the 11 August 1887 General Council Meeting, Jonas Elias was one of the citizens of Walpole Island who voted against the surrender of the Shooting Grounds for leasing purposes; see General Council Meeting held at Walpole Island on August 11th, 1887, RG 10, Volume 2118, File 22,610 Part 1 (Microfilm Reel # C-11,162), Library and Archives Canada (LAC). Jonas Elias's history was revealed by my visit to the Research Center of the Ziibiwing Cultural Center of Anishinabe Culture and Lifeways, Isabella Reservation, Mount Pleasant, Michigan, on 3 April 2006. I am grateful for the assistance of Anita Heard, the centre's research co-ordinator, on this visit.

5 Historical Photos Binder, c. 1890–1950, Walpole Island First Nation, Nin.Da. Waab.Jig.

6 Ebenezer Watson, Indian superintendent, Sarnia, to Sir John A. Macdonald, prime minister and superintendent general of Indian Affairs, 25 August 1882, Binder on "Charles Jacobs Family Tree," Reference No. 1672, Nin.Da.Waab.Jig. Files, Bkejwanong First Nations.

7 Elias, Journal, #8, 1921–22.

8 Registration #001369, Saugeen Township, 22 August 1876, Ontario Marriage Index, Microfilm 19, Provincial Archives of Ontario.

9 Elizabeth Graham, comp., *The Mush Hole: Life at Two Indian Residential Schools* (Waterloo: Heffle, 1997).

10 This information was gathered during visits to Highbanks Cemetery and Nin. Da.Waab.Jig., Walpole Island Heritage Centre, Bkejwanong Unceded Reserve, in February 2004 and on 11 June 2006.

11 See David T. McNab, "'those freebooters would shoot me like a dog': American Terrorists and Homeland Security in the Journals of Ezhaaswe (William A. Elias [1856–1929])," paper given in the workshop on "Lines Drawn upon the Water: Indigenous People and the International Boundary through the Great Lakes Watershed," University of Western Ontario, 12 February 2005, subsequently revised and published as "'those freebooters would shoot me like a dog': American Terrorists and Homeland Security in the Journals of Ezhaaswe (William A. Elias [1856–1929])" in *Lines Drawn upon the Water: First Nations and the Great Lakes Borders and Borderlands*, ed. Karl S. Hele (Waterloo: Wilfrid Laurier University Press, 2008), 115–29; See also David T. McNab, "Centering Identities in Border Places: Oral Traditions and the Written Record in the Journals of William A. Elias (c. 1848–1929), paper given at the American Society for Ethnohistory, Annual Meeting, Santa Fe, NM, 20 November 2005.

12 See II Kings in the Old Testament. This name fits Elias's life as a Methodist missionary.

13 Elias' land remains a black hole in the unceded reserve to this day. To date, nothing has been written about Elias, perhaps because he was an Indigenous person and was thus seen not to be a part of the written history of Canada.

14 Quoted in David McNab, "Herman Merivale and the British Empire, 1806–1874," Ph.D. diss., University of Lancaster, 1978, chap. 5, p. 211.15.

15 Quoted in McNab, "Herman Merivale and the British Empire, 1806–1874," chap. 5, p. 197.

16 See William Westfall, *Two Worlds: The Protestant Culture of Nineteenth-Century Ontario* (Kingston: McGill-Queen's University Press, 1989); Neil Semple, *The Lord's Dominion: The History of Canadian Methodism* (Kingston: McGill-Queen's University Press, 1996).

17 Elias, Journal #1, 1885–87, entry of 6 January 1886. Elias sometimes wrote in the third person.

18 Elias, Journal #1, 1885–87.

19 Elias, Journal #1, 1885–87.

20 Elias, Journal #1, 1885–87, entry of 6 January 1886.

21 Elias, Journal #1, 20 October 1891.

22 David McNab, "Borders of Water and Fire: Islands as Sacred Places and as Meeting Grounds," in *Indigenous Cultural Landscapes*, ed. Jill Oakes, Rick Riewe, et al. (Winnipeg: Indigenous Issues, 2004), 44–45. See, for example, the following reference to Americans fishing: Vankoughnet wrote to his counterpart, Major John Tilton, then the federal deputy minister of Fisheries, on 8 July 1885 regarding the marshes and fishing in Lake St. Clair: "On the occasion of an interview which I had recently with Mr. C.H., Gooderham Esq., and Mr. Bright, of Toronto, who, with others, have a Shooting lease from the Dept. for part of Walpole Island & its marshes, these gentlemen informed me that American fishermen cast their nets near the northern mouth of the streams running through Walpole Island. They do not violate the law exactly by throwing their nets across the streams, but they have them sufficiently far out on each side of the mouth of the streams to impede effectively the passage of the fish up the streams. These gentlemen stated that the streams are ["therefore in consequence" stroked out] consequently almost completely depleted of fish & that the Indians are suffering as a consequence. I feel convinced that I have only to bring this matter under your notice to cause you to have the proper remedy applied." There was no reply from the deputy minister of Fisheries to this letter; RG 10, Volume 2118, File 22,610, Part 1, Microfilm Reel # C-11, 162, LAC.

23 Elias, Journals, 26 May 1888–3 December 1913, entry of 7 January 1898.

24 Elias, Journal #5, 5 October 1903–20 May 1905.

25 David McNab, *Circles of Time: Land Rights and Resistance in Ontario* (Waterloo: Wilfrid Laurier University Press, 1999), 1–10.

26 David McNab, "Of Bears and Birds: The Concept of History in Erdrich's Autobiographical Writings," in *Approaches to Teaching the Works of Louise Erdrich*, ed. Connie Jacobs et al. (New York: Modern Language Association, 2004), 32–41.

27 Elias, Journal #5, 5 October 1903–20 May 1905.

28 Elias, Journal #16, entries of 25–26 March 1925.

29 Elias, Journal #16, 26 March 1925.

CHAPTER 13

A World of Beauty: The Spirits within Nature in the Writings of Louise Erdrich

Ute Lischke

In his published lectures on *Empires of Nature and the Nature of Empires: Imperialism, Scotland and the Environment* (1997), John M. MacKenzie notes the "complexities of imperial rule, ethnic contributions from above and below, the limitations imposed upon policy, and approaches to the conceptualisation of landscape."[1] Louise Erdrich, a writer of fiction, poetry, and autobiography, is a keen observer of nature and landscape, and in her works she embodies the complexities of the issues of imperialism, landscape, and the spirits within nature. In her writings, rich with symbolism and motifs of nature, she evokes snapshots of the natural world, which has a spiritual impact upon her. In this chapter, I will discuss several works of fiction and autobiography that reflect the spiritual impact of nature upon her life and writings.

Erdrich's writings are about communities, especially those Indigenous communities that have been dispossessed of their lands by European settlers, and those communities' struggles for survival. In her narratives, she positions her characters in relation to each other and to other communities, thus showing their resistance from the inside out. Her work has often been compared to the *Little House on the Prairie* series by Laura Ingalls Wilder, whose perspective is that of the European settler—except that Erdrich relates the story from the perspective of the Indigenous families who have been displaced and dispossessed. Erdrich's narratives are significant in redefining the role of Indigenous communities, in understanding their struggles for survival and, importantly, in exploring the role of stories and storytelling within Indigenous communities. Her stories reveal the interconnectedness of our world, our relationship to nature and the spirits within nature as well as to each other.

Route 2 (1991), written with Michael Dorris, is an early travelogue about a circuitous family trip from the East Coast (New Hampshire), where Erdrich was living at the time, to the Pacific West Coast of the United States, returning north of the forty-ninth parallel via Manitoulin Island and back home. *The Blue Jay's Dance* (1995) is an autobiography of a birth year—recollections of Erdrich's life in the country with her young children. I will also briefly address the children's books, *Grandmother's Pigeon* (1996) and *The Range Eternal* (2002), both of which address the home, or the hearth, as a refuge. Her juvenile fiction, *The Birchbark House* (1999), *The Game of Silence* (2005), and *The Porcupine Year* (2008), are significant for demonstrating the relationship between Indigenous peoples and nature. Finally, *Tracks* (1988) and *Four Souls* (2004) illustrate how progress and the destruction of nature/land create havoc in the lives of Indigenous peoples.[2]

On my visit to Birchbark Books in Minneapolis, Minnesota (April 2002), the bookstore owned by Louise Erdrich, it was very evident that spirituality and the natural world have a prominent role in this place. This former butcher's shop has been transformed as landscape. Not only the foodstuffs, such as wild rice (*manomin*), corn (*mandamin*), and licorice, prominently displayed alongside the books on the shelves, but also the playfully decorated confessional from a Catholic church that Erdrich had recently acquired were a testament to the inherent connections between spirituality, nature, and the real world. No doubt the confessional as artefact, related to her novel *The Last Report on the Miracle at Little No Horse* (2001), which deals with Father Damien Modeste, a cross-dressing woman priest living on the reservation at Little No Horse,[3] toys with this spiritual dilemma.

During our conversation, Erdrich emphasized the importance and significance of *place*, or nature—the land where we come from, and its relationship to *home*. She emphasized the significance of her roots and their relationship to her work. Her mother is Chippewa/Cree/Métis from the Turtle Mountain Reservation in North Dakota. Her father, Ralph Erdrich, was born soon after his family emigrated from Germany to the United States in the early 1920s. Her grandfather had been a master butcher in southern Germany, and their ancestral home, Erdrichshof, still stands near Pforzheim. Upon arrival in North America, the Erdrich family had to adapt to new ways; yet they were also still connected to Europe. For example, Erdrich recalled that her grandfather fought for Germany in World War One. However, during World War Two, her father was fighting for the American side, while her German relatives living near Pforzheim were firebombed by the Americans; yet the family held together. Erdrich recalled, "We just had to get through it."[4] This story is just one part of her family history and of herself.

Erdrich tells stories about her landscape and nature. Thomas King has said in *The Truth about Stories* (1993), the truth is that "that's all we are."[5] Stories come from the land, from mother earth—nature. In Erdrich's works, her stories also come from the land and indeed from specific places. In her autobiographical works, we discover where those stories have come from in her own life, to find their way eventually into her fiction.

Route 2

The prolific author of critically acclaimed novels, poetry, and three autobiographical works, Erdrich has shown in the latter how she has progressed in her thinking of and reaction to nature and to the environment. In *Route 2*, coauthored with her then-husband Michael Dorris (1945–97), she begins her journey of self-discovery as a tourist, in awe of the beauty of nature, but ends the book with a visit to Manitoulin Island, the place where the spirits reside. Here she discovers spirituality and a connection to nature and a "glimpse of a world in balance."[6]

In the summer of 1985, Louise Erdrich and Michael Dorris set out in a Dodge Caravan carrying their four children—two babies and two teenagers (Pallas, 1 ½; Persia, 2 ½; Madeline, 11; and Sava, 14)—leaving one son behind to attend an Outward Bound camp in Canada. They head west from their home near Dartmouth in New Hampshire and then east again to discover North America along the historic Teddy Roosevelt Highway known as Route 2. The family makes its way westward, stopping to visit some of Michael's family, and then along the Saskatchewan Border, the Sweet Grass Hills, taking Route 2 to Puget Sound; Route 2 ends on Pacific Avenue, right at the Pacific Ocean. Heading east, they remark on the beauty and size of the country: "Canada is a big country. It takes four large packages of powdered milk to keep two babies marginally content in their car seats from British Columbia to Ontario and at least one water slide a day to subdue older children gone stir crazy in their futile attempts to complete travel bingo cards."[7] In terms of the vastness of the land, the authors comment, "There are stretches of hundreds of miles in British Columbia, Alberta, Saskatchewan and Manitoba with nary a dry cleaner shop, a moving van, or a roadside picnic table to check off and when a featured item does at last appear, the competition to claim it can make the quest for the holy grail look tame by comparison.... But then too there is scenery so distracting, so stunning, that the ordinary contests of confined child vs. parent are temporarily suspended."[8] They are not just consumers of nature. Erdrich also offers insights into the spirits that are part of nature.

Canada is also a "foreign" country,[9] a different nation-state. This becomes evident to the family when they stop at a local bank to change some traveller's cheques into Canadian currency and when they impress the children at a small café by purchasing ice cream bars and soft drinks with exotic, unfamiliar, foreign labels.[10] In high altitude country, Erdrich notices an eagle and remarks, "Kootenai National Park seems to us true wilderness."[11]

The family passes herds of grazing antelopes, flights of geese, skyscrapers in Calgary, and straight, bisecting fields of wheat and oats, as Alberta turns to Saskatchewan. South of Winnipeg, they detour to Wahpeton, North Dakota—a visit to Louise's hometown for a rest. By now their caravan is encrusted with the remains of crackers and fig bars, and pasted with national park permits. But it is after they leave Wahpeton, heading east to Fergus Falls, Minnesota, via Route 2 in Bemidji, to Sault Ste. Marie and into Ontario, that Erdrich's true spiritual journey begins. Their "last major stop on this journey, is a mythic place of origin, the starting point for the tribe to which Louise belongs."[12]

Manitoulin Island is a sacred place, and it is the fourth stopping place in Anishinabe history: "The only indisputable fact known about the place for over a century (1700–1825) is that a great fire raged across the land. Some speculate that it was set intentionally in order to eradicate both evil spirits and disease."[13] Manitoulin Island, the place of the Great Spirit, is the largest freshwater island in the world, located off the north shore of Lake Huron in Ontario, Canada. Anishinabe stories tell us that manitous have always inhabited Manitoulin Island, supernatural beings that guide their lives. Here there is also a significant place, Dreamer's Rock, where many young people go to receive their vision quest.[14] Erdrich has travelled here often, learning to bead and to quill, and practising her skills at speaking Ojibwa. It is the spirituality of the place, the connection to her people that instills her with primal energy:

> Manitoulin figures as a haven where Anishinabec language and custom is forever cherished and revitalized, where a new spirit of optimism and delight constantly is re-formed. Even in myth, it is a place where people come to gain a glimpse of a world in balance, a world as it could be, a world of beauty governed and reflected by art. Honorine's words come back to us as we ride the ferry to Tobermory, as we rush across the final miles and reconnect the loop that began when we left our house in New Hampshire weeks before.[15]

Erdrich tells stories—indeed her life story—to find her own sense of self, her place, and her spirituality, a glimpse of a life in balance. She discovers that her own story has also been shaped by Manitoulin Island.

The Blue Jay's Dance (1995)

Before the Erdrich family ever arrived on North American soil, there existed the romanticized (and male) European notion of wilderness, often defined as wild, uncultivated land inhabited only by wild animals. In this view, all things are categorized and disconnected; and Aboriginal people are noticeable by their absence from this definition. North American Aboriginal people have no such notion of, or word for, *wilderness* in their cultures or languages. Part of this conception of wilderness has to do with Europeans' views of the North as an abstract space. The concept of North is geographically defined according to the compass: for example, a northerly wind or a person from the North. In North America, the North is that which is sparsely populated, pure, untouched by "civilization." However, North for Anishinabe is not abstract but real and practical since it is one of the four sacred directions, and it is a place where the spirits of the Bear dwell.[16] A product of our collective imagination, these ideas of wilderness and the North must also be explored from a female perspective. In her poetry, fiction, and prose, Louise Erdrich evokes a longing and desire for the other that reflects her split Métis self—the European and the Aboriginal.

The Blue Jay's Dance is Erdrich's autobiography of a birth year, a composite of her experiences from her diary of the birth of her children in the early 1990s during her marriage with Michael Dorris. Erdrich recounts her experience of giving birth and reflects on motherhood, as she awaits the birth of the youngest of her three daughters, who joins the family's three adopted children. She now becomes a keen observer and chronicler of nature and "all my relations," evoking seasonal changes parallel to the changes of life, observing animals in their natural habitat in the secluded New Hampshire home that she shared with Dorris. Her descriptions of the natural world around her are very spiritual, but in creating a strong bond with her newborn baby she displays a healthy respect for nature and the environment. Included in her recollections are also several recipes she and Dorris prepare together, including an all-licorice dinner. Family moments such as these evoke memories of her relations and their histories.

Erdrich recalls her family history, noting that on her father's side, the Erdrich family was established near the Black Forest, as "Metzger Meistern" in 1882 when they raised a *Bauernhof* (farm) that still stands in the Renchtal. In the United States, the last of the Indian treaties had been signed, opening up the West. Most of the Anishinabe were concentrated on small parcels of land in the territory west of the Great Lakes.[17] As for her maternal side, she observes that the "land west of the Appalachians was still Indian territory and the people from whom I am descended on my mother's side, the Ojibwa or Anishinabe, lived lightly upon it, leaving few traces of their complicated passage other than their own teeth and bones. They levered no stones from the earth. Their houses, made of sapling frames and birchbark rolls, were not meant to last."[18] The Europeans have left many historical remnants of their presence in Europe, whereas Erdrich's Anishinabe, keepers of mother earth, have left few permanent marks in North America, except for their own survival and presence today and their rich oral traditions. In Erdrich's work, this becomes one of the conjunctions between the German and the Anishnabe. In her writings, the heart of Anishinabe oral traditions parallels and intersects with the pen and ink of the European newcomers. Erdrich has commented about the significance of place in many of her writings. While Europe, especially Germany, is an important factor for her, Erdrich is still very much tied to her family, its history, and the Turtle Mountain reservation in North Dakota.

The Blue Jay's Dance is seasonal in structure, beginning in the winter—the Anishinabe time for telling stories after the first snow has fallen—a time for spiritual renewal among the Cree, Anishinabe, and Métis. The book ends the next fall. Lyrical and haunting, it is a series of thematically connected stories about her family, time, and the birth of her children—magical moments infused with nature. For example, in "The Chickadee's Tongue," she describes her sense of awe:

> Today a chickadee hits the window with a small surprising thunk. I walk outside, pluck it off the warming earth. The bird is stunned, blinking, undamaged. I stand motionless with the bird in my hand, examining it carefully, but not a feather seems to have snapped or ruffled.... I have always wanted to catch a chickadee and look at its tongue, but now that I've got one, my hands seem as big and clumsy as paws. I don't dare try to open its beak. Regaining its wits, the bird seems to trust me—it vibrates, its breath spins, its heart ticks too fast to apprehend, but it doesn't leave the palm of my hand. I wouldn't close my fingers on it for anything, and it knows. It looks up at me, alert and needle-sharp, but very calm, and I feel suddenly that I am an amazingly fortunate woman.[19]

Nature infuses her writings and Erdrich understands that her writing is spiritual, acknowledging in an interview, "Life is religious, I think, and that includes writing." In this respect, she continues, explaining that the "common themes and preoccupations" in her work include "Abandonment and return. Pleasure and denial. Failure. Absurdity. The inability to get a sound night's sleep."[20]

Erdrich explains the spiritual component of her writing: "The world tips away when we look into our children's faces. The days flood by. Time with children runs through our fingers like water as we lift our hands, try to hold, to capture, to fix moments in a lens, a magic circle of images and words. We snap photos, videotape, memorialize while we experience a fast-forward in which there is no replay of even a single instant."[21] The Anishinabe concept of history is specific to a place and infinite—circular, not linear. This explains the difficulties that most readers have with Erdrich's lack of linear chronology in her narratives and with her characters. Her concept of time as a bird and a bear enables her to foretell events through intuition and prophecy.[22]

For Erdrich, time is also connected directly to the female body, and it involves an understanding of narrative about oneself as events take place. The "problem of narrative" is "more than just embarrassment about a physical process." It is the cycle of birth and rebirth: "We're taught to suppress its importance over time, to devalue and belittle an experience in which we are bound up in the circular drama of human fate, in a state of heightened awareness and receptivity, at a crux where we intuit connections and, for a moment, unlock time's hold like a brace, even step from our bodies." This is a narrative of a child, its birth, and its own story. The act of giving birth "often becomes both paradigm and parable."[23] The process of birth and rebirth is connected to the water where time and fish swim and creation begins.

The woman's body in this way "becomes a touchstone, a predictor. A mother or a father, in describing their labour, relates the personality of the child to some piece of the event, makes the story into a frame, an introduction, a prelude to the child's life, melds the labour into the story that is no longer a woman's story or a man's story, but the story of a child."[24] It is abundantly clear that her concept of time is circular and not linear.[25] From this perspective she begins to understand that her home is also a spiritual place. She is from that place having been born on a day of high wind under the grand sky. She cannot share her husband's life.[26]

In "Finches and the Grand Sky," Erdrich observes, "I picture the female goldfinch settling herself into a nest the colour of her husband and suddenly I think—*that's what I've done, moving to this, my husband's farm.* All around me, kind trees and slabs of rocky land, violet and archaic gold shadows that Maxfield Parrish painted into his *Saturday Evening Post* covers. This is a beautiful place but it is not where I belong."[27] It is from this realization that Erdrich went home to the Place of the Grand Sky, Minnesota, and found her own voice, which has shaped her fiction since 1995. In *The Blue Jay's Dance,* she refers to this as her "Horizon Sickness," saying, "I'm homesick." Countered by her husband's response "This is home," Erdrich concludes, "each of us is absolutely right."[28] Her horizon sickness is the desire to return to her family and roots in Minnesota, where one can see earth and sky merge in the distance, and where sunsets linger. For her, place—the place of the Grand Sky—is everything.

Most literary critics have commented on Erdrich's fiction as a place inhabited by dysfunctional and fragmented "Indians"—a view of "Indians" as a twentieth-century vision of poor ignorant savages utterly incapable of dealing with the modern world. It is seen as a bleak view of twentieth-century reservation life filled with violence and fear and danger.[29] Joyce Carol Oates has also stated that her writings can be classified by the term "magic realism."[30] In an interview, Erdrich disclaimed both of these views remarking that her fiction is a natural and a spiritual world and that writing is a holy or religious occupation for her.[31] From her writings, it is evident that her spiritual world is closely tied to nature and her family's stories, and reflects her quest to find a balance in the world.

Children's Literature

Erdrich began to focus on children's books with her first picture book, *Grandmother's Pigeon.* Published in 1996, it is a story of an adventurous grandmother who heads to Greenland on the back of a porpoise, leaving behind grandchildren and three bird's eggs in her cluttered bedroom. The eggs hatch into passenger pigeons, thought to be extinct, through which the children are able to send messages to their missing grandmother.

In her second picture book, *The Range Eternal* (2002), Erdrich pays tribute to her mother Rita Gourneau by reminiscing about the range that stood in her tiny family's cabin at Turtle Mountain (the phrase "The Range Eternal" is emblazoned on the front of the blue enamelled stove,[32] and the words conjure up the past, and the range where the buffalo roam). The story Erdrich tells is one of family and tradition: the wood-burning stove provides warmth and comfort, delicious soups, and hot potatoes to warm cold hands on frozen winter mornings. It is the true centre of the home, reflecting the warmth and care of maternal love. It is about rituals and dynamics that bind family and community.

Historical Events and Juvenile Fiction

In 1837, Ojibwa chiefs and government officials met near present-day St. Paul, Minnesota, resulting in the sale or cession of 13 million acres in east-central Minnesota and northern Wisconsin to the American government. The transaction was contingent on the Ojibwa retaining rights to hunt, fish, and gather on the newly ceded territory. This was followed five years later by a 10-million-acre land cession treaty that opened the south shore of Lake Superior to lumber companies, along with iron and copper mining. Soon these treaties were breeched, and the Ojibwa living east of the Mississippi River were to be removed from their homes. Strong opposition to President Taylor's removal orders at first stopped the removal, but a scheme to lure Ojibwa into Minnesota and trap them there over the winter at Sandy Lake by shifting the site where annuity payments were to be made devastated the Ojibwa.

Further attempts to lure Ojibwa to Sandy Lake were rebuffed by survivors, who referred to this place as a "graveyard." Two years later, when the United States sought Ojibwa land in Minnesota's Arrowhead region, the Ojibwa of Lake Superior region agreed to cede more territory in exchange for permanent reservations in Upper Michigan and Wisconsin through the Treaty of 1854. Driven by the events at Sandy Lake and a love for their homeland and the graves of their forefathers, these Ojibwa were resolved to stay in their traditional villages. Only a few other American Indian tribes successfully saved hunting, fishing, and gathering rights on land they ceded. One hundred and fifty years after the Sandy Lake tragedy, the descendants of the 1850 annuity bands remembered and gathered to dedicate a memorial to those who suffered and died. This is the historical background and geographic setting of Louise Erdrich's juvenile fiction, a trilogy that begins with *The Birchbark House* (1999) and continues with *The Game of Silence* (2005), and *The Porcupine Year* (2008), spanning several decades in the history of the Ojibwa nation.

As cultures live through word of mouth, the art of storytelling, rooted in experience itself, becomes a significant contributor to maintaining cultures. For example, novelists "draw attention to subtle, everyday differences in conduct rooted in experience, including the experience of differing cultural histories."[33] As a storyteller and novelist, Louise Erdrich contributes to the survival of her people by telling the stories of resistance and survival at Sandy Lake. *The Birchbark House* introduces Omakayas (Little Frog), a seven-year-old Ojibwa girl, who lives on an island in Lake Superior at the time when Europeans are beginning to settle the land and displace Native communities. The young girl's days are filled with hard work, but also a love for the old ways;

but the "chimookoman" (white people) hover at the frame of the story,[34] their smallpox decimating the Indigenous population. Erdrich reverses the narrative perspective used in most children's stories about nineteenth-century Native Americans. Rather than looking out at them as dangerous curiosities, Erdrich tells the story from the native perspective, from the inside. Indeed, Erdrich has remarked that she consciously inverted the *Little House on the Prairie* books by Laura Ingalls Wilder to tell the tale of white settlement of Native American lands from the point of view of the dispossessed.[35]

The Game of Silence, the second book of the trilogy, reflects this history of relocation, based on stories told to Erdrich by her mother, Rita Gourneau. It includes this family's Anishinabe/Métis history, how Indigenous families first intermarried with the French voyageurs. In this book, Omakayas, still living with her family on an island in Lake Superior in the 1850s, is aware of how the *chimookomanag*, or white people, have come to settle the land and are forcing the Native people to move further and further west. She knows that her way of life is being threatened by these *chimookomanag*. At the same time, she is also told by her Nokomis (grandmother) of the different relationships various tribes have with the white people:

> "Listen, my little one," she said, "for I'm going to tell you the truth. The chimookomanag we see here are only the first drops of rain. A storm of them lives past the sunrise, in the east. They can flood us like a river."
>
> "Can't we stop them?"
>
> "We have seen what happens to others when they resist, go to war. The river wipes them out. Our way is different. We have always found out how to live with them, work with them trade with them, even to marry them!"
>
> Nokomis's eyes fixed on Omakayas with amusement and Omakayas smiled back. Deydey's [Father's] grandfather had been a French trader, one of the first. Deydey had grown up in a house made of trees, like the cabin he'd built for his family. This alone marked him out as different.[36]

This is an eloquent statement of the nature of empires—sometimes progress cannot be stopped.

The Game of Silence won the Scott O'Dell award, established to encourage writers to focus on historical fiction in order to increase the interest of young readers in the historical background that has helped to shape their country. In *The Game of Silence*, Omakayas is ten years old. Her family has recovered from smallpox, but a greater menace—the white man's government—continues to threaten their existence and will irrevocably change their lives. The book covers the intricacies in the life of Omakayas over the four seasons, and Erdrich deals with the broader meaning of family and Omakayas's coming-of-age on a vision quest.

Erdrich mixes legend and myth with her own family histories, and with a realistic narrative she creates a world in which humans and spirits co-exist. The Ojibwa are matter-of-fact about spirits, which are sometimes frightening and often helpful. Learning to live with them is like learning to live with other people—necessary, but not always easy. In *The Game of Silence*, Omakayas discovers, with some dismay, that she has a special connection with the natural and the spirit worlds. The connection will shape her destiny, as will the American empire.

The Game of Silence takes its title from a system of education—of listening and learning and rewards the Ojibwa use to keep their children quiet when the elders have serious matters to discuss. In the opening pages, Omakayas watches as half-starved refugees arrive at her island in Lake Superior. They are Ojibwa, driven from their homes by government order into the territory of a different tribe. Attacked by that tribe, their village and crops destroyed, they took to canoes and fled to the island where some of their people still live—Omakayas's people.

While the children listen in silence, the new arrivals and the elders discuss why the government is breaking its treaty with them, what they must do, and whether there is a way to stay in their homeland. The Ojibwa understand neither the Europeans' concept of land ownership nor the government's disregard for the treaties it has signed with them. They speculate that an Ojibwa somewhere must have offended the government, perhaps by killing a white man. They decide to send four men on a year's search to the north, south, east, and west, to discover what the offence was.

Between these epochal events, Erdrich continues Omakayas's own story, filling in the outline of her special destiny. Omakayas welcomes her talent for healing but resists her ability to communicate with spirits in her dreams. Eventually, though, after one of her dreams rescues her father from certain death, her grandmother brings her the lump of charcoal that signals an Ojibwa rite of passage: "If she took the charcoal, she would be sent out to the woods to fast and to listen for her spirits.... She didn't want to go.... She was afraid of her dreams. She both wanted to know, and didn't want to know, what they might tell her. Their power frightened her."[37] Power indeed: on her third and last night in the woods, Omakayas foresees her whole future.

Only two men return from their journey, bringing terrible news. What they have found is not a transgression by one of their people, but an American empire bent on seizing land even if it costs many Aboriginal peoples' lives. There will be no reprieve; official orders to move west are on the way. The last chapter tells of the people leaving their island home for an unknown place far away. Still, there is room for individualism. Omakayas's younger brother is loud, greedy, and selfish—the bane of her life—but while everyone shushes him, no one beats him into submission. Two Strike Girl, who would rather be a boy, manages to ignore the standard girls' play to hunt and trap, dodging the less exciting woman's work. The adults discuss her as a problem, but they do not curb her harshly. She will grow up, after all.

The third book in the trilogy, *The Porcupine Year* (2008), continues the story of Omakayas and her brother Pinch. Omakayas is now on the verge of womanhood as her family continues in their struggle for survival. Like other families forced to leave their traditional territory to make room for the increasing number of European settlers, Omakayas and her extended family have made the decision to travel north, fearing war and scarcity of food. They have decided to join their extended family at Lac du Bois in Canada, and en route the family is confronted not only by hunger but also by other enemies and raiding parties—especially one headed by Albert La Pautre, a brother-in-law, whose group steals all of their supplies. Through patience, hard work, and cooperation, the family endures. In this book, too, Omakayas uses her skills and her knowledge of the land to help her family survive. As always, she listens to the spirits around her. For example, right at the beginning of the book, she and her brother Pinch are night hunting for deer in their canoe. Far from camp, Pinch misses his kill and falls into the river. Omakayas is able to rescue him, but the two are caught up in a current and pulled into the rapids. They fight for their lives:

> There was no thinking. All went dark. They were rushing through the night on water they couldn't navigate, past invisible rocks, between black shores. All they could do was swallow their screams and paddle for their lives. Paddle with a wild strength they never knew they had between them. Omakayas felt the cold breath of the rocks as their canoe swept inches from a jagged edge, a monstrous jutting lip, a pointing finger of rough stone. As she paddled she cried out for the rocks, the asiniig, to guide them. Asked them in her mind and then called out again. They seemed to hear her,... They hissed in her ears and she shifted balance, evaded.... But now the clouds lifted and a faint radiance spread around them. They looked at each other—still alive![38]

Both characters know that the spirits have helped them. Later, they see the "memegwesi," or little person on the opposite bank, the spirit that appears mostly to children who still have open hearts and minds. It is this connection to nature and the spirits within nature that ensures survival.

Patience and listening are Ojibwa virtues—and they require a lifetime to learn. Erdrich is a contemporary Native American storyteller, who, through her novels and poetry, relates her tribal and her family histories over a 150-year span from the nineteenth century to the beginning of the twenty-first century. Her storytelling is a blending of the oral traditions derived in part from her Chippewa/Cree/Métis heritage where myths, oral tradition, and culture were an important part of her upbringing. As in all of her writings, she describes not only the daily lives and suffering of Indians, but also reveals their ability to survive through their dignity, humour, and resourcefulness alongside Europeans. They are portrayed as highly complex characters.

Tracks (1988) and *Four Souls* (2004)

One of the most memorable—and there are many such scenes in the stories of Louise Erdrich—is the ending of *Tracks*. The Great War is over but not the environmental devastation created by it. At the time of the Wild Rice Sun in the early fall of 1919, the lumbermen (likely of the Turcot Lumber Company) have come to the shores of Lake Matchimanito to cut down the last remaining stands of timber where Fleur Pillager's log cabin stands and are ready to take her away in her cart. Nanapush, the Ojibwa storyteller, Turtle clan, describes what happens to the Standing People after a breeze comes up and two small trees fall to Mother Earth:

> The wind shrieked and broke, tore into the brush, swept full force upon us. Fleur held to me and gripped my shirt. With one thunderstroke the trees surrounding Fleur's cabin cracked off and fell away from us in a circle, pinning beneath their branches the roaring men, the horses. The limbs snapped steel saws and rammed through wagon boxes. Twigs formed webs of wood, canopies laced over groans and struggles. Then the wind settled, curled back into the clouds, moved on, and we were left standing together in a landscape level to the lake and to the road. The men and animals were quiet with shock. Fearing a second blow, they lay mute in the embrace of the oaks.[39]

This powerful event illustrates Erdrich's understanding of the relationship between Aboriginal peoples, nature and empires in the twentieth and twenty-first centuries.

Taking up where *Tracks* leaves off, in *Four Souls* the strong and compelling woman we remember from *Tracks* decides to leave home, and the story begins. Like *Tracks*, this is the story of the intersection of the empire of nature and the nature of empire. Fleur Pillager takes her mother's name, Four Souls, for strength, and walks from her Ojibwa reservation to the city of Minneapolis. She is seeking revenge on the lumber baron, John James Mauser, who has stripped and cheated her out of her land on her reservation; but revenge is never simple, and she quickly finds her intentions complicated by her own dangerous compassion for the man who wronged her. This novel deals with revenge and healing on various levels, as experienced and told by the three narrators of the novel. It also shows the power of transformation that Fleur exerts on European American women. *Four Souls* continues the Ojibwa saga that began with *Love Medicine,* recounting a way of life slowly being eroded by North American "progress."

Like the German poet Goethe, who once wrote that all writers are homesick, searching for home (something upon which Erdrich herself has reflected upon in the *Blue Jay's Dance*), Erdrich addresses the issue of land and homeland for her people. Consequently strong and vivid characters, both Native American and European, are part of the narrative of *Four Souls*. Chapters move from voice to voice, location to location, and through time. Reflecting upon Native American values, the narrators share their voices and stories. The connection between the stories is the loss of land. Once again, Erdrich is critical of the way the imperialists have stolen the land. Sometimes the criticism is harsh. Sometimes it is delivered with humour, as is often the case when Nanapush, a wise and comic trickster and storyteller, is the narrator. Erdrich's novels reach back and forth from time past to time present, exploring the cultures of and clashes between the Native Americans who first inhabited the land and the government agents and entrepreneurs who wrested it from them. As part of the nature of empires the stories that Erdrich tells here are by turns shocking, heartbreaking, hilarious, and bawdy.

When Fleur Pillager walks from near her reservation to Minneapolis/St. Paul, Minnesota to kill John James Mauser, the lumber baron who stripped so much of her and her tribe's land, she encounters Polly Elizabeth, his sister-in-law, left in charge of his household. Mauser's condition, extensively sweating from an undisclosed illness, keeps him bedridden, and the household requires a new laundress. It is Polly who tells the story of how Fleur appears one day at their doorstep and is hired to replace the laundress who has recently quit. Unable to keep up with the copious loads of laundry produced by Mauser, she is desperate and hires the "Indian."[40] She believes that she has taken a great risk. Polly becomes a witness to and recounts her incredulity at how Fleur, healing Mauser before she will kill him, eventually, becomes passionately enamoured with him and becomes first his mistress and then his wife. Polly Elizabeth is both astounded, yet also intrigued when Mauser annuls his marriage to her sister and marries Fleur. Happy with the financial settlement she and her sister receive, she nevertheless returns to the mansion and ingratiates herself back into Fleur's life out of loneliness and curiosity. When Fleur is pregnant with Mauser's child, to whom she eventually becomes a surrogate and indulgent mother, she describes her role as "Nursemaid, doctor, fictional aunt, slave to the tiny one, servant to the mother too, I was in my correct element."[41]

Fleur never gives the child a spirit name according to native custom. The child is never called by its name, referred to only as "the baby ... the blue-eyed little prince"[42] Fleur refers to him as "my son." By age two, it becomes apparent that he has developmental deficiencies. Officially, for the white paper record, he is John James Mauser II.[43] Fleur's journey into the white man's world for revenge and financial restitution for her land ends in pain. She has destroyed her relationship to her daughter Lulu and has produced a child who is at home neither in the European world nor the native world. The sins of the father seem to be borne by the children.

Four completely new characters of European origin are introduced in *Four Souls*: Polly Elizabeth Gheen, the narrator of six of the seventeen stories; Fantan, the manservant to John James Mauser; Mauser's wife Placide Gheen; and Placide's mother Demeter Gheen. There are three narrators. Nanapush acts as Fleur's conscience. He recounts Fleur's story and tells his own. Polly Elizabeth is a lonely and pretentious spinster at the beginning of the stories; she lives her life through those she lives with. An imperial agent, she makes herself useful to the extent that she has a precarious hold on those around her. At the same time, she is at the beck and call of her sister Placide, who uses her as a model in various disguises as the subject of her paintings. Polly Elizabeth, Placide, and their mother Demeter are characters based on typical classical European mythology. Ironically, Demeter in Greek mythology is the goddess of grain and fertility, yet Demeter's daughters are both sterile. Placide has not borne any children because she practises Karezza, a Buddhist concept of lovemaking based on abstinence, and Polly Elizabeth has no children because she is a spinster, unable to land a husband, despite her desperate attempts to snare the architect of Mauser's house. To her own great surprise, the risk she takes in hiring Fleur Pillager into the Mauser household and into her life effects a transformation that none could have predicted. She is able to free herself from her own family and take a chance with the man with whom she has fallen in love—and to succumb to happiness: "I am that rare thing thought only to exist in death. I am a happy woman."[44]

Polly Elizabeth Gheen is the sister of the upper-crust and fragile Placide, John Mauser's wife, and the daughter of Demeter Hawes Gheen, who sent her daughters off for deportment lessons and had the tires of her automobile washed before an important engagement in Minneapolis. Polly Elizabeth, her face "bleak and martial," voices the accepted bigotry toward American Indians: "Perhaps it is true that Indians are unintelligible, to the civilized mind I mean, as far removed in habit of thought and behaviour as wild wolves from bred hounds."[45] Erdrich initially presents Polly as a cliché, an embittered and lonely sister who clings desperately to her tenuous role as house manager of Mauser's grand estate. She is a bigot, a trivial socialite, an eavesdropper, and an opportunist who draws satisfaction from the power she lords over her ailing brother-in-law. Fleur's arrival sets off a series of events that Polly is unprepared for, but quickly adapts to. Her story is anything but clichéd in its tangled intricacies and the way Erdrich transforms her from an empty, companionless woman into a creature who resists, and is transformed and consumed by love, similar to Agnes DeWitt in *Last Report on the Miracles of Little No Horse* (2001).[46] "Affection," she expounds, "is how a dog survives. Knowing how to exist without it is how a woman wrests her life into her own hands. But when it comes, it takes one by surprise. Affection and freedom and the will to risk. Everything that happened since I answered the door to Fleur was leading up to this"[47] Life is a risk—a gamble.

Fantan, Mauser's loyal manservant whom he had brought back from Europe after they became friends while fighting in World War One, an imperial war, is the lightning rod through which Polly Elizabeth experiences happiness. Like the meaning of his Chinese name (to turn over, or to gamble with cards), Polly discovers in this very quiet, almost mute man a means to her own happiness. Mauser, before leaving Minneapolis to travel the world, leaves Fantan a sum of money. Polly Elizabeth quickly realizes that Fantan has positive qualities and happily twins his life to hers. They will live just outside the reserve and invest in a trading store on the reserve. This will ensure that Polly will continue to remain close to Fleur's boy and read him "sweet poems ... no matter how big he grows."[48] Polly, then, detached from empire, ends up a part of reserve life and of the spirits within.

As Fleur returns to the reserve to regain her land and finalize her act of revenge against Mauser, she realizes that material gains do not bring spiritual well being. She must undergo healing initiated by Margaret. Greed, the spirit of the White Windigo, has become a great affliction, the hallmark of empires and the process of imperialism: "There was no word in our language to describe this urge to own things we didn't need," Nanapush writes.[49] Acquisition leads to Nanapush's conflict with Margaret (over linoleum), in which revenge runs away with them and destroyed them both. Told by Nanapush and Polly Elizabeth and Margaret, from different perspectives, Fleur's story changes shape. We learn about all of the narrators, their individual and collective struggles, their need to survive as individuals and collectively, their desire for vengeance and then acceptance—and most importantly, the restorative power or redemption that stories and storytelling bring. It is through the taking of risks in their lives, opening themselves up to pain, that the restorative powers of transformation are able to take effect. Truly nature is the primary source of Erdrich's spirituality evidenced in her stories.

Conclusion

The nature of empire is a theme in all of Erdrich's writings and through it the complexities of imperialism are revealed. She explores many ideas: the power of motherhood and naming, the dual forces aligned in the narratives, the corrosive nature of vengeance, and the importance of land and of nature. *Four Souls*, for example, ends in a vision that speaks to both loss and possibility, both of which, it is clear, are bound up with the land, which is at issue in all of her works. Erdrich's writings become an extended inquiry into the meaning of ownership, which by all logic should belong to everyone and no one at once.

Another central drama in her writings is the communal decision the Ojibwa must make when American land developers offer to buy their land. Led by Nanapush, the tribe rejects the offer and keeps their land. Fleur shakes off all other obligations—as a mother, daughter, human being—in order to get back her land. She loses her soul—not just once, but four times—in that quest, because the land, after all, was hers. She does get it back and in the end she is healed. In all of her works of fiction and non-fiction, Erdrich aims to maintain a glimpse of a world in balance tied to the land, the source of spirituality. Although aware of her European ancestry, Erdrich's writings are about a strong sense of connection to nature, to her Aboriginal roots, and to Native spirituality. She celebrates nature, love, memory, family, and stories. Her writings are imbued with resistance to empires and a hymn to the spirits within nature.

Notes

1 John M. MacKenzie, *Empires of Nature and the Nature of Empires: Imperialism Scotland and the Environment* (East Linton: Tuckwell, 1997), 4.
2 Louise Erdrich, *Route 2* (Northridge: Lord John Press, 1991); *The Blue Jay's Dance: A Birth Year* (New York: HarperCollins, 1995); *Grandmother's Pigeon* (New York: Hyperion, 1996); *The Range Eternal* (New York: Hyperion, 2002); *The Birchbark House* (New York: Hyperion, 1999); *The Game of Silence* (New York: HarperCollins, 2005), *The Porcupine Year* (New York: HarperCollins, 2008); *Tracks* (New York: Henry Holt, 1988); and *Four Souls* (New York: Harper, 2004).
3 Louise Erdrich, *The Last Report on the Miracle at Little No Horse* (New York: HarperCollins, 2001).
4 Ute Lischke, conversation with Louise Erdrich, April 2002, Birchbark Books Minneapolis, MN.
5 Thomas King, *The Truth about Stories: A Native Narrative* (Toronto: Anansi, 2003), 2.
6 Erdrich, *Route 2*, p. 34.
7 Erdrich, *Route 2*, 15.
8 Erdrich, *Route 2*, 15.
9 Erdrich, *Route 2*, 17.
10 Erdrich, *Route 2*, 17.
11 Erdrich, *Route 2*, 18.
12 Erdrich, *Route 2*, 23.
13 Erdrich, *Route 2*, 25.
14 Erdrich, *Route 2*, 23.
15 Erdrich, *Route 2*, 34.
16 David McNab, "'Time Is a Fish': The Spirit of Nanapush and the Power of Transformation in the Stories of Louise Erdrich," in *(Ad)dressing Our Words: Aboriginal Perspectives on Aboriginal Literature*, ed. Armand Garnet Ruffo (Penticton: Theytus, 2001), 181–204.
17 Erdrich, *Blue Jay's Dance*, 99.
18 Erdrich, *Blue Jay's Dance*, 98.
19 Erdrich, *Blue Jay's Dance*, 82–83.
20 Louise Erdrich, "An Interview with Louise Erdrich," in *Conversations with Louise Erdrich and Michael Dorris*, ed. Allan Chavkin and Nancy Feyl Chavkin (Jackson: University Press of Mississippi, 1994), 228.
21 Erdrich, *Blue Jay's Dance*, 4.
22 Erdrich, *Blue Jay's Dance*, 8.
23 Erdrich, *Blue Jay's Dance*, 44.

24 Erdrich, *Blue Jay's Dance*, 44–45.
25 Erdrich, *Blue Jay's Dance*, 82–84.
26 Erdrich, *Blue Jay's Dance*, 86–88.
27 Erdrich, *Blue Jay's Dance*, 88–92.
28 Erdrich, *Blue Jay's Dance*, 88.
29 See Leslie Marmon Silko's critical review of Erdrich's second novel, *The Beet Queen*, in which Silko denounces Erdrich as a postmodern writer and raises critical issues concerning the relationship between Native American and Western literary traditions and theory. Silko, "Here Is an Odd Artifact for the Fairy-Tale Shelf," *Studies in American Indian Literature* 10, no. 4 (1986): 177–84.
30 Fabienne C. Quennet, *Where 'Indians' Fear to Tread? A Postmodern Reading of Louise Erdrich's North Dakota Quartet* (Hamburg: Lit Verlag, 2001), 85.
31 Ute Lischke, conversation with Louise Erdrich, April 2002, Birchbark Books, Minneapolis, MN.
32 Erdrich, *Range Eternal*, 4.
33 Jane Jacobs, *Dark Age Ahead* (New York: Random House, 2004), 6.
34 Erdrich, *Birchbark House*, 76–77.
35 Erdrich, *Route 2*, 34.
36 Erdrich, *Birchbark House*, 29–30.
37 Erdrich, *Game of Silence*, 223–25.
38 Erdrich, *Porcupine Year*, 5–6.
39 Erdrich, *Tracks*, 222–24.
40 Erdrich, *Four Souls*, 12.
41 Erdrich, *Four Souls*, 68.
42 Erdrich, *Four Souls*, 69.
43 Erdrich, *Four Souls*, 89.
44 Erdrich, *Four Souls*, 161.
45 Erdrich, *Four Souls*, 14.
46 Erdrich, *Last Report*.
47 Erdrich, *Four Souls*, 161.
48 Erdrich, *Four Souls*, 160.
49 Erdrich, *Four Souls*, 76.

CHAPTER 14

Settler Narrative and Indigenous Resistance in *The Baldoon Mystery*

Rick Fehr

> Come roam with me the unsettled forest through
> The settler's farm with the blazing fires o'erspread;
> Where scenes sublime shall meet your wandering view;
> The hunter's cabin and the Indian's shed;
> The log built hamlet, deep in wilds embraced;
> The awful silence of the unpeopled waste.[1]

"Come roam with me"

The opening quotation in Neil T. McDonald's ghost story *The Baldoon Mystery* (1905) reveals a telling relationship between settlers and the land they settled. The analysis herein conveys a relationship set in terms of rigid patriarchy, dualisms of light and dark, and the promise of an agrarian and emerging industrial paradise. Set in the early nineteenth century, the story presents a world in which the river systems of the St. Clair and Channel Ecarte (also known as the Chenail Ecarte, and now commonly as the Snye) become antagonists to the British Empire's desire to pacify both the land and Anishinaabeg of Southwestern Ontario. As a means of establishing that this is a settler narrative first, and not necessarily a treatise on the right of empire, McDonald's opening quotation establishes a paradigm that is entirely resistant to the words God spoke to Adam on the sixth day of Judeo-Christian creation: "Be fruitful and multiply, and replenish the earth and subdue it: and have dominion over the fish in the sea, and over the fowl of the air, and over every living thing that moveth upon the earth."[2]

Instead, the settlers of Baldoon, and specifically John McDonald, the father of Neil T. McDonald and the protagonist of the story, are confronted with an environment that is entirely animate and acts of its own malevolent accord. The contradiction set before the protagonist is therefore a monumental challenge, a challenge that can only be met on familiar political, spiritual, and cultural terms. However, the protagonist never seeks to understand, let alone listen to what these forces might be articulating. Doing so might have offered an altogether different template for living along the St. Clair and Chenail Ecarté rivers. Instead, the forces followed by the protagonist are those most familiar to colonial North America: enlightenment, Judeo/Christian doctrine, and imperialism.

Written as a Romantic tale of overcoming nature in the latter decades of the nineteenth century, *The Baldoon Mystery* employs an ascension and declension narrative previously used by Nathaniel Hawthorne in his story "Young Goodman Brown." Locally, the Baldoon Mystery has often been told as a folk narrative around campfires. As a folk story, it contains elements that make myths effective devices for articulating the origins of the community and the struggles overcome by previous generations. Both the written and spoken accounts offer a series of unexplained phenomena to build the plot. The events that occur are not necessarily portrayed as mythic impressions of an empire and a culture at war with nature; they are instead offered up as actual events that took place (according to the people who witnessed them). As a story that possesses a fragment of mythic resonance, however, *The Baldoon Mystery* offers a dialectic that works through the failure of frontier settlement. This resonance is not limited to the early nineteenth century, as environmental and social tensions similar to those that faced the Baldoon settlement still exist in the region. Neither the publication nor the histories written about the alleged events draw attention to this framework. Instead, the author draws the reader's attention solely to the haunting of the McDonald farm. Witness testimonials are included both in the 1900 and 1905 publications, as well as the 1991 restored edition. Historians, playwrights, and composers often consider the story a series of unexplained events belonging to a mystical and romantic past, rather than on the broader imperial metanarrative present throughout the text. Subsequently, the story is discussed about in a folk or factual context, usually as a feud between two settler families (the McDonalds and Bucanans, who lived nearby on the Sydenham River), with the Anishinaabeg acting as pawns.[3]

As a means of developing a critique of imperialism and its manifestations in the Baldoon Settlement, this study will pick up where ghost stories and historical accounts end. This will be achieved through an accounting of how a simple ghost story is really a mythic template and prophetic device for detailing the British Empire's (and to that extent the settlers') failed attempts at dominion over the lands and waters of Southwestern Ontario. Through this exploration two objectives will be achieved. First and foremost, this study will seek to understand *The Baldoon Mystery* as folklore, or a written story (with mythic resonance) that has endeared itself to a particular community over a period of generations (in this case with nearby Wallaceburg and Walpole Island). As this is being achieved, the broader connections that the *Baldoon Mystery* has to empire and the subjugation of lands and peoples will also be explored in some depth.

"Deep in wild's embrace"

Nature, it has been said, is the feminine personification that occupies a seat beneath God.[4] In the Occidental sense, this definition positions nature in an interesting dichotomy that historian Raymond Williams identified as a being, "[at] one extreme a literal goddess, a universal directing power, and at another extreme (very difficult to distinguish from some non-religious singular uses) an amorphous but still all-powerful creative and shaping force."[5] As the character in a story, nature becomes a highly complex and powerful being. *The Baldoon Mystery* exemplifies this through the story's antagonist, a nameless yet powerful old woman (see figure 14.1). Through her introduction to the story, it is implicitly understood that the author is not only introducing the personification of malevolent nature, but he is also portraying the Anishinaabeg in a particular way:

> It is necessary for the proper development of the thread of this story, that attention be called to another family residing in the neighborhood, whom, as I do not desire to implicate by name, I will for the sake of identification, designate as the people of the Long Low Log house. This family consisted of an old woman, her two sons and one daughter. They were not nice people, but remarkable for a sullen, resentful air, and made few friends. There are few faults less easily condoned in a sparsely settled neighborhood, than unsociability, and it is not surprising that in the course of time the people of the Long Low Log house were not the most popular in the community.[6]

Although the author is reluctant to name the antagonists, one could easily assume he is speaking about the Anishinaabeg community on the Highbanks of Walpole Island. The McDonald farm was built directly across the Chenail

Figure 14.1. Cover image of the *Baldoon Mystery* depicting the antagonist.

Ecarté on land held sacred to the Anishinaabeg, land that surveyor Abraham Iredell indicated as a large village.[7] Having created a paradigm of mistrust with the neighbours, the text then describes the McDonalds as righteous agriculturalists:

> Then spring came after the long winters and each recurrent season saw the frugal Scottish families living in increasing happiness. They had few cares. The earth yielded its increase to their daily labors and they were united by the holy ties of family clanship that they had brought with them from the land of the heather. They were strict Baptists of the old Covenantish character, determined, steady and little likely to be lead away by freaks of the imagination.[8]

With the protagonist and antagonist established, we see the dichotomies of good and bad, righteous and sloven, cast as the ideologies that set the neighbours apart. The McDonald family embodies the imagery of light, while the neighbour embodies all that is dark.

The author offers a veiled allusion to what actually started the haunting that allegedly plagued his family: "Young John McDonald had secured a piece of land which was coveted by these people, who approached him with offers of purchase. These he steadily refused and to the obstinancy on his part he, rightly or wrongly, as the reader may decide himself when he has perused these pages, owes all the miseries he endured during the terrible enactments at the time of the Belledoon Mysteries."[9] Although the author says it is up to the reader to decide whether or not McDonald had actually set in motion the troubles, the dichotomies are already in place to make the decision less difficult. To this extent, the family is portrayed as the victims of malevolent forces time and time again. Throughout the story, the family is beset by a chain of unexplained events: rafters fall from the barn, a ladle chases the family dog all the way to Michigan, and stones come crashing through windows. These stones were painted and thrown into the river; later, these same painted stones would find their way back on the floor, dripping wet. The longer time passes, the more portentous and unsettling the occurrences become. Mysterious orbs fly by the house, setting objects on fire; the baby's cradle rocks violently on its own; an ominous black dog appears and a rogue black goose swims up and down the river. The McDonald family is portrayed as the real victim, and so there can be little or no empathy for the neighbours being refused their offer of purchase.

"The log built hamlet"

Throughout the haunting, there is no indication as to the cause: hence the mystery. As the story builds, there is increasing tension between the settler family and their environment. The protagonist seeks out the advice of travellers and people knowledgeable of witchcraft to find the source and bring resolution to his misery. To this end, McDonald journeys east to meet with the notorious witch hunter of Long Point, Doctor John Troyer, a settler renowned in the lower Great Lakes for his white magic.[10] With the help of a Methodist minister, McDonald takes a path through the Longwood's forest, which seems to come alive with evil spirits at night:

> The tall trees waved in the gentle night breeze and moaned a melancholy dirge over the weary travellers. Now and then a huge white owl would startle their horses with their shrill "to whit! To hoo!" Or a wolf would yelp in the distant underwood. Suddenly as they approached a small clearing and the silver rays of moon fell full upon them, they heard the heavy tramp of a vast multitude coming toward them. Inarticulate voices came to their ears, the crashing of boughs and snapping of twigs were heard, and then the rush as some great host came upon them. But they could see nothing. Poor McDonald's hair stood on end and his teeth chattered with horror. The brave elder, who never for one

> moment during that eventful night swerved from his self imposed duty, struck up in a loud voice a hymn, and bidding his companion follow him, flunged [*sic*] into the dark thicket on his way forward. Then they heard, as it were, another multitude which seemed to meet the first in mortal combat. They heard the groans of the wounded and shrieks of the dying. Then for a time all was still. Close to them from some thicket would come the cry of "Murder! Murder! Help! Help!" until the sounds died away from in the distance as though uttered by some one in extreme peril.[11]

The path through the dark forest is cleared only when the travellers sing hymns to God. Thus the entrance for civilization finds its discourse in the doctrine of scriptural dominion over nature.

Following his journey, McDonald learns that he must also push his neighbours back if he is to bring an end to the haunting. The farmer consults with Troyer's daughter, who is described by the author as having eyes with a "weird, far-away expression."[12] At this meeting, McDonald is told to mould a silver bullet, which he must use to shoot the black goose that has been swimming up and down the river. This act, he is told, will reveal the cause of his family's troubles and subsequently bring them to an end. McDonald acts on this advice close to the end of the story. The goose is shot in the wing and is revealed to be the old woman, who is later spotted wearing a sling to cover her wounded arm. As McDonald raises his gun to fire, two stark images offer contradicting messages about who has won the war between settler and nature: "What a world of hope was in this man's bosom as he gazed on the prospect before him. Here was the beautiful river and the fruitful fields, there the long line of woods, stretching for miles in the distance, and as dark blots in the landscape, the charred remains of his burnt homestead, the ruin of his barn and outbuildings and the mounds, where lay his dumb oxen and cattle.[13] There is an implicit certainty that the author is describing an all-out war between civilization and nature.

This theme runs deep in some of the Romantic authors that may have inspired Neil T. McDonald, such as Nathaniel Hawthorne and Sir Walter Scott. The dichotomies in *The Baldoon Mystery* stretch much further into European and Middle Eastern antiquity. Essayist Frederick Turner has indicated that the dichotomies at play between agriculturalists and the environment are as old as the culture itself. In *Beyond Geography: The Western Spirit Against the Wilderness*, Turner offers one possible root cause of this seemingly endless struggle, one that stretches back thousands of years: "Here in the near East the hard-won evolution from encampments to villages to towns that eventually grew into large cities—achieved over thousands of years in a difficult environment—nurtured the belief that 'civilization' meant the walled, blocked, and grain stocked city and that civilization could only be achieved and perilously maintained by unremitting hand-to-hand combat with a nature that would of itself grant little."[14] The weight of this statement cannot be missed in relation to the struggles being faced by the McDonald family, but more importantly by the Baldoon settlement that preceded the *Baldoon Mystery*.

"The unpeopled waste"

For the more than one hundred crofters who settled the Baldoon lands, the struggle was often defined as a war against the environment. The settlement's patriarch, Lord Douglas Thomas Selkirk V, envisioned an agricultural utopia on the flat, clear land.[15] This vision, however, met with the immediate obstacle presented by the area itself. Wallaceburg historian and hydrology engineer Lloyd Clark points to a unique set of climatic conditions that present the regional hydrology as a highly complex system.[16] The drainage basin that forms through the connection of three river systems is punctuated in the summer by warm air masses that push up from the Gulf of Mexico, and in the winter by frigid polar air masses. Located between lakes St. Clair, Erie, and Huron, the region also faces fluctuating periods of increased precipitation, increased thunderstorm activity,[17] increased snowfall, and frequent freezing of the waterways throughout the winter months. How the longer-term patterns of these climatic conditions play themselves out is just now being realized. The climatic cycles feature significantly higher and lower lake levels that fluctuate over periods of months and years, and sometimes over several decades. For Clark, the failure was not in coming to terms with these cycles, but in acquiring the knowledge to suppress them in order to create farmland. In the abstract to Clark's master's thesis, "The Baldoon Settlement Lands," the failure is presented as a gap between innovation, economy, and the capacity to realize agricultural settlement in the face of greater geo-political struggles:

> The struggles with the lowland environment began with the arrival of Selkirk's dispossessed crofters from the Scottish Highlands in early September of 1804. Rain, flood and disease resulted in considerable loss of life and crops. By 1810, acclimatization of the settlers and, particularly, the installation of a drainage system (in 1806) resulted in a productive Baldoon Farm. But Selkirk's financial problems, the War of 1812 and, more particularly, the rise in lake levels after 1825 to a peak in 1839 were disastrous for the Settlement. The technology of the time was unable to control the drainage problems of the Baldoon lands.[18]

There is an assumption in the above quotation that invokes the necessity of development whereas the hydrologic contours of the land demanded periods of fluctuation and decline. This assumption may be based more on the nineteenth-century European desire of imperial conquest by agriculture, regardless of the risks.

The risks proved fatal both to the settlement and for a number of the settlers, especially in the early years of the settlement. For instance, settlement construction was brought to a near complete halt in the summer of 1804 because of frequent thunderstorms. Only two of fourteen scheduled log houses awaited the settlers' arrival.[19] Work might have resumed in the autumn, but a number of builders fell ill with malaria and subsequently died, including William Burns, the first manager of the settlement. As a result, the settlers were forced to winter in tents. By the following spring, twenty-two people had died from exposure or malaria, including eight of the fifteen family heads.[20] A number of setbacks followed this initial trauma. Though some gains were made, harvests increased, and drainage plans put into place, Selkirk was ultimately forced to sell his holdings in 1818 for fear of further losses. As a result of this disenfranchisement, many of the settlers moved to higher ground further upstream on the Sydenham River, where they founded Wallaceburg.

The failure to immediately convert the land into the agricultural utopia envisioned by Selkirk ultimately manifested itself through the *Baldoon Mystery,* in which the last holdouts of the settlement are determined to usher in a new era. For the second and subsequent generations to achieve a foothold on the floodplain, the settlers sought to tame the region's unique ecological rhythms. These rhythms necessitated the fluctuation of the area's waterways on terms the newcomers could not understand and later would not tolerate. To achieve the pacification of the lands and waters, the *Baldoon Mystery* dictated a means of pacifying not only land, but also the Anishinaabeg who resisted foreign control. While the means the author employed to tell the story are rich in romanticism, they are also entirely hierarchical and patriarchal. At one point a story like the *Baldoon Mystery* may have used mythopoeic elements to describe the environmental causes of failure. Instead, the story centres almost entirely on the power and dominance of male-centred technological innovation as plot resolution.[21] Prior to this development, lessons may have been learned in a world that has power over humans as opposed to one in which man in particular has power over the world. We see this development in characters like John McDonald, who shoots the rogue goose with a bullet he moulded from silver, a symbol of power, wealth, and innovation.

This metaphoric act is in keeping with the drastic transformation from a temperamental hydrologic system to one that passively offers its fertile soil for cash-crop agriculture. If the story is read from the position of imperial dominion, *The Baldoon Mystery* is a story of success. If the story is read from the margins, however, where the environmental degradation and oppression of Indigenous peoples is an everyday reality, *The Baldoon Mystery* becomes a story of technological and imperial land rape.

"The awful silence"

As a story dictated by the imperial desire to pacify land, *The Baldoon Mystery* leaves room for no other narratives. There is no counterargument in the appendix about the cause of the haunting, nor is there room for any voice of dissent. The eyewitness accounts recorded by the author serve to silence any opinions that might suggest other causes of the McDonald haunting. However, differing accounts about the events described in the *Baldoon Mystery* do exist. Not surprisingly, statements given by members of the Anishinaabeg community are highly critical of the McDonald family and the broader colonial society they represent.

Through conversations recorded with two hereditary chiefs, the dichotomies offered by Neil T. McDonald become clouded in a complex account of spiritual, ecological, and social transgressions. At some point in the 1830s, Ojibwa Methodist Minister Reverend Peter Jones[22] spoke with Chief Bauzhigeezhigwaeshikum at Walpole Island about the events, which had by this time been well publicized throughout the region. About seventy years later, in the first decade of the twentieth century, the poet William Leonhardt of Port Lambton spoke to Chief Peterwegeschick (the son of Chief Bauzhigeezhigwaeshikum) about the events.[23] According to the earlier account of Reverend Jones, the events that occurred at the McDonald farmhouse are described as being self-inflicted:

> I asked him [Bauzhigeezhigwaeshikum] what he thought of these strange occurrences among the white people [the McDonalds]. He replied, "O, I know all about it. The place on which the white man's house now stands was the former residence of the *Mamagwasewug*, or fairies. Our forefathers used to see them on the bank of the river. When the white man came and pitched his wigwam on the spot where they lived, they removed back to a poplar grove, where they have been for several years. Last spring this white man went and cleared and burnt this grove, and the fairies have been obliged to remove; their patience and forbearance were now exhausted; they felt indignant at such

> treatment, and were venting their vengeance at the white man by destroying his property." The old chief uttered these words as if fully believed in the existence of these imaginary beings, and in their power to harm those who dared to disturb their habitations.[24]

The description given by Chief Bauzhigeezhigwaeshikum reveals a spiritual element that is not accounted for in Judeo-Christian discourse. The religious elements of the story positions the relationship between John McDonald and the land as being a struggle for power, one that will ultimately result in McDonald claiming dominion over the territory. Once this is achieved, the McDonald family will also fulfill the promise of enlightenment, which throughout the nineteenth century placed an agrarian emphasis on "mixing one's labour with the land"[25] in order to improve it from a state of wilderness into a metaphoric garden. The description shared by Chief Bauzhigeezhigwaeshikum, however, is explicit in its suggestion that the land (and to that extent the water) is already imbued with sacred properties; the transgression on this spot invokes the negative response described by the settlers as a haunting.

Chief Peterwegeschick described quite poignantly the encroachment and its response in the early twentieth century. The poet William Leonhardt later recalled the conversation he had with the chief in an article published in a local newspaper in which Peterwegeschick also considered the actions of the McDonald family to be the source of their trouble. The encroachment described by Chief Peterwegeschick places the settlers along the St. Clair River, at Whitebread Station: "Old Pete, as he was generally called, had been a chief many years and readily told me the cause of the haunted house, or the cause of its being haunted. Over near Whitebread station on a little hill the Indians had erected a medicine lodge, and when the white man interfered with it the spirits of the Indians showed their resentment by haunting the McDonald Homestead. This he was sure of."[26] The account given by Chief Peterwegeschick takes the *Baldoon Mystery* and removes it from the idea of wilderness established by the author in the opening lines of his story. Instead, it is identified as a place within a specific cultural and spiritual context. This encroachment is a spiritual defilement not only of the land, but also of the Anishinaabeg. While Chief Bauzhigeezhigwaeshikum described this assault as being against spirit beings, Chief Peterwegeschick concluded it had been a direct assault against the Anishinaabeg through the destruction of a medicine lodge by the settler family. This assault is significant, as it attempts to simultaneously remove the Anishinaabeg from their territory while at the same time it serves as an act of possession for the settler. The story charts the conversion of Indigenous territory from literary spaces of waste, wilderness, and evil into colonial places marked by productive farmland and sublime Biblical qualities.

Chief Peterwegeschick offers the suggestion that mass encroachment and conversion is marked by a noted decline in ecological diversity. Following his comment about the Medicine lodge, Leonhardt recorded the following, "[his] story was told me in rather a sorrowful tone of voice. He declared that the beaver and other game had been driven away by the white man, and now the few ducks and gulls were all that were left to the Indian."[27] If read from Leonhardt's romantic perspective, the next thought would no doubt lead to the disappearance of the Anishinaabeg;[28] however, the Anishinaabeg have not been relegated to the history books of extinction. There is an irony in the poet's sentiments, as his focus is not at all on the Baldoon settlement, which had by the time of his writing been abandoned more than one hundred years earlier.

"Blazing fires o'erspread"

There is a distinct sense that the McDonald family had been face-to-face with insanity. The author connects this insanity to being abandoned to the wilderness: "We are told that in the old bible days the leper was driven from the tents and cities into the wilderness, forbidden to drink of the stream that flowed by human habitation, to cross the pathway of a fellow creature, or to speak to a living soul. But in this instance the curse fell not only on the hapless man, but on his children, and wherever he went he seemed to carry it with him. The continued dropping of water will wear away the hardest stone."[29] The author had the wilderness of Judeo-Christian doctrine in mind when these lines were written. It is not at all a regenerating force, but one that literally wears down the rock. This is the same wilderness Adam and Eve had been cast into following their fall, the same wilderness in which Moses wandered until Jerusalem was discovered, and the same wilderness where Jesus struggled with Satan for forty days and forty nights.[30] In the *Baldoon Mystery* it is same wilderness the Scottish Highlanders had been sent following the enclosure of their former lands. Here, the elements became demonic, and because the Anishinaabeg (particularly an older woman) were familiar with the territory, they became antagonists.

There was a dogged determination in pressing back the wilderness, satisfying an epistemological need to know the land as they knew it in Europe. In a landscape marked by thick Carolinian forests, the use of fire is often described as the cheapest and easiest means to push back the wilderness. This is noted in the history section on the website of nearby Windsor and Essex County:

> [The] Loyalists who moved here had to chop through one of the thickest walls of forest in North America to reach the soil. The settlers developed a hatred for trees and they "killed" these natural enemies by setting fire to them or by cutting a deep gash through the bark right around the tree to stop the tree from being nourished; the tree gradually died. For fifty years the pioneers of Essex County competed in a race to destroy the dense forest that kept them from the fertile soil. Fire became a symbol of material progress. Citizens of Chicago, 300 miles away, admired the glow in the sky on several occasions when millions of cords of Essex County hardwood (oak and walnut) went up in smoke.[31]

The pacification of the land by means of fire reveals a common exercise in patriarchy. The wilderness, as it is embodied in the *Baldoon Mystery*, is as Don McKay suggested, "the placeless place beyond the mind's appropriations."[32] As a placeless place occupying the unknown, wilderness is something to be feared, as it is the place where one is least likely to find the light of God. Subsequently, wilderness should be pacified and brought to within the mind's appropriations. Once the wilderness had been transformed into the familiar, settlers could then rely on their labour to transform the land into the agrarian paradise envisioned by Selkirk. Reflecting on the one hundred years of Kent County, historian Victor Lauriston relied on patriarchy, aggression, and subjugation to describe the struggle of the Baldoon settlers when he wrote of how they yearned for the dark and attractive fertile soil beneath their feet.[33]

However many gains are made in the settler's struggle, fire is never far behind as a reminder of the force that stands to obliterate his legacy. In the *Baldoon Mystery*, the settler ultimately comes face-to-face with oblivion, with uncontrollable infernos serving as a constant reminder of their place in the wilderness. Fire does so through the most oppressive way the author can imagine, as it threatens the homestead and all that it contains with absolute destruction: "Little balls of fire began to float in the air, and settling in various parts of the house, set it on fire. Fires would break out, too, in every room in the house in the most unaccountable manner. Little bundles of cobwebs, flax, clothing and other combustible things were found constantly, and the harassed family found the greatest difficulty in subduing the flames."[34] By threatening the settler's homestead, fire presents a direct obstacle to the notion of permanent settlement, fulfilling the Judeo-Christian expulsion from the garden. Just as God thrust the flaming sword into the ground preventing his children from returning, the settler too is kept from converting the lands into Utopia.

Fire, in *The Baldoon Mystery*, fulfills simultaneous and contrary roles. It is at once a heathen symbol, bouncing around the house and making the domestic wild, and it is also a symbol of Promethean innovation. In its former role, fire induces a sheer panic in the McDonald family; it is a panic common in Judeo-Christian literature. The prophet Joel prescribes repentance in the face of wildfires to ensure the return of Eden's fruitful soil. The balls of fire in the house, as well as the "ruin of farm and outbuildings," and its associated dumb livestock are all a result of fires that restore wilderness at the expense of civilization. While one could consider this primitive form of law the measure by which civilization can live in a particular place,[35] the author's use of metallurgy (and other symbols of stone) suggests otherwise.

For naturalists like Don McKay, the foundations for patriarchal resistance to wilderness stretch further than religious doctrine and to the cradle of Western civilization in Sumeria. Here, the mythic hero Gilgamesh steps beyond the walls of civilization to conquer the wilderness, which took the form of the forest god Humbaba. Having smashed the god to bits and stripped the sacred Lebanese forest bare, Gilgamesh establishes his fate as a hero. Prior to this act, Gilgamesh justifies his actions against the forest by stating, "I will cut down the tree, I will kill Humbaba, I will make a lasting name for myself, I will stamp my fame on men's minds forever."[36] McKay calls us to think of this monumental act as anything but heroic: "Students of the pathology of abuse will probably recognize the shape of this fury as it is expressed in families. And one may also suspect that we are seeing, in this ancient account of heroism, the foundation of the phenomena known as male rage."[37]

The fate of protagonist John McDonald is enshrined through the shooting of the Black Goose, the feminine embodiment of an unknown elemental nature. The silver bullet moulded by McDonald is symbolic of hydrological advances that allowed the lands adjacent to the Chenail Ecarte and St. Clair River to be drained on an industrial scale, revealing Lauriston's dark and fertile soil. This soil, now put to the labour of man, is assumed to be under the dominion of empire, and no longer is it the unknown. The use of metallurgy speaks to the transformation of wild fires into the domestic, Promethean flame. The metamorphosis of fire had been complete by the time *The Baldoon Mystery* was published. No longer was it under the control of malevolent supernatural forces; its use was shaped by mould of industry and the confines of internal combustion engines. The complete transformation promised untold control of the previously malicious river system through the mass construction of dykes and tile drains, and the use of gas-powered water pumps.

This premonition is offered through McDonald's heroic actions and the defeat of the old hag. The insanity earlier described by the author recalls that even the hardest stone is worn down by water. There is much to be learned from this allusion, as it is much more than just a fitting metaphor for the struggle of settlers. This statement is the point at which the protagonist is at his lowest and must find transcendence. Water is positioned as the ultimate antagonist. Water claimed a number of settlers in the initial settlement years, flooded the fields, prevented the construction of houses through torrential storms, and ultimately defied understanding in its long-term fluctuating cycles. The settlers had crossed the ocean with the promise that they would colonize solid ground. Water ultimately threatens to swallow even the righteous as it conceals beneath the surface everything that is thought to be beyond humanity's grasp, and as a result it is wilderness in the fullest sense.[38] Solid ground is quite different, however, as it provides the foundation to develop both as agriculturalists and industrialists. Solid ground also provides the foundation for monuments to prior struggles against the wilderness, monuments that are meant to stand against time and the wear of water. Monuments to Baldoon, to the settlement and the mystery, are to be found in many places from Wallaceburg to nearby Port Lambton. Monuments are meant to stand against oblivion on a solid ground that details the struggles faced by John McDonald, his family, and by Lord Selkirk and the settlement. Stone, solid ground, and the ability to work the earth offers a promise to John McDonald that he too, like the proverbial Gilgamesh, will transcend the wilderness. One of the tools used by the author, the moonstone, reveals the identity of the antagonist. Subsequently, the bullet formed of molten silver provides the protagonist a weapon to subdue malevolent spirits. In short, the McDonald homestead can only be rebuilt, both physically and metaphysically, with the solidness of earth and a specifically *masculine* ingenuity to manipulate and divine knowledge from it.

Once earth and stone are manipulated, etched and transformed by man, they bear the mark of progress from a state of savagery to civilization. The supposed permanence of words on stone is a testament to the fight against oblivion, the opposite of immortality. Like Gilgamesh, John McDonald is presented as a civilized man, and like Gilgamesh, John McDonald slips into madness when he looks to the nature beyond civilized life. Classics scholar Robert Pogue Harrison describes the decision Gilgamesh makes before challenging Humbaba (the protector of the wild forests) as being a distinction between oblivion and eternity, as well as between insanity and sanity: "With despair in his heart he has looked at the outlying earth: dumb, inert, insurmountable, revolving in her relentless cycles, turning kings into cadavers, waiting impassively to draw all things into her oblivion. Is this not intolerable for someone who is a builder of walls, someone who is devoted to the memorial transcendence of history?"[39]

Like Gilgamesh, John McDonald stands at the precipice of oblivion. He has seen it claim a generation of earlier Baldoon settlers, as well as the settlement itself. Consequently, he resolves to enshrine permanence on a temperamental nature through righteous force. For John McDonald, transcendence also equals legacy, something that can only be realized if he follows a number of steps, the first of which included pacifying the land. Subsequently, this act would guarantee successful crops, which guaranteed the permanence of settlement life. Naturally, the surety of good crops allowed future generations to be born. From here, the story detailing the forebears' struggle against nature is enshrined through writing. Again, the author may have been directly inspired by biblical passages, such as the Book of Joel. An agrarian civilization is literally scorched, flooded, and decimated by plagues, and the prophet announces, "Has anything like this ever happened in your time or the time of your fathers? Tell your children about it; they will tell their children, who in turn will tell the next."[40] Civilization could take root once these steps had been realized, but not before. As for the unknown forces that continually threaten an agriculturalist's livelihood—an unpredictable climate, inclement storms, floods and drought—they could be effectively eliminated through proper planning, engineering, and technological advances. As for the wilderness and its malevolent spirits, they could be marginalized through Judeo-Christian doctrine, the memorializing of their defeat, and ultimately through the promise of the eternal garden.

"Your wandering view"

In the *Baldoon Mystery*, the foreign landscape of Southwestern Ontario, along with its river systems, lakes, marshes, and Carolinian forests, stand in opposition to the goals of civilization. The slight mention of anything resembling sanctity in the new landscape offers an interesting glimpse to the mythic resonance of the story. The settlers till the land in a state of a "[blessed] uneventful peacefulness."[41] The protagonist, John McDonald, and the minister who accompanies him to see the mystic, escape from the dark forest and into the "peaceful sunshine."[42] Finally, the author makes note of the fruitful fields and the bountiful harvests they promise. This occurs just as McDonald is about to shoot the wild and dark goose with his silver bullet. Sanctity, as it appears in the story, is achieved through civilization and its foundational elements of empire, capital, and patriarchy. Each of these elements is found in the promise of the crops that grow on a sexualized virginal ground, and each of these elements is present in the safety promised by the homestead. Thus nature becomes a commodity that promises to feed not only the family, but also the empire that is the family's lifeline. After all, Lord Selkirk's mission was to establish a foothold for the British Empire in a region that was far from home. This is a stark turn from the narratives and mythologies that existed beyond Western European empires and Judeo-Christian doctrine. *The Baldoon Mystery* seeks to explain the right of imperialism where climatic conditions, political contests, and social and cultural beliefs defied dominion. The resonance of myth is there, but the myth as a body of knowledge has been completely turned on its head. As a result, *The Baldoon Mystery* offers the myth of empire building in a way that joins religious doctrine and the enlightenment with the birth of the industrial revolution.

The future promised by such a story offered respite to the Scottish settlers from their own colonization at the hands of the British. Forced from their lands in Scotland, the settlers faced an equally daunting prospect due to climatic and political uncertainty. The *Baldoon Mystery* acts as a manifestation for how that uncertainty is confronted from a distinctly patriarchal perspective. The manner of confronting the challenges before the family ultimately offers a better future for the settler, who eventually prevails in the story. The path to this future is the promise of doctrine and enlightenment (everything presented as light in the story), and that is the ability to push everything that is unknown to the brink (everything presented as dark in the story). Through this process there is a noted absence of engaging with the world *on* the world's terms. Instead, engagement with the world is dictated solely by the demands of man. Again, the missing element in the world becomes sanctity. At one point in time the telling of a story necessitated the significance of place as being the foundation for getting to know the world, as cultural theorist Sean Kane has pointed out:

> Wisdom about nature, that wisdom heard and told in animated pattern, that pattern rendered and in such a way as to preserve a place whole and sacred, safe from human meddling: these are the concepts with which to begin an exploration of myth. Of these, the notion of the sanctity of place is vital. It anchors the other concepts ... once the power of the place is lost to memory, myth is uprooted; knowledge of the earth's processes becomes a different kind of knowledge, manipulated and applied by man.[43]

The author's bright future was shaped and manipulated by a strict utilitarian patriarchy. This representation of the future is one in which the earth was to yield itself in terms dictated by men. The knowledge used to dictate this relationship was imported, and as a result the vision could only grasp the regional climate, ecosystems, and cultures as unknown and foreign. These forces would eventually have to be brought under control as well.

The story can be seen as somewhat prophetic. The terms of control employed in *The Baldoon Mystery* still dictate the terms of control used to convert the land to agriculture and industry. The crisis faced by John McDonald is presented as a story of transcendence. Even when he suppresses the wilderness, it has already razed his farmhouse to ash. This metaphoric defeat is reminiscent of a poem written by Rainer Maria Rilke in the early twentieth century: "Lonelier, turning only towards each other, though still unknown to each other, we build straight roads without lovely curves. The former fires are burning only in boilers, lifting bigger and bigger hammers. But we are losing strength, like swimmers."[44] The path straight and narrow followed by John McDonald has led straight to the social and environmental crisis facing southwestern Ontario. It has given rise to the chemical industry in nearby Sarnia, which for decades has used the St. Clair River as a discharge basin. It is likely that Chief Peterwegeschick could see precisely where the path of the settler was leading. William Leonhardt believed it would lead to the disappearance of the Anishinaabeg of Walpole Island. Instead, it has led to the ongoing resistance on Bkejwanong Territory, one of the few communities directly downstream from the ongoing chemical assault. In Wallaceburg, the path has also led to the bust of the postwar economic boom, in which dominion over the land and community has been increasingly fleeting. The closure of a number of industries, including the town's largest and longest employer (fittingly once named the Dominion Glass Company), which closed in 1999, has brought Wallaceburg full circle to Baldoon, a community that is once again having to uproot to seek better prospects elsewhere.

Notes

1 Neil T. McDonald, *The Baldoon Mystery*, introd. Alan Mann (Wallaceburg, ON: Standard Press, 1991), 1. Originally published 1900. Citations are to the Standard Press edition.

2 Gen. 1:26–30.

3 Victor Lauriston, *Romantic Kent: The Story of a County, 1626–1952* (Chatham, ON: Shepherd Printing Co., 1951); Fred Coyne Hamil, *The Valley of the Lower*

Thames, 1640 to 1850 (Toronto: University of Toronto Press, 1950); A.E.D. MacKenzie, *Baldoon: Lord Selkirk's Settlement in Upper Canada* (London, ON: Phelps, 1979), 70; Frank Mann, *A History of Wallaceburg and Vicinity, 1804 to the Present* (Wallaceburg, ON: Mann Historical Files, 1968), 21; Frank Mann and Al Mann, *Settlement on the Sydenham* (Wallaceburg, ON: Mann Historical Files, 1984), 51.

4 Raymond Williams, *Problems in Materialism and Culture* (London: Verso, 1976), 221.

5 Williams, *Problems in Materialism and Culture,* 221.

6 McDonald, *Baldoon Mystery,* 5.

7 William Leonhardt, "Legends of the St. Clair River," *Sarnia Canadian-Observer,* 18 July 1925; A. Iredell, "Shawanese Township," July 1800, Ministry of Natural Resources, Township Survey Plans, Archives of Ontario, RG 1-470-0-0-324.

8 McDonald, *Baldoon Mystery,* 6.

9 McDonald, *Baldoon Mystery,* 5.

10 James Reaney, "Doctor John Troyer," in *Dictionary of Canadian Biography Online,* ed. John English (University of Toronto/Université Laval), http://www.biographi.ca/EN/ShowBio.asp?BioId=37824&query=Troyer (accessed 8 June 2008).

11 McDonald, *Baldoon Mystery,* 24.

12 McDonald, *Baldoon Mystery,* 25.

13 McDonald, *Baldoon Mystery,* 28.

14 Frederick Turner, *Beyond Geography: The Western Spirit Against the Wilderness* (New York: Viking, 1994), 23.

15 John Morgan Gray, "Douglas, Thomas, Baron Daer and Shortcleuch, 5th Earl of Selkirk," in *Dictionary of Canadian Biography Online,* ed. John English (University of Toronto/Université Laval), http://www.biographi.ca/EN/ShowBio.asp?BioId=36499&query=Selkirk, 2000 (accessed 8 June 2008).

16 Lloyd T. Clark, "The Baldoon Settlement Lands: The Effects of Changing Drainage Technology, 1804 – 1967" (M.A. Thesis, University of Western Ontario, 1970), 17.

17 Environment Canada describes nearby Windsor as having a substantially higher number of lightning strikes any other region in Canada on an ongoing annual basis. See Meteorological Service of Canada, "Lightning Maps and Statistics," 28 July 2011, Environment Canada, http://www.ec.gc.ca/foudre-lightning/default.asp?lang=En&n=C4E86962-1 (accessed 19 August 2012).

18 Clark, "Baldoon Settlement Lands," iii.

19 MacKenzie, *Baldoon,* 45.

20 MacKenzie, *Baldoon,* 46.

21 Turner, *Beyond Geography*, 30.
22 Peter Jones, *History of the Ojebway Indians* (New York: Books for Library Press, 1971). Originally published 1861.
23 Leonhardt, "Legends of the St. Clair River."
24 Jones, *History of the Ojebway Indians*, 159.
25 C.B. MacPherson, *The Political Theory of Possessive Individualism: Hobbes to Locke* (Toronto: Oxford University Press, 1964), 202.
26 Leonhardt, "Legends of the St. Clair River."
27 Leonhardt, "Legends of the St. Clair River."
28 Leonhardt wrote a poem about his encounter, titled "The River St. Clair"; in keeping with popular Romanticism, the subject of his poem is pushed off of the landscape while industrial European settlers fill the void left by its former inhabitants.
29 McDonald, *Baldoon Mystery*, 14–15.
30 William Cronon, "The Trouble with Wilderness; or, Getting Back to the Wrong Nature," in *Uncommon Ground: Toward Reinventing Nature*, ed. William Cronon, (New York: W.W. Norton, 1995), 70–71.
31 Essex, "Early Municpal History of Essex County," *County of Essex: The Sun Parlor of Canada*, http://www.countyofessex.on.ca/wps/wcm/connect/coe/coe/about+essex+county/history+of+essex+county/early+history+of+essex+county+%281792+-+1924%29/04+early+municipal+history+of+essex+county (accessed 8 September 2012).
32 Don McKay, *Vis à Vis: Field Notes on Poetry and Wilderness* (Kentville, NS: Gaspereau, 2001), 87.
33 Lauriston, *Romantic Kent*, 51.
34 McDonald, *Baldoon Mystery*, 12.
35 Stephen J. Pyne, *Fire in America: A Cultural History of Wildland and Rural Fire* (Princeton NJ: Princeton University Press, 1982), 68.
36 *Gilgamesh: A New English Version*, transl. Stephen Mitchell (Toronto: Free Press, 2004), 27.
37 Don McKay, *Deactivated West 100* (Kentville, NS: Gaspereau, 2005), 23.
38 Robert Pogue Harrison, *The Dominion of the Dead* (Chicago: University of Chicago Press, 2005), 13.
39 Robert Pogue Harrison, *Forests: In the Shadow of Civilization* (Chicago: University of Chicago Press, 1992), 16.
40 Joel 1:2–3.
41 McDonald, *Baldoon Mystery*, 5.
42 McDonald, *Baldoon Mystery*, 24.
43 Sean Kane, *Wisdom of the Mythtellers* (Peterborough, ON: Broadview, 1998), 50.

44 Rainer Marie Rilke, "Sonnets to Orpheus," in *Rilke's Late Poetry*, transl. and introd. Graham Good (Vancouver: Ronsdale, 2004), 82.

CHAPTER 15

The Great Indian Bus Tour: Mapping Toronto's Urban First Nations Oral Tradition

Jon Johnson

Toronto, Canada's largest city and the capital of the province of Ontario, is a bustling economic and political centre whose growth and development over time has greatly altered the physical and cultural landscape of the Greater Toronto Area. At the same time, the City of Toronto is built atop lands that have constituted part of the traditional territories of Anishnabe and Haudenosaunee peoples and their ancestors for millennia before the arrival of European settlers on the continent. Despite historical and ongoing forms of colonialism, assimilation, displacement, and discrimination that are well-cited effects of early Canadian empire building, First Nations peoples have continuously occupied the Greater Toronto Area for millennia before the arrival of Europeans, and presently there exists a vibrant urban First Nations community in Toronto with an intact oral tradition that preserves an awareness of the Greater Toronto Area as traditional Indigenous territory. This paper underscores the integrity and substance of this oral tradition through an examination of the Great Indian Bus Tour, a tour operated by the Native Canadian Centre of Toronto as part of the centre's community programming. The Great Indian Bus Tour constitutes a rich collection of traditional urban oral knowledge that in many ways parallels the oral traditions that are practised, shared, and written about more conventionally in non-urban settings. As an example of urban Indigenous storytelling, the bus tour provides an alternative vision of Toronto that demonstrates the historical contributions and ongoing presence of First Nations people in the city and instructs Indigenous and non-Indigenous people to see how the empire of nature persists despite European expansionism, urban development, and the colonial subjugation of Indigenous cultures.

Understanding Urban Territory as Traditional Indigenous Territory

First Nations have continuously occupied Canadian urban centres since their inception. While government relocation policies led to a decline in the number of First Nations people living in cities prior to the twentieth century, as early as the late 1930s numerous push and pull factors such as residential schooling, poor economic and social conditions on reserves, termination of treaty rights, and education and employment opportunities led to steadily increasing First Nations populations in cities.[1] The 2006 Canadian census statistics indicate that currently 54 percent of all Aboriginal people in Canada live within urban centres, up from 50 percent in 1996.[2]

The increasing numbers of Indigenous people living within urban areas is not a recent trend. Evidence of the steadily growing urban Aboriginal population has been available for approximately fifty years, yet relatively little scholarly attention has focused on the existence and character of the cultural knowledge and traditions of Indigenous peoples living in cities. Much has been written on Indigenous knowledge and traditions as they are practiced by First Nations peoples living in more natural rural, wilderness, or reserve environments.[3] These studies discuss the importance of storytelling in the ongoing maintenance of First Nations culture and traditions, document the deeply rooted experiential and spiritual connections that First Nations people have with their local landscapes, illustrate the suitability of their oral traditions for living sustainably in those environments, and demonstrate the tenacity of Indigenous oral traditions despite myriad colonial interventions. However, most of the literature that addresses urban Indigenous populations tends to fall under what Rick Ponting and Cora Voyajeur call the "deficit paradigm."[4] Issues such as assimilation, loss of Indigenous culture and identity, and urban maladaptation in the form of addiction, abuse, homelessness, alienation, unemployment, poverty, suicide, diabetes, HIV/AIDS, and tuberculosis dominate the literature on urban First Nations. These are serious ongoing concerns, and literature that addresses these concerns usually represents well-intentioned (albeit sometimes paternalistic) attempts to formulate solutions to the problematic issues under examination. However, the predominant emphasis on the deficit paradigm perpetuates an unquestioned assumption that that the only issues of importance relating to urban Indigenous people are the problems they continue to face, that contemporary Indigenous peoples are passive victims of colonization,[5] and that urban ecologies are antithetical to Indigenous culture.

Much of the deficit paradigm literature emerges from the large body of policy research that was produced in the 1950s, 1960s, and 1970s in response to the perceived problems associated with the migration of First Nations peoples to urban centers.[6] Indeed, much of the more recent policy research on urban Aboriginal peoples continues to construct these populations as problematic. Evelyn Peters suggests that the nature of the academic literature on urban First Nations populations reflects prevailing ideas about the relationship between First Nations culture and city life.[7] Citing various academic and government reports, she argues that "a common theme in the literature on aboriginal urbanization before the 1980s was that aboriginal culture presents a major barrier to successful adjustment to urban society" and focused on "the incompatibility of aboriginal culture and urban life and the need to abandon cultural values in order to adapt to the urban setting."[8] These assimilationist arguments are implicitly based on an essentialist dichotomy that suggests that autochthonous Indigenous knowledge and traditions are incompatible with modern, Euro-American cities.[9] Insofar as these essentialist notions continue to go unquestioned, literature on Indigenous people living in cities will continue to be skewed toward examination of problems, precluding any understanding of the unique cultural forms manifested by these communities by virtue of their urban location.

Many First Nations writers and cultural authorities have countered this traditional-rural / modern-urban duality, arguing instead that supporting and enhancing traditional Indigenous culture is often a precondition for successful adjustment to city life.[10] David R. Newhouse, Cora J. Voyajeur, and Dan Beavon have suggested that "themes of persistence of identity and the adaptability of aboriginal peoples are the keys to understanding aboriginal history,"[11] and this applies equally to urban Indigenous populations. The recent Urban Aboriginal Peoples Survey, which interviewed Aboriginal people across eleven Canadian cities, found that "Canadian cities are become sites of connection, engagement and cultural vitality for a large number of Aboriginal peoples."[12]

Toronto is home to a large and growing First Nations population. Although the 2006 census enumerated 26,575 individuals of Aboriginal descent living within the city, Toronto-based Aboriginal service providers estimate that the actual population is closer to 60,000 residents. The discrepancies are due to "a large transient and homeless population who are not enumerated as well as a large, stable group. The large, stable group is also reluctant to be enumerated."[13] It notable that, for the first time since Jesuit missionaries first arrived in the region in the 1640s, the current Aboriginal population of Toronto parallels the 65,000 First Nations people estimated to have been living in the Toronto area prior to European exploration.[14] Additionally, Indigenous people residing in Toronto were among the most likely of all those included in the Urban Aboriginal Peoples Survey to relate a strong sense of pride in and connection to their Aboriginal identity and to state that cultural activities were widely available in their city.[15]

Although urban territories may present some challenges to practising Indigenous knowledge and traditions that are based on observation of and engagement with ecological relationships in the natural world, it is nevertheless important not to underestimate the ongoing relevance and adaptability of traditional Indigenous knowledge to metropolitan locales. Some have observed that while built environments are much different from rural ones, urban territories still possess ecology and it is still possible to learn from and commune with urban ecological relationships. Referring to Toronto, Howard has written that although "the landscape is changed, it is no less connected to Native identity. As I have heard Elder Lilian McGregor remark on many occasions, 'the sidewalks are cement, but that cement is made of the earth and water.' The city is reducible to its basic elements, and that connection between aboriginal people ... and the land, is not broken in the contemporary discourses of urban Native people"[16] The empire of nature, which I understand to be the fundamental logic of place, or *genius loci*, which emerges from the cumulative work of innumerable reciprocal, ecological relationships within that place, is still accessible by those peoples who know how to work sympathetic magic with the natural world. A. Rodney Bobiwash, a prominent member of Toronto's First Nations community and founder of the Great Indian Bus Tour, expressed his holistic awareness of the enduring empire of nature within cities and its relevance for Toronto's Native community during an interview aired posthumously on TVOntario:

> There's a medicine that grows on the sidewalk called plantain. It grows anywhere—in dusty lots, the cracks of sidewalks—and if you pick it up and clean it and put it on a wound, it will take infection out and promote healing. In a lot of ways, the plantain is very similar to the history of Indian people in the city. They may be obscure and they may be sort of growing between the cracks in the sidewalk, but when they're brought back to who they are, then there's an immense amount of power, and there's an immense amount of healing.[17]

Others have argued that the characterization of a territory as traditional from an Indigenous perspective has little to do with the presence or absence of built form. Rather, a major part of what makes a territory traditional is the existence of an oral tradition that represents the historical Indigenous occupation of that territory.[18] Vine Deloria Jr. and James Treat echo this notion in their writings about Crazy Horse, a renowned Lakota leader and warrior who lived in the nineteenth century. When Crazy Horse was asked to identify where his lands were, he replied that they were located where his people were buried. Deloria and Treat suggest that when Crazy Horse said this, he was thinking of "the immediate past deeds of his generation. These had imprinted on the land new stories and experiences that gave the Sioux a moral title to the lands."[19] The protocols for determining territories as traditionally Indigenous, from the view of at least some First Nations people, transcend any rural–urban dichotomy since traditional territories are more properly defined by the persistence of stories that document the use and occupation of those lands by Indigenous people historically and in the present.

Placing Time: Traditional Indigenous Storytelling Methodologies

Among First Nations groups, storytelling continues to be a preferred methodology for sharing knowledge, teaching values, and entertaining. These stories maintain cultural traditions and sovereignty, and encode multiple levels of practical and spiritual knowledge about the landscape. Many scholars have noted the abundance of practical and ecological knowledge about the local landscape that is often encoded in traditional Indigenous stories. Things that are important to remember, such as migration routes, hunting routes, and the locations of campgrounds and medicines are examples of information that are commonly encoded in traditional First Nations stories. Some stories act as maps of large territories and contain lengthy and detailed histories about how First Nations peoples lived in those territories.[20]

Although the content of traditional First Nations stories varies, they tend to illustrate relationships between things—between people, animals, plants, the land, the sky, the sacred and secular, the past and present. The nature of these relationships is derived from generations of engagement with the ecologies of Indigenous traditional territories and, in turn, informs First Nations understandings of the world and the roles and responsibilities of everything within it.[21] Time, in this holistic and relational cosmology, is not understood "as a linear sequence of events as related by Western historians, but rather as a "mythic world of 'biological' time, which is 'eternal, cyclical, endlessly repetitive, powered by Nature, and cosmogonic.'"[22] Or as David McNab succinctly states, "The oral tradition is a holistic view of history within circles of time."[23] In this sense, the past, present, and future are understood as interconnected. This view of time mirrors the many cyclical relationships in the natural world that ecologists are just beginning to understand. The seasons, of course, are cyclical as is the global flow of water and moisture. Animal populations grow and shrink in a cyclical pattern, and life itself can be understood as an endless cycle of birth, death, and rebirth.

Indigenous storytelling and ecology appear to track each other closely. Ecological cycles and relationships act as schema for the organization of Indigenous thought and influence the nature of Indigenous oral storytelling traditions, which, in turn, give expression to a group's deep relationship with its ancestral territory. The incorporation of features of the local landscape within stories is an ancient and effective methodology for encoding and remembering traditional Indigenous knowledge. For instance, Deloria Jr. and Treat write that "Tribal histories, for the most part, are land-centered. That is to say, every feature of a landscape has stories attached to it. If a tribal group is very large or has lived on a particular piece of land for many generations, some natural features will have many stories attached to them."[24] During her fieldwork among elderly Athapaskan speakers in the Canadian subarctic, Julie Cruikshank recorded a bewildering array of place names labelling specific areas of the local landscape, all of which had one or more stories associated with them.[25] She eventually learned that the association of place names and stories was a powerful way of keeping and sharing Indigenous historical, ecological, and cultural knowledge. Place names helped storytellers recall an impressive amount of detail regarding the history of those places and related cultural knowledge because places act as mnemonic aids for the lessons and knowledge contained in stories.

Features of the landscape serve as excellent markers because they persist through time and can therefore act as constant reminders of the events, stories, and lessons associated with them. The integrity of these places through time also helps to authenticate the events of the story and to affirm the continued relevance for traditional knowledge in the present.[26] Cruikshank found that her informants narrated their own life histories using place names.[27] Place names, and thus the places themselves, were inscribed with cultural knowledge and oral history. It is in this vein that McNab has written that "rather than being separate cultural categories, landscape and memory are, in fact, inseparable. Aboriginal tradition sees humankind, as one with, and inseparable from, nature. Without "pen and ink," First Nations remember and understand their internal and external landscapes, using their oral traditions and their stories.[28] Similarly, Keith Basso found that descriptive place names are considered important among the Western Apache.[29] Through place names, every culturally significant feature of Apache territory was mapped with stories. These stories often contained important lessons about cultural mores and values. As the place names and stories were learned, the mere mention of a place name would sometimes be enough to recall an important lesson or correct a perceived transgression. The methodology of associating local places with stories has the power to establish enduring bonds between people and specific features of the landscape. As one Apache woman stated, "The land makes people live right."[30] Indeed, the Apache report that upon hearing place names or the stories associated with them "A psychological balance has been restored ... [and] that a 'sickness' (nezgai) has been 'healed' (nabilziih)."[31]

Mapping Toronto's First Nations Oral Tradition on the Great Indian Bus Tour

While much has been written on Indigenous storytelling traditions practised in more natural wilderness and reserve environments, the false assumption that Indigenous culture is incompatible with urban environments has precluded sufficient examination of the presence and nature of urban Indigenous storytelling traditions. Among many members of Toronto's First Nations community, there exists an intact and vibrant oral tradition that defies any notion of the First Nations experience of Toronto as purely pejorative. This oral tradition describes an urban First Nations community that has strong roots in the Toronto area. Based on her fieldwork among the Toronto First Nations community, Howard notes, "Native people in Toronto have actively formed a discourse around this city as a Native territory. The pre-contact history and sacred nature of the area, particularly in Anishnaabe lore, is a significant part of contemporary discourse in the Toronto Native community."[32]

The Great Indian Bus Tour, operated by the Toronto Native Community History Program at the Native Canadian Centre of Toronto, constitutes but one highly visible example of an urban First Nations storytelling tradition that in many ways parallels the traditional Indigenous stories that have been shared and passed down across countless generations. The Great Indian Bus Tour was conceived and developed in 1995 largely by A. Rodney Bobiwash, a university educator, community activist, and former executive director of the Native Canadian Centre of Toronto, to raise awareness about the heritage and enduring presence of First Nations in Toronto, and to promote a connection to Toronto's landscape and a sense of cultural pride among the city's First Nations community.[33] In the TVOntario interview mentioned previously, Bobiwash stated,

> When we do the Great Indian Bus Tour, we essentially want people getting off the bus at the end of the day with a different set of eyes ... if we can get people to govern their relationships with that different set of eyeballs, then we've really come to some useful purpose in history.... Most cities in North America, of course, are built on Native land. Most don't acknowledge that. Most have very little knowledge, of the presence of Native people, either historic or contemporary, within the urban-scape.[34]

The bus tour, which usually lasts from three to five hours, takes passengers on a journey through Toronto and to various places in the city that have First Nations significance. The information that constitutes the tour was initially researched and assembled primarily by A. Rodney Bobiwash and his wife Heather Howard, who served as co-ordinator of the Toronto Native Community History Program, a part of the Native Canadian Centre. Information sources for the tour include a mix of archaeological evidence, historical and archival research, and the oral accounts of Toronto's First Nations elders, teachers, and other community members about the city. All of these are interwoven into the numerous stories that the bus-tour guide relates throughout the tour.

Just as in the traditional Indigenous stories mentioned previously, the history of places across Toronto's urban-scape is prominently featured during the tour in ways that establish the Greater Toronto Area as First Nations traditional territory. The numerous prehistoric and historic Native archaeological sites located throughout Toronto that are mentioned on the tour testify to the approximately 11,000 years of occupation of Toronto by Native people.[35] It is noted that numerous Indigenous sites dot the Rouge, Don, and Humber River valleys. The tour guide relates that "the Rouge Valley in Scarborough is rich for archaeological resources, there's a number of sites there. In fact there's over 100 identified in the Rouge Valley alone; sites that contain things like single arrowheads, fire pits, entire village sites. So the Rouge Valley was incredibly rich for Indian people."[36] Several large First Nations village sites are known to have existed within the city limits. One such village site was located at what is now called Baby Point, a wealthy neighbourhood near Jane and Bloor streets that is situated atop a bluff overlooking the Humber River. Archaeological and historical sources both document that this bluff was the foundation for a large Seneca village called Teiaiagon (roughly meaning "the knife that cuts through the river at the falls") that was occupied during the seventeenth century.[37] Further south, where the Humber River meets Lake Ontario, is the site of a large Mississauga village site (dated to around 1800), although the site was destroyed during the construction of the Humber Sewage Treatment Plant.[38] Another large Seneca village called Ganatsekwyagon (dating from the mid-seventeenth century) is located along the Rouge River, a little north of Lake Ontario.[39]

There is also a great amount of oral knowledge about the First Nations legacy of Toronto that strengthens the notion that Toronto is First Nations traditional territory. Significantly for Anishnabe peoples, it is noted on the tour that Toronto is along the route of the great Anishnabe migration from the East Coast into the interior of North America: "on the East Coast it was a time of turmoil and they looked to the Creator for an answer. And the answer was a migration through the guidance of a megis shell that they saw in the sky. There would be many stopping places along this migration ... Kingston, Walpole Island, Toronto Islands ... this is all part of traditional tribal lands."[40] In the oral account of this great journey, some Anishnabe people settled at each of the stopping points along the way. Thus, oral history suggests that the Toronto area was settled by Anishnabe people during the great migration and Toronto is therefore represented in Anishnabe oral tradition as a part of this group's traditional territory.

In addition to pointing out the ancient historical presence of First Nations in the city, the bus tour also demonstrates that First Nations people have continuously occupied the Greater Toronto Area. Numerous stories are told about the more recent activities and accomplishments of First Nations residents of Toronto. For instance, Dr. Peter Martin (Oronhyatekha), a Haudenosaunee man from Six Nations who in 1864 became Toronto's first Native physician. Dr. Oronhyatekha was a prominent philanthropist and an advocate for Toronto's Indigenous community. One story relates how Dr. Oronhyatekha helped many First Nations residents at the time to procure life insurance as a "bulwark against poverty and misfortune,"[41] sparing some children from the horrors of residential school in the event of their parents' deaths. Oronhyatekha's former home in Toronto is located on Carlton Street, near Allen Gardens park in downtown Toronto. Stories are also told of the community activism of individuals like Rodney Bobiwash, who struggled against racism in all its forms and devoted much time and energy toward educating people about First Nations culture, history and rights.[42] These stories underscore the fact that First Nations people have always lived in, visited, and contributed to the City of Toronto, and that the contemporary First Nations community continues this legacy.

In addition to establishing Toronto as traditional First Nations territory, the bus tour also imparts quite a bit of practical information for contemporary residents about how to live successfully as First Nations people in Toronto. The practical knowledge about the city related during the bus tour can be compared to the abundance of practical ecological knowledge encoded in traditional Indigenous stories. Urban territories have their own rhythms and requirements, so it is appropriate that urban Indigenous stories encode and pass on urban ecological knowledge that is reflective of these cosmopolitan landscapes. Especially while traveling through the downtown core of the city, the bus tour guide devotes a significant amount of time listing the names and locations of popular hangouts, craft shops, and many of the cultural and service agencies that cater to the city's Indigenous population. Often, this information is shared through stories about the history of the places in question. For instance, the tour guide discusses the importance of Spadina Avenue, a major north–south route running through downtown Toronto, for contemporary Indigenous residents: "Spadina factors hugely in the Native community; you'll find a lot of Native agencies on Spadina. That is Anduhyaun. Anduhyaun is a Native women's shelter, a place of refuge for women and their children and families."[43] The importance of cultural and service organizations cannot be underestimated for the urban First Nations community, which is widely scattered throughout Toronto. Indeed, some have argued that the urban First Nations community is actualized through these organizations, which provide convenient meeting places where one is sure to find other members of the community.[44] Speaking about the Native community in Toronto, the tour guide suggests that "how we gather is through our agencies. We have the Council Fire which is also a hostel, the Native Women's Resource Center, Anishnawbe Health, which practices both Western and traditional medicine and Miziwe Biik (an employment agency)."[45] James Mason, a well-known and respected First Nations oral historian of the Toronto Native community, suggested that stories of Toronto, told from a First Nations perspective, "are adapted to the specific context of Native life in the city" and contribute to what he referred to as the "urban Native 'survival camp.'"[46]

Numerous place names are also shared during the Great Indian Bus Tour in ways congruent with the methodologies used by the Western Apache and Athapaskan groups studied by Basso and Cruickshank.[47] Perhaps the most prominent and well-known First Nations place name persists in the name for the city itself—Toronto. Although its meaning has been interpreted variously, one widely accepted interpretation suggests that *Toronto* comes from a Wendat or Mohawk word for a fishing weir, a structure of stakes placed together at the mouth of a river to gather and catch fish. From this, Toronto has been interpreted as a gathering place or a meeting place.[48] The tour guide relates that Toronto has long been a meeting place for Aboriginal people, as archaeological evidence and the oral history of Anishnabe and Haudenosaunee peoples attests. It is also pointed out that currently Toronto is popularly regarded as one of the most multicultural cities in the world, which demonstrates the continued recognition of Toronto as a meeting place for a diversity of people. The Urban Aboriginal Peoples Survey found that First Nations people were among the most likely in all participating cities to feel very close connections to people from other First Nations groups and were also found to be widely accepting of non-Aboriginal people in the city.[49] This suggests that the fundamental character of Toronto as a gathering or meeting place for a diversity of people remains unaltered in Indigenous discourse about the city—it is the past, present, and future of the land marked by this place name.

Another example of a prominent Toronto-based First Nations place name that is mentioned during the tour is the previously discussed Spadina Avenue. The tour guide explains that the word *spadina* is derived from the Anishnabe term *Ishpaadina*, which translates into English as "to go up the hill" or "the rise in the land," and which was subsequently adopted by European settlers. This phrase likely refers to the large bluff upon which Casa Loma was built.[50] The high concentration of Native agencies along and around Spadina Avenue, paired with the realization that the name Spadina has an Indigenous origin, reinforces the significance of this route for the Indigenous community.

Several other place names, most with known significance and stories attached to them, are also mentioned during the tour. Similar to the place names studied by Basso and Cruikshank,[51] the urban place names related during the tour act as compact mnemonic devices that allow quick recall of the stories and information with which they are associated. Through the use of landmarks and place names alone, the tour guide expertly recalls and relates five hours of Indigenous history and stories about the Toronto area. Wherever possible, stories about local places are told when the bus is in proximity to the places themselves, enabling the tour participants to more directly experience these places as the tour guide relates the appropriate story. The Indigenous history of Toronto is not related chronologically on the bus tour, as in Euro-American literate storytelling traditions, but rather topographically. Proximity to places of First Nations significance in the urban landscape control the tempo and ordering of the narratives on the tour, rather than an external, linear temporal framework. The past, present, and future of the First Nations heritage of Toronto are related synchronically through these places.

This topographical chronology is embedded in the route of the bus tour, which is roughly structured according to the four directions of the medicine wheel (or the circle of life), a widely used traditional teaching model among many First Nations. The medicine wheel is usually conceptualized as a circle with a centre and four sections representing cardinal directions (north, east, south, and west). These directions are also used to discuss the four seasons (winter, spring, fall, and summer), the four aspects of self (physical, mental, emotional, and spiritual) and the four sacred medicines (tobacco, sweetgrass, cedar, and sage).[52] As such, the medicine wheel is a powerful tool for metaphorically illustrating relationships among many seemingly separate domains of experience.

In accordance with some medicine wheel teachings, the tour generally starts at the Native Canadian Centre of Toronto, which can be conceived as the centre of the medicine wheel. This is appropriate since it is a central gathering spot for many in the First Nations community. Established officially in 1962 (from its earlier roots in the YMCA's Indian Social Club), "the Centre occupies a sacred place among Native people in Toronto. The Centre is important symbolically as the 'heart' or 'mother' of organizations that form the infrastructure of what is considered 'the Toronto Native community.'"[53] Many of the diverse organizations and agencies catering to the Aboriginal population of Toronto started within or were initially supported by the Native Canadian Centre of Toronto.[54] There is a strict prohibition against alcohol consumption while on the centre's grounds, largely out of "respect for the sacredness of the Centre, the Elders present there, and medicines and sacred items that are located there."[55] The centre is also the site of a totem pole that was carved by a Haida artist and subsequently gifted to the centre. Although totem poles are conventionally most representative of coastal Indigenous cultures, the pole at the Native Canadian Centre of Toronto is notable because the totems (or dodems) were carved to represent eastern clan symbols and thus commemorate the Indigenous peoples of the Toronto area.[56]

From the centre, the tour bus travels northward toward the site of Casa Loma, where the tour bus makes its first stop to talk about the First Nations heritage of that location. The focus of this stop is not the castle itself but rather what it obscures. It is said that Casa Loma is built atop a Mississauga council ground, which existed before the land was appropriated from the Mississaugas and subsequently developed.[57] The tour guide also informs the group that the bluff upon which Casa Loma sits marks a section of the original shoreline of 12,000-year-old glacial lake that archaeologists call Lake Iroquois.[58] As the tour participants gaze southward from the top of the bluff across the city below, they are encouraged to imagine that at one point, all the land south of the bluff was underwater. At the base of this bluff runs Davenport Road. The tour guide points out that, while most of central Toronto's streets are laid out in a rigid grid pattern, Davenport Road instead follows the base of the bluff in a curving and meandering fashion. The reason for this anomaly is that Davenport Road actually follows the route of an ancient trail that was used by First Nations for hundreds or thousands of years after the glacial waters receded. This trail was subsequently used by European settlers, and eventually the route was paved without significantly altering its trajectory.[59] The tour guide illustrates how Davenport Road, although now a paved street, recalls the original trail, whose function remains intact in the present.

From Casa Loma, the tour bus proceeds eastward toward its second stop in Scarborough, where an archaeological site known as Tabor Hill is located. Tabor Hill is a burial mound, or ossuary, dated to the fourteenth or fifteenth century, which contains the remains of approximately 500 Native ancestors.[60] At this stop, the bus tour participants ascend the slope of the burial mound and form a circle at it apex. The history and sacred nature of Tabor Hill is noted, an honour song is performed, and tobacco offerings are made to pay respect to the ancestors buried there.

The bus then travels in a southwesterly direction toward the shore of Lake Ontario. As the bus makes its way along the lakeshore, the First Nations heritage of various sites along the way is noted. The Toronto Islands are highlighted as a place that has long been recognized by First Nations as a place of ceremony, healing, and rejuvenation. The tour guide then explains how these qualities are still associated with the islands today—it is a place that remains relatively undeveloped, where there is no traffic, and where people come to relax and enjoy a natural setting.[61] Stories are told about how Indigenous artefacts were found while construction crews were digging the foundations for the CN Tower, and about the contributions of First Nations sharpshooters who helped defend Fort York during the War of 1812, as the bus approaches those sites. As the bus reaches the site of the Canadian National Exhibition, the tour guide discusses the long First Nations trading history of the Toronto area. The exhibition grounds mark the site of the earliest European settlement in the area—a French fur-trading post called Fort Rouillé. Established around 1750, Fort Rouillé was a significant site of early trade between Europeans and First Nations people.[62] After the establishment of the exhibition, this tradition of trading between First Nations and Europeans continued as local First Nations people sold crafts and food items that catered to a European clientele.[63] Indeed, archaeological and oral evidence suggest that the Toronto area was a prominent trading centre well before the arrival of Europeans in the area. Archaeologists have unearthed artefacts from various sites across the city that originated from as far away as the Ohio Valley, the Gulf of Mexico, the north shore of Lake Superior, James Bay, the western plains, and the Pacific Coast.[64] This accumulated evidence supports the interpretation that Toronto has been a site of significant trade and intercultural exchange for thousands of years. Today, as Canada's current economic capital, Toronto persists in its legacy of trade, originally established by (although eventually largely bypassing) First Nations people.

Along the lakeshore, the bus proceeds west to the bay of the Humber River where there is yet another stop. At this stop, the tour group stands at the mouth of the river while the guide notes various features with First Nations significance. The role of Toronto as a meeting place and trading centre is re-emphasized through discussion of the Toronto Carrying Place trail, a major trading route connecting Lake Simcoe to Lake Ontario via the Humber and Rouge rivers that was long used by Indigenous peoples and later, European settlers and traders.[65] Today, the mouth of the Humber River is straddled by a suspension bridge that incorporates stylized Thunderbird motifs, common among many First Nations myths, within its metallic frame. From here, the bus heads back to the Native Canadian Centre of Toronto, the beginning and ending point for the bus tour. In this way, the route of the bus maps the medicine wheel through the city, with stops in three of the four cardinal directions (north, east, and west). This roughly circular route provides a way of understanding the First Nations heritage of Toronto using a traditional Indigenous framework.

Conclusion

First Nations people have continuously occupied most Canadian cities since the time of their inception, and currently over half of Canada's Aboriginal people now live in urban areas.[66] Despite this recognition, there exists a predominant conceit that traditional Indigenous culture is incompatible with or irrelevant to urban areas. This conceit is at least partially based on the assumption that, since Indigenous knowledge is highly based on observation of natural ecological relationships and cities are built landscapes that many consider to be outside of nature, cities are not conducive to the survival of Indigenous knowledge and culture. However, cities still possess natural ecology as well as a *genius loci* that is still enacted and expressed through built form. The endurance of the empire of nature within cities suggests that Indigenous knowledge and cultures can remain relevant and important for Indigenous people living in urban areas. As they have done in a variety of natural ecologies across Turtle Island, Indigenous knowledge and cultures are also capable of adapting to the requirements of urban rhythms and urban form, and just as they do in non-urban environments, the stories kept and told about the urban landscape play an important part in the maintenance of urban First Nations culture. The content of urban stories differs from stories told about rural settings, but they are different precisely because these stories emerge from a way of engaging with local environments that is similar in both contexts. Marie Battiste and James Youngblood Henderson have suggested that traditional knowledge is defined not by its antiquity, but rather by its adherence to protocols for learning and sharing knowledge that have been identified by Indigenous people living in specific locales to be appropriate to those places.[67] Indigenous knowledge and traditions emerged from generations of deep observation of and participation within the ecologies of different traditional territories, and Indigenous land-based stories must be reflective of and relevant to the environments in which they emerged.

The Great Indian Bus Tour of Toronto is a specific example of urban Indigenous storytelling that appears to maintain epistemological consistency with other traditional topocentric storytelling protocols. The whole structure of the Great Indian Bus Tour, from the topographical ordering of communal tribal memories, to the synchronic comparisons made about places mentioned, to the urban ecological knowledge they encode, and the way they establish the urban landscape as part of traditional Indigenous territory, is comparable to Indigenous storytelling traditions more conventionally associated with rural and reserve territories. Regardless of the presence or absence of built form, the existence of an oral tradition representing a particular territory as Indigenous is a primary precondition for labelling that territory "traditional." The First Nations oral tradition of Toronto, as expressed through the Great Indian Bus Tour, demonstrates that Toronto can legitimately be called traditional territory for Anishnabe and Haudenosaunee peoples. It is also demonstrated, through stories of the accomplishments of First Nations residents of Toronto, that the city's First Nations heritage continues to unfold in the present. The persistence of place names throughout this territory is a testament to the long occupation of this landscape by First Nations people. Similar to traditional stories told in and about wilderness environments, the bus tour provides a wealth of information about Toronto that connects people to the hangouts and agencies in which Toronto's First Nations community gathers. In this sense, then, the bus tour contains numerous examples of what might be considered urban Indigenous ecological knowledge—knowledge of places or services in the city that urban First Nations individuals might find useful and that in turn connect them to other members of the First Nations community. This knowledge helps First Nations people to find the tools necessary to live and thrive as a First Nations people in the city. This oral tradition defies any notion that urban environments are incompatible with First Nations culture.

The bus tour helps people to see how, despite the drastic changes to First Nations territories and people that have been wrought by European colonialism, expansionism, displacement, and material and technological change, Toronto has a deeper, more fundamental *genius loci* that, although not always easy to perceive, still persists today. The resilience of the empire of nature in Toronto is such that although it has been obscured in some ways by built form, the landscape's fundamental character, as represented by Toronto's Indigenous storytellers, is still intact. The tenacity and strength of First Nations people and culture in the Toronto area draws, at least in part, from the resilience of the empire of nature. Rodney Bobiwash wrote that "for Aboriginal people living in the Toronto area, there is a long history of Native occupation which Toronto's modern towers of concrete and steel may obscure but cannot eradicate."[68] The Great Indian Bus Tour remains a monument to Rodney Bobiwash's holistic understanding of the city. However, I would also argue that the Great Indian Bus Tour, as an urban extension of First Nations storytelling traditions, promotes the idea that Toronto's urban form is deeply inscribed by the area's First Nations legacy—that the presence of Toronto's urban form continues to represent the First Nations heritage of the area, if one is properly taught how to see it. This emphasizes that Toronto is indeed a traditional Indigenous territory, not simply despite the presence of urban form, but rather by virtue of it.

Notes

1 Heather Howard, "Dreamcatchers in the City: An Ethnohistory of Social Action, Gender and Class in Native Community Production in Toronto" (Ph.D. dissertation, University of Toronto, 2005), 31–34.

2 Statistics Canada, "Aboriginal Peoples in Canada in 2006: Inuit, Métis and First Nations, 2006 Census," 27 August 2011, http://www12.statcan.ca/census-recensement/2006/as-sa/97-558/p3-eng.cfm.

3 Naomi Adelson, *"Being Alive Well": Health and the Politics of Cree Well-Being* (Toronto: University of Toronto Press, 2000); Keith Basso, *Wisdom Sits in Places: Landscape and Language among the Western Apache* (Albuquerque: University of New Mexico Press, 1996); Hugh Brody, *Maps and Dreams* (Vancouver: Douglas and McIntyre, 1988); Bruce Chatwin, *The Songlines* (London: Jonathan Cape, 1987); Julie Cruikshank, "Getting the Words Right: Perspec-

tives on Naming and Places in Athapaskan Oral History," *Arctic Anthropology* 27, no. 1 (1990): 52–65; and, Julie Cruikshank, *Life Lived like a Story: The Stories of Three Yukon Native Elders* (Lincoln: University of Nebraska Press, 1990).

4 Rick J. Ponting and Cora A. Voyajeur, "Multiple Points of Light: Grounds for Optimism among First Nations in Canada," in *Hidden in Plain Sight: Contributions of Aboriginal Peoples to Canadian Identity and Culture*, ed. David R. Newhouse, Cora J. Voyajeur, and Dan Beavon (Toronto: University of Toronto Press, 2005), 425.

5 David R. Newhouse, Cora J. Voyajeur, and Dan Beavon, "Introduction," in *Hidden in Plain Sight: Contributions of Aboriginal Peoples to Canadian Identity and Culture*, ed. David R. Newhouse, Cora J. Voyajeur, and Dan Beavon (Toronto: University of Toronto Press, 2005), 5.

6 Howard, "Dreamcatchers in the City," 28.

7 Evelyn Peters, "'Urban' and 'Aboriginal': An Impossible Contradiction?" in *City Lives and City Forms: Critical Research and Canadian Urbanism*, ed. Jon Caufield and Linda Peake (Toronto: University of Toronto Press, 1996), 315.

8 Peters, "'Urban' and 'Aboriginal,'" 316, 318.

9 Howard, "Dreamcatchers in the City," 35; Peters, "Urban' and 'Aboriginal,'" 319.

10 Peters, "'Urban' and 'Aboriginal,'" 320.

11 Newhouse et al., "Introduction," 8.

12 Environics Institute, *Urban Aboriginal Peoples Study: Toronto Report* (Toronto: Environics Institute, 2010), 9.

13 Native Canadian Centre of Toronto, *In the Spirit of Unity: A Synopsis of Programs and Services Available to the Urban Aboriginal Population in the Greater Toronto Area* (Toronto: Native Canadian Centre of Toronto, 2002), 17.

14 A. Rodney Bobiwash, "The History of Native People in the Toronto Area: An Overview," in *The Meeting Place: Aboriginal Life in Toronto*, ed. Frances Sanderson and Heather Howard-Bobiwash (Toronto: Native Canadian Centre of Toronto, 1997), 11.

15 Environics Institute, *Urban Aboriginal Peoples Study*, 22.

16 Howard, "Dreamcatchers in the City," 65.

17 Quoted in Howard, "Dreamcatchers in the City," 236.

18 Doug Williams, director of studies for the PhD program in Indigenous Studies, Trent University, personal communication, 2004.

19 Vine Deloria Jr. and James Treat, *For This Land: Writings on Religion in America* (New York: Routledge, 1999), 253.

20 Basso, *Wisdom Sits in Places*; Cruikshank, "Getting the Words Right"; Cruikshank, *Life Lived Like a Story*; and Brody, *Maps and Dreams*.

21 Vine Deloria Jr. and Daniel R. Wildcat, *Power and Place: Indian Education in America* (Golden, CO: Fulcrum Resources, 2001).
22 James Axtell, "The Ethnohistory of Native America," in *Rethinking American Indian History*, ed. Donald L. Fixico (Albuquerque: University of New Mexico Press, 1997), 22.
23 David T. McNab, "'Water Is Her Lifeblood': The Waters of Bkejwanong and the Treaty-Making Process," in *Earth, Water, Air and Fire: Studies in Canadian Ethnohistory*, ed. David T. McNab (Waterloo: Wilfrid Laurier University Press, 1998), 37.
24 Deloria Jr. and Treat, *For This Land*, 252.
25 Cruikshank, "Getting the Words Right"; Cruikshank, *Life Lived Like a Story*.
26 Cruikshank, "Getting the Words Right," 62.
27 Cruikshank, "Getting the Words Right"; Cruikshank, *Life Lived Like a Story*.
28 McNab, "Water Is Her Lifeblood," 38.
29 Basso, *Wisdom Sits in Places*.
30 Quoted in Basso, *Wisdom Sits in Places*, 38.
31 Basso, *Wisdom Sits in Places*, 92.
32 Howard, "Dreamcatchers in the City," 65.
33 Monica Bodirsky, co-ordinator of Getekindaswingamig: The Toronto Native Community History Program, conversation with author, 2006.
34 Quoted in Howard, "Dreamcatchers in the City," 236.
35 Bobiwash, "History of Native People," 7.
36 Alanis King, "The Great Indian Bus Tour" (Getekindaswingamig: Toronto Native Community History Program. Toronto, 2005); Howard, "Dreamcatchers in the City," 102.
37 Mima Kapches, "An Archaeological View of Toronto: Life in the Past Lanes," *Rotunda* 19, no. 4 (1987): 21–22.
38 Toronto Historical Association, *A Glimpse of Toronto's History: Opportunities for the Commemoration of Lost Historic Sites*. Toronto: Toronto Historical Association, 2001.
39 Toronto Historical Association, *Glimpse of Toronto's History*.
40 King, "Great Indian Bus Tour."
41 Bobiwash, "History of Native People," 20.
42 King, "Great Indian Bus Tour."
43 King, "Great Indian Bus Tour."
44 King, "Great Indian Bus Tour."
45 King, "Great Indian Bus Tour."
46 Quoted in Howard, "Dreamcatchers in the City," 249.
47 Basso, *Wisdom Sits in Places*; Cruikshank, "Getting the Words Right."

48 Bodirsky, conversation with author.
49 Environics Institute, *Urban Aboriginal Peoples Study*, 33, 56.
50 Bodirsky, conversation with author, 2006; and King, "Great Indian Bus Tour."
51 Basso, *Wisdom Sits in Places*; Cruikshank, "Getting the Words Right."
52 Ann N. Dapice, "The Medicine Wheel," *Journal of Transcultural Nursing* 17, no. 3 (2006): 252.
53 Howard, "Dreamcatchers in the City," 102.
54 Roger Obonsawin and Heather Howard-Bobiwash, "The Native Canadian Centre of Toronto: The Meeting Place for the Aboriginal Community for 35 Years," in *The Meeting Place: Aboriginal Life in Toronto*, ed. Frances Sanderson and Heather Howard-Bobiwash (Toronto: Native Canadian Centre of Toronto, 1997), 25–59.
55 Howard, "Dreamcatchers in the City," 102.
56 Howard, "Dreamcatchers in the City," 198.
57 King, "Great Indian Bus Tour."
58 P.F. Karrow and B.G. Warner, "The Geological and Biological Environment for Human Occupation in Southern Ontario," in *The Archaeology of Southern Ontario to A.D. 1650*, ed. Chris J. Ellis and Neal Ferris (London, ON: London Chapter of the Ontario Archaeological Society, 1990), 15.
59 King, "Great Indian Bus Tour."
60 Christine F. Dodd, D. Poulton, Paul A. Lennox, David G. Smith, and Gary A. Warrick, "The Middle Ontario Iroquoian Stage," in *The Archaeology of Southern Ontario to A.D. 1650*, ed. Chris Ellis and Neal Ferris (London, ON: Ontario Archaeological Society, 1990), 353.
61 King, "Great Indian Bus Tour."
62 Bobiwash, "History of Native People," 11.
63 King, "Great Indian Bus Tour."
64 Bobiwash, "History of Native People," 8–9.
65 King, "The Great Indian Bus Tour."
66 Statistics Canada, "Aboriginal Peoples in Canada in 2006," 2011.
67 Marie Battiste and James Youngblood Henderson, *Protecting Indigenous Knowledge and Heritage: A Global Challenge* (Saskatoon: Purich, 2000).
68 Bobiwash, "History of Native People," 5.

Bibliography

I. Archival Collections

Library and Archives Canada, Ottawa, ON

Indian Affairs, RG10

"Band Council Resolution #13," 16 March 1971. Vol. 10300, File 493,8-2-7-7, Reel T-7577.

"Memorandum from Cameron to Regional Director," 22 March 1971. Vol. 10300, File 493,8-2-7-7, Reel T-7577.

"Letter from Maurice Foster, MP to William McKim," 31 March 1971. Vol. 10300, File 493,8-2-7-7, Reel T-7577.

"Letter from McKim to Foster," 20 April 1971. Vol. 10300, File 493,8-2-7-7, Reel T-7577.

"Letter from McGilp to Chief Johnston," 14 April 1971. Vol. 10300, File 493,8-2-7-7, Reel T-7577.

General Council Meeting held at Walpole Island on August 11th, 1887. Vol. 2118, File 22,610 Part 1, Reel # C-11,162.

Privy Council Office, RG2

"Cabinet Conclusions," 10 June 1960. Vol. 2746, File C. 17 May–30 June, 3.

"Cabinet Conclusions," 30 June 1960. Vol. 2746, File C. 17 May–30 June, 4.

Industry, Trade, and Commerce, RG20

"A Report on Progress: Noranda Mines, Limited, 1961." Vol. 775, File 23-100-N17.

"A Report on Progress: Noranda Mines, Limited, 1959." Vol. 775, File 23-100-N17.

Archives of Ontario

Indian Affairs Diffusion Materials, Record Group 10, Series 2, Vol. 4, Reel 1221.

B-39, "A Sketch of Part of the Western District for A.T. Iredell, London office, Newark, 2 August 1795. D.W. Smith, Act. Surv. Gen., No. 15."

B-67 (photostat), Lake St. Clair and Vicinity, McNiff, 1797.

RG 1-470-0-0-324 Shawanee (Sombra Tp), [N-2290], "Sombra, formerly Shawanese W.D." [Western District] A. Iredell, 9 July 1800.

RG 1, A-I-1, Vol. 3, Detroit, letter, 26 Sep 1793, from Patrick McNiff to Lt. Col. England, p. 68.

RG 1, A-1-6, MS 30/5, Vol. 27, No. 220. Letter 12 June 1804, Iredell to Chewett & Rideout.

F47-5-1-0-44.2, [untitled]. Showing "A schedule of all the lots on this [U.S.] side of the River [Detroit River]" and "Schedule of the lots on this [Sandwich Tp] side of the River [Detroit River]." n.d.

Ontario Marriage Index, Microfilm 19, Registration #001369, Saugeen Township, August 22nd, 1876-on-line April 4th, 2006.

Wayne County

"Potawatomi and Ottawa deed to Antoine Beaubien, Jean Marie Beaubien at River Raisin." Register of Deeds, Reel no. P8, 200-201.

Minister of Natural Resources

Surveys Branch,

Field Notes Transcribed from Original Books, Vol. 3, 10, 13

Field Note Book 537.

Plans

Rochester 2492 K19

Sandwich 2034 D14.

Sandwich 2425 K18.

Tilbury West 91245 Y51-15.

Rochester 1989 C8.

Instructions to Land Surveyors, Ontario, Crown Surveys, 16 October 1792–7 May 1796, Vol. 2.

Instructions to Land Surveyors, Ontario, Crown Surveys, 1 June 1796–6 December 1819. Vol. 3.

Shawanaga First Nation, Ontario

Elias Journals

Ziibiwing Cultural Center , Isabella Reservation, Mount Pleasant

Genealogical files.

Walpole Island First Nation

Nin.Da.Waab.Jig., Historical Photos Binder, c. 1890–1950.

Binder, "Charles Jacobs Family Tree," Reference No. 1672.

II. Government Documents

Canada. Aboriginal Affairs and Northern Development. "Copy of the Robinson Treaty Made in the Year 1850 with the Ojibewa Indians of Lake Huron Conveying Certain Lands to the Crown," *Aboriginal Affairs and Northern Development Canada*, http://www.aadnc-aandc.gc.ca/eng/1100100028984.

———. An Act for the gradual enfranchisement of Indians, the better management of Indian affairs, and to extend the provisions of the Act 31st Victoria, Statutes of Canada 1869, c. 6 (32 Vict.). In *Pre-Legislation Concerning Indians: A Selected and Indexed Collection*, ed. Thomas Isaac, 52–55. Saskatchewan: Native Law Centre, 1993.

———. Act for the protection of the Indians in Upper Canada from imposition, and the property occupied or enjoyed by them from trespass and injury, Statutes of the Province of Canada, 1850, c. 74. In *Pre-Legislation Concerning Indians: A Selected and Indexed Collection*, ed. Thomas Isaac, 42–46. Saskatchewan: Native Law Centre, 1993.

———. An Act to encourage the gradual Civilization of the Indian Tribes in this Province, 1857, 22 Vict., c. 26. In *Pre-Legislation Concerning Indians: A Selected and Indexed Collection*, ed. Thomas Isaac, 11–15. Saskatchewan: Native Law Centre, 1993.

———. An Act providing for the organisation of the Department of the Secretary of State of Canada, and for the management of Indian and Ordnance Lands, 1868. In *Indian Acts and Amendments 1868–1975: An Indexed Collection*, ed. Sharon Venne, 1–10. Saskatchewan: Native Law Centre, 1981.

———. Constitution Act, 1982, Schedule B to the *Canada Act* 1982 (UK), 1982, c. 11.

———. Environment Canada. *The State of Canada's Environment—1996*. Ottawa: Government of Canada, 1996.

———. Health Canada. "First Nations and Inuit Health." First Nations and Inuit Health. http://www.hc-sc.gc.ca/fnihb-dgspni/fnihb/phcph/fnihccp/training/ahrds.htm.

———. Indian Act, Revised Statues of Canada 1985, c. I-5.

———. Indian Act, Statutes of Canada 1876, c. 18.

———. *Indian Treaties and Surrenders*. Vol. 1. 1902. Saskatoon, Fifth House, 1992.

———. Meteorological Service of Canada. "Lightning Maps and Statistics." 28 July 2011. Environment Canada, http://www.ec.gc.ca/foudre-lightning/default.asp?lang=En&n=C4E86962-1.

———. Parliament. House of Commons. Standing Committee on Aboriginal Affairs and Northern Development. Slaughtering of Inuit Sled Dogs. Meeting 23. Ottawa, 11 March 2005.

———. Royal Commission on Aboriginal Peoples. *People to People, Nation to Nation: Highlights of the Final Report of the Royal Commission on Aboriginal People.* Ottawa: Canada Communication, 1996.

———. Royal Commission on Aboriginal Peoples. *Report.* Ottawa: Canada Communication, 1996.

———. Statistics Canada. "Aboriginal Identity Population by Age Group, Median Age and Sex, 2006 counts, for Canada, Provinces and Territories." 6 October 2010, http://www12.statcan.ca/census-recensement/2006/dp-pd/hlt/97-558/pages/page.cfm?Lang=E&Geo=PR&Code=01&Table=1&Data=Count&Sex=1&Age=1&StartRec=1&Sort=2&Display=Page.

———. Statistics Canada. "Aboriginal Peoples in Canada in 2006: Inuit, Métis and First Nations, 2006 Census." 27 August 2011. http://www12.statcan.ca/census-recensement/2006/as-sa/97-558/p3-eng.cfm.

———. Statistics Canada. "Aboriginal Peoples of Canada in Census 2001." www12.statcan.ca/english/census01/products/analytic/companion/abor/canada.cfm#2.

———. Statistics Canada. *Ontario (Code 35): Aboriginal Population Profile, 2006 Census* [table]. Cat. no. 92-594-XWE. Ottawa: Statistics Canada, 2007. http://www12.statcan.ca/census-recensement/2006/dp-pd/prof/92-594/index.cfm?Lang=E.

Essex. "County History: Early Years." http://www.countyofessex.on.ca/countyhistory/earlyyears_home.asp.

London. *An Affordable Housing Strategy for the City of London.* London: London City Hall, 2005.

New Zealand Parliamentary Commissioner for the Environment. *See Change: Learning and Education for Sustainability.* Wellington, NZ: Parliamentary Commissioner for the Environment, 2004. Accessed 6 February 2006, http://www.pce.parliament.nz/assets/Uploads/Reports/pdf/See_change_report.pdf.

Ontario. Ministry of Education. *Acting Today, Shaping Tomorrow: A Policy Framework for Environmental Education in Ontario Schools.* Toronto: Queen's Printer, 2009. http://www.edu.gov.on.ca/curriculumcouncil/ShapeTomorrow.pdf.

———. Ministry of Education. *Environmental Education: Scope and Sequence of Expectations.* Toronto: Queen's Printer, 2011. http://www.edu.gov.on.ca/eng/curriculum/elementary/environ18curr.pdf.

———. Ministry of Education. *Ontario Secondary Schools, Grades 9–12: Program and Diploma Requirements.* Toronto: Queen's Printer for Ontario, 1999.

———. Ministry of the Environment. Industrial Spills in Ontario. May 2005. PIBS 5085e.

———. Working Group on Environmental Education. *Shaping Our Schools, Shaping Our Future: Environmental Education in Ontario Schools.* Toronto: Working Group on Environmental Education, 2007.

United Nations Education, Scientific, Cultural Organisation (UNESCO). *United Nations Decade for Education for Sustainable Development (2005–2014): Draft International Implementation Scheme.*" October 2004. Accessed 26 June 2012, http://portal.unesco.org/education/en/file_download.php/03f375b07798a2a55dcdc39db7aa8211Final+IIS.pdf.

III. Newspapers

Anishinabek News (North Bay, ON)
The Dominion (Toronto)
The Financial Post (Toronto)
The Gazette (Montreal)
The Journal (Kingston)
Indian News (Ottawa)
London Free Press (London, ON)
The Nation (Montreal)
National Post (Toronto)
Sarnia Canadian-Observer (Sarnia)
The Standard (Elliot Lake)
The Star.com (Toronto)
The Sudbury Star (Sudbury)
The Globe and Mail (Toronto)

IV. Unpublished work

Berman, Morris. "Science after Deconstruction: A Second Look at the Sociology of Knowledge." Presented at "Emerging Approaches to Inquiry" conference 5, Hawkwood, 1994.

Blondin, George. "My Life in the Sahtu." Submission to Royal Commission on Aboriginal Peoples, June 1993, 8–9.

Bourgeois, Paul. "An Ojibwe Conceptual Glossary." Draft, Major Glossary Paper, York University (26 February 1998).

Darnell, Regna. "Qualitative Demographics of Aboriginal Urban–Rural Migration: The Persistence of Nomadic Habits." Paper presented at the Canadian Anthropology Society, Halifax, 2003.

Jacobs, D. "The Great Lakes Today: A View of Bkejwanong." Presented at Reddin Symposium XI: The Environment of the Great Lakes, Canadian Studies Centre, Bowling Green State University, 1988.

———. ICI Canada vs. Ontario Consolidated Hearings Board. Witness Statement. *Transcription of Hearing Proceedings* 19, no. 1 (1996), 1–13. Walpole Island Heritage Centre Archives.

McNab, David. "Centring Identities in Border Places: Oral Traditions and the Written Record in the Journals of William A. Elias (1856-1929)." American Society for Ethnohistory, Annual Meeting, Santa Fe, New Mexico, 20 November 2005.

———. "'those freebooters would shoot me like a dog': American Terrorists and Homeland Security in the Journals of Ezhaaswe (William A. Elias (1856-1929))." Workshop on "Lines Drawn upon the Water," Aboriginal People and the International Boundary through the Great Lakes Watershed, University of Western Ontario, 12 February 2005.

Simpson, L. "Effects on Aboriginals from the Great Lakes Environment E.A.G.L.E. PROJECT: Sociocultural Pilot Project Technical Report." Assembly of First Nations/Chiefs of Ontario/Health Canada Partnership, 2001.

Stephens, C.V. "From Scourges and Historical Traumas to Environmental Health Fears: A Multi-temporal Case Study of Discursive (Re)Constructions of Health and Well-being at the Walpole Island First Nation." Presented at the Annual Meeting of the American Society for Ethnohistory. Doubletree Hotel, Tulsa, Oklahoma, 2007.

———. "A Preliminary Overview of the Nineteenth Century Health History of the Walpole Island First Nation: With Special Focus on the Historical Documents Contained in the Reverend Andrew Jamieson Collection." Research Report. McMaster University, 2004.

———. "Toxic Talk": Calibrating Divergent Aboriginal and Biomedical Conceptualizations and Understandings of Risk and Environmental Illness in a Contemporary Native Community. Presented at the Annual Meeting of the American Society for Ethnohistory. Hilton Hotel, Eugene, Oregon, 2008.

———. "Where the Waters Divide: Water Quality and Human Health at the Walpole Island First Nation—Preliminary Findings." 2005 Richard F. Salisbury Award for Applied Anthropology Presentation. Canadian Anthropology Society (CASCA) Annual Conference, Concordia University, Montreal, Canada, 2006.

Stephens, C.V., and R. Darnell. "Water Quality Issues in the WIFN Community." In "Feasibility of Conducting Epidemiological Studies to Assess the Health Risk of the Walpole Island First Nation Community from Exposure to Environmental Contaminants," ed. J.R. Bend, B.A. Corbett, R. Darnell, et al. Research Report. Environmental Contaminants Health Program, First Nations and Inuit Health Branch, Canada, 2005.

V. Published Works, Theses, and Dissertations

Aberley, Doug. "Interpreting Bioregionalism: A Story from Many Voices." In *Bioregionalism*, ed. Michael Vincent McGinnis, 13–42. London: Routledge: 1999.

Aborigines Protection Society. *Report on the Indians of Upper Canada*. London: William Ball, Arnold, 1839.

Abram, David. *The Spell of the Sensuous: Perception and Language in a More-Than-Human World*. New York: Pantheon, 1996.

Adelson, Naomi. *"Being Alive Well": Health and the Politics of Cree Well-Being*. Toronto: University of Toronto Press, 2000.

Adelson A. *Health Beliefs and the Politics of Cree Well Being*. New Delhi: Sage, 1998.

Akii Kwe (formerly The Women of Bkejwanong). "Minobimaatisiiwin—'We Are to Care for Her.'" Position Paper. n.d.

Akwesasne Notes, ed. *Basic Call to Consciousness*. Rooseveltown, NY: Mohawk Nation, 1978. Rpt. Summertown, TN: Native Voices, 2005.

Allen, Robert S. *His Majesty's Indian Allies: British Indian Policy in The Defense of Canada, 1774–1815*. Toronto: Dundurn Press, 1992.

Anand, S.S., S. Yusuf, et al. "Risk Factors, Atherosclerosis, and Cardiovascular Disease among Aboriginal People in Canada: The Study of Health Assessment and Risk Evaluation in Aboriginal Peoples (SHARE-AP)." *Lancet* 358, no. 9288 (2001): 1147.

Angus, Charlie, and Brit Griffin. *We Lived a Life and Then Some: The Life, Death, and Life of a Mining Town*. Toronto: Between the Lines, 1996.

Ani, Marimba. *Yurugu: An African-Centered Critique of European Cultural Thought and Behavior*. Trenton, NJ: African World Press, 1994.

Animals' Voice. "Working in the Front Line: Kashechewan Spay North 2006." Summer 2006, 16.

Anonymous. "Kashechewan: Water Crisis in Northern Ontario." *CBC News*. 9 November 2006. http://www.cbc.ca/news/background/aboriginals/kashechewan.html.

Apffel-Marglin, Frederique, ed. *The Spirit of Regeneration: Andean Culture Confronting Western Notions of Development*. New York: Zed, 1998.

Appadurai, Arjun. *Modernity at Large: Cultural Dimensions of Globalization*. Minneapolis: University of Minnesota Press, 1996.

Arnold, David. *The Problem of Nature: Environment, Culture and European Expansion*. Oxford: Oxford University Press, 1996.

Assembly of First Nations. *The E.A.G.L.E Project: The Effects on Aboriginal Peoples from the Great Lakes Environment: Annual Report*. Ottawa: Health Canada, 1995. http://www.chiefs-of-ontario.org/sites/default/files/files/socio-c.pdf.

Bibliography

Augustine, Stephen. "Traditional Aboriginal Knowledge and Science versus Occidental Science." Prepared for the Biodiversity Convention Office of Environment Canada, 1997. http://www.quechuanetwork.org/ yachaywasi/Stephen_Augustine1.doc.

Axtell, James. "The Ethnohistory of Native America." In *Rethinking American Indian History*, ed. Donald L. Fixico, 11–27. Albuquerque: University of New Mexico Press, 1997.

Babbie, E.R. *Survey Research Methods*. 2nd ed. Belmont: Wadsworth, 1990.

Bankoff, Greg. "Winds of Colonisation: The Meteorological Contours of Spain's Imperium in the Pacific, 1521–1878." *Environment and History* 12, no. 1 (2006): 65–88.

Basso, Keith. *Wisdom Sits in Places: Landscape and Language Among the Western Apache*. Albuquerque: University of New Mexico Press, 1996.

Battiste, Marie. "Enabling the Autumn Seed: Toward a Decolonized Approach to Aboriginal Knowledge, Language, and Education." *Canadian Journal of Native Education* 22, no. 1 (1998): 16–27.

———. *Reclaiming Indigenous Voice and Vision*. Vancouver: UBC Press, 2000.

———. "Micmac Literacy and Cognitive Assimilation." In *Indian Education in Canada*, vol. 1, *The Legacy*, ed. Jean Barman, Yvonne Hébert, and Don McCaskill, 32–44. Vancouver: University of British Columbia Press, 1989.

Battiste, Marie, and James Youngblood Henderson, *Protecting Indigenous Knowledge and Heritage: A Global Challenge*. Saskatoon: Purich, 2000.

Beinart, William, and Lotte Hughes. *Environment and Empire*. Oxford: Oxford University Press, 2007.

Beinart, William, and Joann McGregor, eds. *Social History and African Environments*. Oxford: James Currey, 2003.

Beinart, William, and Karen Middleton. "Plant Transfers in Historical Perspective: A Review Article." *Environment and History* 10, no. 1 (2004): 3–30.

Benjamin, Walter. *Selected Writings: Walter Benjamin*. Ed. Marcus Bullock and Michael W. Jennings. Cambridge: Belknap, 1996.

Bennett, Judith A. "War, Emergency and the Environment: Fiji, 1939–1946." *Environment and History* 7, no. 3 (2001): 255–88.

Benton-Banai, Edward. *The Mishomis Book: The Voice of the Ojibway*. St. Paul, MN: Indian Country Press, 1979. Rpt. Hayward, WI: Indian Country Communications, 1988.

Berg, Peter, and Raymond F. Dasmann. "Reinhabiting California." In *Home! A Bioregional Reader*, ed. Van Andruss, Christopher Plant, Judith Plant, and Stephanie Wright. Philadelphia: New Society, 1990.

Berman, Morris. "Science after Deconstruction: A Second Look at the Sociology of Knowledge." Edited transcript of presentation given at the conference Emerging Approaches to Inquiry 5, Hawkwood, 1994.

Bernard, H.R. *Research Methods in Anthropology: Qualitative and Quantitative Approaches*. Thousand Oaks: Sage, 1994.

Berry, Thomas. *The Great Work: Our Way into the Future*. New York: Bell Tower, 1999.

Berry, Wendell. *What Are People For?* New York: North Point, 1990.

Bkejwanong. *Approaches to Environmental Management: The Experience of Walpole Island First Nation*. http://www.bkejwanong.com/waters/waterinfo.html.

Bobiwash, A. Rodney. "The History of Native People in the Toronto Area: An Overview." In *The Meeting Place: Aboriginal Life in Toronto*, ed. Frances Sanderson and Heather Howard-Bobiwash, 5–24. Toronto: Native Canadian Centre of Toronto, 1997.

Boldt, Menno. *Surviving as Indians*. Toronto: University of Toronto Press, 1993.

Boldt, Menno and Anthony Long. "Native Indian Self-Government: Instrument of Autonomy or Assimilation?" In *Governments in Conflict? Provinces and Indian Nations in Canada*, ed. Anthony Long, Menno Boldt, and Leroy Little Bear, 38–56. Toronto: University of Toronto Press.

Bordo, Jonathan. "Jack Pine: Wilderness Sublime or the Erasure of the Aboriginal Presence from the Landscape." *Journal of Canadian Studies* 27, no. 4 (1993): 98–128.

Borrows, John. "Constitutional Law from a First Nation Perspective: Self-Government and the Royal Proclamation." *UBC Law Review* 28 (1994): 1–47.

———. "A Genealogy of Law: Inherent Sovereignty and First Nations Self-Government." L.M. thesis, University of Toronto, 1991.

———. "Wampum at Niagara: The Royal Proclamation, Canadian Legal History, and Self-Government." In *Aboriginal and Treaty Rights in Canada*, ed. Michael Asch, 155–72. Vancouver: University of British Columbia Press, 1997.

Bowers, Chet A. *Educating for Eco-justice and Community*. Athens: University of Georgia Press, 2001.

———. *Let Them Eat Data: How Computers Affect Education, Cultural Diversity, and the Prospects of Ecological Sustainability*. Athens: University of Georgia Press, 2000.

———. "The Role of Education and Ideology in the Transition from a Modern to a More Bioregionally-oriented Culture." In *Bioregionalism*, ed. Michael Vincent McGinnis, 191–204. London: Routledge, 1999.

Bowler, R. Arthur, and Bruce G. Wilson. "John Butler." In *Dictionary of Canadian Biography Online*, Library and Archives Canada. http://www.biographi.ca/EN/.

Boyarin, Jonathan, and Daniel Boyarin. *Powers of Diaspora: Two Essays on the Relevance of Jewish Culture*. Minneapolis: University of Minnesota Press, 2002.

Bradley, Raymond S., and Philip D. Jones, eds. *Climate since 1500*. London: Routledge, 1992.

Braziel, Jana Evans, and Manita Mannur, eds. *Theorizing Diaspora*. Oxford: Blackwell, 2003.

Brockington, Dan. *Fortress Conservation: The Preservation of the Mkomazi Reserve, Tanzania* Oxford: International African Institute with James Currey, 2002.

Brody, Hugh. *Maps and Dreams*. Toronto: Douglas and McIntyre, 1988.

Brooking, Tom, and Eric Pawson, eds. "New Zealand," special issue, *Environment and History* 9, no. 4 (2003).

Brownlie, Robin Jarvis. *A Fatherly Eye: Indian Agents, Government Power, and Aboriginal Resistance in Ontario, 1918–1939*. Don Mills, ON: Oxford University Press, 2003.

Bumsted, J. M. *The Scots in Canada*. Ottawa: Canadian Historical Association, 1982.

Byatt, A.S. *On Histories and Stories: Selected Essays*. London: Chatto and Windus, 2000.

Byles, J., N. Higginbotham, and R. Heller. "How to Perform Transdisciplinary Research: Epidemiological Study Designs." In *Health Social Science: A Transdisciplinary and Complexity Perspective*, ed. N. Higgenbotham, G. Albrecht, and L. Connor, 206–26. Oxford: Oxford University Press, 2001.

Cajete, Gregory. "Chapter 6: Sense of Place." In *Native Science: Natural Laws of Interdependence*, 178–213, Santa Fe, NM: Clear Light, 2000.

———. *Look to the Mountain: An Ecology of Indigenous Education*. Durango: Kivaki, 1994.

Calder, Jenni. *The Scots in Canada*. Edinburgh: Lauth, 2003.

Calliou, Sharilyn. "Peacekeeping Actions at Home: A Medicine Wheel Model for a Peacekeeping Pedagogy." In *First Nations Education in Canada: The Circle Unfolds*, ed. M. Battiste and J. Barman, 47–72. Vancouver: University of British Columbia Press, 1995.

———. "Us/Them, Me/You: Who? (Re)thinking the Binary of First Nations and non–First Nations." *Canadian Journal of Native Education* 22, no. 1 (1998): 28–52.

Calloway, Colin G. *Crown and Calumet: British–Indian Relations, 1783–1815*. Norman: University of Oklahoma Press, 1987.

———. *New for All: Indians, Europeans and the Remaking of Early America*. Baltimore: Johns Hopkins University Press, 1997.

Canadian Press. "Number of Aboriginal People Living in Toronto Continues to Grow." CBC *News*, 15 January 2008. http://www.cbc.ca/canada/toronto/story/2008/01/15/tto-census.html/.

Carpenter, C., and L. Sattenspiel. "The Design and Use of an Agent-based Model to Simulate the 1918 Influenza Epidemic at Norway House, Manitoba." *American Journal of Human Biology* 21, no. 3 (2009): 290–300, http://www.3interscience.wiley.com.

Centre for Sustainable Community Development, "What Is Sustainable Community Development?" Simon Fraser University, http://www.sfu.ca/cscd/about-us/what-is-sustainable-community-development.html.

Certeau, Michel de. *The Practice of Everyday Life*. Los Angeles: University of California Press, 1984.

Chatwin, Bruce. *The Songlines*. London: Jonathan Cape, 1987.

Chavkin, Allan, and Nancy Feyl Chavkin,. "An Interview with Louise Erdrich." In *Conversations with Louise Erdrich and Michael Dorris*, ed. Chavkin, Allan, and Nancy Feyl Chavkin, 20–53. Jackson: University Press of Mississippi, 1994.

Chiarappa, Michael J. "Overseeing the Family of Whitefishes: the Priorities and Debates of Coregonid Management on America's Great Lakes, 1870–2000." *Environment and History* 11, no. 2 (2005): 163–94.

Churchill, Ward. *Acts of Rebellion: The Ward Churchill Reader*. New York: Routledge, 2003.

Chute, Janet. "Pursuing the Great Spirit's Plan: Nineteenth-Century Ojibwa Attitudes Towards the Future of Logging and Mining on Unsurrendered Indian Lands North of Lakes Huron and Superior." In *Social Relations in Resource Hinterlands: Papers from the 27th Annual Meeting of the Western Association of Sociology and Anthropology*, ed. Thomas W. Dunk, 173–203. Thunder Bay: Lakehead University Centre for Northern and Regional Studies, 1991.

Circle of Turtle Lodge. *Anishnabe 101: The Basics of What You Need to Know to Begin Your Journey on the Red Road*. Golden Lake, ON: Circle of Turtle Lodge, 2002.

Clarke, John. "Geographical Aspects of Land Speculation in Essex County to 1825: The Strategy of Particular Individuals." In *Historical Essays on Upper Canada: New Perspectives*, ed. J.K. Johnston and Bruce G. Wilson, 81–129. Ottawa: Carleton University Press, 1991.

———. *Land, Power and Economics on the Frontier of Upper Canada*. Montreal: McGill-Queen's University Press, 2001.

Clark, Lloyd Thomas. "The Baldoon Settlement Lands: The Effects of Changing Drainage Technology, 1804–1967." M.A. thesis, University of Western Ontario, 1970.

Clifford, James. "Notes on (Field)notes." In *Fieldnotes The Makings of Anthropology*, ed. Roger Sanjek, 47–70. Ithaca, NY: Cornell University Press, 1990.

———. *Routes, Travel and Transformation in the late Twentieth Century*. Cambridge: Harvard University Press, 1997.

Cohen, Robin. "Diaspora and the Nation-state." *International Affairs* 72, no. 3 (1996): 507–20.

Cohen-Cruz, Jan. "General Introduction." In *Radical Street Performance*, 1–6. New York: Routledge, 1998.

Colborn, T.E., A. Davidson, S.N. Green, R.A. Hodge, C.I. Jackson, and R.A. Liroff. *Great Lakes, Great Legacy?* Harper: Conservation Foundation and the Institute for Research on Public Policy, 1990.

Colorado, P. "Bridging Native Science and Western Science." *Convergence* 21, no. 2/3 (1988): 49–68.

Colson, Elizabeth. "Forced Migration and the Anthropological Response." *Journal of Refugee Studies* 11 (2003): 1–18.

The Compact Oxford Dictionary. 2nd ed. Rev. ed. Ed. Catherine Soanes. Oxford: Oxford University Press, 2003.

Connor, L., C. Treloar, and N. Higgenbotham. "How to Perform Transdisciplinary Research: Qualitative Study Designs and Methods." In *Health Social Science: A Transdisciplinary and Complexity Perspective*, ed. N. Higgenbotham, G. Albrecht, and L. Connor, 227–66. Oxford: Oxford University Press, 2001.

Conte, Christopher A. *Highland Sanctuary: Environmental History in Tanzania's Usambara Mountains*. Athens: Ohio University Press, 2004.

"Copy of Indenture Made between Chippewa Chiefs and James A. May, Jacob Bogart and Bernarbus Harson, 1797-02-04." In *Michigan Pioneer and Historical Collections*, vol. 8, 498–500. Pioneer Society of the State of Michigan, 1885.

Crosby, Alfred W. *Ecological Imperialism: The Biological Expansion of Europe, 900–1900*. Cambridge: Cambridge University Press, 1986. Rpt. 2004.

———. *The Columbian Exchange: Biological and Cultural Consequences of 1492*. Westport, CT: Greenwood Press, 1972. Rpt. 2003.

———. *Germs, Seeds, and Animals: Studies in Ecological History*. Armonk, NY: M.E. Sharpe, 1994.

———. "The Past and Present of Environmental History." *American Historical Review* 100, no. 4 (1995): 1177–89.

Cruickshank, Julie. *Do Glaciers Listen? Local Knowledge, Colonial Encounters and Social Imagination*. Seattle: University of Washington Press, 2005.

———. "Getting the Words Right: Perspectives on Naming and Places in Athapaskan Oral History." *Arctic Anthropology* 27, no. 1 (1990): 53–65.

———. *The Social Life of Stories: Narrative and Knowledge in the Yukon Territory*. Lincoln: University of Nebraska Press, 1998.

———. "Oral History, Narrative Strategies and Native American Historiography: Perspectives from the Yukon Territory, Canada." In *Clearing a Path: Theorizing the Past in Native American Studies*, ed. N. Shoemaker, 3–27. London: Routledge, 2002.

Cruikshank, J., A. Sidney, K. Smith, and A. Ned. *Life Lived Like a Story: Life Stories of Three Yukon Elders*. Lincoln: University of Nebraska Press, 1990.

Cummins, Bryan D. *First Nations, First Dogs*. Calgary: Detselig Enterprises, 2002.

Cunningham, Alain. *Canadian Indian Policy and Development Planning Theory*. New York: Garland, 1999.

Dale, Ann. *At the Edge: Sustainable Development in the 21st Century*. Vancouver: University of British Columbia Press, 2001.

Daloz, Laurent A. Parks. "Transformative Learning for Bioregional Citizenship." In *Learning Toward an Ecological Conciousness: Selected Transformative Practices*, ed. Edmund O'Sullivan and Marilyn Taylor, 29–46. Hampshire, UK: Palgrave Macmillan, 2004.

Dapice, Ann N. "The Medicine Wheel." *Journal of Transcultural Nursing* 17, no. 3 (2006): 251–60.

Darnell, Regna. "Canadian Anthropologists, the First Nations and Canada's Self-Image at the Millennium." *Anthropologica* 42 (2000): 165–74.

———. "Qualitative Demographics of Aboriginal Urban–Rural Migration: The Persistence of Nomadic Habits." In *Proceedings of the 35th Algonquian Conference*, ed. H. Wolfart, 75–89. Winnipeg: University of Manitoba Press, 2004.

———. "Rethinking Band and Tribe, Community and Nation: An Accordion Model of Nomadic Native North American Social Organization." In *Papers of the 29th Algonquian Conference*, ed. David Pentland, 90–105. Winnipeg: University of Manitoba, 1998.

Darnell, Regna, and María Cristina Manzano-Munguía. "Nomadic Legacies and urban Algonquian residence." In *Papers of the 36th Algonquian Conference*, ed. H.C. Wolfart, 173–86. Winnipeg: University of Manitoba, 2005.

Darnell, Regna, and C.V. Stephens. "Keepers of the Water, Keepers of the Fire: Building Bridges Between Academic and Indigenous Knowledges in Environmental Health Research." *International Journal of the Humanities* 5, no. 10 (2007): 105–14.

———. "Species at Risk, Language at Risk: Reflections on Biodiversity and Translation at the Walpole Island First Nation." In *Proceedings of the 38th Annual Algonquian Conference*, ed. C. Wolfart, 129–42. Winnipeg: University of Manitoba Press, 2007.

Das, Veena, and Deborah Poole. "State and Its Margins: Comparative Ethnographies." In *Anthropology in the Margins of the State*, ed. Veena Das and Deborah Poole, 3–34. Santa Fe, NM: School of American Research Press, 2004.

Deiter, Connie. *Human Security and Aboriginal Women in Canada*. Ottawa: Status of Women Canada, Policy Research, 2005.

Deloria, Vine. "Conclusion: Anthros, Indians and Planetary Reality." In *Indians and Anthropologists*, ed. Vine Deloria Jr., 209–21. Tucson: University of Arizona Press, 1997.

———. *Custer Died for Your Sins: An Indian Manifesto*. New York: Macmillan, 1969.

———. *Red Earth, White Lies*. New York: Scribner, 1995.

Deloria, Vine, Jr., and James Treat. *For this Land: Writings on Religion in America*. New York: Routledge, 1999.

Deloria, Vine, Jr., and Daniel R. Wildcat. *Power and Place: Indian Education in America*. Golden, CO: Fulcrum Resources, 2001.

Denzin, Norman, and Yvonna Lincoln. *Handbook of Qualitative Research*. London: Sage, 1994.

Devereux, Paul. *Re-visioning the Earth: A Guide to Opening the Healing Channels Between Mind and Nature*. New York: Fireside, 1996.

Devine, T.M. *Scotland's Empire, 1600–1815*. London: Allen Lane, 2003.

Diamond, Jared. *Guns, Germs, and Steel: The Fates of Human Societies*. New York: W.W. Norton, 1997.

Dickason, Olive Patricia. *Canada's First Nations: A History of Founding Peoples from Earliest Times*. Oxford: Oxford University Press, 2002.

Dixon, Catharine. *The Power and the Promise: The Elliot Lake Story*. Elliot Lake: Gillidix, 1996.

Dodd, Christine F., D. Poulton, Paul A. Lennox, David G. Smith, and Gary A. Warrick, "The Middle Ontario Iroquoian Stage." In *The Archaeology of Southern Ontario to A.D. 1650*, ed. Chris Ellis and Neal Ferris, 321–59. London: Ontario Archaeological Society, 1990.

Dowd, Gregory Evans. "The French King Wakes Up in Detroit: 'Pontiac's War' in Rumor and History." *Ethnohistory* 37, no. 3 (Summer 1990): 254–78.

———. *War under Heaven: Pontiac, The Indian Nations, and the British Empire*. Baltimore: Johns Hopkins University Press, 2002.

Druke, Mary A. "Iroquois Treaties: Common Forms, Varying Interpretations." In *The History and Culture of Iroquois Diplomacy*, ed. Francis Jennings, 85–98. New York: Syracuse University Press, 1985.

Dumont, James. "Journey to Daylight-land: Through Ojibwa Eyes." In *The First Ones: Readings in Indian/Native Studies*, ed. David R. Miller, Carl Beal, James Dempsey, and R. Wesley Heber, 75–80. Craven, SK: Saskatchewan Indian Federated College, 1992.

Dunlap, Thomas R. *Nature and the English Diaspora: Environment and History in the United States, Canada, Australia and New Zealand*. Cambridge: Cambridge University Press, 1999.

Dunn, J., S. Taylor, S. Elliot, and S. Walter. "Psychosocial Effects of PCB Contamination and Remediation: The Case of Smithsville, Ontario." *Social Science and Medicine* 39, no. 8 (1994): 1093–104.

Edelstein, M.R. *Contaminated Communities: The Social and Psychological Impacts of Residential Toxic Exposure*. Boulder: Westview, 1988.

Egan, C. "Inuit Women's Perceptions of Pollution." Ph.D. diss., University of Manitoba, Winnipeg, 1999.

Egan, Kieran. "Individual Development in Literacy." In *Literacy, Society, and Schooling: A Reader*, ed. Suzanne de Castell, Allan Luke, and Kieran Egan, 243–55. Cambridge: Cambridge University Press, 1986.

Ekos Research Associates and Anishinabek Consultants Incorporation, *Survey of First Nations People Living Off-reserve, Metis and Inuit: Final Report to the Indian and Northern Affairs Canada*. Ottawa: Ekos Research Associates Incorporation, 2006.

Eliot, T.S. *Four Quartets*. San Diego: Harcourt, 1971.

Eliot, Sir Charles. *The East Africa Protectorate*. London: F. Cass, 1905.

Environics Institute. *Urban Aboriginal Peoples Study, 2010*. Scarborough: Environics Institute, 2010. http://uaps.ca/wp-content/uploads/2010/03/UAPS-Main-Report_Dec.pdf.

Environmental Education Ontario (EEON). "About EEON." 2007. http://www.eeon.org/about.html.

———. *Greening the Way Ontario Learns: A Public Strategic Plan for Environmental and Sustainability Education—Summary*. Toronto: EEON, 2003. http://www.eeon.org/pdf/greeningsummaryint.pdf.

Erdrich, Louise. *The Antelope Wife*. New York: HarperCollins, 1998.

———. *The Birchbark House*. New York: Hyperion, 1999.

———. *The Blue Jay's Dance: A Birth Year*. New York: HarperCollins, 1995.

———. *Four Souls*. New York: HarperCollins Publishers, 2004.

———. *The Game of Silence* Toronto: Harper Trophy Canada, 2005.

———. *Grandmother's Pigeon*. New York: Hyperion, 1996.

———. *The Last Report on the Miracles at Little No Horse*. New York: HarperCollins, 2001.

———. *The Porcupine Year*. New York: HarperCollins, 2008.

———. *The Range Eternal*. New York: Hyperion, 2002.

———. *Route 2*. Northridge: Lord John Press, 1991.

———. *Tracks*. New York: Harper Collins, 1988.

Escobar, Arturo. "The Making and Unmaking of the Third World through Development." In *ThePost-Development Reader*, ed. Majid Rahnema and Victoria Bawtree, 85–93. Nova Scotia: Fernwood, 1997.

Esteva, Gustavo. "Basta! Mexican Indians Say 'Enough!'" In *The Post-Development Reader*, ed. Majid Rahnema and Victoria Bawtree, 302–6. Nova Scotia: Fernwood, 1997.

Fagan, Kristina. "What's the Trouble with the Trickster? An Introduction." In *Troubling Tricksters: Revisioning Critical Conversations*, ed. Deanna Reder and Linda M. Morra, 3–20. Waterloo: Wilfrid Laurier University Press, 2010.

Fan Hitch. "The Qikiqtani Inuit Association Soon to Embark on Truth Commission Hearings." 10, no. 1 (2007). http://homepage.mac.com/puggiq/V10N1/V10,N1News.html.

Farmer, Paul. *Infections and Inequalities: The Modern Plagues*. Berkeley: University of California Press, 1999.

———. *Pathologies of Power: Health, Human Rights and the New War on the Poor*. Berkeley: University of California Press, 2003.

Fawcett, Leesa. "Animal Stories and the Struggle against Forgetting." *Pathways: The Ontario Journal of Outdoor Education* 11, no. 2 (1999): 19–22.

Fenton, William N. "Structure, Continuity, and Change in the Process of Iroquois Treaty Making," In *The History and Culture of Iroquois Diplomacy: An Interdisciplinary Guide to the Treaties of the Six Nations and Their League*, ed. Francis Jennings et al., 3–36. New York: Syracuse, 1995.

Fernandez, Eduardo Grillo. "Development or Cultural Affirmation in the Andes?" In *The Spirit of Regeneration: Andean Culture Confronting Western Notions of Development*, ed. Frederique Apffel-Marglin, 124–45. New York: Zed Books, 1998.

Fetterman, David. *Ethnography: Step by Step*. Applied Social Research Methods no. 17. London: Sage, 1998.

Fichten. J.M. "When Toxic Chemicals Pollute Residential Environments: The Cultural Meaning of Home and Home Ownership." *Home Organization* 48, no. 4 (1989): 313–24.

Fimreite, N., W.N. Holsworth, J.A. Keith, P.A. Pearce, and I.M. Gruchy, "Mercury in Fish and Fish-Eating Birds near Sites of Industrial Contamination in Canada," *Canadian Field-Naturalist* 85 (1971): 211–20.

Fixico, Donald. *The Urban Indian Experience in America*. Alburqueque: University of New Mexico Press, 2000.

Flores, Dan. "Place: Thinking about Bioregional History." In *Bioregionalism*, ed. Michael Vincent McGinnis, 43–60. London: Routledge, 1999.

Foucault, Michael. "An Interview with Michel Foucault. October 25th, 1982." In *Technologies of the Self: A Seminar with Michel Foucault*, ed. L.H. Martin, H. Gutman, and P. Hutton, 9–15. London: Tavistock, 1998.

Fox, N.J. *Beyond Health: Postmodernism and Embodiment*. London: Free Association, 1999.

Franklin, Ursula M. *The Real World of Technology*. Etobicoke, ON: Anansi, 1999.

Freire, Paulo. *Pedagogy of the Oppressed*. New York: Continuum International, 2000.

Frost, Warwick. "'Did They Really Hate Trees?' Attitudes of Farmers, Tourists and Naturalists Towards Nature in the Rainforests of Eastern Australia." *Environment and History* 8, no. 1 (2002): 3–20.

Gibb, L.M. *Love Canal: The Story Continues ...* Stony Creek, CT: New Society, 1998.

Gilbertson, Michael. "Injury to Health: A Forensic Audit of the Great Lakes Water Quality Agreement (1972–2005) with Special Reference to Congenital Minamata Disease." Ph.D. diss., University of Sterling, 2008.

Gilgamesh: A New English Version. Ed. and transl. Stephen Mitchell. Toronto: Free Press, 2004.

Gill, Jill H. *Native Worldviews: An Introduction*. New York: Prometheus, 2002.

Gillespie, Greg. *Hunting for Empire: Narratives of Sport in Rupert's Land, 1840–70*. Vancouver: University of British Columbia Press, 2007.

Gilroy, Paul. "The Black Atlantic as a Counterculture of Modernity." In *Theorizing Diaspora*, ed. Jana Evans Braziel and Manita Mannur, 49–80. Oxford: Blackwell, 2003.

Glaser, B., and A. Strauss. 1967. *Discovery of Grounded Theory: Strategies for Qualitative Research*. Chicago: Aldine de Gruyter.

Graham, Elizabeth, comp. *The Mush Hole: Life at Two Indian Residential Schools*. Waterloo, ON: Heffle, 1997.

Gramsci, Antonio. *Selections from the Prison Notebooks*. Ed. and transl. Quintin Hoare and Geoffrey Nowell Smith. New York: International, 1971.

Great Lakes Indian Fish and Wildlife Commission. *Sandy Lake Tragedy and Memorial* [pamphlet]. Odanah, WI: Great Lakes Indian Fish and Wildlife Commission, n.d.

Great Lakes Information Network (GLIN). *Areas of Concern in the Great Lakes Region*. http://www.great-lakes.net/envt/pollution/aoc.html#overview.

Grey, John Morgan. "Douglas, Thomas, Baron Daer and Shortcleuch, 5th Earl of Selkirk." *Dictionary of Canadian Biography Online*. http://www.biographi.ca/EN/ShowBio.asp?BioId=36499&query=Selkirk.

Grove, Richard H. *Ecology, Climate and Empire: Colonialism and Global Environmental History, 1400–1940*. Cambridge: White Horse, 1997.

———. *Green Imperialism: Colonial Expansion, Tropical Island Edens and the Origins of Environmentalism, 1600–1860*. Cambridge: Cambridge University Press, 1995.

Gruenewald, David A. "Accountability and Collaboration: Institutional Barriers and Strategic Pathways for Place-based Education." *Ethics, Place and Environment* 8, no. 3 (2005): 261–83.

———. "The Best of Both Worlds: A Critical Pedagogy of Place." *Educational Researcher* 32, no. 4 (2002): 3–12.

Gwyn, Julian. "Sir William Johnson." In *Dictionary of Canadian Biography Online*, Library and Archives Canada. http://www.biographi.ca/EN/.

Hackett, P. *A Very Remarkable Disease: Epidemics in the Petit Nord, 1670 to 1846*. Winnipeg: University of Manitoba Press, 2002.

Haffner, G.D., V. Glooschenko, C.A. Straughan, C.E. Herbert, and R. Lazar. "Concentrations and Distributions of Polychlorinated Biphenyls, Including Non-ortho Congeners, in Mink Populations from Southern Ontario." *Journal of Great Lakes Research* 24, no. 4 (1998): 880–88.

Hamil, Fred Coyne. *The Valley of the Lower Thames, 1640 to 1850*. Toronto: University of Toronto Press, 1951.

Hamilton, Milton W. *Sir William Johnson: Colonial American, 1715–1763*. New York: Kennikat, 1976.

Hampton, Eber. "Towards a Redefinition of Indian Education." In *First Nations Education in Canada: The Circle Unfolds*, ed. M. Battiste and J. Barman, 5–46. Vancouver: University of British Columbia Press, 1995.

Harada, Y. "Congenital Minamata Disease." In *Minamata Disease*, ed. T. Tsubaki and K. Irunkayama, 209–39. New York: Elsevier Scientific, 1977.

Harper, Marjory, and Michael E. Vance, eds. *Myth, Migration and the Making of Memory: Scotia and Nova Scotia, c. 1700–1990*. Halifax: Published for the Gorsewood Research Institute for Atlantic Canada Studies by Fernwood and John Donald, 1999.

Harring, Sidney L. *White Man's Law: Native People in Nineteenth-Century Canadian Jurisprudence*. Toronto: University of Toronto Press, 1998.

Harrison, Robert Pogue. *The Dominion of the Dead*. Chicago: University of Chicago Press, 2005.

———. *Forests: The Shadow of Civilization*. Chicago: University of Chicago Press, 1992.

Havlick, David, and Marion Hourdequin. "Practical Wisdom in Environmental Education." *Ethics, Place and Environment* 8, no. 3 (2005): 385–92.

Heard, Shawn. "The City of Elliot Lake to 1991: Before the Roof Fell In." In *Boom Town Blues Elliot Lake: Collapse and Revival in a Single-Industry Community*, ed. Anne-Marie Mawhiney and Jane Pitblado, 21–35. Toronto: Dundurn, 1999.

Hefferman, Theresa. "Power in the Clown." *Toronto Theatre Magazine*, Fall 1998.

Helling, Rudolf A. *Elliot Lake ... Beginning*. Windsor: Assumption University of Windsor, 1960.

Henley, Thom. Rediscovery: *Ancient Pathways, New Directions*. Edmonton: Lone Pine, 1996.

Herring, D. Ann. "'There were young people and old people and babies dying every week': The 1918–19 Influenza Pandemic at Norway House." *Ethnohistory* 41, no. 1 (1994): 73–105.

———. "Toward a Reconsideration of Disease and Contact in the Americas." *Prairie Forum* 17 (1992): 1–13.

Herring, D. Ann, and Robert D. Hoppa. "Endemic Tuberculosis among Nineteenth Century Cree in the Central Canadian Subarctic." *Perspectives in Human Biology* 4, no. 1 (1999): 189–99.

Herriot, Trevor. *River in a Dry Land: A Prairie Passage*. Toronto: Stoddard, 2000.

Hodgins, Bruce W. "Gary G. Potts." In *Blockades and Resistance: Studies in Actions of Peace and the Temagami Blockades of 1988–89*, ed. Bruce W. Hodgins, Ute Lischke, and David T. McNab, 19–22. Waterloo: Wilfrid Laurier University Press, 2003.

Homer-Dixon, Thomas. *The Upside of Down: Catastrophe, Creativity, and the Renewal of Civilization*. Toronto: Vintage Canada, 2006.

Hoppa, Robert D. "Mortality in a Northern Ontario Fur-trade Community: Moose Factory, 1851–1964." *Canadian Studies in Population* 25, no. 2 (1998): 175–98.

Horsman, Reginald "Matthew Elliot." In *Dictionary of Canadian Biography Online*, Library and Archives Canada. http://www.biographi.ca/EN/.

Howard, Heather. "Dreamcatchers in the City: An Ethnohistory of Social Action, Gender and Class in Native Community Production in Toronto." Ph.D. diss., University of Toronto, 2005.

Howard, Heather, and Craig Proulx, eds. *Aboriginal Peoples in Canadian Cities: Transformations and Continuities*. Waterloo: Wilfrid Laurier University Press, 2011.

Hutchison, David. *Growing Up Green: Education for Ecological Renewal*. New York: Teachers College Press, 1998.

Hutchison, George, and Dick Wallace. *Grassy Narrows*. Toronto: Van Nostrand Reinhold, 1977.

Ingold, Tim. *The Appropriation of Nature: Essays on Human Ecology and Social Relations*. Manchester: Manchester University Press, 1986.

Ingold, Tim, David Riches, and James Woodburn, eds. *Hunters and Gatherers: History, Evolution and Social Change*. New York: Berg, 1988.

Institute of Environmental Research (IER), Inc. "Environmental Impact Protection Program (Summary Progress Report). 3 April 1984.

Irukayama, K. "The Pollution of Minamata Bay and Minamata Disease." *Advanced Water Pollution Research* 3 (1966): 150–65.

Isaac, Thomas. *Aboriginal Law: Commentary, Cases and Materials*. Saskatoon: Purich, 2004.

Jacobs, Jane. *Dark Age Ahead*. New York: Random House, 2004.

Jacobs, Wilbur R. *Wilderness Politics and Indian Gifts: The Northern Colonial Frontier, 1748–1763*. Lincoln: University of Nebraska Press, 1950.

Jennings, Francis. *The History and Culture of Iroquois Diplomacy: An Interdisciplinary Guide to the Treaties of the Six Nations and Their League*. Syracuse: Syracuse University Press, 1995.

Johnson, William. *The Papers of Sir William Johnson*. 13 vols. Ed. Milton W. Hamilton. Albany: University of the State of New York, 1921–1962.

Johnston, Basil. *Ojibwa Heritage*. Toronto: McClelland and Stewart, 1990.

———. *Ojibway Ceremonies*. Toronto: McClelland and Stewart, 1982.

Johnston, Darlene. *The Taking of Indian Lands in Canada: Consent or Coercion?* Saskatoon: University of Saskatchewan Native Law Centre, 1989.

Jones, Dorothy V. *License for Empire: Colonialism by Treaty in Early America*. Chicago: University of Chicago Press, 1982.

Jones, Rev. Peter. *History of the Ojebway Indians*. 1861; Rpt., New York: Books for Library Press, 1971.

Kane, Sean. *Wisdom of the Mythtellers*. Peterborough: Broadview, 1995.

Kapches, Mima. "An Archaeological View of Toronto: Life in the Past Lanes." *Rotunda* 19, no. 4 (1987): 18–24.

Karrow, P.F., and B.G. Warner. "The Geological and Biological Environment for Human Occupation in Southern Ontario." In *The Archaeology of Southern Ontario to A.D. 1650*, ed. Chris J. Ellis and Neal Ferris, 5–35. London, ON: London Chapter of the Ontario Archaeological Society, 1990.

Kaufert, P., and J. O'Neil. "Analysis of Dialogue on Risks in Childbirth." In *Knowledge, Power and Practice*, ed. S. Lindenbaum and M. Locke, 32–54. Berkeley: University of California Press, 1993.

Kelly, Robert L. *The Foraging Spectrum: Diversity in Hunter-Gatherer Lifeways*. Washington: Smithsonian Institution Press, 1995.

Kincheloe, J.L.. "Critical Ontology: Visions of Selfhood and Curriculum." *Journal of Curriculum Theorizing* (2003): 47–64.

King, Alanis. "The Great Indian Bus Tour." *Getekindaswingamig: The Toronto Native Community History Program*. Toronto: n.p., 2005.

King, Thomas. *The Truth about Stories: A Native Narrative*. Toronto: Anansi, 2003.

Kitson, Josey. *Northern Dogs: A Summary of the 2007 Conference. Toronto: International Fund for Animal Welfare, 2008*. http://www.wspa.ca/nd/Conference_Summary.pdf.

Kremer, Jurgen. "Indigenous Science: Introduction." *ReVision* 18, no. 3 (1995): 2–5.

Kulchyski, Peter, Don McCaskill and David Newhouse, eds. *In the Words of Elders: Aboriginal Cultures in Transition*. Toronto: University of Toronto Press, 2003.

Kulisek, L.L. "William Caldwell." *Dictionary of Canadian Biography Online*, Library and Archives Canada. http://www.biographi.ca/EN/.

LaDuke, Winona. *All Our Relations: Native Struggles for Land and Life*. Cambridge, MA: South End, 1999.

Lajeunesse, Ernest J. *The Windsor Border Region: Canada's Southernmost Frontier; A Collection of Documents.* Toronto: Champlain Society, 1960.

Lanigan, Mary Anne. "Aboriginal Pedagogy: Storytelling." In *As We See... Aboriginal Pedagogy*, ed. L.A. Stiffarm, 103–20. Saskatoon: Extension Division at the University of Saskatchewan, 1998.

Lauriston, Victor. *Romantic Kent: The Story of a County, 1626–1952.* Chatham: County of Kent, 1952.

Lawrence, Bonita. *"Real" Indians and Others: Mixed-Blood Urban Native Peoples and Indigenous Nationhood.* Lincoln: University of Nebraska Press, 2004.

Leighton, Douglas. "Simon Girty." In *Dictionary of Canadian Biography Online.* Library and Archives Canada. http://www.biographi.ca/EN/.

Leopold, Aldo. *A Sand County Almanac: With Essays on Conservation from Round River.* 1949. Rpt. New York: Oxford University Press, 1966.

Lesser, Alexander. *History, Evolution and the Concept of Culture: Selected Papers by Alexander Lesser.* Cambridge: Cambridge University Press, 1985.

Life after People: The Series, History Channel, A & E Television Networks, accessed 19 Oct. 2009, www.history.com/content/life_after_people/about-the-show.

Lindon, E. "Lost Tribes, Lost Knowledge." *Time*, 23 Sept. 1991, 44–56.

Lischke-McNab, Ute. Conversations with Louise Erdrich, Minneapolis, April 11, 2002.

Little Bear, Leroy. "Aboriginal Relationships to the Land and Resources." In *Sacred Lands: Aboriginal World Views, Claims and Conflicts*, ed. J. Oakes, R. Riewe, K. Kinew, and E. Maloney, 15–20. Winnipeg: Canadian Circumpolar Institute and Department of Native Studies, 1998.

Little Bear, Leroy, Menno Boldt, and J. Anthony Long, eds. *Pathways to Self-determination: Canadian Indians and the Canadian State.* Toronto: University of Toronto Press, 1984.

Loppie-Reading, C., and F. Wein. "Health Inequalities and Social Determinants of Aboriginal Peoples' Health." Report of National Collaborating Centre for Aboriginal Health, 2009.

http://www.nccah-ccnsa.ca/docs/social%20determinates/NCCAH-Loppie-Wien_Report.pdf.

Louv, Richard. *Last Child in the Woods: Saving out Children from Nature-Deficit Disorder.* Chapel Hill, NC: Algonquin Books of Chapel Hill, 2005.

Luke, T.W. "Education, Environment and Sustainability." *Educational Philosophy and Theory* 33, no. 2 (2001): 187–202.

Lytwyn, Victor, and Dean Jacobs. "'For Good Will and Affection': The Detroit Indian Deeds and British Land Policy, 1760–1827." *Ontario History* 92, no. 2 (2000): 9–29.

MacKenzie, A.E.D. *Baldoon: Lord Selkirk's Settlement in Upper Canada.* London: Phelps, 1979.

MacKenzie, John M. "Art and the Empire." In *The Cambridge Illustrated History of the British Empire,* ed. P.J. Marshall, 296–315. Cambridge: Cambridge University Press, 1996.

———. "Chivalry, Social Darwinism and Ritualised Killing: The Hunting Ethos in Central Africa up to 1914." In *Conservation in Africa: People, Policies and Practice,* ed. David Anderson and Richard Grove, 41–62. Cambridge: Cambridge University Press, 1987.

———. "Empire and the Ecological Apocalypse: The Historiography of the Imperial Environment." In *Ecology and Empire: Environmental History of Settler Societies,* ed. Tom Griffiths and Libby Robin, 215–28. Edinburgh: Keele University Press, 1997.

———. *The Empire of Nature: Hunting, Conservation and British Imperialism.* Manchester: Manchester University Press, 1988.

———. *Empires of Nature and the Nature of Empires: Imperialism, Scotland and the Environment.* East Linton: Tuckwell, 1997.

———. "Green Pasts and Presents: The Paradox of Environmental Histories and Current Anxieties of Damage and Destruction." In *How Green Was Our Empire: Environment, Development and the Colonial Service,* ed. Terry Barringer, 145–51. London: Institute of Commonwealth Studies, OSPA Research Project, 2005.

———. "Hunting and the Natural World in Juvenile Literature." In *Imperialism and Juvenile Literature,* ed., Jeffrey Richards, 144–72. Manchester: Manchester University Press, 1989.

———. "Hunting in Eastern and Central Africa in the late Nineteenth Century, with Special Reference to Zimbabwe." In *Sport in Africa: Essays in Social History,* ed. William J. Baker and James A. Mangan, 172–95. New York: Africana, 1987.

———, ed. *Imperialism and the Natural World.* Manchester: Manchester University Press, 1990.

———. "Missionaries, Science and the Environment in Nineteenth-century Africa." In *The Imperial Horizons of British Protestant Missions, 1880–1914,* ed. Andrew Porter, 106–30. Grand Rapids, MI: W.B. Eerdmans, 2003.

———. "People and Landscape: The Environment and National Identities in Museums." In *National Museums: Negotiating Histories,* ed. Darryl McIntyre and Kirsten Wiener, 173–82. Canberra: National Museum of Australia, 2001.

———. *The Scots in South Africa: Ethnicity, Identity, Gender and Race.* Manchester: Manchester University Press, 2007.

———. "'This year's forest is next year's fire': The Colonial Official and the Environment." In *How Green Was Our Empire: Environment, Development and the Co-

lonial Service, ed. Terry Barringer, 7–22. London: Institute of Commonwealth Studies, OSPA Research Project, 2005.

MacPherson, C.B. *The Political Theory of Possessive Individualism: Hobbes to Locke*. Toronto: Oxford University Press, 1964.

Mann, Frank. *A History of Wallaceburg and Vicinity, 1804 to the present*. Wallaceburg, ON: Mann Historical Files, 1968.

Mann, Frank, and Alan Mann. *Settlement on the Sydenham*. Wallaceburg: Mann Historical Files, 1984.

Mannion, A.M. *Global Environmental Change*. Harlow: Prentice Hall, 1991.

Manzano-Munguía, Maria Cristina. "Conceptualizing Native Non-Government Organizations in Canada: An Ethnographic Approach." *International Journal of Interdisciplinary Social Sciences* 2, no. 1 (2007): 449–59.

———. "Indian Policy and Legislation: Aboriginal Identity Survival in Canada." *Journal of Studies in Ethnicity and Nationalism* 11, no. 3 (2011): 404–26.

———. "Mediating Aboriginal–State Relations Through Native Non-Governmental Organizations and Aboriginal Leaders: An Alternative Model." Ph.D. diss., University of Western Ontario, 2009.

Marchand, S.J. *Environmental Impacts on the Lake St. Clair Fishery: A Case Study of Mercury Pollution and Its Effects on Walpole Island Reserve*. Occasional paper no. 11. Walpole Island: Nin Da Waab Jig Heritage Centre, 1986.

Marglin, Stephen A. "Farmers, Seedmen, and Scientists: Systems of Agriculture and Systems of Knowledge." In *Decolonizing Knowledge: From Development to Dialogue*, ed. Frédérique Apffel-Marglin and Stephen A. Marglin, 142–82. Oxford: Clarendon Press, 1996.

Marshall, Katherine, and Gretchen Rossman. *Designing Qualitative Research*. 2nd ed. London: Sage, 1995.

Massey, Doreen, John Allen, and Steve Pile, eds. *The Economy in Question*. London: Sage, 1999.

McDonald, Neil T. *The Baldoon Mystery*. 1905. Rpt. Wallaceburg, ON: Standard, 1991.

McElroy, A., and P.K. Townsend. *Medical Anthropology in Ecological Perspective*. 4th ed. Boulder: Westview, 2004.

McKay, Don. *Deactivated West 100*. Kentville, NS: Gaspereau, 2005.

———. *Vis à Vis: Field Notes on Poetry and Wilderness*. Kentville, NS: Gaspereau, 2001.

McNab, David. "Borders of Water and Fire: Islands as Sacred Places and as Meeting Grounds." In *Aboriginal Cultural Landscapes*, ed. Jill Oakes, Rick Riewe, et al., 35–45. Winnipeg: Aboriginal Issues Press, 2004.

———. *Circles of Time: Aboriginal Land Rights and Resistance in Ontario.* Waterloo: Wilfrid Laurier University Press, 1999.

———, ed. *Earth, Water, Air and Fire: Studies in Canadian Ethnohistory.* Proceedings of a Conference in Bkejwanong, ON, 12–14 May 1994. Waterloo: Wilfrid Laurier University Press, 1998.

———. "Herman Merivale and the British Empire, 1806–1874," Ph.D. diss., University of Lancaster, 1978.

———. "Sovereignty, Treaties and Trade in the Bkejwanong Territory." *Journal of Aboriginal Economic Development* 3, no. 2 (2003): 52–66.

———. "'those freebooters would shoot me like a dog': American Terrorists and Homeland Security in the Journals of Ezhaaswe (William A. Elias (1856–1929))." In *Lines Drawn upon the Water: First Nations and the Great Lakes Borders and Borderlands,* ed. Karl S. Hele, 115–30. Waterloo: Wilfrid Laurier University Press, 2008.

———. "'Time is a Fish': The Spirit of Nanapush and the Power of Transformation in theStories of Louise Erdrich." In *(Ad)dressing Our Words: Aboriginal Perspectives on Aboriginal Literature,* ed. Armand Garnet Ruffo, 181–204. Penticton: Theytus, 2001.

———. "'Water Is Her Lifeblood': The Waters of Bkejwanong and the Treaty-Making Process." In *Earth, Water, Air and Fire: Studies in Canadian Ethnohistory,* ed. David T. McNab, 35–63. Waterloo: Wilfrid Laurier University Press, 1998.

McNab, David T., Bruce W. Hodgins, and Ute Lischke. *Blockades and Resistance: Studies in Actions of Peace and the Temagami Blockades of 1988–89.* Waterloo: Wilfrid Laurier University Press, 2003.

Millennium Ecosystem Assessment Board. *Living Beyond Our Means: Natural Assets and Human Well-being.* March 2005. www.millenniumassessment.org/documents/document.429.aspx.pdf.

Moffat, Robert. *Missionary Labours and Scenes in Southern Africa.* London: John Snow, 1846.

Moogk, Peter N. "Lÿdius." *Dictionary of Canadian Biography Online.* Library and Archives Canada. http://www.biographi.ca/EN/.

Moseley, William G., and B. Ikubolajeh Logan, eds. *African Environment and Development.* Aldershot: Ashgate, 2004.

Native Canadian Centre of Toronto. *In the Spirit of Unity: A Synopsis of Programs and Services* Toronto: Native Canadian Centre of Toronto, 2002.

Nelson, Larry L. *A Man of Distinction Among Them: Alexander McKee and the Ohio Frontier, 1754–1799.* Kent: Kent State University Press, 1999.

Nelson, Melissa. "Reclaiming an Indigenous mind." *Ecopsychology Newsletter,* Fall 1994, 1–3.

Newhouse, David. "Urban Life: Reflections of a Middle-Class Indian." In *Aboriginal Peoples in Canadian Cities: Transformations and Continuities*, ed. Heather Howard and Craig Proulx, 23–38. Waterloo: Wilfrid Laurier University Press, 2011.

Newhouse, David R., Cora J. Voyageur, and Dan Beavon. "Introduction." In *Hidden in Plain Sight: Contributions of Aboriginal Peoples to Canadian Identity and Culture*, ed. David R. Newhouse, Cora J. Voyajeur, and Dan Beavon, 3–13. Toronto: University of Toronto Press, 2005.

Nichols, Roger. *Indians in the United States and Canada: A Comparative History*. Lincoln: University of Nebraska Press, 1999.

Nin Da Waab Jig. *Minishenhying Anishnaabe-aki: Walpole Island: The Soul of Indian Territory*. Walpole Island: Nin Da Waab Jig Heritage Centre, 1987.

Nin Da Waab Jig Heritage Centre, R. Darnell, and C.V. Stephens. *E-Niizaanaag Wii-ngoshkaag Maampii Bkejwanong: Species at Risk at the Walpole Island Nation (Ojibwe version)*. London: University of Western Ontario, 2006.

North American Association for Environmental Education (NAAEE). *Excellence in Environmental Education: Guidelines for Learning*. Washington, D.C.: NAAEE, 2004.

Obonsawin, Roger, and Heather Howard-Bobiwash. "The Native Canadian Centre of Toronto: The Meeting Place for the Aboriginal Community for 35 Years." In *The Meeting Place: Aboriginal Life in Toronto*, ed. Frances Sanderson and Heather Howard-Bobiwash, 25–59. Toronto: Native Canadian Centre of Toronto, 1997.

Ontario Society for the Prevention of Cruelty to Animals (OSPCA). "Ontario SPCA Deploys Staff to Kashechewan for Emergency Evacuation of Pets Due to Flooding." Media Release. 25 Apr. 2006. www.ontariospca.ca/press_releases/2006/2006_apr25.html.

———. "Ontario SPCA Spay North Team Flying to Kashechewan First Nation Community to Spay/Neuter and Offer Additional Veterinary Services." Media Release. 9 Feb. 2006. www.ontariospca.ca/press_releases/2006/2006_feb09_1.html.

Ontario Society for Environmental Education (OSEE). "Information about OSEE." Toronto: OSEE, 1995. www.osee.org.

Opekokew, Delia. *The Political and Legal Inequities among Aboriginal Peoples in Canada*. Kingston, ON: Institute of Intergovernmental Relations, 1987.

Oppenheim, A.N. *Questionnaire Design, Interviewing and Attitude Measurement*. London: St. Martin's, 1992.

O'Riley, Patricia A. *Technology, Culture and Socioeconomics: A Rhizoanalysis of Educational Discourses*. New York: Peter Lang, 2003.

Orr, David. *Ecological Literacy: Education and the Transition to a Postmodern World.* New York: State University of New York Press, 1992.

Orr, Willie. *Deer Forests, Landlords and Crofters.* Edinburgh: John Donald, 1982.

Osawabine, Joe, "Artistic Statement," Debajehmujig Theatre Group, 2006, http://www.debaj.ca/content/Artistic-Director?q=content/About-Company-Artistic-Statement.

Osborne, Brian S. "The Iconography of Nationhood in Canadian Art." In *The Iconography of Landscape: Essays on the Symbolic Representation, Design and Use of Past Environments,* ed. Denis Cosgrove and Stephen Daniels, 162–78. Cambridge: Cambridge University Press, 1988.

Par, Eileen. "A Clown for Our Times." *En Route Magazine,* December 1981.

Park, Geoff. *Nga Ururoa: Ecology and History in a New Zealand Landscape.* Wellington: Victoria University Press, 1995.

Pawson, Eric, and Tom Brooking, eds. *Environmental Histories of New Zealand.* Oxford: Oxford University Press, 2002.

Peat, David. *Lighting the Seventh Fire.* New York: Birch Lane, 1994.

Peters, Evelyn. "Emerging Themes in Academic Research in Urban Aboriginal Identities in Canada 1996–2010." *Aboriginal Policy Studies* 1, no. 1 (2011): 78–105.

———. "'Urban' and 'Aboriginal'": An Impossible Contradiction?" In *City Lives and City Forms: Critical Research and Canadian Urbanism,* ed. Jon Caufield and Linda Peake, 62–82. Toronto: University of Toronto Press, 1996.

Peters, Diane. "Fears of a Clown." *Eyeopener,* 22 March 1995.

Ponting, J. Rick, and Roger Gibbins. *Out of Irrelevance: A Socio-Political Introduction to Indian Affairs in Canada.* Toronto: Butterworths, 1980.

Ponting, J. Rick, and Cora J. Voyajeur. "Multiple Points of Light: Grounds for Optimism among First Nations in Canada." In *Hidden in Plain Sight: Contributions of Aboriginal Peoples to Canadian Identity and Culture,* ed. David R. Newhouse, Cora J. Voyajeur, and Dan Beavon, 425–54. Toronto: University of Toronto Press, 2005.

Ponting, Clive. *A Green History of the World: The Environment and the Collapse of Great Civilizations.* New York: Penguin, 1991.

Proulx, Craig. "Aboriginal Identification in North American Cities." *Canadian Journal of Native Studies* 26, no. 2 (2005): 405–38.

———. *Reclaiming Aboriginal Justice, Identity and Community.* Saskatoon: Purich, 2003.

Puk, Tom, and Dustin Behm. "Ecological Literacy as the First Imperative: The Role of Government in Developing Ecological Literacy in Ontario Secondary Schools; The Diluted Curriculum." Research report, Faculty of Education, Lakehead University, 2002. http://flash.lakeheadu.ca/~tpuk/Ecological%20Literacy%20as%20the%20First%20Imperative%20Research%20Report.PDF.

Pyne, Stephen J. *Fire in America: A Cultural History of Wildland and Rural Fire.* Princeton, NJ: Princeton University Press, 1982.

Quaife, Milo M., ed. *The John Askin Papers.* Vol. 2. Detroit: Detroit Library Commission, 1928.

Queen's Journal. "Where Was the Outcry?: At the G20 Conference, Stephen Harper Claims that Canada Has 'no history of colonialism.'" 29 Sept. 2009. www.queensjournal.ca/story/2009-09-29/opinions/where-was-outcry/.

Quintana, Jorge. "American Indian Systems for Natural Resource Management." *Akwekon* 9, no. 2 (1992): 92–97.

Rapport, Nigel, and Joanna Overing. *Social and Cultural Anthropology: The Key Concepts.* New York: Routledge, 2000.

Reaney, James. "Doctor John Troyer." In *Dictionary of Canadian Biography Online.* www.biographi.ca/EN/ShowBio.asp?BioId=37824&query=Troyer.

Regnier, Robert. "The Sacred Circle: An Aboriginal Approach to Healing Education at an Urban High School." In *First Nations Education in Canada: The Circle Unfolds,* ed. M. Battiste and J. Barman, 313–29. Vancouver: University of British Columbia Press, 1995.

Rekmans, Lorraine, Keith Lewis, and Anabel Dwyer, eds. *This Is My Homeland: Stories of the Effects of Nuclear Industries by People of the Serpent River First Nation and the North Shore of Lake Huron.* Cutler: Serpent River First Nation, 2003.

Rice, Brian "A Methodology Based on Rotinonshonni Traditions." In *Native Voices in Research,* ed. Jill Elizabeth Oakes, Rick Riewe, Alison Edmunds, Alison Dubois, and Kimberley Wilde, 171–82. Winnipeg: Aboriginal Issues Press, 1994.

Riddell, R.G. "A Study of the Land Policy of the Colonial Office, 1763–1865." *Canadian Historical Review* 18 (1937): 385–405.

Rilke, Rainer Maria. *Sonnets to Orpheus, 1922.* Ed. and transl. Graham Good. Vancouver: Ronsdale, 2005.

Roberts, Leslie. *Noranda.* Toronto: Clarke Irwin, 1956.

Robinson, E.J., and M.E. Moffatt. "Outbreak of Rotavirus Gastroenteritis in a James Bay Cree Community." *Canadian Journal of Public Health* 76, no. 1 (1985): 21–24.

Rogers, Edward. "The Algonquian Farmers of Southern Ontario, 1830–1945." In *Aboriginal Ontario: Historical Perspectives on the First Nations,* ed. Edward S. Rogers and Donald B. Smith, 122–66. Toronto: Dundurn, 1994.

Rosaldo, Renato. *Culture and Truth.* Boston: Beacon, 1989.

Roy, Arundhati. *The Cost of Living.* New York: Modern Library, 1990.

Ryan, Allan J. *The Trickster Shift.* Vancouver: University of British Columbia Press, 1999.

Sabathy-Judd, Linda. *Moravians in Upper Canada: The Diary of the Indian Mission of Fairfield on the Thames, 1792–1813.* Toronto: Champlain Society, 1999.

Sahlins, Marshall. "Notes on the original affluent society," In *Man the Hunter*, ed. R. Lee and I. DeVore, 85–89. Chicago: Aldine, 1968.

———. *Stone Age Economics.* Chicago: Aldine-Atherton, 1974.

Saunders, Robert E. "What Was the Family Compact?" *Ontario History* 49, no. 4 (1957): 165–78.

Sawchuk, Joe. "Negotiating an Identity: Métis Political Organizations, the Canadian Government, and Competing Concepts of Aboriginality." *American Indian Quarterly* 25, no. 1 (2001): 73–84.

Schama, Simon. *Landscape and Memory*. New York: Knopf, 1995.

Schechner, Richard. *The Future of Ritual: Writings on Culture and Performance.* New York: Routledge, 1995.

Schensul, Stephen, Jean Schensul, and Margaret LeCompte. *Essential Ethnographic Methods: Observations, Interviews, and Questionnaires.* London: Altamira, 1999.

Schmaltz, Peter S. *The Ojibwa of Southern Ontario.* Toronto: University of Toronto Press, 1991.

Scott, James. *Seeing Like a State: How Certain Schemes to Improve the Human Condition Have Failed.* New Haven: Yale University Press, 1998.

Semple, Neil. *The Lord's Dominion: The History of Canadian Methodism.* Montreal: McGill–Queen's University Press, 1996.

Sheffer, Gabriel. *Diaspora Politics: At Home Abroad.* Cambridge: Cambridge University Press, 2003.

Shkilnyk, Anastasia M. *A Poison Stronger Than Love: The Destruction of an Ojibwa Community.* New Haven: Yale University Press, 1985.

Simpson, L., D. Martin-Hill, P. Driben, and M. Wheatley. "Effects on Aboriginals from the Great Lakes Environment E.A.G.L.E. Project: Sociocultural Pilot Project Technical Report." Assembly of First Nations/Chiefs of Ontario/Health Canada Partnership, 2001.

Skaria, Ajay. *Hybrid Histories: Forests, Frontiers and Wildness in Western India.* Delhi: Oxford University Press, 1999.

Smith, Derek G., ed. *Canadian Indians and the Law: Selected Documents, 1663–1972.* Toronto: McClelland and Stewart, 1975.

Smith, Gregory. "Cultivating Care and Connections: Preparing the Soil for a Just and Sustainable Society." *Educational Studies* 36, no. 1 (2004): 73–92.

———. *Education and the Environment: Learning to Live with Limits.* Albany: State University of New York Press, 1992.

Smith, Theresa S. *The Island of the Anishnaabeg: Thunderers and Water Monsters in the Traditional Ojibwe Life-World.* Idaho: University of Idaho Press, 1995.

Smith, Tuhiwai Smith. *Decolonizing Methodologies: Research and Indigenous Peoples.* London: Zed Books, 1999.

Sobel, David. *Beyond Ecophobia: Reclaiming the Heart in Nature Education*. Great Barrington, MA: Orion Society and Myrin Institute, 1996.

Southcott, Chris. *The Aboriginal Population and the Economy of Northern Ontario*. Census Research Paper Series Report no. 12. Thunder Bay: Local Boards of Northern Ontario, 2009.

Spradley, J.P. *The Ethnographic Interview*. New York: Holt, Reinhart and Winston, 1979.

Stacey, C.P "Jeffery Amherst." *Dictionary of Canadian Biography Online*, Library and Archives Canada. http://www.biographi.ca/EN/.

Stagg, Jack. *Anglo-Indian Relations in North America to 1763 and an Analysis of the Royal Proclamation of 1763*. Ottawa: Indian and Northern Affairs Canada, 1981.

Standen, Dale, and David McNab, eds. *Gin Das Winan: Documenting Aboriginal History in Ontario*. Occasional Papers of the Champlain Society no. 2. Toronto: Champlain Society, 1996.

Stanley, George. "As Long as the Sun Shines and Water Flows: An Historical Comment." In *As Long as the Sun Shines and Water Flows: A Reader in Canadian Native Studies*, ed. Ian Getty and Antoine Lussier, 1–26. Vancouver: University of British Columbia Press, 1983.

Steckley, John. *Full Circle Canada's First Nations*. Toronto: Prentice Hall, 2001.

Steele, Ian K. *Warpaths: Invasions of North America*. New York: Oxford University Press, 1994.

Steen, Sandy. "Bastions of Mechanism, Castles Built on Sand: A Critique of Schooling from an Ecological Perspective." *Canadian Journal of Environmental Education* 8 (2003): 191–203.

Steinhart, Edward I. *Black Poachers, White Hunters: A Social History of Hunting in Colonial Kenya*. Oxford: James Currey, 2006.

Stephens, C.V. "'She was weakly for a long time and the consumption set in': Using Parish Records to Explore Disease Patterns and Causes of Death in a First Nations Community." In *Research in Anthropology and Linguistics (RAL-e) Monograph Series*, ed. J. Littleton, J. Park, A. Herring, and T. Farmer, 134–48. Auckland: Department of Anthropology, University of Auckland, 2008.

———. "Syndemics, Structural Violence and the Politics of Health: A Critical Biocultural Approach to the Study of Disease and Tuberculosis Mortality in a Parish Population at Walpole Island (1850-1885)." In *Proceedings of the 39th Annual Algonquian Conference*, ed. Karl S. Hele and Regna Darnell, 581–613. London: University of Western Ontario, 2008.

———. "Toxic Talk at Walpole Island First Nation: Narratives of Pollution, Loss and Resistance." Ph.D. diss., McMaster University, 2009.

Stephens, C.V., and R. Darnell. "The Interdisciplines of Ecosystem Health: As Revealed in First Nations Collaborations." *International Journal of Interdisciplinary Social Sciences* 3, no. 1 (2008): 147–60.

Strauss, A., and J. Corbin, eds. *Basics of Qualitative Research: Techniques and Procedures for Developing Grounded Theory.* Newbury Park, CA: Sage, 1990.

———. *Grounded Theory in Practice.* Thousand Oaks, CA: Sage, 1997.

Surtees, Robert. "Canadian Indian Policies." In *Handbook of North American Indians History of Indian–White Relations*, ed. William Sturtevant and Wilcomb Washburn, 81–95. Washington: Smithsonian Institution, 1998.

———. "Land Cessions, 1763–1830." In *Aboriginal Ontario: Historical Perspectives on the First Nations*, ed. Edward S. Rogers and Donald B. Smith, 92–121. Toronto: Dundurn, 1994.

Suzuki, David. "Foreword." In *Rediscovery: Ancient Pathways: New Directions*, ed. Thom Henley, 11–14. Edmonton: Lone Pine, 1996.

Taylor, Peter Shawn. "The Myth of the Sled Dog Killings." *Maclean's*, 1 Jan. 2007.

Tedlock, Barbara. "Boundaries of Belief." *Parabola: Myth and the Quest for Meaning* 4, no. 1 (1979): 70–77.

Tehanetorens. *Wampum Belts.* 1972. Rpt. Oshweken, ON: Iroqrafts, 2003.

Tobias, John L. "Protection, Civilization, Assimilation: An Outline History of Canada's Indian Policy." In *As Long as the Sun Shines and the Water Flows: A Reader in Canadian Native Studies*, ed. Ian A.L. Getty and Antoine S. Lussier, 39–55. Vancouver: University of British Columbia Press, 1983.

Toronto Historical Association. *A Glimpse of Toronto's History: Opportunities for the Commemoration of Lost Historic Sites.* Toronto: Toronto Historical Association, 2001.

Transformative Learning Centre—OISE/UT. "The TLC Approach to Transformative Learning: Grounded Hope." Toronto: OISE/UT, 2007. tlc.oise.utoronto.ca/about.html.

Trostle, J.A. *Epidemiology and Culture.* New York: Cambridge University Press, 2005.

Trouillot, Michel-Rolph."The Anthropology of the State in the Age of Globalization: Close Encounters of the Deceptive Kind." *Current Anthropology* 42, no. 1 (2001): 125–38.

Tsubaki T., and K. Irunkayama, eds. *Minamata Disease.* New York: Elsevier Scientific, 1977.

Turner, Nancy J. *The Earth's Blanket: Traditional Teachings for Sustainable Living.* Seattle: University of Washington Press, 2005.

Turner, Frederick. *Beyond Geography: The Western Spirit Against the Wilderness.* 5th ed. New York: Viking, 1994.

Van Der Ryn, Sim, and Stuart Cowan. *Ecological Design.* 10th anniversary ed. Washington: Island Press, 2007.

Van Wyck, Sheila. "Harvests Yet to Reap: History, Identity and Agriculture in a Canadian Indian Community." Ph.D. thesis, University of Toronto, 1992.

Vecsey, Christopher. "Grassy Narrows Reserve: Mercury Pollution, Social Disruption, and Natural Resources: A Question of Autonomy." *American Indian Quarterly* 11, no. 4 (Autumn 1987): 287–314.

Wainwright, Nicholas B. *George Croghan: Wilderness Diplomat.* Chapel Hill University of North Carolina Press, 1959.

Waldram, J.B., D.A. Herring, and T.K. Young. *Aboriginal Health in Canada: Historical, Cultural and Epidemiological Perspectives.* 2nd ed. Toronto: University of Toronto Press, 2006.

Walia, Harsha. "Really, Harper: Canada Has No History of Colonialism?" *Dominion,* 28 Sept. 2009. http://www.dominionpaper.ca/articles/2943.

Wallace, Ian. "Waving Goodbye to Someone You Love." *Impact,* Fall 1989.

Wanyeki, L. Muthoni, ed. *Women and Land in Africa: Culture, Religion and Realizing Women's Rights.* London: Zed, 2003.

Warry, Wayne. *Ending Denial: Understanding Aboriginal Issues.* Toronto: Broadview, 2007.

Weaver, Sally. *Making Canadian Indian Policy: The Hidden Agenda, 1968–1970.* Toronto: University of Toronto Press, 1981.

Weaver, John C. "Concepts of Economic Improvement and the Social Construction of Property Rights: Highlights from the English Speaking World." In *Despotic Dominion: Property Rights in British Settler Societies,* ed. John McLaren et al., 79–102. Vancouver: University of British Columbia Press, 2005.

Weenie, Angelina. "Aboriginal Pedagogy: The Sacred Circle Concept." In *As We See ... Aboriginal Pedagogy,* ed., L.A. Stiffarm, 59–66. Saskatoon: Extension Division at the University of Saskatchewan, 1998.

Weisman, Alan. "Earth Without People: What Would Happen to Our Planet If the Mighty Hand of Humanity Simply Disappeared?" *Discover Magazine,* Feb. 2005. http://discovermagazine.com/2005/feb/earth-without-people/article_view?b_start:int=1&-C=.

Westfall, William. *Two Worlds: The Protestant Culture of Nineteenth-Century Ontario.* Montreal: McGill-Queen's University Press, 1989.

White, Richard. *The Middle Ground: Indians, Empires and Republics in the Great Lakes Region, 1650–1815.* Cambridge: University of Cambridge Press, 1991.

Widdowson, Frances, and Albert Howard. *Disrobing the Aboriginal Industry.* Montreal: McGill-Queen's University Press, 2008.

Williams, Paul. "Oral Tradition on Trial." In *Gin Das Winan: Documenting Aboriginal History in Ontario,* Occasional Papers of the Champlain Society no. 2, ed. Dale Standen and David McNab. Toronto: Champlain Society, 1996.

Williams, Raymond. *Problems in Materialism and Culture*. London: Verso, 1980.

Windeyer, Chris. "Qikiqitani 'Not Satisfied' with Dog Slaughter Report." *Northern News Service Online*, 4 December 2006. nnsl.com/frames/newspapers/2006-12/dec4_06dg.html.

Withers, Charles W.J. *Geography, Science and National Identity: Scotland since 1520* Cambridge: Cambridge University Press, 2001.

Wolf, Eric. *Pathways of Power: Building an Anthropology of the Modern World*. Berkeley: University of California Press, 2001.

Wong, Lloyd, and Vic Satzewich. "Introduction: The Meaning and Significance of Transnationalism." In *Transnational Identities and Practices in Canada*, ed. Vic Satzewich and Lloyd Wong, 1–18. Vancouver: University of British Columbia Press, 2006.

Wooseter, Margaret. *Living Waters: Reading the Rivers of the Lower Great Lakes*. Albany: State University Press of New York, 2009.

The Contributors

Heather Marie Annis is a Toronto-based playwright, performer, theatre creator, clown, and academic. She is a graduate of York University, with a BFA in Theatre as well as a master's in Environmental Studies with a focus on theatre for social change. She is very involved in community arts, having written several plays, such as *The Longest Way Around* (in association with Shawanaga First Nation), *The Way* (Bareback Theatre); *Evicted* (Toronto Community Housing and Mixed Company Theatre), and *A Fine Line* (Mixed Company Theatre). She has also co-written eight shows as part of UNIT, which features the clown sisters Morro and Jasp and has toured Canada, garnering the 2010 Canadian Comedy Award nomination and a 2012 Dora Award. She is also a therapeutic clown who works in elder-care settings and is currently involved in a research project administered by Toronto Rehabilitation Institute–University Health Network on elder-clowning for residents with dementia in long-term-care facilities.

Alesha Jane Breckenridge is from Huntsville, Ontario. She is currently teaching science at City Adult Learning Centre in Toronto. Her educational background includes a master's degree in environmental studies, a diploma in education for the environment and sustainability, and a bachelor of education. Alesha is the co-director of Willoway, a non-profit organization focused on education for the environment.

Regna Darnell is Distinguished University Professor of Anthropology and First Nations Studies at the University of Western Ontario with a cross-appointment to ecosystem health in the Schulich School of Medicine and Dentistry. She has published widely on First Nations languages and cultures, ethnohistory, and history of anthropology.

Rick Fehr is an assistant professor in First Nations Studies and Geography at Western University. His research interests are nineteenth-century historical relations between Canada and First Nations peoples in southwestern Ontario. His recent research focuses on ecological perceptions and environmental change in Upper Canada.

Lori-Beth Hallock has a master's degree in environmental studies from York University, Canada. She has an honours bachelor of arts in Canadian studies and history from the University of Toronto. Born and raised in Sudbury, Ontario, her interests include Aboriginal issues, education, and northern history. She is currently a senior policy advisor for the Government of Ontario.

Karl S. Hele is a member of Garden River First Nation. He teaches in and is the director of First Peoples studies at Concordia University, where is he an associate professor of First Peoples studies in the School of Community and Public Affairs. He has served as the joint editor of the Algonquian Proceedings and edited *Lines Drawn upon the Water*; he has presented and published several papers on the history of the Anishinabeg and Métis communities in the Sault Ste. Marie region.

Jon J. Johnson teaches in the Department of Social Sciences at York University and has been working within Toronto's Indigenous community since 2003. He completed a B.A. and M.A. in anthropology at the University of Western Ontario and is about to complete a Ph.D. in the communication and culture program at York University. His doctoral dissertation is focused on First Nations oral traditions told within and about Toronto and their importance to the ongoing health of First Nations people living within the city.

Lianne C. Leddy is a member of the Serpent River First Nation and an assistant professor in the Department of History at Memorial University. She has continued her work on the effects of the uranium mining industry on the Serpent River Anishinaabek, which led to her current research on gendered postwar Indigenous–settler relations in Canada.

Ute Lischke, professor, teaches Indigenous literature and film in the Department of English and Film Studies, Wilfrid Laurier University. She is the co-editor of *Walking a Tightrope: Aboriginal People and Their Representations*, *The Long Journey of a Forgotten People: Métis Identities and Family Histories*, and *Blockades and Resistance: Studies in Actions of Peace and the Temagami Blockades of 1988–89*. She is currently working on Indigenous film in Canada.

John M. MacKenzie is professor emeritus of imperial history at Lancaster University and holds honorary professorships at Aberdeen, Stirling, St. Andrews, and Edinburgh universities. He is the author of *Propaganda and Empire* (1984), *The Empire of Nature* (1988), *Orientalism* (1995), *The Scots in South Africa* (2007) and *Museums and Empire* (2009). Among a number of edited books, the most recent are *European Empires and the People* (2011) and *Scotland and the British Empire* (2011). He has edited the journal *Environment and History* (2000–2005) and since 1986 has been general editor of Manchester University Press's Studies in Imperialism series.

María Manzano-Munguía is a professor and researcher at the Institute of Social Sciences and Humanities in the Benémerita Universidad Autónoma de Puebla, Pue, Mexico. She is currently conducting research on Indigenous forced transnationalism across the borderlands (Mexico and the United States). She has published on issues related to Aboriginal–state relations, Indian policy and legislation, Native non-governmental organizations, and Aboriginal leaders in urban centres.

David T. McNab is a Métis historian who has worked for almost forty years on Indigenous land and treaty rights issues in Canada. David teaches Indigenous thought and Canadian studies in the Departments of Equity Studies/Humanities in the Faculty of Liberal Arts and Professional Studies at York University, in Toronto. In addition to more than eighty articles, David has published nine books, including his recent publications *No Place for Fairness: Indigenous Land Rights and Policy in the Bear Island Case and Beyond* (2009); and (with Olive Patricia Dickason), the fourth edition of *Canada's First Nations: A History of Founding Peoples from Earliest Times* (2009). He is currently working on, among other book projects, the fifth edition of *Canada's First Nations.*

Brian Rice is an enrolled member of the Mohawk Nation and is currently teaching in the Department of Education at the University of Winnipeg. He regularly teaches courses in Aboriginal history and culture both national and global. He graduated with a Ph.D. in traditional knowledge at the California Institute of Integral Studies, the only all-Indigenous Ph.D. program in existence in the world. He has written two books: *Encounters Between Newcomers and Aboriginal Peoples in the East* (2006) and *Seeing the World with Aboriginal Eyes* (2005), used in several academic institutions. Additionally he has published on Aboriginal rights, reconciliation, and Rotinonshonni traditions. His dissertation entitled *The Rotinonshonni Through the Eyes of Taharonhiawako and Sawiskera: A Traditional History of the Iroquois People for Modern Times,*is now undergoing final review at Syracuse University Press.

Maureen Riche is a Ph.D. student in the Department of Humanities at York University, Toronto. Her main area of research interest is the dog in Indigenous cultures. She has written and presented on trauma, memory, and the demise of the Inuit sled dog in Canada's North, as well as on dog people in the fiction of Ojibwa writer Louise Erdrich. Maureen is originally from Newfoundland and Labrador.

Christianne V. Stephens is a medical anthropologist and a Sessional Assistant Professor in the Department of Anthropology at York University. She earned her Ph.D. in the anthropology of health at McMaster where she studied under the supervision of Ann Herring. Christianne has conducted ten years of ethnographic fieldwork and archival research at the Walpole Island First Nation (Canada). Her research focuses on Aboriginal health, environmental health, risk perception and risk communication, illness narratives, syndemics, cultural epidemiology, and structural violence.

Rhonda Telford has been professionally involved with First Nation land claims and other land and resource issues for more than twenty-five years. She has presented widely at conferences and in First Nation communities, has a number of published articles, and has interviewed dozens of elders. She has been working with the Union of Ontario Indians for more than a decade. Her 1996 Ph.D. dissertation concerned First Nation ownership of minerals, including oil and gas in Ontario.

Karen J. Travers is currently completing her Ph.D. in the Department of History at York University, Toronto. Her dissertation examines the confluence of policy, personalities, and economies in the settlement history of Anishinabe peoples and Euro-Canadians between 1790 and 1871 in present-day Lambton County, Ontario.

Index

Index

Books in the Indigenous Studies Series

Published by Wilfrid Laurier University Press

Blockades and Resistance: Studies in Actions of Peace and the Temagami Blockades of 1988–89 | Bruce W. Hodgins, Ute Lischke, and David T. McNab, editors | 2003 | 0-88920-381-4

Walking a Tightrope: Aboriginal People and Their Representations | Ute Lischke and David T. McNab, editors | 2005 | 978-0-88920-484-3

*Indian Country: Essays on Contemporary Native Cultur*e | Gail Guthrie Valaskakis | 2005 | photos | 978-0-88920-479-9

Words of the Huron | John L. Steckley | 2007 | 978-0-88920-516-1

Essential Song: Three Decades of Northern Cree Music | Lynn Whidden | 2007 | 978-0-88920-459-1

The Long Journey of a Forgotten People: Métis Identities and Family Histories | Ute Lischke and David T. McNab, editors | 2007 | 978-0-88920-523-9

From the Iron House: Imprisonment in First Nations Writing | Deena Rymhs | 2008: 978-1-55458-021-7 hardcover | 2016: 978-1-55458-580-9 paper

Lines Drawn upon the Water: First Nations and the Great Lakes Borders and Borderlands | *Karl S. Hele, editor* | 2008: 978-1-55458-004-0 hardcover | 2016: 978-1-55458-487-1 paper

Troubling Tricksters: Revisioning Critical Conversations | Linda M. Morra and Deanna Reder, editors | 2009 | 978-1-55458-181-8

Aboriginal Peoples in Canadian Cities: Transformations and Continuities | Heather A. Howard and Craig Proulx, editors | 2011 | 978-1-055458-260-0

Bridging Two Peoples: Chief Peter E. Jones, 1843–1909 | Allan Sherwin | 2012 | 978-1-55458-633-2

The Nature of Empires and the Empires of Nature: Indigenous Peoples and the Great Lakes Environment | Karl S. Hele, editor | 2013: 978-1-55458-328-7 | 2016: 978-1-55458-488-8 paper

The Eighteenth-Century Wyandot: A Clan-Based Study | John L. Steckley | 2014 | 978-1-55458-956-2

Indigenous Poetics in Canada | Neal McLeod, editor | 2014 | 978-1-55458-982-1

Literary Land Claims: The "Indian Land Question" from Pontiac's War to Attawapiskat | Margery Fee | 2015 | 978-1-77112-119-4

Learn, Teach, Challenge: Approaching Indigenous Literatures | Deanna Reder and Linda M. Morra, editors | 2016 | 978-1-77112-185-9

Arts of Engagement: Taking Aesthetic Action In and Beyond the Truth and Reconciliation Commission of Canada | Dylan Robinson and Keavy Martin, editors | 2016 | 978-1-77112-169-9

Why Indigenous Literatures Matter | Daniel Heath Justice | 2017 | 978-1-77112-176-7

Read, Listen, Tell: Indigenous Stories from Turtle Island | Sophie McCall, David Gaertner, Gabrielle L'Hirondelle Hill, and Deanna Reder, editors | 2017 | 978-1-77112-300-6

Violence Against Indigenous Women: Literature, Activism, Resistance | Allison Hargreaves | 2017 | 978-1-77112-239-9

Activating the Heart: Storytelling, Knowledge Sharing, and Relationship | Julia Christensen, Lisa Szabo-Jones, and Christopher Cox, editors | 2017 | 978-1-77112-219-1